AF599230

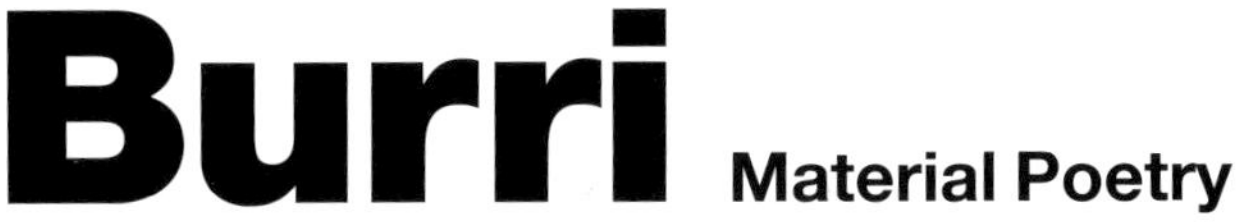

Burri Material Poetry

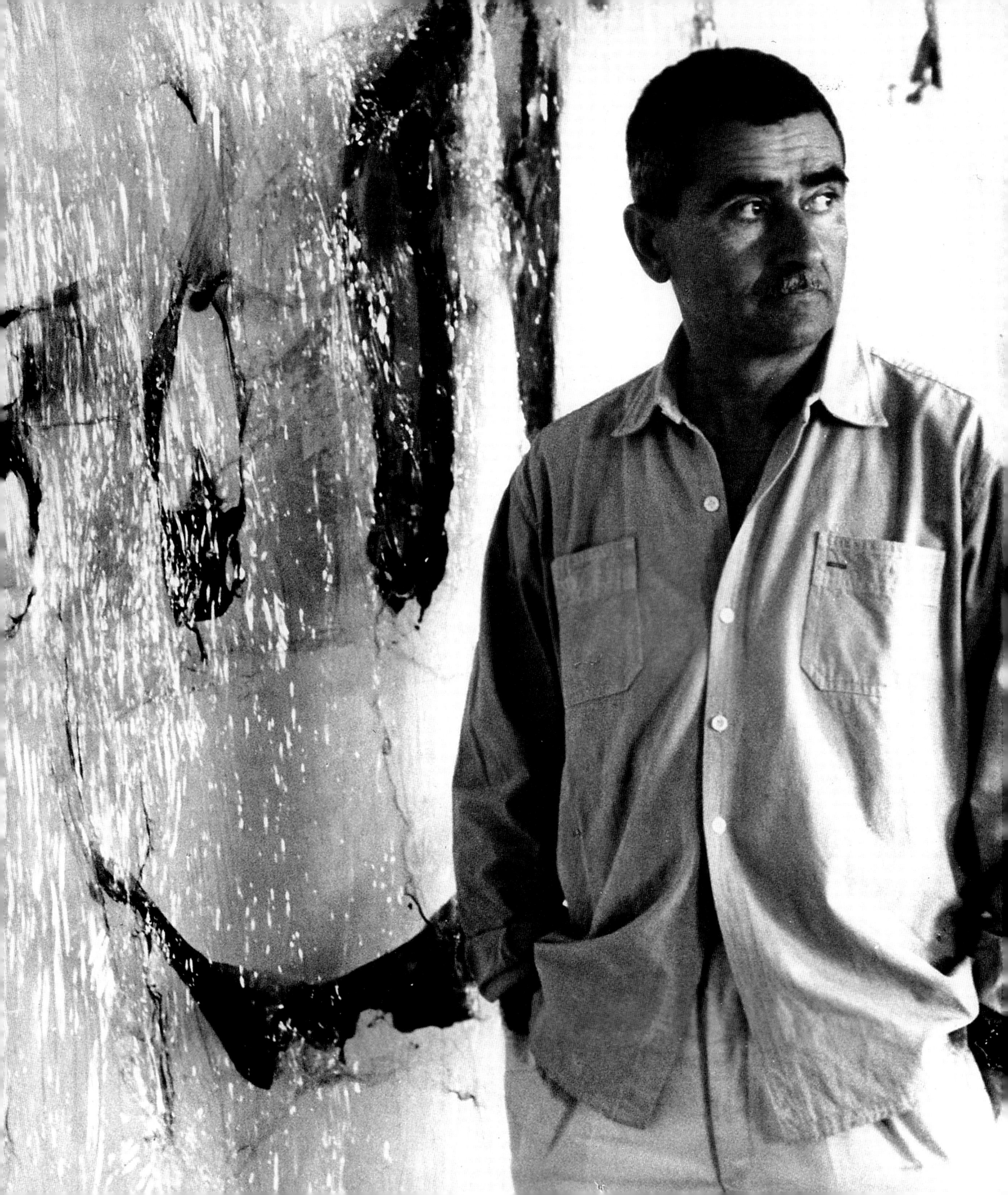

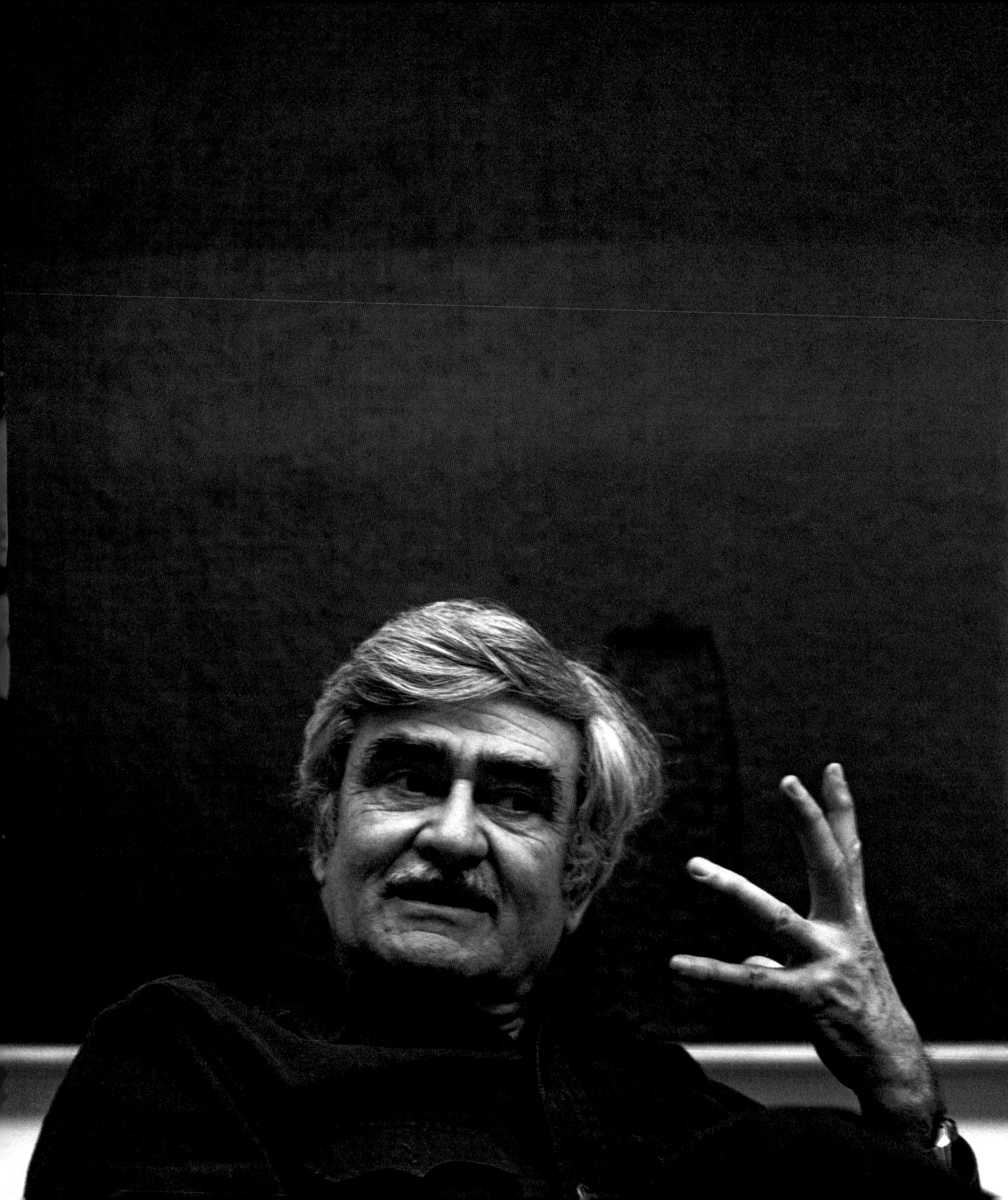

Burri

Material Poetry

edited by Bruno Corà

SKIRA

Medal of the President of the Republic

Burri
Material Poetry

curated by Bruno Corà

Alba, Fondazione Ferrero
9 October 2021–30 January 2022

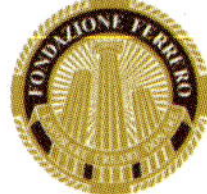

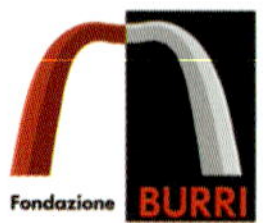

Exhibition promoted and organized by
Fondazione Piera Pietro e Giovanni Ferrero Onlus
in collaboration with
Fondazione Palazzo Albizzini Collezione Burri

With the contribution of
Fondazione Compagnia di San Paolo
Francesco Profumo, President
Alberto Anfossi, General Secretary

Under the patronage of
Comune di Alba
Carlo Bo, Mayor
Carlotta Boffa, Town Councillor for Cultural Policies

Exhibition project and curatorship
Bruno Corà

General and technical coordination
Anna Maria Traversini for the Fondazione Burri
Elena Torchio for the Fondazione Ferrero

Layout design project
Tiziano Sarteanesi for the Fondazione Burri
Danilo Manassero
in collaboration with Flavio Bonifacio for the Fondazione Ferrero

Exhibition Setup
Tiziano Sarteanesi

Condition reports and courier for the Fondazione Burri
Greta Boninsegni

Exhibition promotional campaign concept and development
Ferrero Pubbliregia

Media Planning
Alberto Scanavacca

Press Office
PCM Studio di Paola Manfredi
with the collaboration of Margherita Campanello for the Fondazione Ferrero and Mirna Ventanni for the Fondazione Burri

Cultural mediation
Formazione, Giorgina Bertolino,
Fondazione Sandretto Re Rebaudengo

Mediation and educational staff
Roberta Aureli, Mattia Azeglio, Rosario Calabrese, Sara Catalani, Francesca Cerutti, Edi Guerzoni, Chiara Lo Bello, Sofia Malizia, Chiara Marchetti, Irene Perosino, Giulia Perrucci, Lucia Pessina, Giulia Proglio, Jacopo Tanzi

Our special thanks go to
Giulia Cavallo and Claudio Cocino, Ferrero Human Resources

Educational activities
Atlante Servizi Culturali: Gregorio Battistoni, Lavinia Bonucci, Giulia Grassini, and Lorenzo Martinelli
With the supervision of
Rosario Salvato for the Fondazione Burri and Emanuela Delpiano for the Fondazione Ferrero

We wish to thank all the owners and staff of the companies that have provided services for the realisation of the exhibition structures

Insurance
Aon S.p.A. Insurance & Reinsurance Brokers, AXA XL principal company
Our special thanks go to
Alberto Tinivella and Anna Garelli of Ferrero Group

Transport
Arterìa

Exhibition installation and dismantling
Laboratorio Pagliero Cesare

The exhibition project, conceived and realised in collaboration with the Fondazione Palazzo Albizzini Collezione Burri, also involved the following institutions with regard to the works on loan:

Galleria Civica d'Arte Moderna e Contemporanea, Turin
Riccardo Passoni, *Director*

Fondazione Magnani-Rocca, Mamiano di Traversetolo, Parma
Stefano Roffi, *Scientific Director*

Gallerie d'Italia, Milan
Michele Coppola, *Executive Director of Art, Culture and Historical Heritage Historical, Archaeological and Artistic Heritage Division – Intesa Sanpaolo*

Tornabuoni Arte, Florence
Roberto Casamonti

We wish to thank all the private collectors who have loaned their works preferring to remain anonymous for their kindness and willingness to assist

Special thanks to Eva Menzio

From 9 October 2021 to 30 January 2022, in the Exhibition Space of the Fondazione Banca d'Alba at Via Cavour 4, to complement the exhibition held in the rooms of the Fondazione Ferrero, it is possible to visit the exhibition *Burri. Il Cretto di Gibellina,* curated by Bruno Corà, Tiziano Sarteanesi and Stefano Valeri, with the collaboration of Arti Binarie and Danilo Manassero

Our special thanks go to
Tino Cornaglia, *President*
Riccardo Corino, *General Director*
Paolo Taricco, *Head of External Relations*

Catalog
edited by Bruno Corà

Texts by
Bruno Corà
Mario Diacono
Thierry Dufrêne
José Jiménez
Petra Richter

Biographical Chronology
Greta Boninsegni

Apparatuses and Bibliographical Research
Greta Boninsegni, Rita Olivieri, Luca Petricci, Linda Cala Scarcione

Photographic materials and IT documents management
Nicola Cavargini

Audiovisual media
Alberto Brizzi and Marco Capaccioni for Arti Binarie
Livio Sacco for Audiosystem

Legal consultancy
Marco Gervasio, Giorgia Lugato

Health & Safety
Marzia Genta, Carlo Bonino

Security
Nicola Ricchiuti, Dario Fessia

Thanks
The organizers and the curator wish to express their most heartfelt gratitude to all those who have cooperated in any way in the realization of the exhibition, apologizing as of now for any involuntary omission.

Nicola Angerame, Manuele e Piero Apolli, Pierangelo Battaglino, Christian Beccafichi, Arianna Bona, Giampaolo Canu, Sara Cappa, Luca Carrà, Edoardo Casolari, Francesca Cattoi, Francesca Ceriani, Laura Corino, Fabiana Dadone, Mafalda De Carolis, Pietro De Carolis, Giovanni De Logu, Angela Dierna, teachers and students of the Liceo Artistico P. Gallizio in Alba, Ursula Esposito, Federica Farci, Elena Ferrero, Elena Finazzi, Giusy Fortarezza, Augusto Frachey, Giovanna Gaj, Arturo Galansino, Stefano Giubboni, Giovanni Grasso, Rada Kratchanova, Isabella Lastrucci, Camilla Lumini, Luciano Marengo, Ivano Martinetti, Teresa Mascolo, Liana Mattacchini, Claudia Melagrana, Guido Oldani, Marta Onali, Cristina Pereno, Roberto Peruzzi, Silvia Santinelli, Chiara Sarteanesi, Piero Negri Scaglione, Anna Scaperrotta, Chiara Sozzi, Gelsomina Spione, Bruno Strumia, Simone Strummiello, Studio Saracco Associati, Umberto Tersigni, Gaia Toninelli, Maurizio Torcellan, Gaia Torregrossa, Paolo Virilli, Elena Volpato, Claudia Zunino

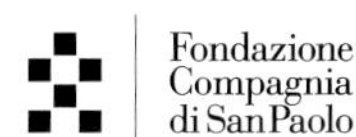

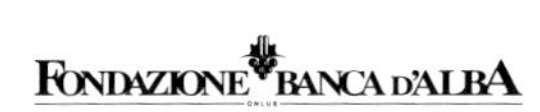

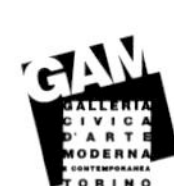

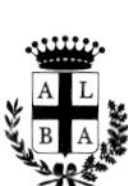

Three years after the exhibition *Dal Nulla al Sogno*, I am pleased, as is my family, that the Foundation desired and created by my husband Michele is now ready to host an exhibition dedicated to Alberto Burri (Città di Castello 1915–Nice 1995). An exhibition that we have greatly looked forward to in the very long and difficult times experienced by every country in the world during the pandemic, and that witnessed the Fondazione Ferrero's firm solidarity alongside the health professionals and authorities, reinforcing the commitment in favor of people, its core mission, through its medical and social services.

Over the past three years, during meetings and conversations either in person or remotely with Professor Bruno Corà, President of the Fondazione Palazzo Albizzini Collezione Burri and curator of our exhibition, I had a chance to appreciate just how solid Burri's roots were in the city of his birth, and the extent to which he was inspired by the fifteenth- and sixteenth-century artists from that territory, Piero della Francesca and Raphael in particular.

My knowledge of the artist's work, to whom we are dedicating this monographic retrospective, also reminds me of the value of friendship, having shared with remarkable people and persons of unparalleled humanity, like the founder of FAI, Giulia Maria Crespi, the emotions that are triggered when observing a "painting" by Burri in a silence that is at the same time filled with vitality and deep spirituality.

"My last painting is the same as my first one," the artist would often say, an artist who discovered his true, profound vocation after working as a frontline physician during World War II. The reflection on his artistic trajectory encompasses the theme of life that continues, notwithstanding the adversities, to manifest itself in its eternal becoming.

Professor Corà, with the unequalled knowledge about Burri that distinguishes him, has chosen to emphasize one aspect that, I am sure, will arouse interest and touch all the visitors' heartstrings: *material poetry*.

Burri's painting, as he himself defines it, is an "irreducible presence" capable of inspiring a silent contemplation and the meditated composure with which one approaches prayer and poetic interpretation.

Maria Franca Ferrero
President, Fondazione Ferrero

More than five years after internationally celebrating the anniversary of the birth of Alberto Burri (1915–1995) and commemorating his death over a quarter of a century ago, we can safely say that this exhibition in Alba dedicated to his "Material Poetry" at the Fondazione Ferrero is testimony to the historical dimension of this great twentieth-century artist.

On this occasion it seemed important to me to underscore in Burri's works a tacit significance, because this was hermetically part of his art. To do so the reference to Horace's formula "*ut pictura poesis*" was implemented, which can be used to connote the artist's painting that burst onto the contemporary art scene in such an incredible way.

During visits to the Fondazione Ferrero in Alba, thanks to the unforgettable hospitality of the President Maria Franca Ferrero, whom I wish to thank here also on behalf of the members of the Fondazione Burri who worked on creating this exhibition, we observed numerous cultural ties between our two foundations, as well as between Alba and Città di Castello. These concern several historical and artistic aspects, as well as the productive and entrepreneurial activity of their respective citizens in sectors like the agricultural and food supply chains. These are all common denominators that engender the perception of wide-ranging and well-established affinities, favorable to honing the prestige and reciprocal recognition of initiatives already undertaken together, and others yet to be undertaken in what we hope will be the making of a successful future.

Bruno Corà
President, Fondazione Palazzo Albizzini Collezione Burri

With all the enthusiasm prompted by a new beginning that had been so greatly desired, I gladly accepted the invitation to welcome the important exhibition that the Fondazione Ferrero will open in the autumn.

The Fondazione Ferrero confirms its vocation for gifts and donations that is engraved in its symbol, with an event of international importance that will enable the knowledge of a major Italian artist to be advanced.

And I believe there is no greater gift than culture, understood in its broader sense of the diffusion of knowledge, to raise the spirits.

In its now long historical path of exhibitions, the Fondazione Ferrero has demonstrated that it gives precedence to contemporary art, adding a period that is closest to the artistic knowledge of all of us, but often also less known.

I am referring to that twentieth century that school curriculums often do not succeed in reaching and that we do not have the capacity to interpret by ourselves.

In recent years the Fondazione Ferrero has given all of us, even those less familiar with art, a major opportunity to immerse ourselves in a world rich in stimuli and attractions, a world that we have each processed in our own way, even if simply cherishing the memory of the feelings provoked by the work that most grabbed our attention at the time.

I am certain that this exhibition will also have the same success as past ones and that it will provide many art enthusiasts with the opportunity to visit our city and our splendid hills.

This is a second reason why we must thank the Ferrero family, who continue to have a profound effect on the development of a territory that is unique in the world for its nature, but also for the way it has been able to forge the steadfastness of its inhabitants.

I heartily recommend that you all read the critical essay by Bruno Corà, the exhibition curator, an extensively documented and richly worded text that has succeeded in transposing the poetry that gives the exhibition its title onto the written page.

Finally, I must express my gratitude to the Fondazione Palazzo Albizzini Collezione Burri for its work in conserving the master's works and for their generous willingness to assist, which has enabled the event to take place.

I hope you all enjoy your visit, and also that it will encourage you to regain knowledge of great contemporary Italian art and a poetic dimension in life.

Carlo Bo
Mayor of Alba

Making culture in a courageous way is a concept that might only apparently be in contradiction with our bank's main activity.

No economic reality, today, can set to one side the democratic sharing of art and culture, clearly seen in all their multiple variants.

Art and culture are strategic engines driving the development of our territory, instruments that, with the pandemic, have even more urgently become an authentic and tangible expression of civil, but also economic, growth.

Making "courageous culture" is a role entrusted to the protagonists of a far-sighted and generous entrepreneurial sector, represented first and foremost, in Alba, by the Ferrero family.

We are proud to collaborate with and place ourselves at the service of the Fondazione Ferrero and the Fondazione Burri, which have conceived, completed, supported, and sponsored the exhibition *Burri. Material Poetry*, curated by Bruno Corà.

Our exhibition space, in the heart of the city, will host the focus devoted to *Burri. Il Cretto di Gibellina* and will be an ideal driving force, acting as a reference point and a resonance chamber for the largest exhibition staged in the rooms of the Fondazione Ferrero.

I am profoundly convinced that it is the task of each of us, today more than ever, to start again from the manifestations of beauty that Nature and Art offer us.

With the exhibition devoted to Alberto Burri and presented in two venues, the Fondazione Ferrero and the Fondazione Burri have offered the Fondazione Banca d'Alba the opportunity to give back "cultural oxygen," well-being for the heart and mind, to all the people who will visit our city in the next four months.

Tino Cornaglia
Chairman, Fondazione Banca d'Alba

The Fondazione Compagnia di San Paolo strongly believes in supporting the knowledge, conservation, and valorization of the cultural heritage as a tool that can foster community development. It is committed to promoting the most qualified cultural institutions that are capable of organizing events that can contribute to the collective good.

The decision to support the exhibition events proposed by cultural institutions that actively advance research in the art history sector and fuel reflections useful for the growth of the public falls within the scope of this general aim.

Burri. Material Poetry is indeed a significant exhibition thanks to the curatorial project that will greatly contribute to a deeper knowledge of the practice and figure of Alberto Burri, casting light on a number of lesser known aspects of his art.

Lastly, also thanks to the free admission to the exhibition, the vast educational program, and the presence of cultural mediators, this initiative helps people from all walks of life to learn about art.

Sincerest thanks to all those who have worked on the exhibition, the result of a successful collaboration between the Fondazione Ferrero and the Fondazione Palazzo Albizzini Collezione Burri.

Fondazione Compagnia di San Paolo

It is with great pleasure that we have decided to participate once again in a new exhibition venture of the Fondazione Ferrero in Alba.

We have regularly shared exhibition projects: starting from lending works for past exhibitions dedicated to Pinot Gallizio, Giorgio Morandi, and Carlo Carrà, and all the way to events related to the monographic exhibitions presented in Alba. Cases in point are the exhibitions of the works of Felice Casorati (*Il pensiero assorto*) and Giacomo Balla *(ProtoBalla. La Torino del giovane Balla)* which were held in Wunderkammer, here at the GAM, in 2014 and 2016, respectively.

We were able to lend *Grande Ferro* for this important event dedicated to Burri's work and prepared by the Fondazione Ferrero in collaboration with the Fondazione Palazzo Albizzini Collezione Burri in Città di Castello.

Alberto Burri was a "poor" artist, but also intense and determined in his research into the potential of the material, capable of offering a hard and new reading of the aesthetic dimension of the work of art. He radicalized all the fears that were expressed in the renewal of Italian art in the post-World War II period, at the height of the existential ferment, and he opened many doors for the research of the future generations.

Naturally, we will try to continue our collaboration with the future projects of the Fondazione Ferrero, based on consolidated modalities, or by developing innovative forms of collaboration, as will be the case for the support of our *I Maestri serie Oro* project, the winner of the PAC – Piano per l'Arte Contemporanea competition, developed by the Ministry of Culture.

Riccardo Passoni
Director, GAM – Galleria Civica d'Arte Moderna
e Contemporanea di Torino

Pages 4–5
Alberto Burri, Rome, Grottarossa, 1962

Page 6
Alberto Burri, Città di Castello,
Casenove di Morra, 1982

Design
Marcello Francone

Editorial Coordination
Vincenza Russo

Editing
Roberta Rita Pertegato

Layout
Evelina Laviano

Translations
Robert Burns and Leslie A. Ray
for Language Consulting Congressi, Milan
Charles Davis and Madeleine Brook
for NTL, Florence
Sylvia Notini

Photo Credits
© Agenzia Fotogramma 1984: p. 199
© Archivio dell'Arte – Luciano Pedicini: p. 203
© John David O'Brien, Los Angeles: p. 201
Aurelio Amendola: pp. 6, 18, 34, 44, 70, 184–185, 194, 201, 205, 206, 208–209
Gabriele Basilico: p. 215
Vittorugo Contino: pp. 80, 211
Plinio De Martiis: p. 56
Lionello Fabbri: p. 217
Marvin Lazarus: p. 82
F. Polchi for Artibinarie: pp. 37, 68
Josephine Powell: p. 254
Sergio Rossi: p. 72
Alessandro Sarteanesi: pp. 202, 212, 214
Sandro Visca: p. 197

For all other photos of the works and Alberto Burri © Fondazione Palazzo Albizzini Collezione Burri, Città di Castello – by SIAE 2021
© Joseph Beuys, Jean Dubuffet, Renato Guttuso by SIAE 2021
© Basaldella Afro by SIAE 2021
© Association Marcel Duchamp by SIAE 2021
© The Willem de Kooning Foundation, New York by SIAE 2021
© Succession Yves Klein by SIAE 2021
© Kounellis by SIAE 2021
© Robert Rauschenberg Foundation by SIAE 2021
© Comissió Tàpies by SIAE 2021

First published in Italy in 2021 by
Skira editore S.p.A.
Palazzo Casati Stampa
via Torino 61
20123 Milan
Italy
www.skira.net

Printed and bound in Italy. First edition:
Petruzzi s.r.l.
Città di Castello, Perugia

ISBN: 978-88-572-4675-8

Distributed in USA, Canada, Central & South America by ARTBOOK | D.A.P. 75 Broad Street Suite 630, New York, NY 10004, USA.
Distributed elsewhere in the world by Thames and Hudson Ltd., 181A High Holborn, London WC1V 7QX, United Kingdom.

Contents

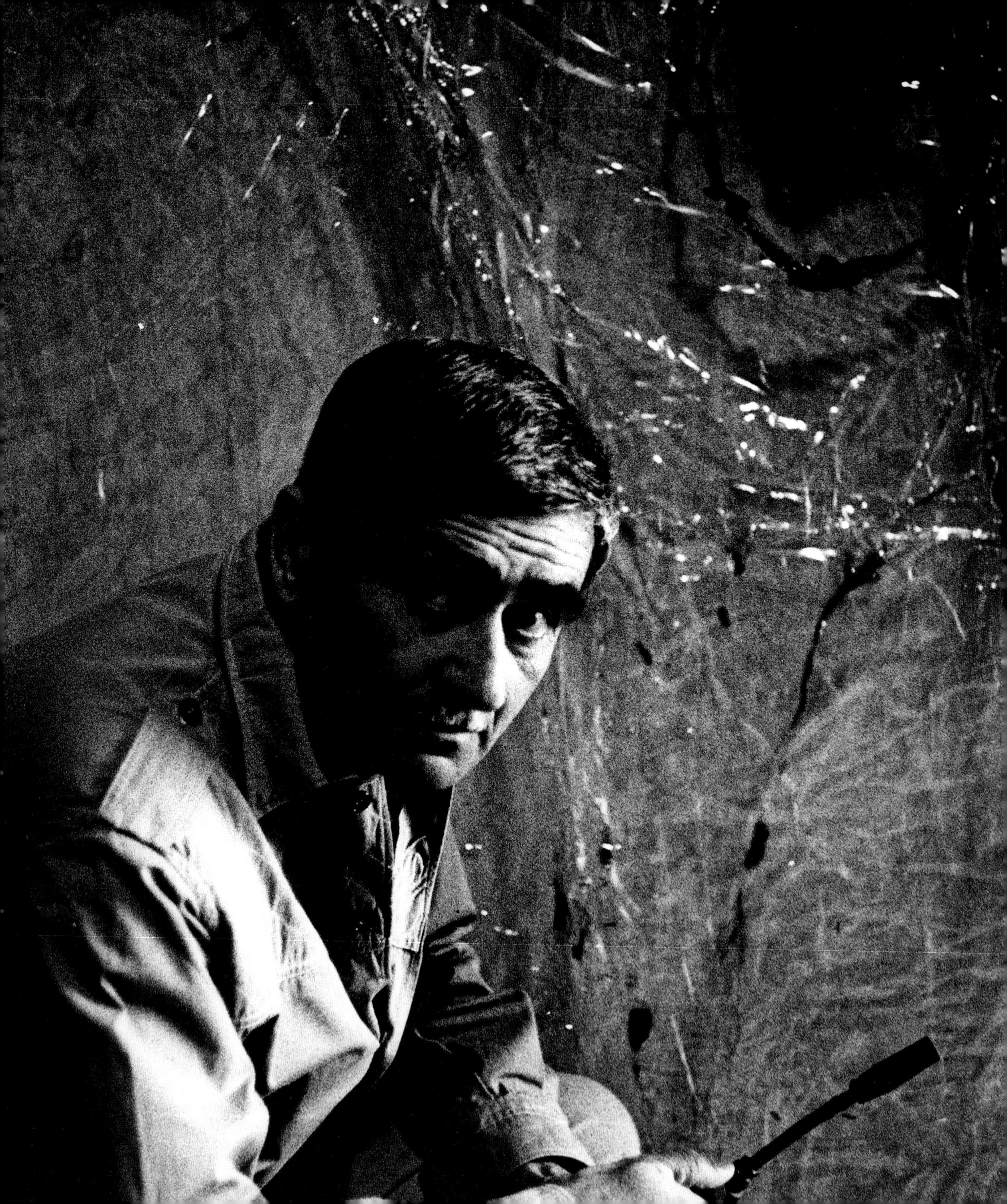

Burri. Material Poetry

Bruno Corà

Giuseppe Ungaretti, one of the highest oracular voices in twentieth-century poetry, said something unforgettable about the art of Alberto Burri: “I love Burri because he is not only today’s greatest painter, but he is also my principal source of envy: he is today’s greatest poet.”[1] If we add this affirmation to the many other statements, as well as poetic and poetic-critical writings both during and after Burri’s life (De Libero, Sinisgalli, Villa, Diacono, Pieyre de Mandiargues, Zeichen, and others), the theme and need for this exhibition are clear.

In this hermeneutic vein, we had already begun thinking a few years ago about how to bring out Burri’s relationship with poetry. On that occasion[2] I presented numerous circumstances that evidenced Burri’s reservations regarding critical words and writings or alternatively his openness to and great interest in the poetic words of Sappho, D’Annunzio, Pound, Ungaretti, and his first exegete, the poet Emilio Villa. I did not hesitate to point out how “Burri’s creative partnership with Villa [. . .] is one of the most meaningful episodes in his attention to the use of words in art together with the choice to join his works with the poetic words of Villa.”[3]

Similarly, on that same occasion, Tonino Sicoli argued cogently that in the exo-editorial work with Villa to create the artist’s book *17 variazioni su temi proposti per una pura ideologia fonetica* (1955), Burri

> reveals himself to be a refined draftsman and skilled arranger of minute materials, a builder of subtle weaves hinting at a spatiality [. . .] lying at the very origin of languages still indistinct between graphics and drawing, between writing and matter, between the void and the first interventions of a creation that still has a lot of the immaterial in it. In this way, Burri places his genetic footprint on Visual Poetry too, becoming with Villa the precursor of those artists who explore writing as an image and representing continuity with the futurist Paroliberismo emerging in 1912 from the provocatory intuition of Filippo Tommaso Marinetti and with Guillaume Apollinaire’s *Calligrammes*, composed in 1913–17 with drawings.[4]

Those observations were followed by a number of equally meaningful considerations relating to our interpretive interest: “if we really think about it, words are the material of poetry that the poet uses as writing but also as sound; equally so paint is the material of vision that the painter uses in its density and chromatic efficacy. Words create visions and the image stimulates thought, revealing the drama of existence, giving a spatiality that is also an inner dimension. Burri thus aspires to a total language, supreme Poetry.”[5]

Alberto Burri, ca. 1966

Ut pictura poesis

It is clear from those considerations that Burri's painting, together with its innovative linguistic and revolutionary attributes (pictorial material, color, form, and space), also gives new meaning to the formula *ut pictura poesis* from classical antiquity. Expressing an aesthetic principle spanning the centuries, Horace's words, "poetry is a speaking picture, painting a silent poetry"—taken from a verse by the Latin poet Simonides of Keos and coming to us via Plutarch—appear to have found an extraordinary interpreter in Burri.

After the concepts expressed by Leon Battista Alberti (1404–1472) in *De pictura* on the parallelism between the two humanistic disciplines of painting and poetry, after Leonardo's (1452–1519) treatises distinguishing the temporality of the expressive immediacy of painting and literature, after the "dispute" in Benedetto Varchi's (1503–1565) *Lezzioni*, and after the thoughts of Giovanni Paolo Lomazzo (1538–1592) in his *Trattato dell'Arte della pittura* on the relationship between the communicative effectiveness of the painted image as opposed to the "mental images of the poet," at the height of the twentieth century a formidable example of the Horatian theme reappeared in Burri's paintings.

While Burri made his debut in Rome in 1946, his vocation for it had taken concrete form during his imprisonment in Hereford, Texas starting in May 1943. Recent historical studies and research into that affair offer a broad and detailed report on Burri's "purgatory" in those years. Flavio Giovanni Conti writes:

> After beginning his medical studies he volunteered for the Ethiopian War, enlisting in the Voluntary Militia for National Security. He was awarded his degree in 1940

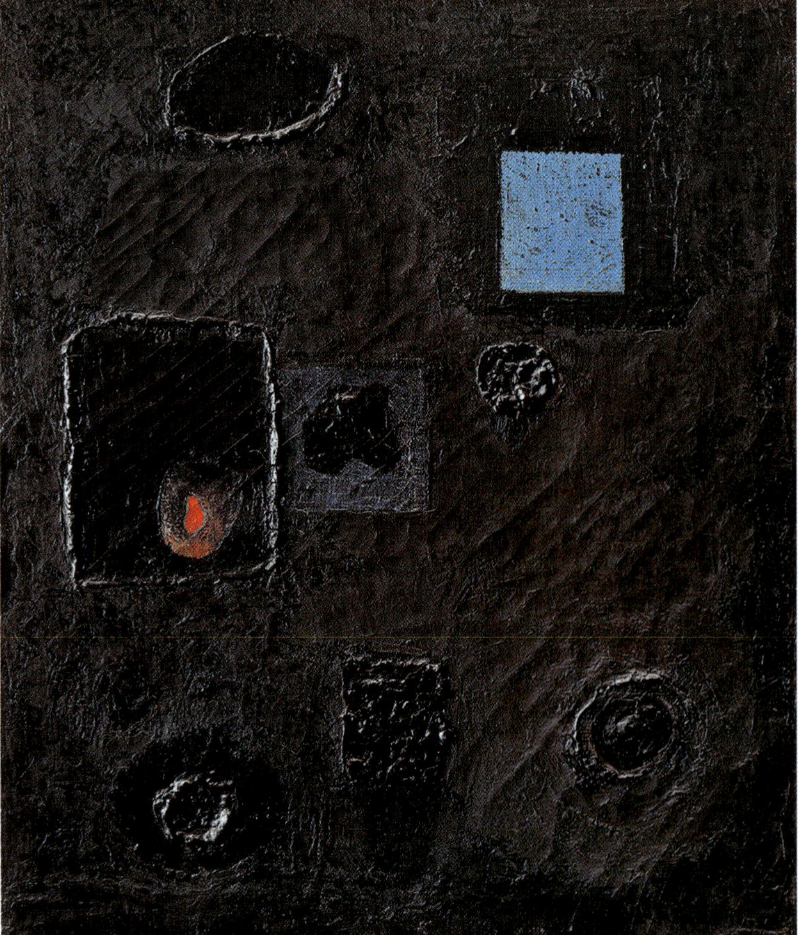

1. Alberto Burri, *Nero 1*, 1948
Città di Castello, Fondazione Palazzo Albizzini Collezione Burri

2. Alberto Burri,
SZ1, 1949
Città di Castello,
Fondazione Palazzo
Albizzini Collezione Burri

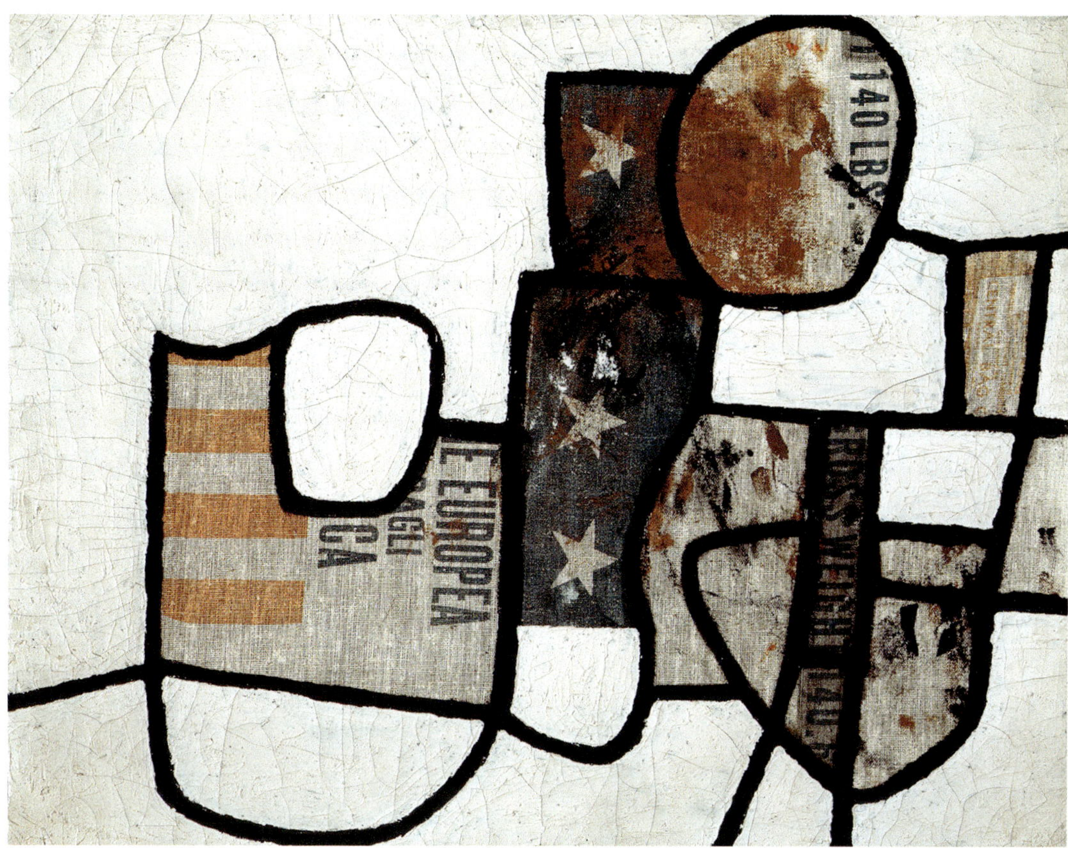

and was called to arms when war broke out. He was initially sent to the Yugoslavian front and then to North Africa in the role of medical officer until he was captured in Tunisia in May 1943. During his internment in Hereford, he declined to practice his profession to protest American restrictions on the liberty of imprisoned physicians [. . .]. Burri considered his imprisonment to be the turning point in his decision to work as an artist.

Immersing himself in painting was a way of escaping the reality of war and detention. However, the artist always denied any explicit connection between his war experience and the development of his original painting techniques: "actually, there is no relation between my medical work during the war and my artistic pursuits. I have never had—as some have hypothesized—flashbacks of any sort to bandages, blood, wounds, or other such things. The only relationship is consequential, that is, during those years of imprisonment in the concentration camp, I refused to practice medicine and immersed myself completely in painting."

Burri describes the genesis of his vocation as follows: "in those years I understood that I *had* to be a painter. The paintings I did then are just as valid as my most recent works, no more no less, in terms of pictorial intensity. I recall that I kept changing subjects, painting new pictures and changing them again, an endless number of times. That was how I really began as a painter; the medical gauze, blood, and burns from war have nothing to do with it. All inventions."[6]

After returning to Italy in 1946 and spending two years in Rome, and exhibiting solo twice there, in 1949 he created the assemblage *SZ1* (fig. 2), a painting-collage using burlap recovered from sugar sacks distributed by the United Nations Relief and Rehabilitation Administration as part of Marshall Plan aid to Italy. *SZ1* features a patch of fabric printed

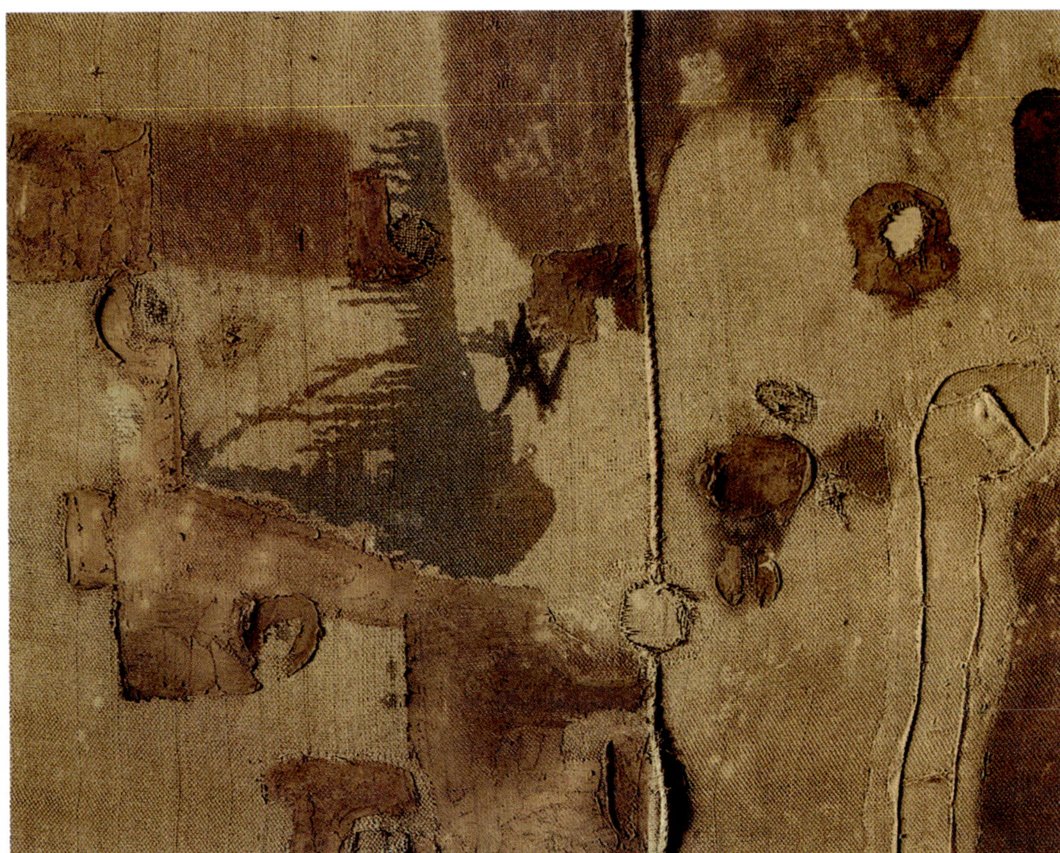

3. Alberto Burri,
Sacco, 1950
Città di Castello,
Fondazione Palazzo
Albizzini Collezione Burri

with the stripes of the U.S. flag and words about the subsidies to Europe. The following year, Burri created a new work, *Sacco*, 1950, made entirely of a ripped jute sack mounted on a stretcher and featuring stitching, patches, and bits of diluted brown color (fig. 3).

Both those novel apparitions caused quite a stir on the artistic and cultural scene, triggering wonder mixed with bewilderment and also broad failure to grasp their significance. If we exclude the very few positive reviews,[7] the critics were generally unable to appreciate the innovative linguistic style introduced by Burri with those paintings and other analogous works that he had created in the meantime.

Subverting grand established tradition, Burri replaced the use of color, line, and the usual canvas support—upon which to represent and bring to life an image—with matter itself, physically "displayed" with no mimetic pretension. He worked with the contiguity of material and material, on surface variations, the replacement of a color with materials of similar color but containing much more information in their physical composition, their previous use, what they had lived through. Lastly, he worked by bringing out contrasts among different materials in an instinctive geometrical layout of the image he was seeking. He deliberated freely based on his own creative logic, guided by his intuition for form and space, like a dowser guided by the magnetic presence of water in the subsurface. But it cannot be overstated that Burri's use of materials in his work was purposeful from the beginning; the most important thing to the artist was the achievement of meaningful form and space in his painting, seeking and finding an equilibrium among the different textural elements in each of his works.

The Discovery of Matter-Color

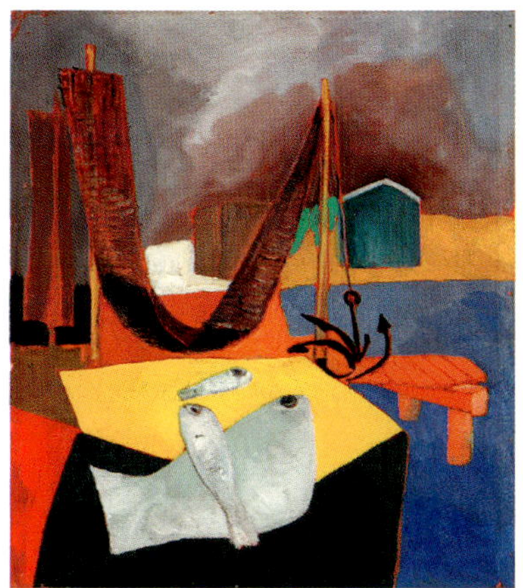

4. Alberto Burri, *Pesca a Fano*, 1947 Perugia, Accademia di Belle Arti

5. Alberto Burri, *Sacco S3*, 1953 Città di Castello, Fondazione Palazzo Albizzini Collezione Burri

After abandoning his early figurative expressions and elaborations, in 1948 (fig. 4), Burri drew on a source of poetic tension guided by an inner intuition and purposeful drive, free of concerns for the artistic sphere and the trends of the time. He concentrated on the inalienable principles of his own identity, memory, conscience, and desire to subvert the conditions imposed by a post-war reality of existential discomfort and the impulse to re-affirm his own inner imaginative flame.

The compositional focus and the ideational rigor of form, space, and equilibrium in the conception of the image that informed his works from the beginning were so evident and powerful as to indicate objectives far different from those suggested by some critics, who used the metaphors of “wound,” “blood,” and “surgical acts” (as hypothetical reminiscences based on his past profession as a physician, a connection consistently denied by Burri), or other sophisticated but hardly credible analyses that fell short of the full and well deserved acknowledgement of his art. As I see it, Burri’s painting is the outcome of the conscious elaboration of a very lucid poetic tension and a precision the artist himself called “infallible” as regards the concrete achievement of the objective of revolutionizing the tradition of painting of which, from a certain point on in his life, he saw himself as a historical depositary.

The enterprise followed a meditated process of unswerving poetic and cognitive determination in pursuing ideal artistic directions, choices, and solutions demanded of he who would prove to be one of the great epoch-making interpreters.

In the aftermath of a tragedy of unparalleled proportions such as World War II and as a man of proud temperament subjected to humiliation and deprivation during some three years of imprisonment, the young painter developed a *Weltanschauung* that allowed him to poetically elaborate the unspeakable dramas he had been through and get on with his life. Challenging norms and wielding a visual language that diverged radically from the prevail-

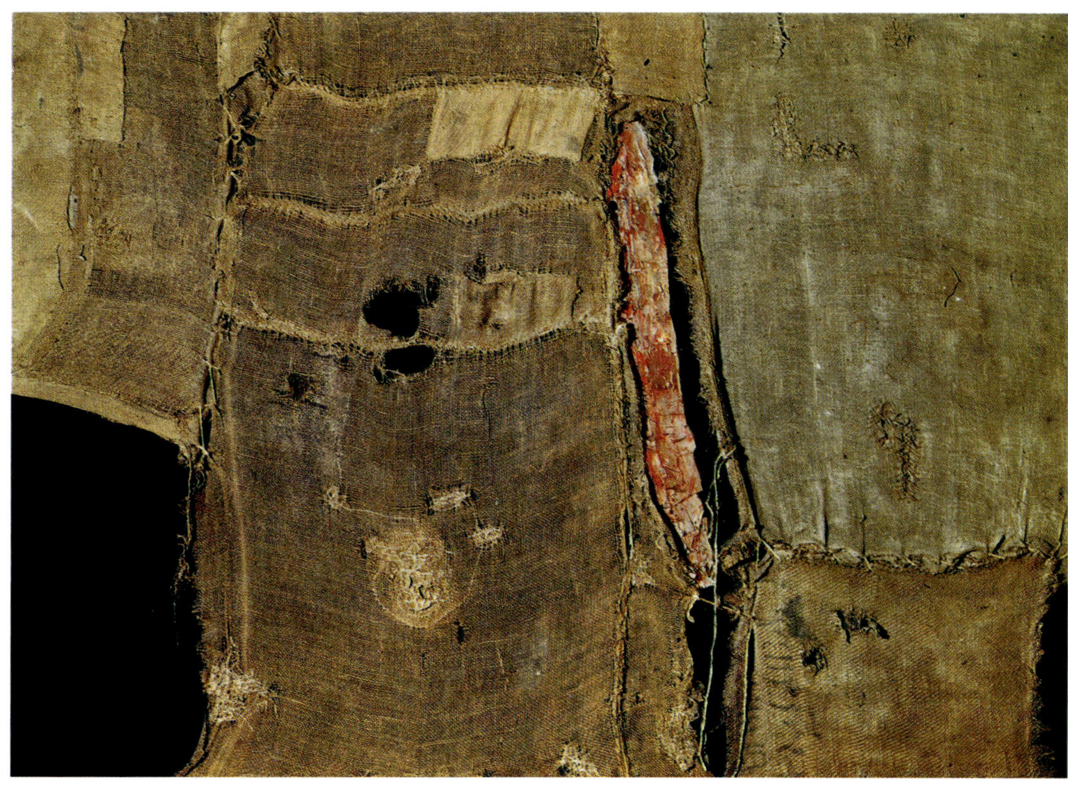

ing idiom, he demonstrated the strength and irrepressibility of the processes of imagination that feed the thoughts of a man and his potential to free himself through art and poetry.

The readiness to take up a challenge, his ethical fiber, his inclination towards his compositional faculties, his innate sense of measurement and geometry, the ease with which he manipulated any material available to him—probable legacy of the Robinson Crusoe life in the Hereford camp—and his desire to use it to surprise and amaze by transforming it into art guided Burri towards a totally novel idiom. His need for absolute equilibrium in his work and the executive rigor he put into it steered the qualities and objectives of the painter, destined to influence, starting in the post-war period, the sensibilities of painting and sculpture in the Italian and international art scene, opening up orientations that had never been considered before.

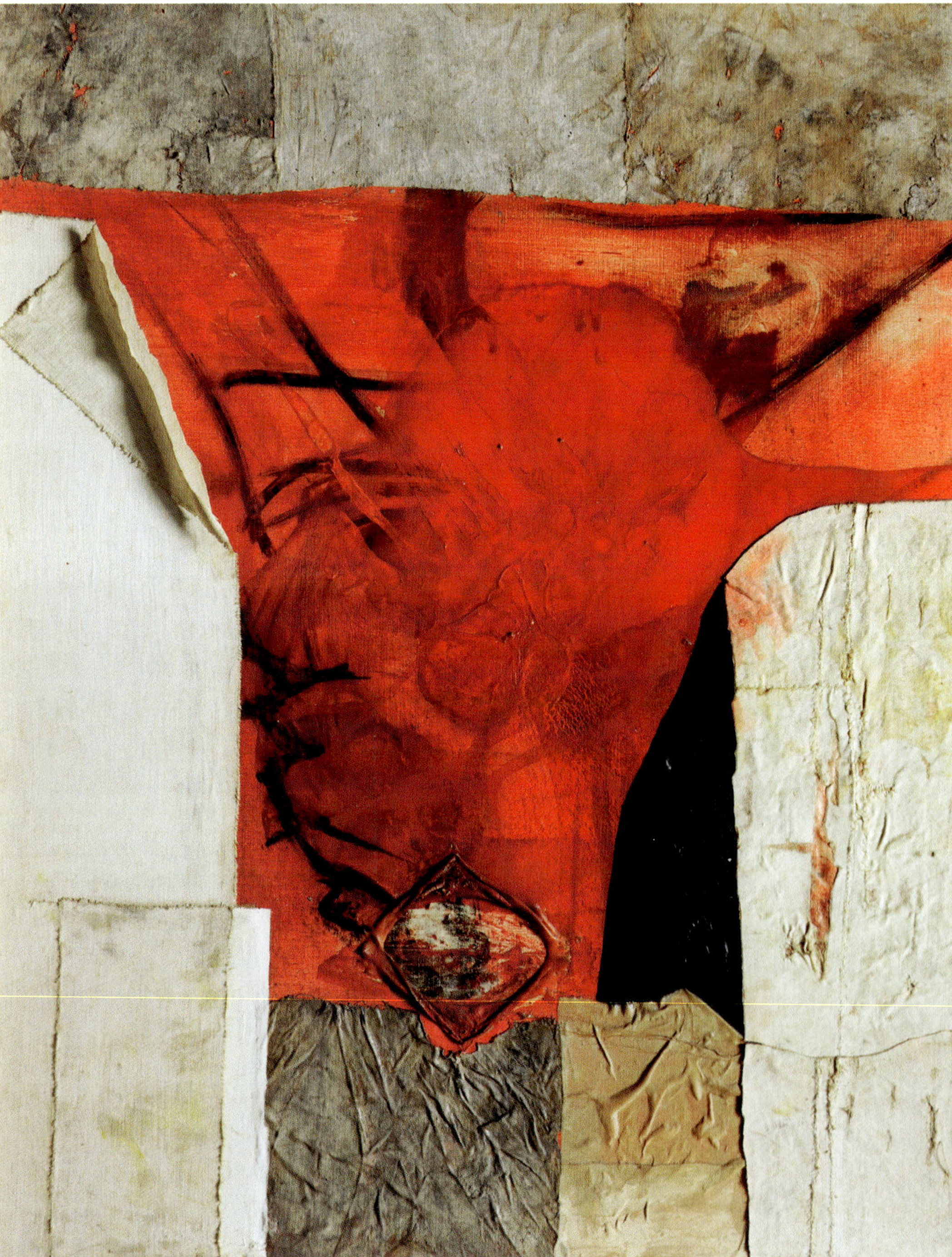

6. Alberto Burri,
Rosso, 1953
Private collection

7. Alberto Burri,
Rosso Gobbo, [1954]
Città di Castello,
Fondazione Palazzo
Albizzini Collezione Burri

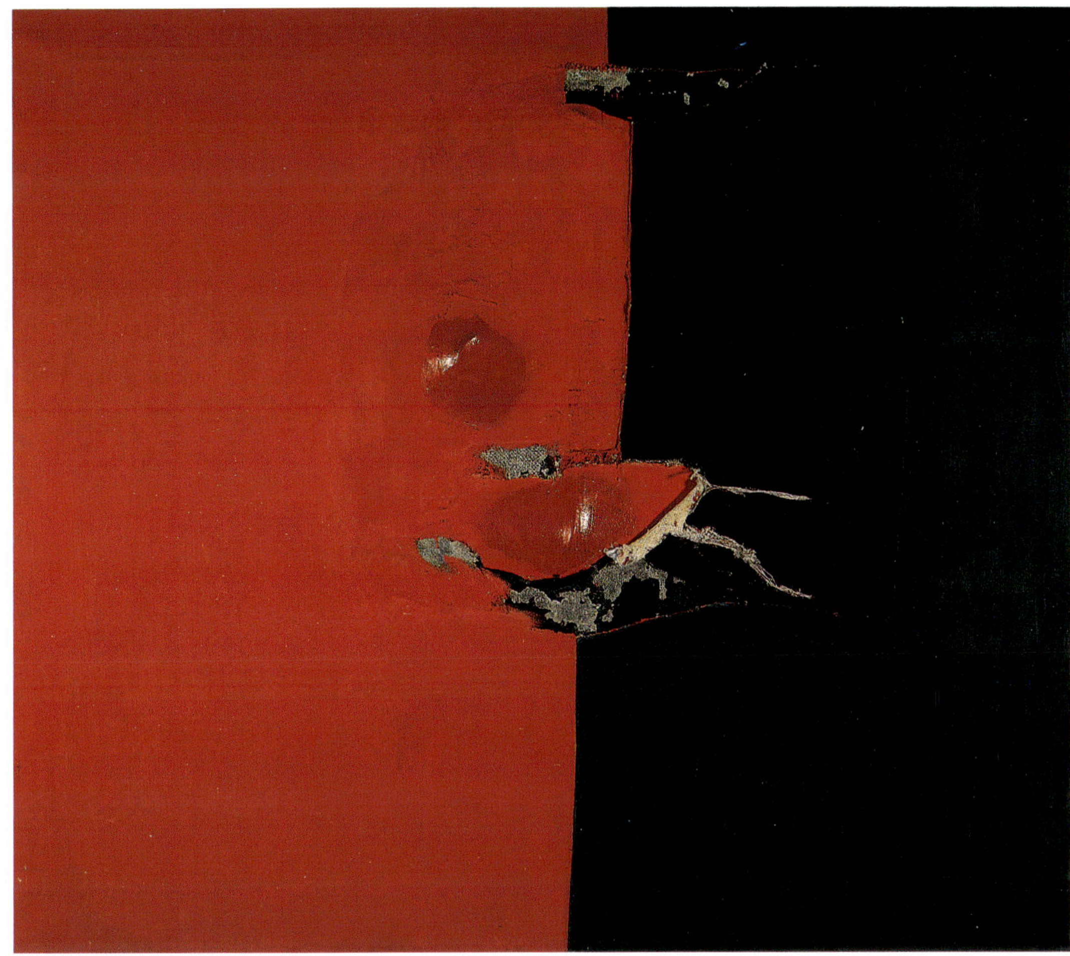

By the true display of the matter through painting, Burri overturned all precedents of representational value. Moving at the opposite extreme, he presented its form as a spatial equilibrium intuited almost rhabdomantically and then effectively offered in the work in a wholly novel poetic language.

At stake was the release from any condition limiting or inhibiting free imagination; the possibility to conceive and even access a new level of space, form, and beauty—the poetic level—that constituted the stage for a new artistic and anthropological venture after the loss of moorings suffered during the war. Challenge and wager underpinned a silent but no less incisive protest, when they are given voice in an image that Burri composed with a determination that borders on the drama of a scream, lacking any aesthetic filter that might blunt its impact on the observer. Burri knew that his pictorial logic and linguistic innovation pushed the extremes of the observer's emotional tolerance for broken rules. But he moved towards and even forced that limit, already having a clear idea in his mind about painting—as Cennino Cennini said—as "an art [. . .] for which we must be endowed with both imagination and skill in the hand, to discover unseen things concealed beneath the obscurity of natural objects, and to arrest them with the hand, presenting to the sight that which did not before appear to exist."[8] No less, as Leonardo said, it is a "mental discourse" that has to become as *subtle* as philosophy, responding to the intuitions and thoughts of a logic spoken by every artist who seeks to visualize their imagination.

Burri's matter painting made its poetic debut between 1945 (his first oil painting on canvas, *Texas*) and 1949 (an oil on burlap sack, *SZ1*). Burri followed the perfected imaginative resolve of *Sacco* (1950) with *Gobbo* (1950) (fig. 9) and *Sabbia* (1952), and also with two

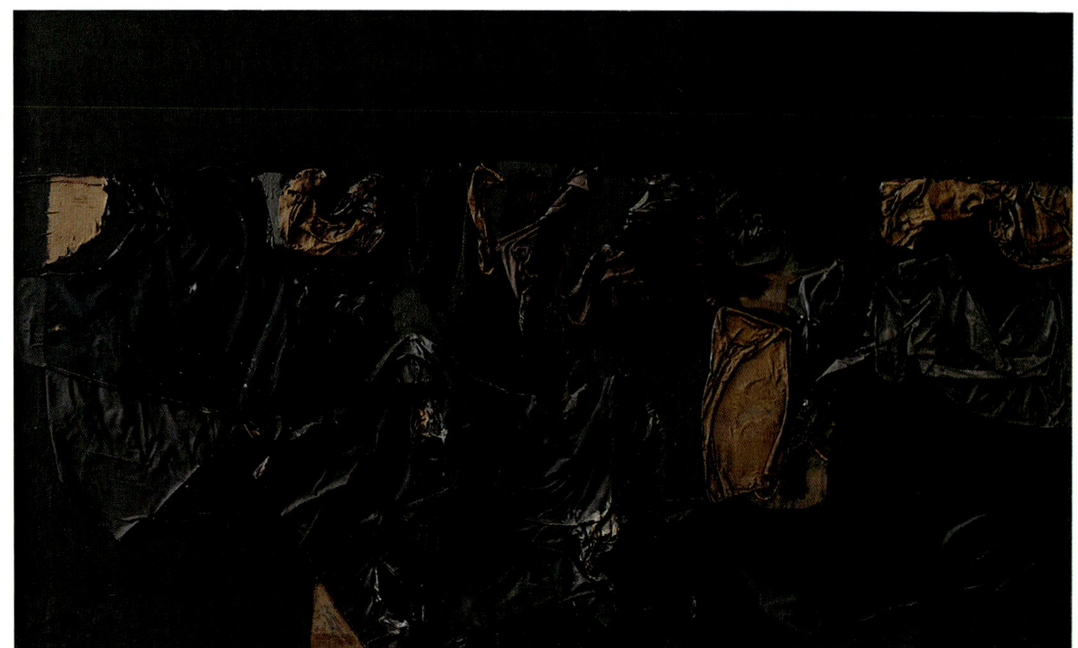

8. Alberto Burri,
Tutto Nero, 1956
Città di Castello,
Fondazione Palazzo
Albizzini Collezione Burri

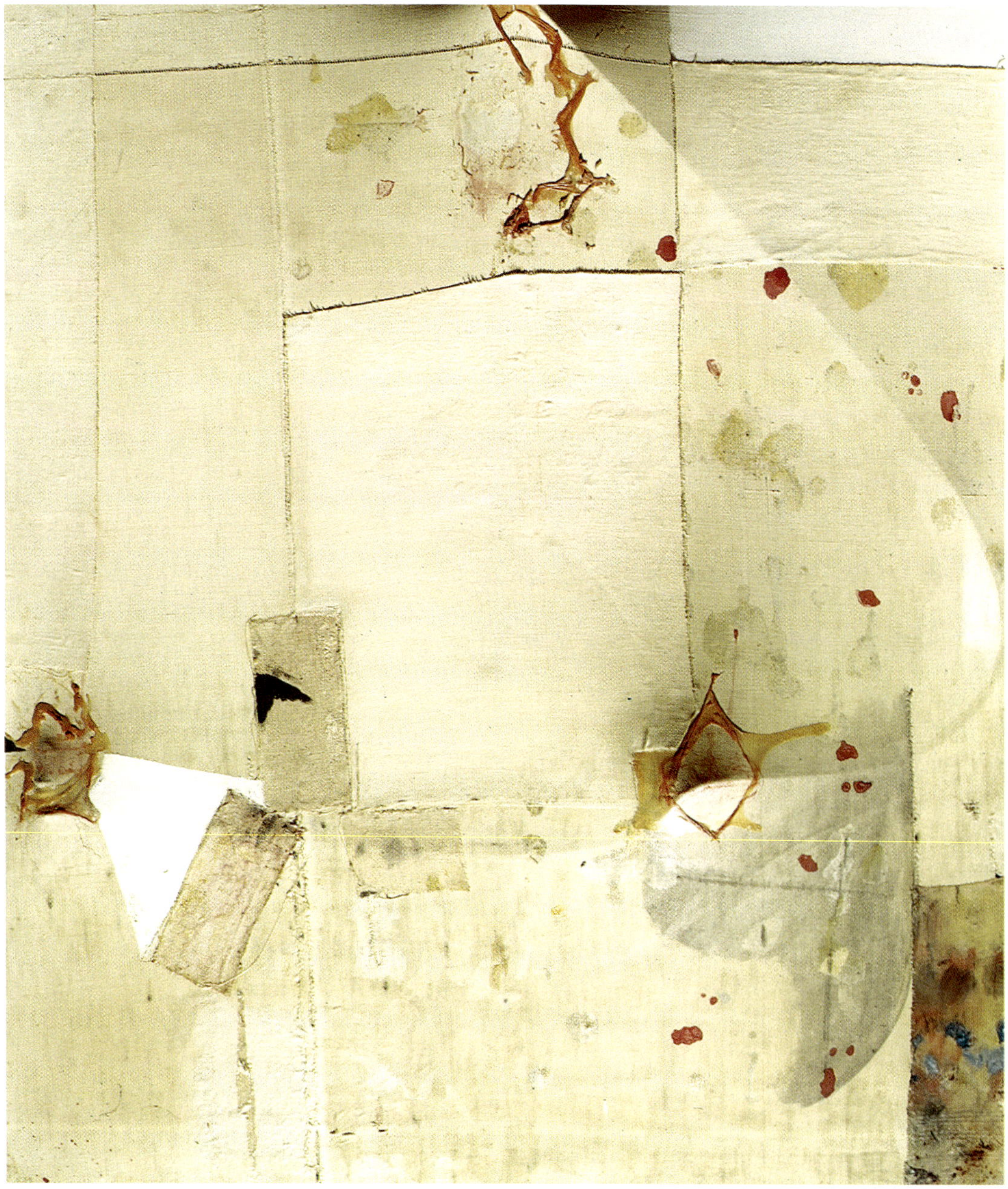

9. Alberto Burri,
Gobbo, 1952
Città di Castello,
Fondazione Palazzo
Albizzini Collezione Burri

10. Alberto Burri,
Rosso, 1956
Città di Castello,
Fondazione Palazzo
Albizzini Collezione Burri

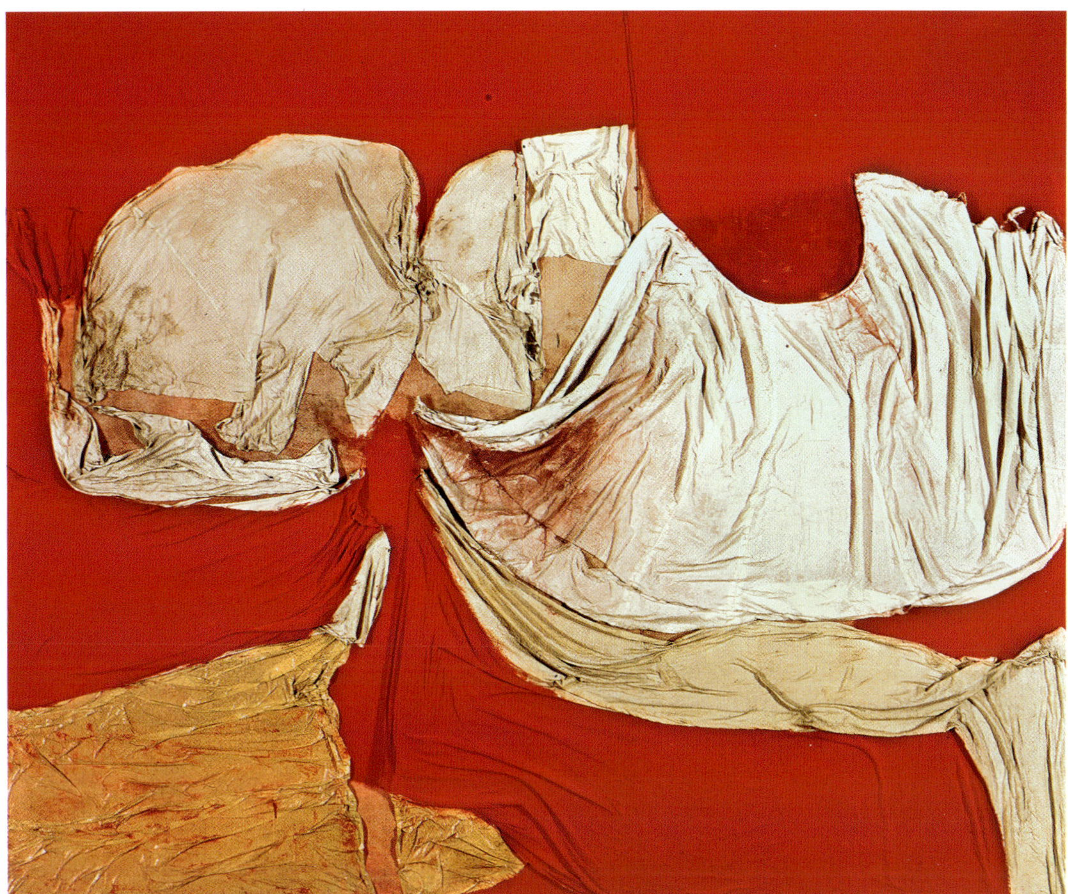

works that Robert Rauschenberg viewed in 1953 during his stay in Rome, when he visited the artist's studio: *Grande Bianco* (1952) (in the Burri Collection) and *Grande Sacco* (1952) (now in the Valsecchi Collection). The vivid impression would resurface the following year in Rauschenberg's *Combine Paintings*, as Charles F. Stuckey noted in the catalog of the retrospective at the Solomon Guggenheim Museum of New York in 1997–98. Emily Braun added to the story and extended the influence to Cy Twombly in her careful, well documented essay in the catalog to the 2015 Burri retrospective at the same museum. Braun refers to the use of white, an aspect of Burri's work that had certainly impressed Twombly on a return visit to Rome after his trip with Rauschenberg in 1953.

In spite of the regular use of different materials, drawing from them the same expressive power and analogous idiomatic results, Burri never exalted matter in its own right, that is, as a purpose for his poetics, rather he considered it to be a basic real element with which to achieve a quality of space and a form that he did not hesitate to define "unbalanced equilibrium, but equilibrium nevertheless," evoking its essence in the image.

The material, while being of central importance in the preparation of the work, has always been at the service of a poetic image-idea that affirmed, through sapient formalization acts, its innate momentum and gravity.

The Display of Matter

We should now investigate what moved Burri to complement his initially figurative painting by scandalously displaying matter as an emblem of itself, an original entity, a pure ontological *spectaculum* put to observation. Starting from the premise that Burri's birth into

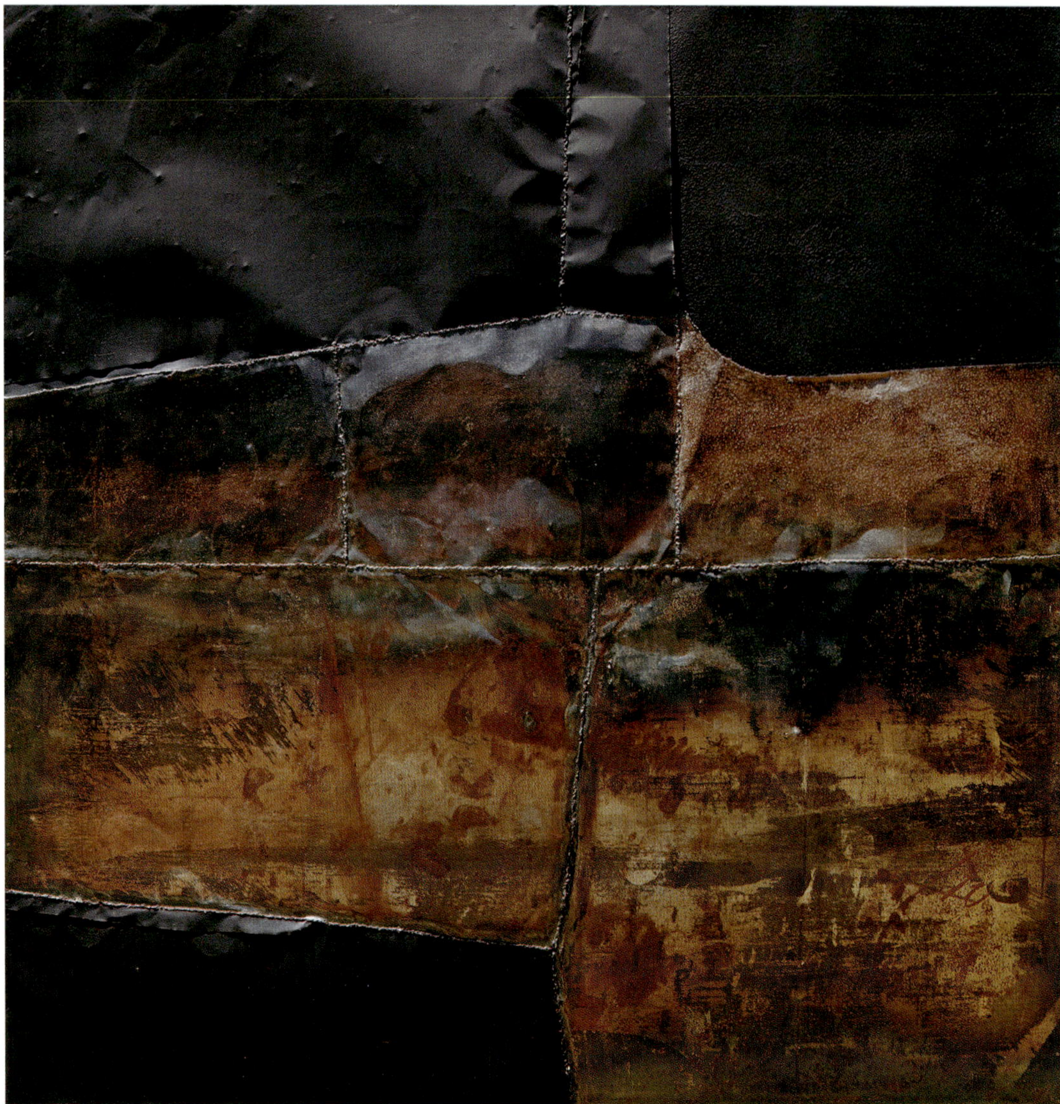

11. Alberto Burri, *Ferro*, 1959 Città di Castello, Fondazione Palazzo Albizzini Collezione Burri

painting was by palingenesis, any *logos* not radically cued to life dramatically lived was delegitimized in Burri's mind and useless to his poetic thought.

If the Greek *légein* means "gather," "choose," "count," and only later "narrate," the matter in Burri's first *Catrami* (1948) (fig. 1) coheres and is offered to the observer in the manner of a startling epiphany and laically "religious" experience. To get back to reality and communicate it to others—after the difficult consequences of the war—Burri had to identify an objective vehicle in painting for an individual regeneration that otherwise would not be believable to his own eyes. No previous experience he had had nor path taken in painting by others was capable of responding to his profound need to reset codes laden with meaning and history and thus having objectively reached the dead and existentially dramatic end of informal painting.

Among rare explicit statements, he said, "Words mean nothing to me; they speak about painting. What I want to express appears in painting"[9] and "Words do not help me when I wish to talk about my painting. It is an irreducible presence that refuses to be translated into any other form of expression. It is a presence that is at once immanent and active."[10] We may discern here certain fundamentals of that poetic tension resolved not in literary or narrative means, but in silent painting. Above all, Burri believes in painting as an independent, untranslatable idiom. Furthermore, the "presence" of painting involves the authentic "display" of matter considered by him to be a residual yet germinal element of every observation of reality, detached from prejudices or symbolic/meaningful projections. Moving on from the perspectival mode of representing reality, Mondrian's neoplastic grid had already led everyone to an "end of the line". Conscious of that terminal result, that wall, Burri looked to the material, mastering new liberty drawn from it to create space and offer it as a new possible dimension of painting.

In the post-war years, Burri envisioned this dimension in painting far removed from any previous illusory vocation it had had. The *tabula rasa* he prepared starting in 1948 accommodated nothing more than the simple revelation of what is true and real at the zero setting of bare matter in all its cognitive and poetic tension.

At the opposite extreme from the "fully worked" quality of representational painting, even abstract, Burri could accept only the non-contamination in his painting of something desert-like, pre-logical, primal. This embryonic matter set Burri off on his journey in painting.

In Fautrier, Dubuffet, and Prampolini himself or Schwitters, it had been observed that matter had assumed values, respectively, of "presages and anguish of flesh destined for

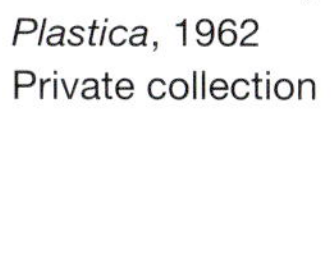

12. Alberto Burri, *Plastica*, 1962
Private collection

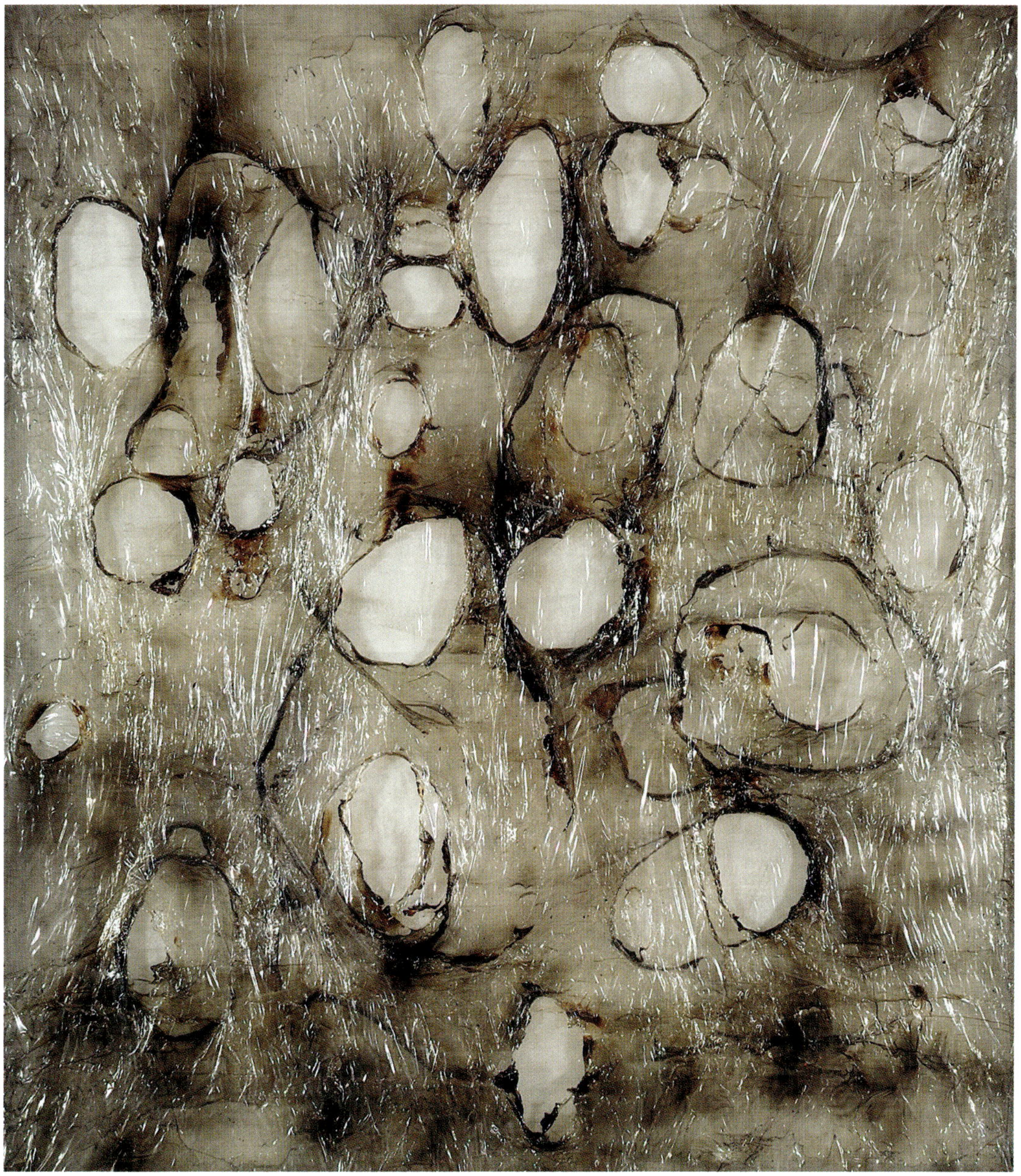

the earth," "irregular surfaces of different nature," and "futurist and constructivist polymaterialism."[11] But in all these and other cases, in its bare presentation the matter never rose to naked protagonism or ostentation. Even when unusual, the material in painting almost always accompanies or relates something other than itself and, in any case, lacks the ontological or frontal presence (Cesare Brandi's *astanza*) found in the work of Burri. What happened here is that Burri decided, starting in 1948, to obtain "action," meaning, and pictorial quality from the gesture of a composed and balanced "display" of the essential matter itself, eschewing any possible metaphorical value previously ascribed to it.

After the momentous announcement of his startling appearance in the agon of painting with the new language of the *Sacchi*, it was the sulfureous poetic writing of Emilio Villa (1951) to celebrate his advent:

> Alberto Burri cultivates, as if *in vitro*—nay, as if in linen—these contractile anatomies of unexpressed, uncertain organisms somewhere between the appearance of disused biological materials and an ideal of fulminous universes somewhere between

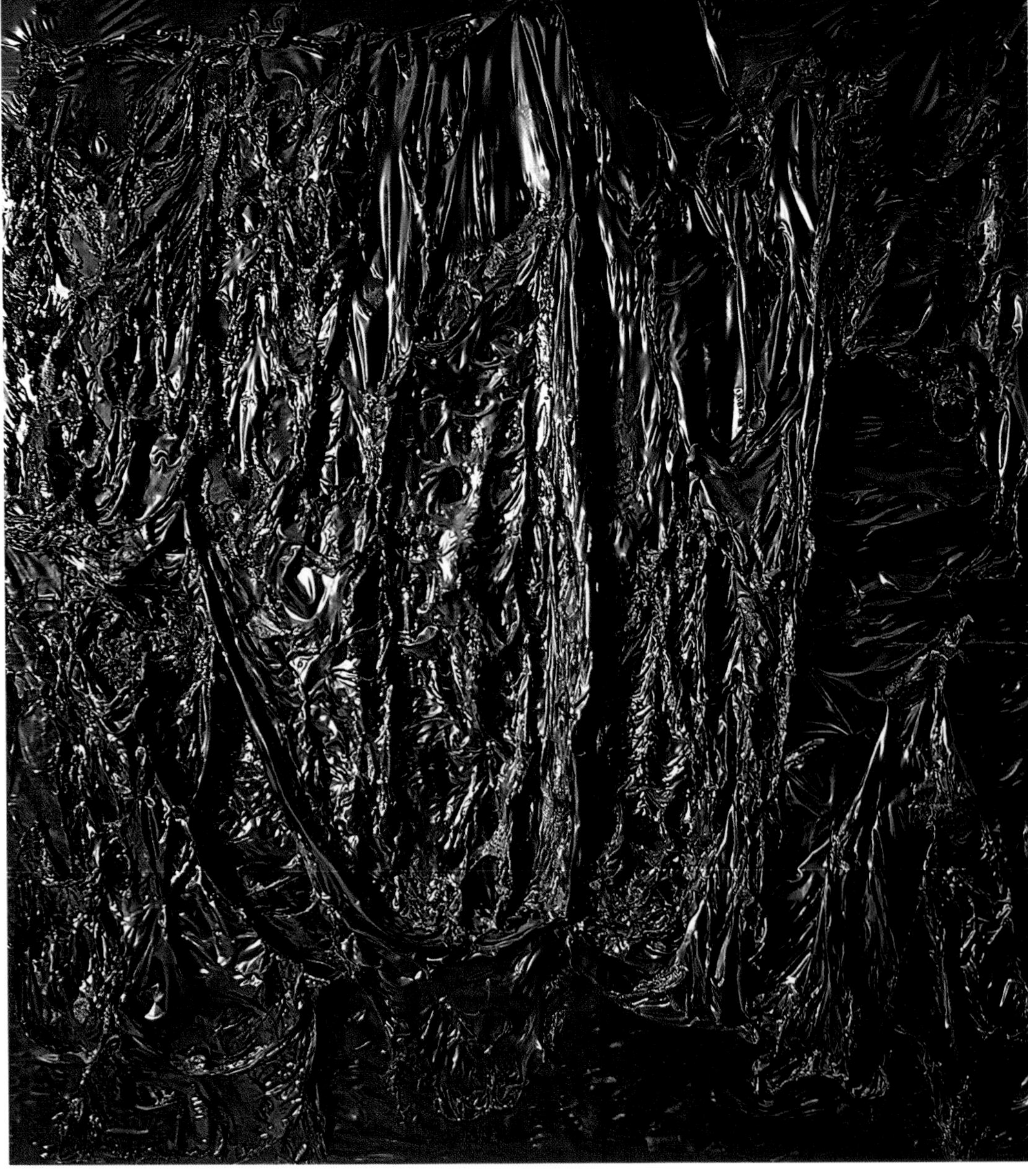

13. Alberto Burri, *Grande Nero Plastica*, 1964 Città di Castello, Fondazione Palazzo Albizzini Collezione Burri

> gigantic and super minimal [. . .], a lamenting cosmogony supposed with the simple innocence of ordinary materials, cast-off neighborhood rags, poor quality paints, amorphous pastes between decay and crystallization, scrap lumber destined for water or fire, asphalts, mucilage. A world of everyday wastes can be analogous and congenial to the most powerful imaginations: in any point in the world an alert and disinterested eye like the one that gives sight to Alberto Burri can surprise and draw out an image originating in higher sources, whence emanates exactly the meaning of our popular lay epic [. . .]. I remember Burri's great invention: the opaque, daring opacity after everything, drawn up from the depths of the *other* colors, and formed in highly expressive concretions, the existence of the world in its pure state, almost elegance, lightness conceived within the matter, before unity and before separations.[12]

Thus, from the *Muffe* and the *Catrami*, and then, in a more conspicuous way, with the *Sacchi* and the *Gobbi*, Burri began his method of displaying the matter that, demanding an active audience, quickly turns *in utero* towards a dramaturgic phenomenology of the work.

Cesare Brandi recognized Burri's intuition in later reflections where he asserted that this fully objective display of matter by Burri was "exactly reflected in the initial reactions of the public, which took affront at the humble material" and also stated that "this innovator [. . .] had understood right from the beginning the presentational role that the matter had to assume in his painting, and how he cared about that role and not about the matter in and of itself [...]; the *Gobbi* paintings confirm the role of matter in Burri's works, which is that of forcing the observer to react directly."[13]

If the *Catrami* and *Muffe* marked Burri's novitiate with heterogeneous materials that guided him towards meaningful outcomes, the *Sacchi* and the sensitivity he had gained for materials led him to an irrepressible spring, bountiful and clear.

The anonymous "life experience" that they display and the zero degree of their appreciable materiality as "things" are aspects that, determining the imagination of their use, prompted Burri, almost on a dare, to consider them key elements in his action of requalifying painting: crude, de-signified matter to display in the work by formalizing and qualifying its spatiality with extraordinary compositional skill, achieving unerring equilibrium among the parts.

The material elaborated by Burri in pronounced contrasts of color and surface textures often achieves a theatrical quality likening it to that of certain chiaroscuro works by Caravaggio. In many works that perception is generated by the pregnancy of the matter-colors struck by light in the foreground, contrasting with backgrounds lying black and dark beyond the holes, broad gaps and lacerations, both in the *Sacchi* and in the *Plastiche*.

Burri also resorted, perhaps as inclination, to the theatricality of matter in his large theatre scene paintings. They were clearly akin, except in scale, to the works in his most successful cycles. This ability to move from the scale of original conception to micro or macro realizations, without altering the aesthetic outcome, is yet more proof of how Burri sought and found, in all conditions, balance and quiet in the unpredictability of his "displays" of matter.

If we look into the core of this unrenounceable search for equilibrium in Burri's painting we must necessarily think in terms of quantitative-perceptual weights and measures of the matter-colors used in each of his works. In a certain sense, Burri assesses the power of a matter-color by considering its specific position, a specific quantity-measure, its relationship of contiguity with other "presences." In many parts of Burri's oeuvre there seems to be an active ordering principle that I would define an "organic equivalence", running in an undercurrent of rules belonging as much to nature as to art. Burri's is an equilibrium obtained mainly from a genealogical aptitude for discerning the golden measures in the art of his place of origin and from the centuries preceding him, and also from alternations of color and spatial distribution observed in nature, both in the agricultural design of his Umbria and in the desert expanses he initially experienced in Africa and later in California (Death Valley), without any interest in translating them into naturalistic painting, but instead as purely metric-chromatic-spatial suggestions.

The matter displayed by Burri gives origin to a linguistic leap he intuited by turning his back on the narrative and "metaphoric representation" of painting before him. Burri's insight interpreted matter as the genesis of a language that is open to the recognition of the "true" as the "real" that asks to be epiphanically "seen" and comprehended in its ontological magnitude. The *hic et nunc* often evoked regarding the material in Burri's work is thus the distinctive *quid* of its antimimetic presence.

This is the step taken by Burri in displaying matter. He also displayed its compositional equilibrium, absent which matter would have remained unqualified as a mere hackneyed ready-made in a chaotic residual state.

If Burri's grand pictorial oeuvre is recapitulated in cycles that revolve, each time, around a preselected material—tar, sackcloth, wood, steel, plastic, Cellotex—each one becoming protagonist of his painting, it is through their very *mise-en-scène* that the strenuous and tenacious action of Burri is evidenced, aiming at achieving form and space as objectives of the equilibrium that is always reached, in different ways and nearly infallibly. Burri engaged every cycle with the same principles and intensity. Any time he felt that a specific material's potential to stimulate his imagination had ceased, he moved on to a new and different one.

The lexical material in Burri's work is accompanied with equal frequency by other no less meaningful aspects emerging from the combination of organizing acts: sewing, cutting, gluing, burning, welding, shaping, connecting, and others allowing expression of manual skill and artistic sensitivity. Hence, while the contrasts in the chromatic juxtapositions of patches of different fabrics appear determining in the *Sacchi*, no less eloquent are the interrelations among their parts via seams, mends, overlaps, and borders that provide the work with a solid range of compositionally harmonious elements emphasizing tension among elaborative gestures.

In the mid-1950s, after having given life to some of the most significant phases in his experimentation with materials such as tar, pumice, white glue, sackcloth, gold, Cellotex, sawdust, cloth, rope, sand, tow, plaster, and oil, Burri introduced flame as a formative action in the work, determining its substance and image.

Fire, Blowing, and the Manual Control of Chance in the *Combustioni*

Without delving into its symbolic, anthropological, magical-ritual, or phenomenological value, it is unquestionable that Burri's use of flame to condition his various materials introduced an incisive poetic element whose disruptive power would produce significant outcomes in his work and that of others (fig. 16). In a slow but constant crescendo starting in 1951, he employed combustion in works such as *Senza titolo* (1951), *Dittico* (1952), and *Bianco* (1952), then in *Rosso* (1953) (fig. 6), and later with decreasing frequency in 1954–1956 in works such as *Tutto Nero 2 T* (1954), *Sacco* (1955), *Rosso e Sacco* (1956),

14. Alberto Burri,
Rosso Plastica, 1964
Città di Castello,
Fondazione Palazzo
Albizzini Collezione Burri

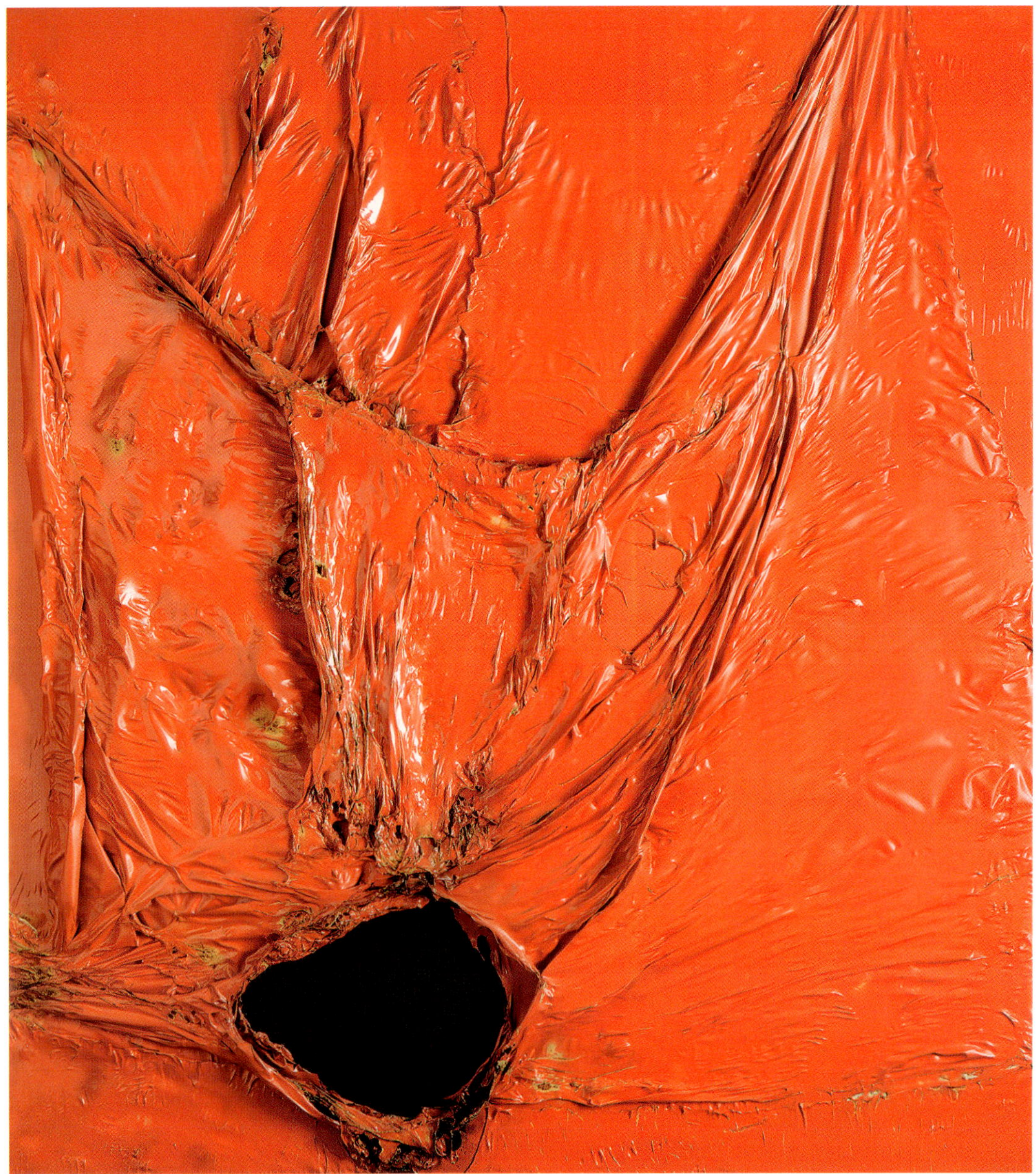

or *Nero con punti rossi* (1956). It became a fully recognizable method, producing veritable masterpieces when Burri began working with wood and plastic. Many works using his combustive method merit reference; Burri practiced "combustion" for more than twenty years, from 1951 to 1971, finally abandoning it on the threshold to his *Cretti*, fully defined already in 1971.

Legni, *Ferri*, and *Plastiche*

The *Legni*, sheets of veneer composed in serial structures, lacerated and blackened with burnt craters and crevasses, and the various *Plastiche* with their different thicknesses and colors—mainly whites, reds, and blacks, but after 1961 also transparent—took form under Burri's incessant action, wielding the torch to open gaps in the uniform surfaces and burn the central zones and boundaries of an uncharted territory of painting.

They marked new experiential forays for Burri: after the *Muffe*, *Catrami*, and *Sacchi*, it was the time of the paper *Combustioni*, the *Legni*, and *Plastiche*, which gave him access

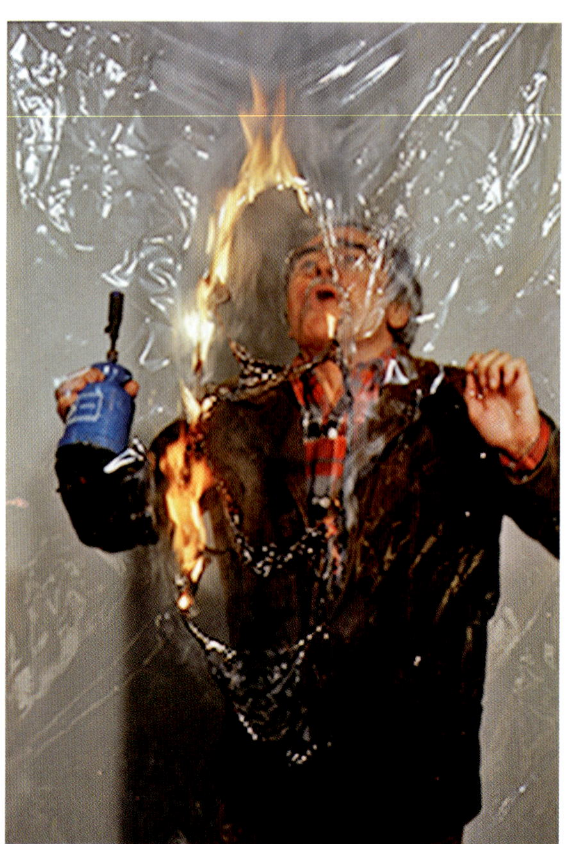

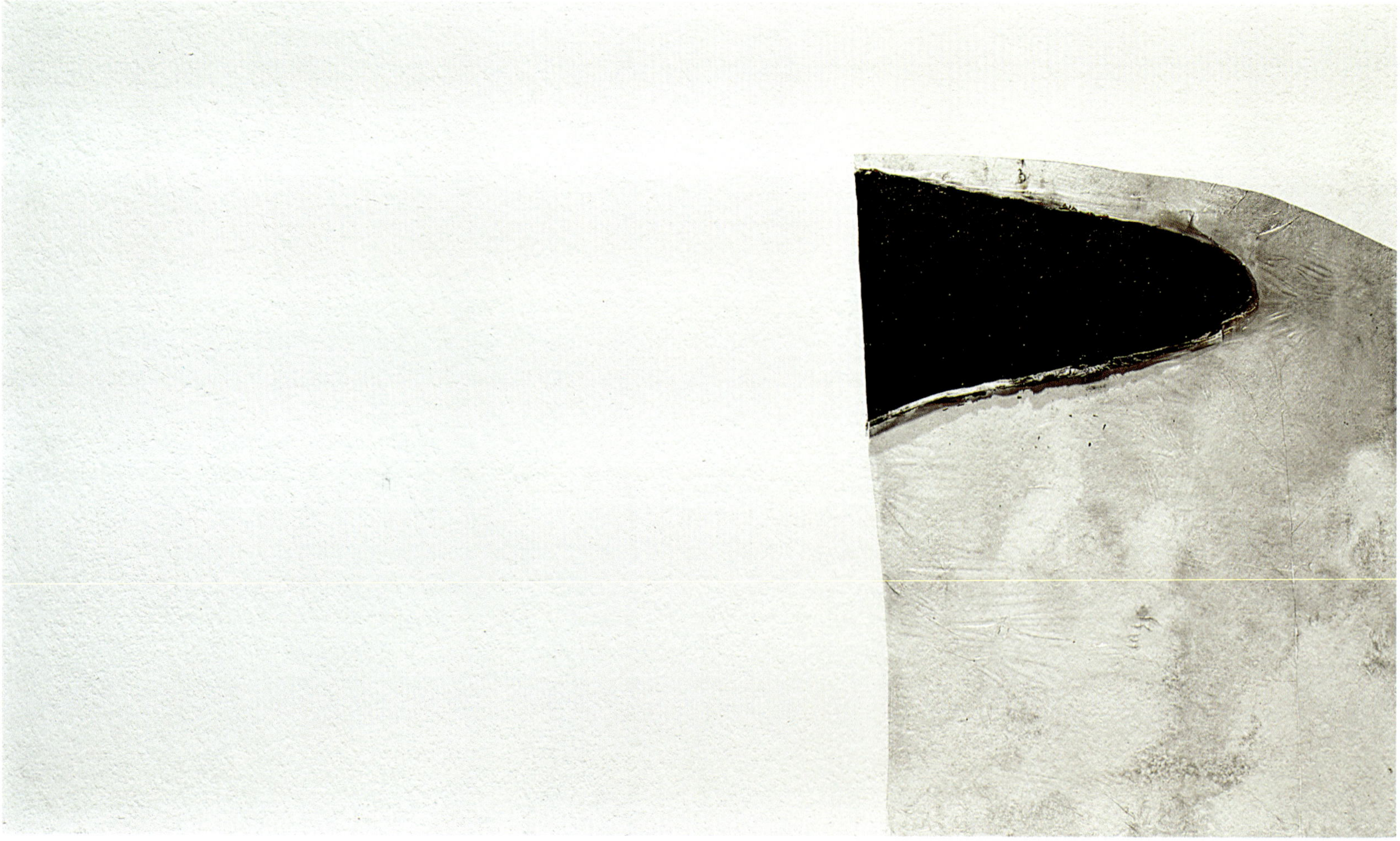

15. Alberto Burri,
Bianco Cretto, [1973]
Città di Castello,
Fondazione Palazzo
Albizzini Collezione Burri

16. Alberto Burri working on a *plastica*, 1976
Casenove di Morra,
Città di Castello

17. Alberto Burri,
Grande Bianco B 2, 1966
Città di Castello,
Fondazione Palazzo
Albizzini Collezione Burri

to shadows and phantasmagorias. He was not unlike an archaic shaman working before the wall of a paleolithic cave or a fifteenth-century fresco painter confronting a wall of a palazzo. Using new materials, Burri made his way back to the same path via the same inexhaustible artistic act. Like any great subversive dramatic poet—from Dante Alighieri to Arthur Rimbaud—engaged in the "descent into hell," which Pieyre de Mandiargues recognized early on in Burri's artistic path, he passed through arduous stages and learning experiences whose visionary narration is transcribed in works that configure—in a now-supra-historical spatio-temporality—the spiritual odyssey of a survivor returning from the historical catastrophes and abysses of twentieth-century imagery.

Burri also used the cleansing fire to give form to his *Ferri* (1958–1961) (fig. 11), composing and welding—like the *miglior fabbro* [14]—pages of rare poetic power. The *Ferri* meet the observer's gaze with the ardent pride of civil forms recalling the workshops of proto-Medieval Europe, where armor and armets were forged, but also gold and silver altar frontals, and that are still intact nowadays.

Flame, like painting, is difficult if not impossible to define. If we look at photos or watch films of Burri using a flame to lacerate transparent plastic surfaces and shape them with his hands, we comprehend that those images are worth more than any words to signify his formative acts. Burri's action with flame is strongly attractive because it transgresses an archaic social prohibition on knowledge. And it is doubly so because fire, seeming to destroy, is used by the artist to construct something hitherto unknown and to renew form at the root. It is desire, rather than need, that drives Burri's poetic excitation in using the flame. "Fire," writes Gaston Bachelard, "suggests the desire to change, to speed up the passage of time, to bring all of life to its conclusion, to its hereafter. In these circumstances the reverie becomes truly fascinating and dramatic; it magnifies human destiny."[15] But in the compositional will driving Burri's formative act on wooden, plastic, and metallic materials there is an ordering principle that Bachelard also accurately identified: "fire separates substances and destroys material impurities. [. . .] that which has gone through the ordeal of fire has gained in homogeneity and hence in purity."[16]

From the elemental primariness of fire, Burri shifts smoothly to other material essences: earth, air, water. As we will see, these elements are recapitulated in the *Cretti*.

The exhibitions of the *Ferri* at Peppino Palazzoli's Galleria Blu in Milan (1958) and the transparent *Plastiche* at the Marlborough Gallery in Rome (1962) marked, for many reasons, a significant junction that was every bit as relevant as the *Sacchi* and other stations on Burri's linguistic journey. And in achieving from those refractory and hostile materials an effectively "groundbreaking" and qualified image, he performs yet another miracle of transformation.

As regards the *Plastiche*, it has been observed that Burri showed an interest in this material as far back as the 1950s. In that period he created various works, such as *Sacco 5P* (1953) with a number of plastic inserts and later *Tutto Rosso P* (1956), *Rosso P_1* (1956), *Combustione Plastica Rosso e Nero* [1956], and *Nero Rosso Combustione P57* (1957), followed in 1958 by five *Combustione plastica*, three of which were small format, and finally *Nero* (1961), *Rosso Plastica 3* (1961), and two *Rosso Plastica* (1961), both of small dimensions. After that, almost in a gradual growth of executional difficulty but also aesthetic revelation, with the combustions of the transparent *Plastiche* exhibited at the Marlborough in Rome in 1962 the empty space of the lacerations and craters produced together with the black of the burnt material and its residues, the faint graded shadows produced by the flame and smoke, and the many needles of light released on the surfaces achieved a complexity that amounted to a poetic peak for Burri. With the red and black *Plastiche*, the artist abandoned transparency in favor of a frontal confrontation that prevented any penetration by the gaze. The observer is forced to seek bearings in the irreducible presence of the lacerated material, at times shining like glossy drool in *Nero Plastica* (1964), at times matte with shadows generated by the flame, at times uniformly black and abysmal in the featureless acrylic grounds of cratered zones, as exemplified in this exhibition by *Rosso Plastica* (1962).

18. Alberto Burri, *Grande Cretto Gibellina*, 1985–2015

The convulsive transformation of the red and black plastic surfaces created until 1964 in Burri's combustions took physical modification of standard materials to the level of a dramatic elaborative *furor* brought to bear on the plastic. Countless folds and gravid recursive deposits of material emerge from the post-combustive cooling and in the drawn thickenings of material. Burri created them instinctively, guided by an innate talent for calling forth an echo in our memories that reawakens not only the pain of hundreds of holy depositions in European painting from the thirteenth to the sixteenth century but also the more recent Deleuzian reflections on the aesthetics of the Baroque fold or those on the "fallen drapery" explored by Didi-Huberman.[17]

Starting in those same years, Burri worked on an extensive new conception of plastic combustions that require further and different observation. Among them we distinguish the group of small-format plastic combustions, structured as thin sheets of transparent, colorless cellophane on masonite, Cellotex, or hardboard supports and the much more solemn and powerful group of the *Bianco Plastica*, which the artist produced from 1965 to 1968, providing veritable masterpieces, a selection of which were exhibited by Burri in the personal room at the XXXIII Biennale Internazionale d'Arte di Venezia in 1966. Of those works, this exhibition features *Bianco Plastica B5* (1965) and *Bianco Plastica* (1967).

We must augment our observations of fire and the process of combustion in the development of the *Plastiche* with a number of considerations regarding both the cinereal matter deriving from the action of the flame on the plastic, and the action of the "puffs" from Burri's mouth towards the flame, no less important than the manual shaping action on the liquefying plastic. As it has been noted, the edges of the plastic rent by the flame present an "extinguished" quality of black that only the most expert chalcography is able to equal.[18]

Ash too is a material considered by Burri for its chromatic value and yet more symptomatic evidence of the transformation and physical disappearance of the plastic. It is not possible here to refer to "the traces that remain" as masterfully penned by Jacques Derrida in certain inimitable pages,[19] or by Nietzsche in reference to the life–death dyad.

The act of combustion is destructive and the ash is the trace of the destruction of the plastic wrought by Burri. However, it is also the construction of a new image, a vital work in that its form announces a new possible order of space and a equilibrium among signifiers contained within it.

In the films showing Burri intent on executing his plastic combustions, we observe the gesture of his hands shaping the lacerations as he produces them, not without, however, having first blown hard on the plastic that burns forming gaps within it. This blowing is thus an additional technique that cannot be discounted in the work of combustion. Emitted by Burri's mouth, it is coordinated with the gesture that shapes and observes a rhythm modulated by breathing as well as by the feverish craftsman's inclination to intervene and modify the free and casual combustion of the plastic. We no longer have the cave painter here, but the most audacious modern artist!

Manifested and renewed in these works by Burri—as would occur in an obvious way in the *Cretti*—is the desire to unleash chance, but also the challenge of controlling, con-

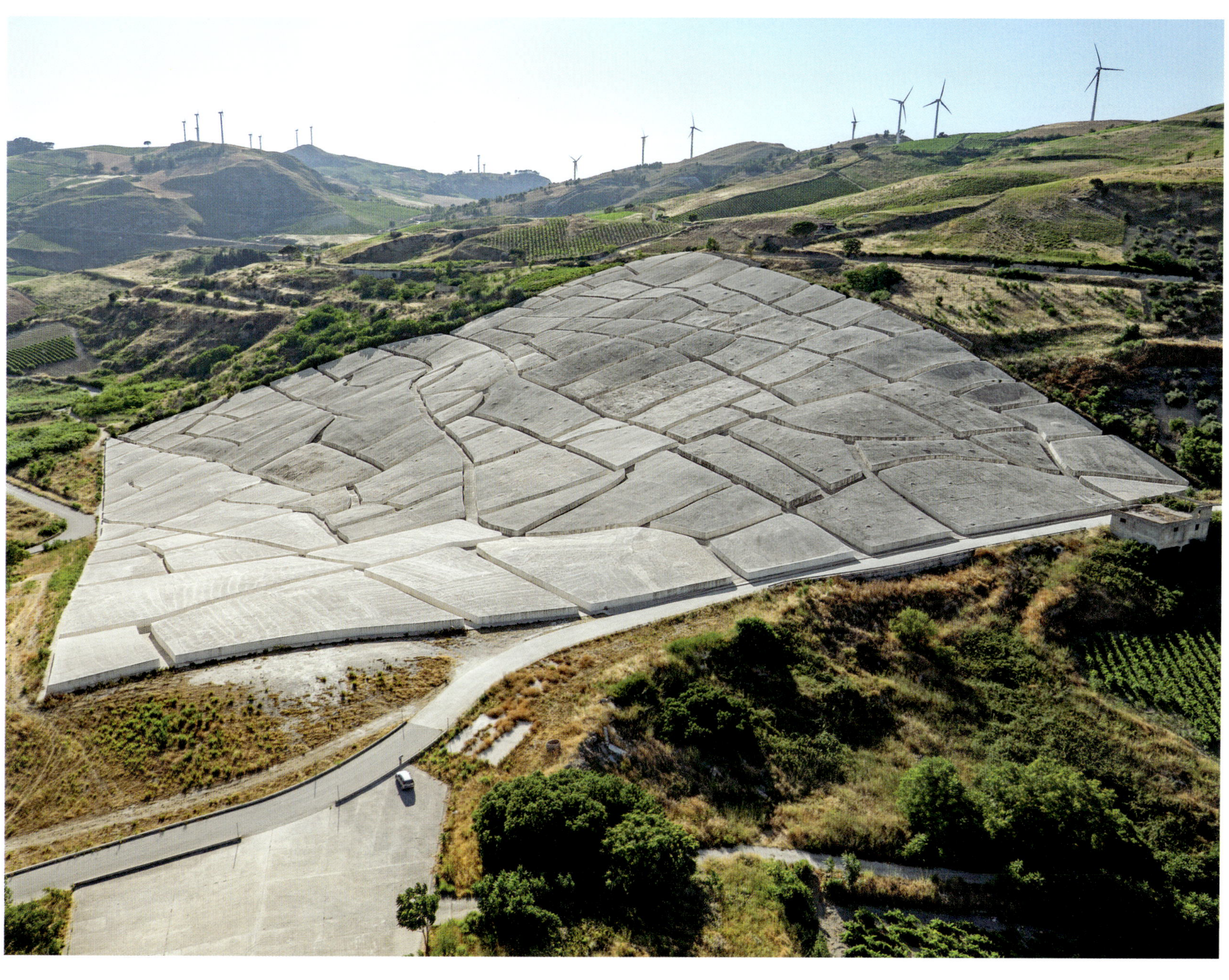

taining, and steering. An evident eros produced by the combustive action and its duration in time, accompanied by the risk of uncontrolled destruction, is manifested in the eyes of the observer beholding Burri in an *élan vital* that reveals his powerful emotions.

The blowing, the air, the breath, even if invisible and absent in the *Plastiche*, were elements as determining as was fire, it too now absent but leaving its effects in the *Plastiche*. The voids of the lacerations and craters present in the *Plastiche* were dimensioned and defined by Burri's blowing and his expert hands, the artist also calculating the "missing parts" in developing his works. Thinking of the holes, the fissures, the voids in the burnt plastic as a puff of Burri's breath helps us better comprehend the complex and novel spatiality well beyond the visible aspects of these works.

As has been acutely observed, when we exhale, what we are internally made of seems to spread through the surrounding space. "Darwin [. . .] hypothesized also that *breath* constitutes the quintessential *formant* of our affections, and thus of our gestures and our lineaments marked by emotion."[20]

19. Alberto Burri,
Nero A3 80, 1987
Private collection

The *Cretti*

Burri worked assiduously on his *Cretti* from 1973 to 1976, during which time he created the largest number of acrovinyls on Cellotex. Nevertheless, anyone observing the entire repertory of the *Cretti* will realize that Burri had already had the revelatory experience of that image in 1958 in *Tutto Nero* and *Tutto Bianco*, both from the same year. He decided

to include them among the *Cretti* in the systematic catalog he organized in 1990. Furthermore, he included *Cretti* dating from 1969 to 1972, as well as those from 1977, 1978, and 1979, years during which he also created the monumental ceramics of the *Grande Cretto* of Los Angeles [1977] and the *Grande Cretto Nero* of Capodimonte [1978]. All this to show that the generative development starting from a given material and specific methods frequently began before or extended after the period of his most intensive work in that medium. No less important, we may observe that while Burri was working intensively on the *Cretti*, he had already begun developing his *Cellotex*, created with materials he had been using for a longer time.[21] However, these overlaps of different material expressions are frequent in Burri's oeuvre, demonstrating a freedom unconcerned with classification schemes.

If we exclude the ceramic and metal versions, all of Burri's *Cretti* were created using acrovinyl glue mainly on Cellotex supports, with only a very few on masonite, paper or pasteboard, zinc sheets, canvas, or plywood.

Although each of these works is completely unique, we may note dominant aspects in their rigorous spatial configuration. Some of them exhibit broad curved forms obtained from the pure contrast between the crackled surfaces and the rest, predominantly smooth and monochromatic. Burri's *Cretti* are either black or white (with the exception of one work with both colors).

Chance and Imaginative Determination

Within Burri's oeuvre, the *Cretti* constitute an extraordinary demonstration of the artist's aptitude for triggering amazement that he consciously sought and achieved in various circumstances in working with each of his materials. The formation of the image in the *Cretti* is the result of a careful measuring and control of the artist's processes of destructuring the layers of acrovinyl glue; Burri conceived every step in the process all the way to the desired outcome.

Whatever the suggestions from nature, it is clear that they are the starting point for a process of qualification of the material that he guides through formative actions towards the achievement of the image. He does so embracing chance elements and stimuli, harnessing and working them into the equilibrium of form and space that fully resolves and realizes his poetic intuition. In each of these works, there is always a guiding action leading to the form to be achieved even though incidental content is produced; new manifestations of the deep, inner life of the material, which, depending on case and need, and under the looming specter of latent entropy, transforms and changes, bringing into evidence imponderable forces and tensions. Rather than opposing them, Burri goes with them, guiding his action to achieve the morphological qualities of his poetic imagery.

It is not within the scope of this essay to establish the deep and unknown phenomena to which the material in question was subjected, but rather to guide perception of how the formative thought and hand of the artist willfully guided those processes to the desired outcome. More than the numbers, weights, and percentages of the elements brought into play, we are more interested in noting that the *risk* undertaken in his game amounts to defying chaos and working towards the realization of new norms, new equilibria, novel qualities both envisioned and achieved. The rest follows from there, the questions that the works raise, each in its own way. But clear in all of them is Burri's desire to influence the randomness of material processes and guide them towards outcomes he has preordained.

What are the seats of thought, of consciousness, and of the senses that each of the *Cretti* arouses in different ways? What is the individual's gaze exposed to when it observes the secret motives arranged by the artist in each of them? In each *Cretto* we observe we may see what Burri has always called "control of the unforeseen."

The congenital absence of any human sentiment in the material objectively obligates us to consider it alien to any vice or virtue, any pathos or pleasure, to any projection of the psyche onto it. It thus makes no sense to attribute any symbolic meaning to the *Cretti*. Nor, on the other hand, can they be considered merely the expression of meaningless material. Burri, like any great artist, has aroused entities of meaning in these works that must be sensed. We can only dwell on their material and formal qualities, their design, their image, sense their feedback, and perceive what our gaze encounters. The consideration of the extent of the pervasive fracture that cleaves the acrovinylic compound is certainly the first aspect that cannot be avoided because of its evocatively dramatic power.

Gilles Deleuze's ponderous and keen analysis of the "fold" helps us understand how the crack, like the fold, has neither beginning nor end, eludes any resolution, and is a combination of the incommensurable and the measure, of the resistance and yielding of the material.

A crack in the ground may be due to drought, to the lack of moisture, to failed irrigation. It expresses a deficit that if protracted would lead to the extinction of all forms of life. Stripping the phenomenon of its naturality, Burri assumed its catastrophic and thanatological value, having epiphanically glimpsed in it a chthonic archetype more than an offbeat *vanitas*. It is probable that he had discerned the morphological aspect, exalting its coefficient of trauma.

Unlike in a natural landscape, the regulated, guided, composed fracture in the *Cretto* does not speak only of unknown and catastrophic elemental forces, but becomes the mirror of thought, of its insistent, thirsting, unquenchable questioning. If it is true that the work of art does not give answers, it does make it possible to pose ceaseless questions.

The space of the *Cretto* obliges the gaze to trace its fractures like a wayfarer lost among the streets of a deserted, abandoned city would do: the solid mass of incidents of a Burrian acrovinyl has the labyrinthine structure of the cerebrum and thought constantly seeking a way out towards a goal.

Burri's *Grande Cretto Gibellina* (1981, 1984, 2015) (fig. 18) has a body that can be traveled through; it contains the ruined fabric of an unfortunate village in the Sicilian Valle del Belice, snuffed out by an earthquake one winter night in February 1968. Entering its fissures, getting lost in the maze, the old streetscape of the town, we are reminded each time of the condition of those who lived in these lands. The *Grande Cretto*, a humanistic, mnemonic, and sublime work, evokes both the catastrophe and the inexpugnability of memory that both veils and highlights. Beholding the *Grande Cretto Gibellina* we understand that form is what allows us to comprehend the phenomenic essence of reality and that artistic space is a powerful thought giving meaning to things, in the most eloquent of silences.

Together with Picasso's *Guernica* (1937), Burri's *Grande Cretto Gibellina* is one of the most historically and civilly significant works of the twentieth century.

The invention of the "morphology" of the *Cretto* indirectly serves as a warning against the irreversible and catastrophic warming of a planet scientifically diagnosed as victim. Art sometimes expresses such premonitions.

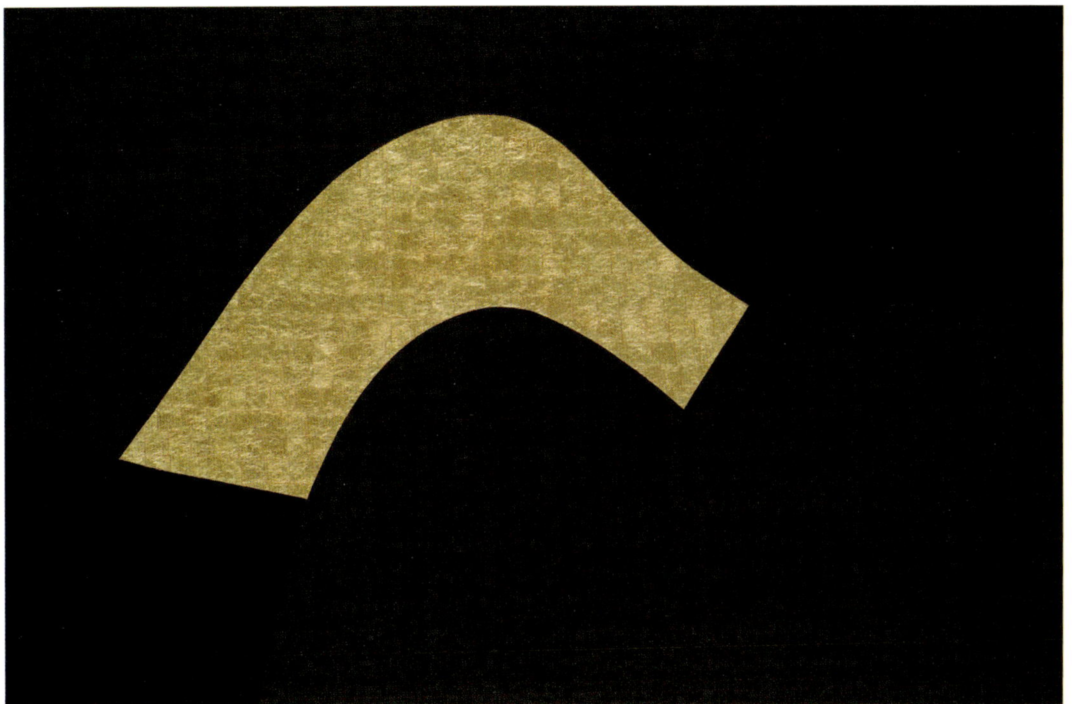

20. Alberto Burri,
Nero e Oro, [1993]
Private collection

Form, Space, and Equilibrium of the Unforeseen: the *Cellotex*

In his trails through material (and his art includes a nomenclature for the painting cycles that alludes to that metaphor of his existence: from *il Viaggio*, 1979, to *Sestante*, 1982, Burri included Cellotex among his repertory of materials (as a support) since 1950, thus quite early on, after his first abstractly structured paintings. In assessing the intensity and affirmation of values of form, space, and equilibrium of the unforeseen over the course of Burri's career, we may also note that, among all the materials he contemplated, he preferred Cellotex. Unlike the other materials he used, it never sated his desire to elaborate it. As stated above, Burri always stopped using a material, avoiding repetition, as soon as he sensed that he had exhausted its potential or become bored using it. At the height of Burri's artistic maturity, Cellotex turns out to be the material that expresses all the technical mastery and poetic, formal, and spatial expression of the master from Città del Castello.

Within the long timespan of Cellotex use, from 1949 to 1994, Burri used tools and methods starting in the 1970s that were as elementary as were the results, in terms of their spare essentialness and pure aesthetic tension. Through the skillful and measured use of PVA glue (Vinavil) and also acrylic, coupled with a technique involving a knife to remove Cellotex surface layers, Burri succeeded in composing images dominated by geometrical patterns of impressive proportions, but also with sensual qualities due to the chromatic breadth achieved in the use of a single color: black, red, or white.

Interesting in this exhibition is the apparently monochrome black *Cellotex* (1975, 150 x 249 cm) that is actually bichrome for the range of its blacks. Particularly effective is also the ocher and black *Cellotex* (1978, 126.5 x 211.5 cm) containing geometries evoking the "golden ratio."

Our wonder is always aroused by the sapient structuring, the different levels of articulation of the surface of the work accomplished via peeling, drawing, and black acrylic paint, and with gold leaf in the incised zones.

Burri's artistic trajectory concludes under the banner of gold and black. With *Nero e Oro* (1993) (fig. 20), full of light and shadow, not without byzantine echoes brought into its present, Burri's path reaches a sublime degree of spatiality akin to the majestic form and equilibrium of his first works.

Regarding the final phase of Burri's painting, defined as "serene classicism," Dieter Ronte writes:

> These figurative harmonies complete our aesthetic knowledge and invite us to serenity and meditation. The ideals of a classical "beauty," the traditions of the "Italian spirituality" become clearly evident in great works. The artist's materials and magic merge in paintings of great evocative power. Burri's technical independence ensures him autonomy and freedom of spirit. He opens new aesthetic horizons for us of hitherto unknown seriousness and dignity.[22]

[1] Ungaretti wrote the original statement in his own hand on a copy of the book by Bruna Bianco, Giuseppe Ungaretti, *Dialogo* (Turin: Fogola Editore, 1968) as a dedication for Burri having created a *Combustione* to accompany that edition. The exemplar is on display at the Fondazione Burri.

[2] *Alberto Burri e i poeti. Materia e suono della parola*, curated by Bruno Corà and Tonino Sicoli, Rende, MAON – Museo d'Arte dell'Otto e Novecento, 11 November 2015–28 February 2016. The initiative owes a great deal to the work of Tonino Sicoli, director of the MAON, recently deceased.

[3] Bruno Corà, "Burri e la parola poetica," in Bruno Corà and Tonino Sicoli, eds., *Alberto Burri e i poeti. Materia e suono della parola* (Città di Castello: Fondazione Palazzo Albizzini Collezione Burri, 2015), 13.

[4] Tonino Sicoli, "Burri e la poesia," in Corà and Sicoli, *Alberto Burri e i poeti*, 14–15.

[5] *Ibid.*, 17.

[6] Flavio Giovanni Conti, *Hereford. Prigionieri italiani non cooperatori in Texas* (Bologna: il Mulino, 2021), 297–298.

[7] Angelo Canevari, "Burri," *Spazio* 3, no. 6 (December 1951–April 1952); Lorenza Trucchi, "Dal casto Omiccioli all'alchimia di Burri," *Il momento* (18 January 1952).

[8] Christiana J. Herringhan, ed., *The Book of the Art of Cennino Cennini* (New York: Routledge, 2018), chap. 1, 4.

[9] Alberto Burri, quoted in Milton Gendel, "Burri Makes a Picture," *Art News* 8 (December 1954).

[10] Alberto Burri, in Andrew Carnduff Ritchie, ed., *The New Decade. 22 European Painters and Sculptors* (New York: The Museum of Modern Art, 1955), 82.

[11] Maurizio Calvesi, "Alberto Burri e i mutamenti dell'arte," in Maurizio Calvesi and Italo Tomassoni, eds., *Burri, gli artisti e la materia 1945-2004* (Cinisello Balsamo: Silvana Editoriale, 2005), 20.

[12] Emilio Villa, "Burri," in *Arti Visive*, I series, nos. 4–5 (May 1953); republished in Emilio Villa, *Pittura dell'ultimo giorno* (Florence: Le Lettere, 1996), 11–12.

[13] Cesare Brandi, *Burri* (Rome: Editalia, 1963), 30.

[14] Appellative attributed by T. S. Eliot to Ezra Pound in the opening to *The Waste Land*, Pound having masterfully intervened in the English poet's versification before Eliot published his masterpiece.

[15] Gaston Bachelard, *Psychoanalysis of Fire*, tr. Alan C. M. Ross (Boston: Beacon Press 1987), 16.

[16] *Ibid.*, 103–104.

[17] See Gilles Deleuze, *The Fold: Leibniz and the Baroque*, tr. Tom Conley (Minneapolis: Un. of Minnesota Press, 1993); Georges Didi-Huberman, *Ninfa moderna. Essai sur le drapé tombé* (Paris: Gallimard, 2001).

[18] The etchings on paper done by Burri first with the assistance of Edizioni Castelli (1959) and then of Stamperia 2RC (1964–1965), directed by Valter Rossi, provided exemplary results of what can be achieved in simulating the "burned" and ashes using different techniques.

[19] Jacques Derrida, *Cinders*, tr. Ned Lukacher (Minneapolis: Un. of Minnesota Press, 2014).

[20] Georges Didi-Huberman, *Gesti d'aria e di pietra. Corpo, parola, soffio, immagine*, tr. Chiara Tartarini (Reggio Emilia: Diabasis, 2006), 26–27. Originally published as *Gestes d'air et de pierre. Corps, parole, souffle, image* (Paris: Minuit, 2005).

[21] Bruno Corà, "Burri e i Cellotex: un denominatore comune nella pittura di materia," in Bruno Corà, ed., *Alberto Burri. Opera al nero* (Milan: Skira, 2021), 11–45.

[22] Dieter Ronte, "Material und Magie/Materiale e Magia," in Alberto Burri and Dieter Ronte, *Alberto Burri, Cellotex und Multiplex* (Città di Castello: Rubini & Petruzzi, 1981).

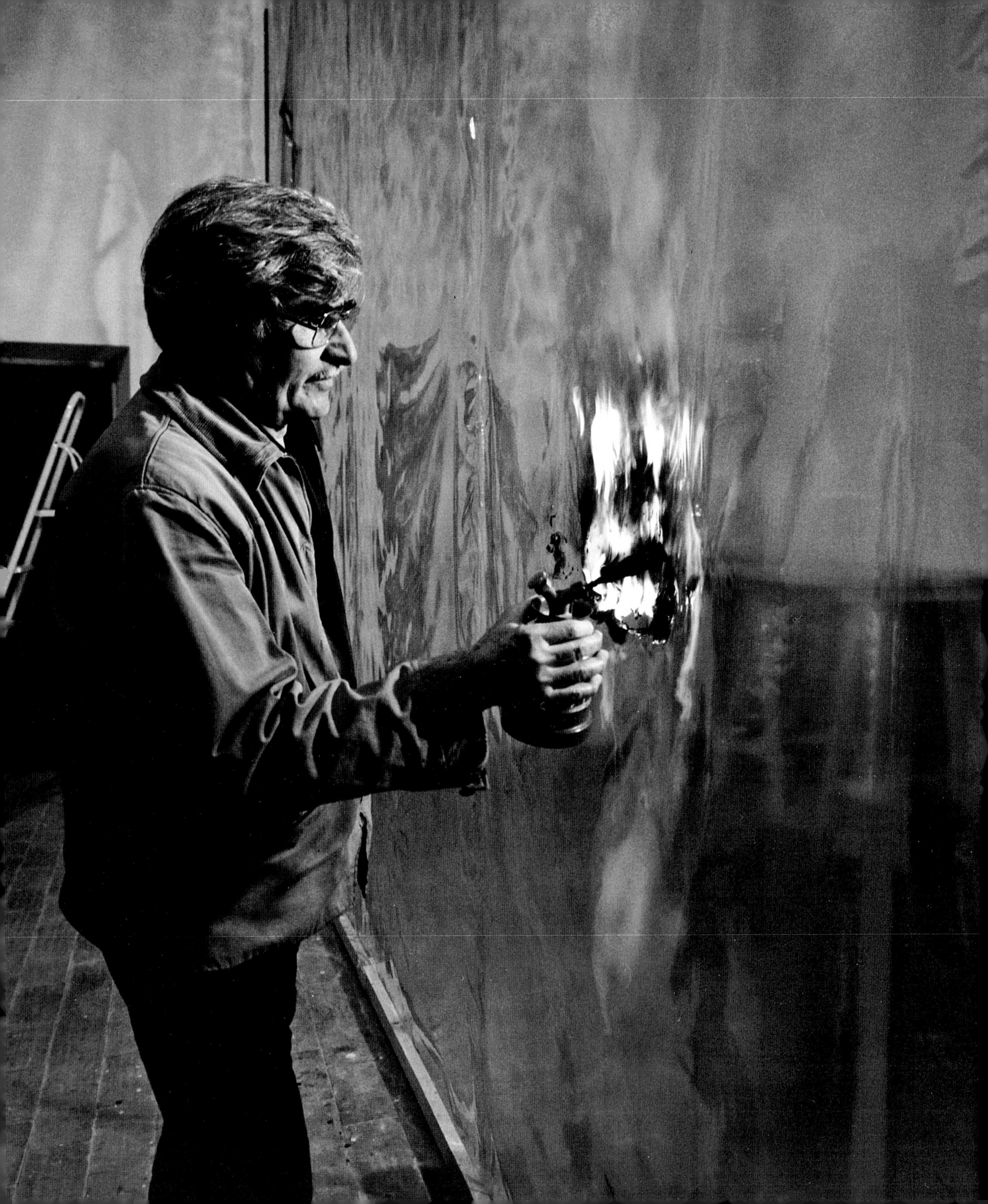

Matter Speaks

José Jiménez

Alberto Burri's artistic work is among the most original and valuable to have been developed in the 20th century. At its core lies his will to make matter speak through painting. Burri identifies it—matter—as a mirror of what we feel as human beings in our lives. The craters, hollows, cuts, and tears that animate his painterly language lead us to see ourselves in our inevitable fragility: we are fragile.

Burri acts by shaping matter with complete freedom, without ever subjecting the form to mere external replication. The forms we find in his works spring from the interiority of matter through interrogation of our senses and our mind. All this takes place in the unfolding of a process which, in the course of the 20th century, produces what we might call "the explosion of form," an intensely plural search for modes of representation that address the possibility of going beyond traditional imitation of external reality.

Such approaches are commonly labelled "abstraction" or "informalism." These terms seem to me unsuitable, the former because the visual arts in all their variants have a central core of abstraction contained within their forms, and the latter because without forms there is no visual representation; forms are constantly present in every kind of visual art. So I think the most appropriate way of precisely locating the sphere occupied by Burri's work, and that of other artists who converge in the same direction, is to speak of "non-figurativism," as opposed to figurative art (at once abstract and formal).

In that non-figurative sphere of the explosion of form, Burri's way of working is never intuitive or improvised. On the contrary, he always deploys a very precise and controlled use of his artistic working technique, as he himself pointed out in 1965, for example, in relation to his work with plastics:

> I am looking for elasticity, but I can also make the color split whenever I want to achieve those white surfaces with all the cracks, by varying the thickness and quantity of material. You have to be able to control the material and that comes with experience. For example, with these burned plastics, I am in control of my technique from start to finish.[1]

Control and *precision*: for Burri, painting does not arise from mere chance, nor from rejecting given forms. To my mind, all this is also profoundly related to certain decisive aspects of his life: his medical training, his enlistment as a volunteer military doctor during World War II, his capture in Tunisia, and his internment in a prison camp in Texas, which is where he decided to abandon working as a doctor and devote himself to painting.

Alberto Burri, Casenove di Morra, Città di Castello, 1976

During the terrible war years Burri had had the profound experience of the destruction of life, the search for supports and signs of recovery, the solidity of materials that remain

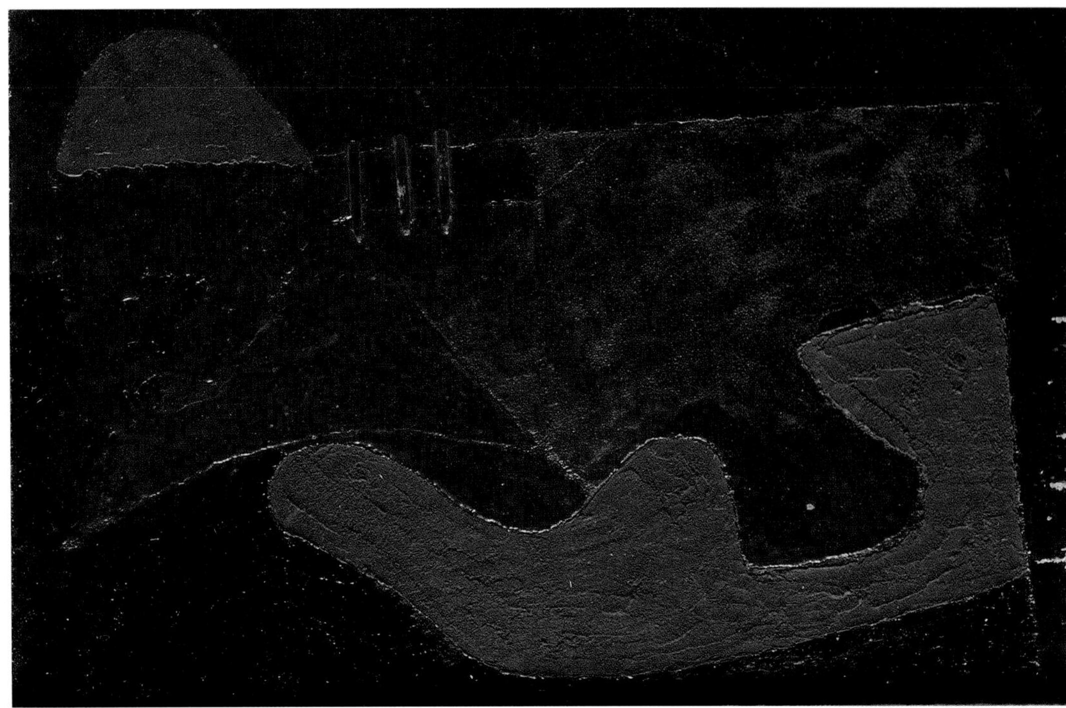

1. Alberto Burri, *Nero*, [1950]
Private collection

alive in spite of tears and cracks . . . Obviously, the craters, hollows, cuts, and tears that characterize his work are lingering echoes of those experiences, always visualized through the deep gaze of a doctor. The pains of matter mirror the pains of humanity.

Although he had already painted landscapes as a student, in Umbria, what had been a pastime then, as Burri himself points out, turned into something very different in the prison camp: "What a difference!," he confesses. "Back then it was just a pastime, a form of relaxation. But at Hereford painting began to fill my life and give me strength."[2]

That was when he found "true freedom" in painting, and when he noticed its complex nature and the impossibility of translating it into any other medium of expression: "When I started to paint, I think my work allowed me to find true freedom. [. . .] If I try to talk about painting, I realize once again that it is *an irreducible presence that refuses to be translated* into any other form of expression."[3]

Alberto Burri leads us here to a consideration of *painting* as *a fully autonomous language*, which could not be translated into another type of language. The fact is that the non-figurative painterly language he develops in his works has no immediate correlation with the visual perception of external reality, which can be perceived in figurative painting (regardless of its degree of abstraction). In Burri it is a question of making *visual poetry*, with intense, completely open meanings: never one-directional, using the registers and material supports we find in life as media of expression . . . *Matter speaks*.

That search for a more inner understanding of forms than we get from immediate figurative representation leads us to the level of "inner form." This is a concept formulated by Ernst Bloch, the great philosopher of utopia, in one of his first books: *The Spirit of Utopia* (revised edition of 1923, originally published in 1918). The explosion of form in modern art made it possible to "steer toward our true home," providing access to the deeper meaning of aesthetic experience, the necessary leap "into self and truth, into the power of the seal and into expression, into the ideogram of revealed inwardness, of the figure of life, of humanity."[4]

What is thus revealed is "the secret human form," the "image of the innermost shape."[5] Works of art act as "mirrors of the world," in which the heart of man and the heart of the world are found, and in which "sounds of the invisible world" take shape. And thus, when artworks reflect our innermost form, which always remains hidden, they illuminate the desire and nostalgia that dwell in our hearts: "finally see the human countenance," "the mysterious outline of the human countenance."[6] That is where Burri's works lead us: to the inner form of what we are, feel and think, through its echoes and reflections in matter.

In all these questions we find substantial levels of convergence with the approach of Antoni Tàpies, an artist who also constantly seeks to represent *inner form* by making *matter think* and *speak*. Tàpies himself, after pointing out that he had sometimes been compared to Alberto Burri, qualified his closeness to him by explaining that Burri "follows the principle of subordinating composition and expressiveness of color, shape, and texture to highly deliberate visual ideas. This is the opposite of what happens in my work, where textures are combined with signs, with symbolic and personal allusions."[7] And this last point is quite accurate: the use of signs involving symbolic and personal associations is a central feature of the works of Antoni Tàpies, unlike what we find in Alberto Burri.

But certainly, the issue that most suggests a closeness between the works of the two artists is an *interest in matter*. And even in what Tàpies conveys on this question we can find an important biographical parallel, in their experiences of *sanatoria* and *war*:

> It could be said that my inclination as an artist began in a sanatorium bed. Those years I spent in a sanatorium coincided with World War II, and they were also the years when news was starting to reach us of scientific studies on the constituent elements of matter, atoms, subatomic particles, and of course the explosion of the

2. Alberto Burri, *Plastica T*, 1962
Città di Castello, Fondazione Palazzo Albizzini Collezione Burri

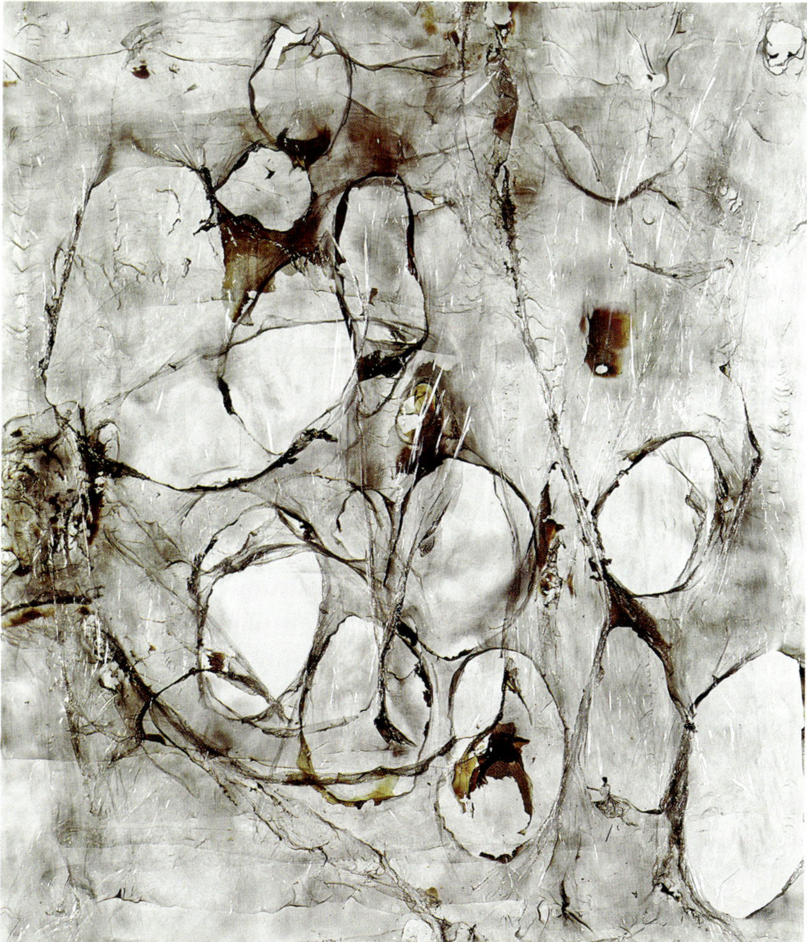

atomic bomb. All this became extremely topical, and perhaps my use of matter, and my fondness, as you might say, for closely analyzing and studying matter, comes from the fact that the whole of society at that time was concerned to know what matter was and what was the nature of that energy capable of creating such a terrible explosion as the one in Japan.[8]

In the light of all these considerations, where does Antoni Tàpies place the boundary between what is and is not "art"? Through his works, always highly concentrated visually, Tàpies teaches us to look with different eyes at our everyday surroundings, the materials, and supports that do not usually attract our gaze. However, the roots of visual expression are common to all human beings. And patches, tears and scribbles are links that tend towards fullness of expression.

From surrealist automatism, the painter goes beyond painting. Thick superimposed layers. Scratches. Extravagant profusion of collage: paper, string, thread . . . To the point of aesthetically interrogating material objects, which become "an extension of reality." If the eye and the hand are interconnected, so are repetitive expressive babble and the emergence of signs. Taking interrogation of the visual world to its ultimate extreme, as Tàpies does, therefore involves radically rethinking the boundaries of art.

All the more so if our gaze lingers on the spiritual framework of things, that ideal undercurrent that allows us to see the entire universe concentrated in a geometric point, or latent life in a tiny grain of sand. Everything in everything. But then a wall is not simply a wall. Nor is a torn stretcher mere broken wood and fabric. Nor are the traces and incisions that impregnate and perforate materials meaningless remains.

On the contrary. The roots of art spring from the simple act of marking or touching. At the moment when our hands or our feet come into contact with any kind of matter in the world, natural or artificial, they leave the trail of a sign in their impressions. And the world is populated by signs. Incisions. Lines: vertical and horizontal, straight and curved. Colors. Strokes. Stairs. Crosses. Letters. Marks. Arrows. Graffiti. Scribbles. Pictograms. Figures. Chairs. On canvas. On the rough surface of a wall. Or on the vegetative skin of wood. A rainbow of signs displayed in the works of Tàpies.

In an intense parallel with Alberto Burri's expressive procedures, Antoni Tàpies is *a writer of bare forms*. In his work perspective as an artist, everything non-essential that sometimes accompanies our idea of art is unmasked. The chromatic asceticism so common in his painting should be understood as an attempt to oppose the instrumental use of color, and at the same time as a way of establishing a color range capable of "communicating" with our necessary inner silence, so troubled, so beleaguered in this world of noise and vanities.

In his own words: "Being constantly surrounded by the impact of the advertising and signage typical of our society also led me to look for a more internalized color, which could be defined as half-light, the light of our dreams and our inner world."[9] The artistic has nothing to do with the ornamental. It is a fundamental questioning of the origin of the senses. Why is life not just drifting, dissolving into the emptiness of material existence? Because matter has a life of its own: spiritual breath. And the human eye, through the hand, reveals the intense, open process of communication between all forms of life and experience. Art is the resonator of the spirit of the universe.

This attitude means going beyond the positivist register which has so strongly conditioned Western culture through the expansion of modern technology. Through art, Tàpies has managed to transcend it, by establishing an intense contact with Eastern spirituality, and

3. Alberto Burri,
Sacco 5P, 1953
Città di Castello,
Fondazione Palazzo
Albizzini Collezione Burri

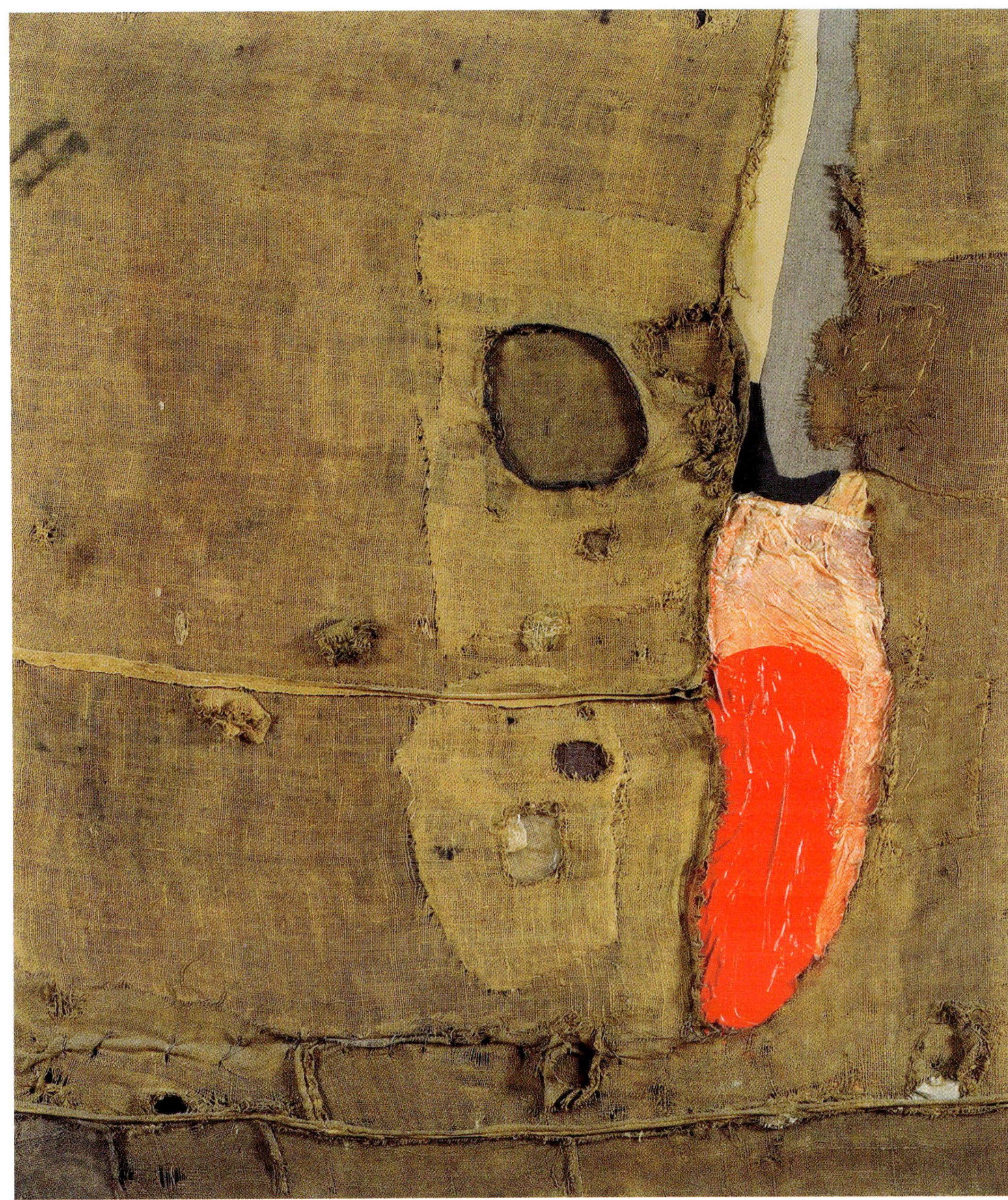

at the same time with the anti-positivist disposition of the new science. So his artistic will also tends to overcome the barriers—cultural, social, political—interposed between people. If forms of basic expression are the same for all human beings, whatever their position or their history, art becomes one of the best arguments in favor of the unity of the human spirit, and of the possibility of that spirit communicating with the artificial world, created by man, and with the natural world, from which it comes and to which it must return.

But what is important, in Tàpies, is that this universalist spirituality by no means implies abstract uniformity, but rather a love of differences, which preserve the particularity of signs. This, when deployed, is what gives various forms of life, language and cultural traditions breath of their own. Hence the constant personal references that appear in his work: the signs that refer to himself, his loved ones, biographical material and the objects present in his life.

Another decisive feature is that neither is it a passive form of spirituality. It is not a matter of replacing the former spiritual force of religion with art, after secularization and the

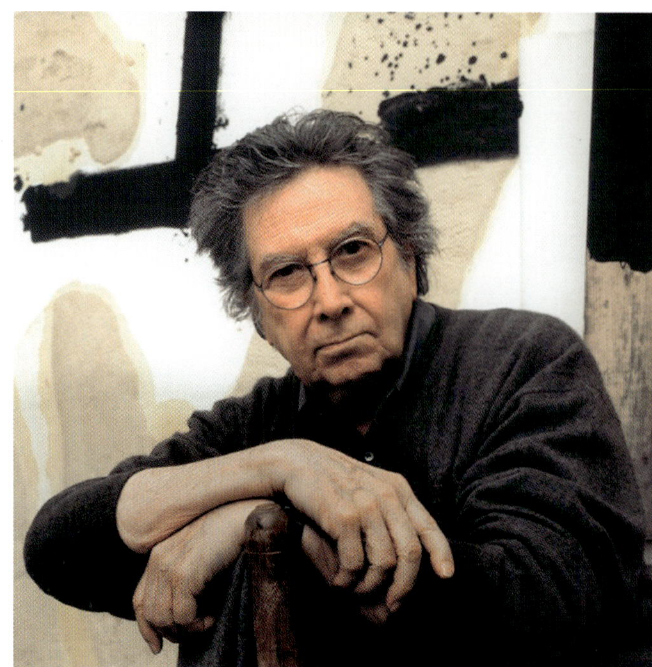

4. Antoni Tàpies

public decline of religion in the modern process of our culture. The spirituality of Tàpies's work demands that the viewer participate and interact with the signs, materials and objects that speak, at once, to the feelings and the mind.

The centrality of the communicative dimension is what gives all his pieces a very profound evocative capacity and at the same time an off-putting quality that repels the superficial gaze, the kind that is content with the mere liturgy of approaching artworks and retreating in confusion. All this connects with Tàpies's interest in alchemy, magic, and transmutation. However important it may be, a work of art is not an end in itself. It is a triggering element, an aesthetic cipher intended to provoke a reaction in anyone who approaches it, leading to their possible transformation and human enrichment.

And this is concentrated in what Tàpies calls "the meditative element," which he sees as the central feature of his contribution to art, replete with secular spirituality:

> The central purpose of my work is that the painting should be like a talisman, an object or a mechanism to help people who see it to change their normal mindset and be transported to this state we call contemplation of profound reality, cosmic consciousness, the absolute, or, for believers, the face of the divine. So that in this way they can discover their own nature.[10]

The keyword for understanding the scope of Tàpies's works is poetry. *Visual poetry*. Ranging inquisitively over the registers and modulations of matter until it locates the sign, at once familiar and strange, of humanity and its inscription in nature and work. At this point, meditation on painting and transmutation of the object or its metamorphosis into sculpture become a revelation of the visible: not only does it change the world we live in, but above all the way we look at things and at ourselves. A scale of meaning is thus articulated in his works, through matter, signs, and traces. Moving on that scale, Tàpies, the writer of bare forms, takes us from matter to spirit.

Paint and materials: sand, wood, bronze, canvas. Objects articulated with supports: string, envelopes, plates, white canvas fabric. Tàpies transmutes both the flowing expressi-

5. Antoni Tàpies,
Caja de cartón desplegada, 1960

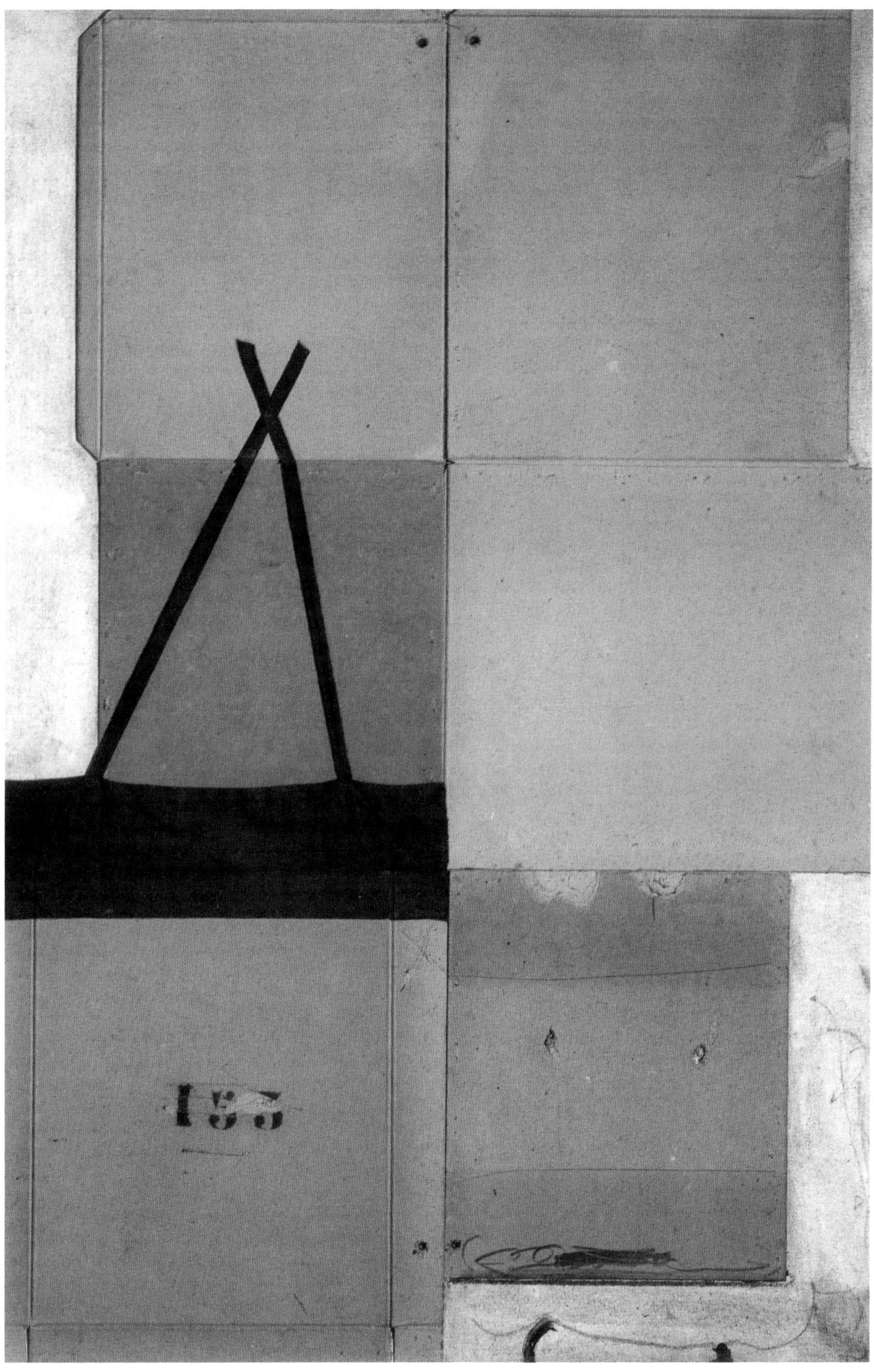

veness of the materials and the form of the everyday objects into a synthesis that leads us to the lightning flash of illumination. As always in his visual journey, it is a matter of avoiding any temptation to indulge in grandiloquence or solemnity. On the contrary: the visual gesture flows from the materiality itself, which is usually disregarded. But this is precisely a way of performing an alchemical transformation, similar to that alchemy of the word which Arthur Rimbaud described as the foundation of poetic language.

These pieces achieve a kind of salvaging of temporal experience, a recovery, through form, of what must remain and give density to human experience. Fullness of time crystallized in a work of art. Antoni Tàpies himself has referred in his writings to the constitutive nature of the "instant of art," which Zen thought called "the path of instantaneous awakening," specifying that it has nothing to do "with improvisation or speed, as has sometimes been thought, but rather refers to a kind of loving clarity which, with intense insight, fully brings to life all the dynamics [. . .] of the here and now."[11]

Fixing in material and everyday form that which transcends it. The artist, a *poet of forms*, provides another angle to our gaze, stimulating our ability to see, and thereby to pass from the external world to our deepest intimacy. Surmounting the overload of well-worn images and deafening noise of the present world. Leading us to the inner light, to the silence of form. To the fullness of the moment.

If we can describe both Alberto Burri and Antoni Tàpies as *poets of forms*, as makers of *visual poetry*, it is not surprising that both have aroused profound echoes in the sphere of verbal poetry. An especially significant example, in the case of Tàpies, is the way in which his works have resonated and given rise to a dialogue with one of the most important contemporary poets in Spanish: José Ángel Valente (1929–2000).

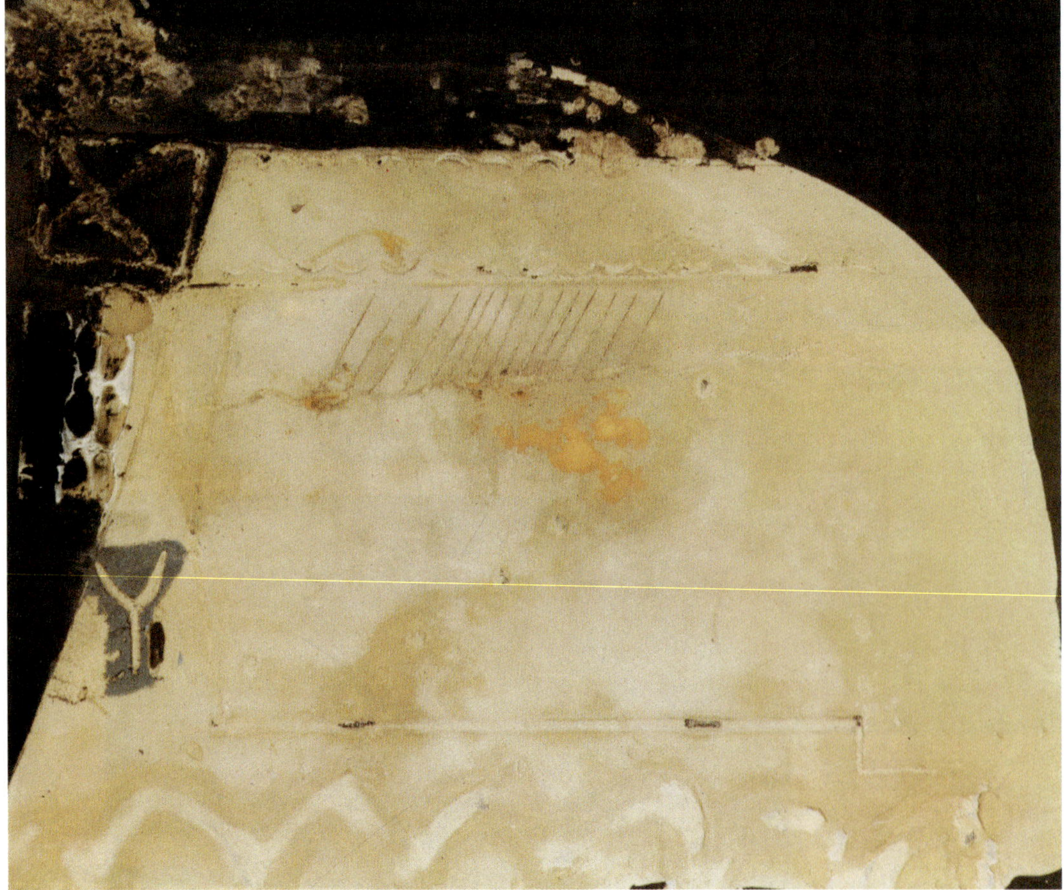

6. Antoni Tàpies, *Marrón y ocre*, 1959

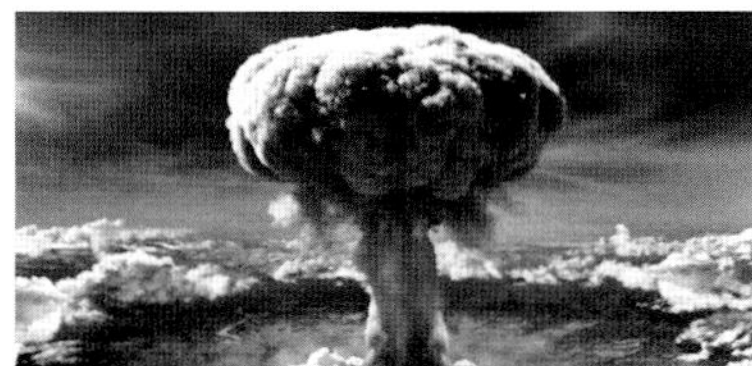

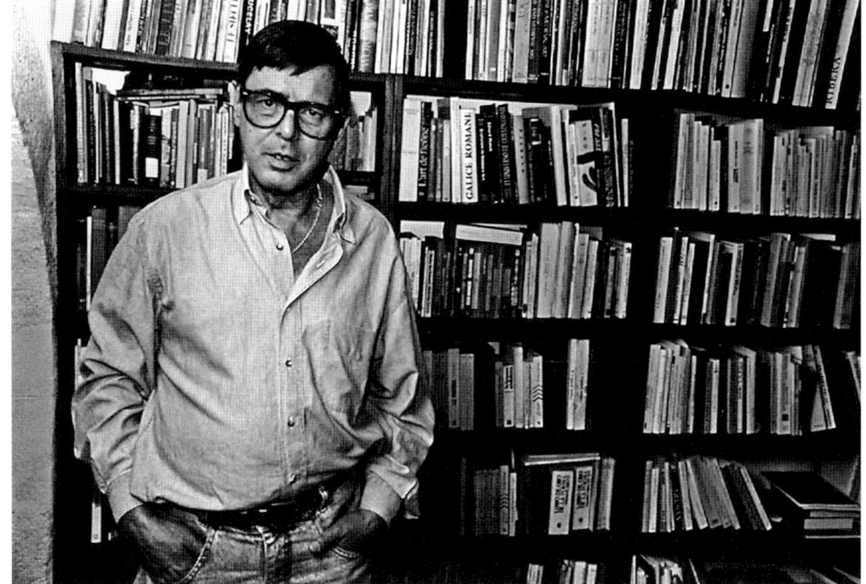

7. Atomic bomb explosion in Hiroshima, 1945

8. José Ángel Valente

Valente's work is highly diverse and plural in its illumination and interests: not just in *poetic matter* itself. He also cultivated the introspection of the essay, which he always approached through the interiority of texts, as in a play of mirrors in which he himself was reflected, revealing at once the weight and importance of physical distance, of exile from what is closest, as a necessary step to attain literary universality. And also dialogue with the other arts, and in a very special way with painting and sculpture, in which he saw a link of continuity with the course of words in flight.

"Flight" is an accurate term to locate his poetic perspective, because he himself pointed out that the poet "is an extramural bird," not shut in a cage. And at the same time, it is a "solitary bird" (*Monticola solitarius*, the blue rock thrush), whose scale or "conditions" are summed up as follows by Valente, who suggests that children should learn them by heart and sing them at school: "The first is that it flies to the highest place; the second, that it cannot bear company, even of its own kind; the third, that it puts its beak in the air; the fourth, that it has no particular color; the fifth, that it sings sweetly."[12] He is obviously alluding here to the idea that the flight of the blue rock thrush leads us to a profound synthesis of all the supports susceptible of meaning. Or in other words, to the interconnection of all the arts.

The "solitary bird" (*pájaro solitario*), as the blue rock thrush is called in Spanish, is also popularly known as the "crazy bird" (*pájaro loco*), and its sweet song resembles that of the blackbird. The bird, with its flight, is an expression of the ultimacy of language and of the leap or flight beyond it, to the image. As Gaston Bachelard notes, "the bird in full flight constitutes a center of poetic space."[13] The "solitary" bird that reaches the highest scale in poetic language also leads us to birds in the music of the great composer Olivier Messiaen: *Le Merle noir* (1952), *Réveil des oiseaux* (1953), *Catalogue des oiseaux* (1956–58).

And that is where José Ángel Valente is located: "I strive to decipher a bird." What sign inhabits that image? It is *an enigma*, which arises from the fragmentary and corporeal nature of language. And it is also an enigma that expresses the transgressive force of poetic language. This leads us to a set of decisive *words/images* for establishing a poetic map of his creativity: memory, word, water, bird, light, death, body, cloud, air, tree, matter, love, fire . . . A journey to the farthest reach of the possible or a link to the impossible: the *leap* or *flight of the image*. A place beyond, reached by words, in their essential search, by leaping over themselves. A place where language undergoes its most radical metamorphosis, where it turns into an *image*.

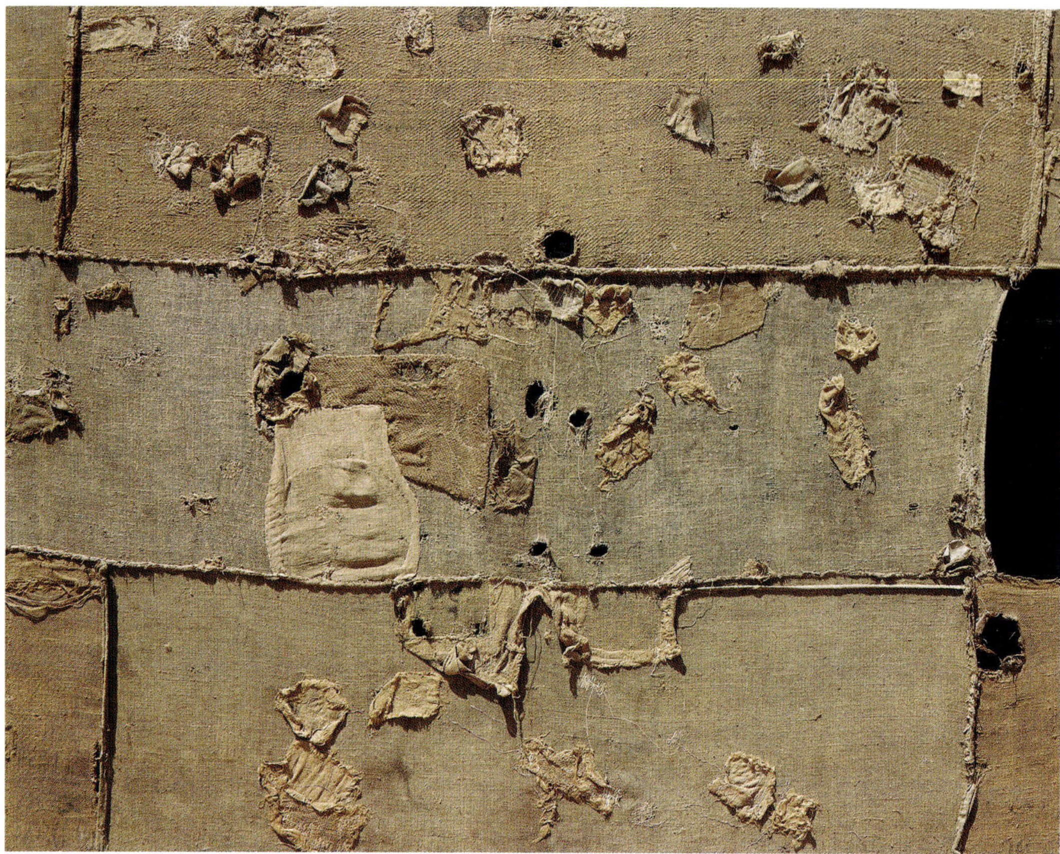

9. Alberto Burri,
Grande Sacco, 1957/1958
Città di Castello,
Fondazione Palazzo
Albizzini Collezione Burri

In one of his poems from the 1989 collection *Al dios del lugar*, the enigmatic question is expressed in concrete form in the image of the word that takes flight and reaches the light:

> Vértice
> de la luz, el pájaro,
> su vuelo detenido, signo de qué,
> en la raíz o en la consumación
> del vuelo [14]

In that poetic flight José Ángel Valente focuses his attention by ascending towards painting with "Cinco fragmentos para Antoni Tàpies" a set of prose texts placed as the conclusion of his book *Material memoria* (1979), later included in a collection of his writings, with the same title, in 1992. In number III of these fragments Tàpies's work is described as "a supreme contemplation of matter" *in dialogue with forms*, with the processes of *formation*: "A radical presence of matter which reaches form, but which is above all formation: forms that dissolve themselves in the primordial nostalgia for the formless, for that which is strictly indifferent to change and can therefore change in every way and be the infinite root of all possible forms."[15]

And he emphasizes what Tàpies gives us in his paintings and sculptures, in a process that is at once elevated and bare, of intense *visual poetry*:

> In Tàpies's art it does not make sense to speak of abstraction and figurativism. Form does not figure: it is. Form is matter. Matter—the matter in a painting or a composition—is not a support for anything superimposed on it. It is not matter of any form,

but the absolute form of itself. There is perhaps no artist in modern times who has taken this process of the unification of matter itself to a more advanced extreme. Être la matière!, as Flaubert wrote.[16]

That, in short, is where Valente's dialogue with Tàpies leads us: to visualize the forms of matter as the core of his artistic work. That autonomy of the forms of matter is clearly also a central issue in the work of Alberto Burri.

Burri, Tàpies, Valente . . . Through matterist visual poetry, or verbal poetry, they lead us to matter itself, the root from which we spring. Our bodies and minds are matter that has learned to feel, speak, and think. That is why we can find senses, types of language and thoughts mirrored in the various supports of matter. To do so, we need to open our vision and our sensibility: to *know how to see* in the primary registers of matter, to *know how to feel* in its echoes and projections, and thereby *come to think and know*, entering into a profound dialogue with the roots of our being in the world. *Matter speaks*.

1 Marcello Venturoli, "Il pennello di fuoco," in Bruno Corà, *BURRI: Plastiche* (Florence: Forma, 2018), 74. First pub. in *Le Ore* (12 August 1965).
2 Franco Simongini, "Il suo mondo bruciato," in Corà, *Burri: Plastiche*, 91. First pub. in *Il Messaggero* (11 September 1971).
3 Venturoli, "Il pennello di fuoco," 74, (italics mine).
4 Ernst Bloch, *The Spirit of Utopia*, trans. Anthony Nassar (Stanford, CA: Stanford Un. Press, 2000), 115.
5 Ibid., 26.
6 Ibid., 32–33.
7 Manuel J. Borja-Villel, "Conversaciones con Antoni Tàpies (1985–1991)," in *Tàpies: Comunicació sobre el mur* (Barcelona: Fundació Antoni Tàpies, 1992), 285.
8 Ibid.
9 Ibid., 287.
10 Sol Alameda, "La predestinación," interview by Sol Alameda, *El País Semanal* (12 February 1995), n.p.
11 Antoni Tàpies, "El instante del arte," in *La realidad como arte. Por un arte moderno y progresista* (Murcia: Colegio Oficial de Aparejadores y Arquitectos Técnicos de Murcia, 1989), 46, originally published in *La Vanguardia* (14 May 1975).
12 José Ángel Valente, "*Variaciones sobre el pájaro y la red, precedido de La piedra y el centro"* (Barcelona: Tusquets, 1991), 21.
13 Gaston Bachelard, *Fragments of a Poetics of Fire*, ed. Suzanne Bachelard, trans. Kenneth Haltman (Dallas, TX: Dallas Institute of Humanities and Culture, 1990), 95.
14 José Ángel Valente, *Material memoria (1979–1989)* (Madrid: Alianza, 1992), 206. [Apex / of light, the bird, / its flight arrested, a sign of what, / at the root or at the consummation / of flight.]
15 Ibid., 42.
16 Ibid., 43.

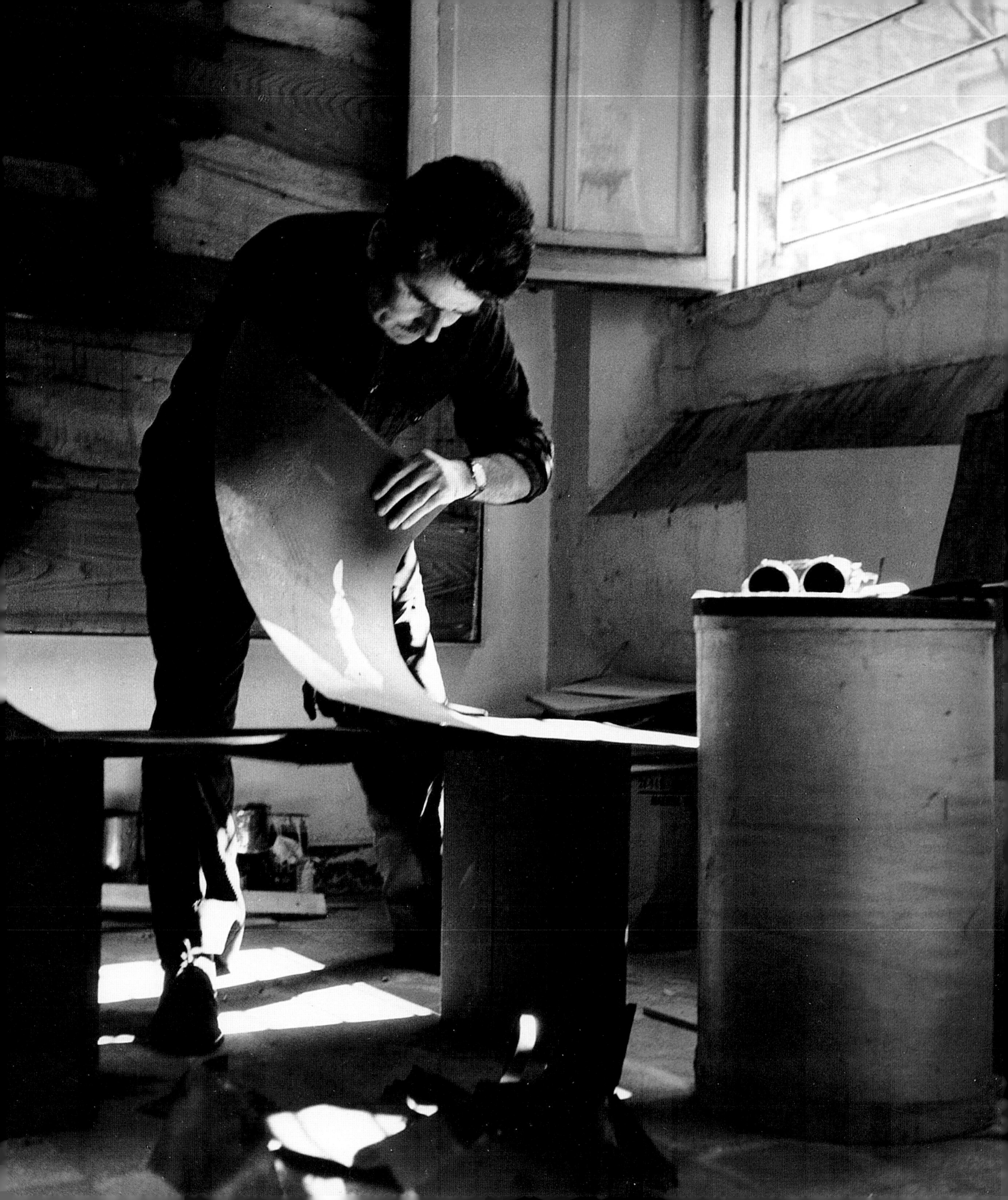

Burri: Towards a New Pact between the Artist and Nature

Thierry Dufrêne

All Alberto Burri's work is permeated by the desire, alternately triumphant and desperate, to reverse the signs of destruction and creation, to avert the fatal opposition between the poles of matter and spirit, of industry and technology on the one hand and nature on the other, so as to make artistic activity the visible manifestation of the living energy that creates and regenerates the world. Burri's "cosmic" art can be revisited today in the light of the ecological questions of our time. His work can be seen as the site of tensions and expressions in which an awareness, torn between fear and promise, of man's relationship to nature in the Anthropocene era was already forming. Burri initially regarded a painting as a field or a body given over to exploration, exploitation, even degradation, but equally, in a final impulse, to restitution, suturing, regeneration. He then managed to create natural phenomena within the ecosystem of the painting, using combustion and atmospheric and chemical transformation of industrial materials, producing an unstable equilibrium between creative force and destructive power. Finally, having attained the maturity of his art, he turned to the memory of painterly tradition, where he sought to graft together art as practiced in the studio and the culture of the landscape in the *Cretti* series (fig. 1), finding the common root of art (*ars*), as a product of the human imagination, and cultivation (*coleo*), in the sense of care of the environment and the land: culture.

The Work as a Field and a Body

Following Giotto, artists of the Quattrocento detached the bodies of the figures in their paintings from the ethereal divine space created for them by the gold background inherited from Byzantine art. From now on, those bodies rooted in cities or humanized landscapes were available for action, offering the artist a repertoire of forms that expressed intentions (Michael Baxandall). And there the history of art remained for long centuries. But modern art autonomized forms and colors and detached them from the bodies of figures, to the point of abandoning figurativism for abstraction. However, the American art critic Clement Greenberg noted a change of direction in the abstract expressionism of the 1950s, particularly with Willem De Kooning's *Women* (1952–55) (fig. 2), which he described as "homeless representation": "I mean by this a plastic and descriptive painterliness that is applied to abstract ends, but which continues to suggest representational ones."[1] He was referring to the fact that the manner of painting was clearly abstract, in the sense that the brushstrokes and colors were self-sufficient, but that at the same time characters or three-dimensional objects could be recognized. Similarly, Burri's contemporaries remarked that his *Sacchi* (fig. 3) were abstract compositions but also made one think of bodies—and we know that de Kooning was very important to Burri. Thus in 1961 Françoise Choay, recalling that Burri

Alberto Burri, Via Nera, Rome, 1959

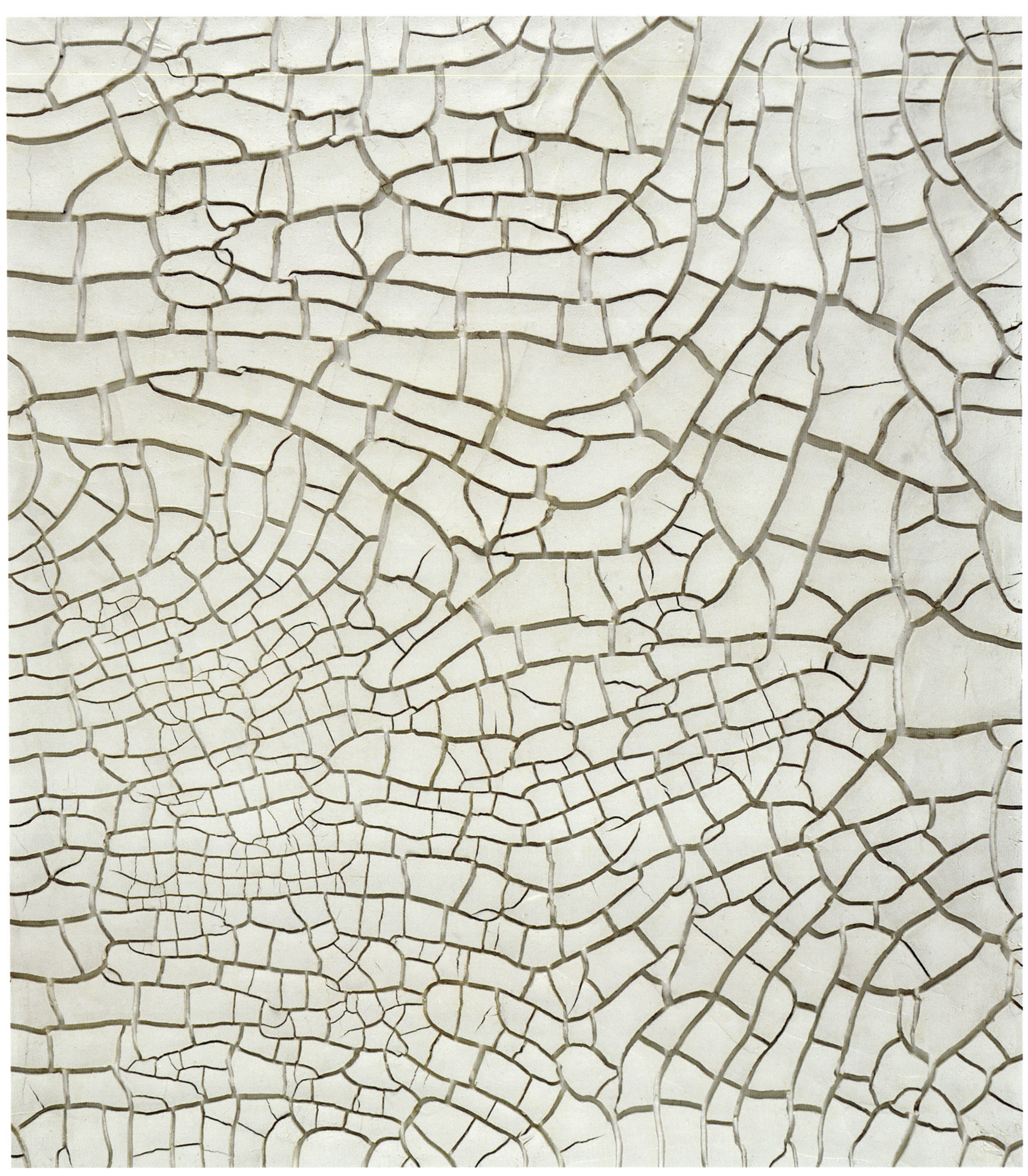

1. Alberto Burri, *Cretto G3,* 1975 Private collection

was a doctor, established a parallel between his work on jute sacking and a "penetrating trauma in the patient's flesh."[2] She too saw a body in the abstract form. *Sacchi* could be compared to the *Hautes pâtes* of the French artist Jean Dubuffet. Michel Tapié, who saw Burri's work as "Neo-Dadaism," also had the feeling that his art was a revival of ancestral magic, with objects of enchantment.[3] This required the work to stand in a relationship of contiguity, or of metonymy (the part for the whole), to the living body (that of the artist, that of the viewer) or the social body (depicted by the objects exchanged there, which have their place in society's set of symbolic values). That body for which the canvas serves as a proxy would be merely a skin if it were not pierced, lacerated, stitched: so it becomes a symbolic expression and a talisman.

A talisman or a relic (derived from a body) is also what the writer André Pieyre de Mandiargues saw on first encountering a work by Burri in a gallery in Rome, just after the war: "a small but remarkable collection of scraps of various fabrics," of which he says: "such an object, which combined the ravishing beauty of a hothouse flower with the mysterious impurity of a healing wound, seemed fascinating to me."[4] But the writer also makes another comparison to which we will return later: "the wounds of a recent work of man, those of industrial material, resemble the wounds of the human body." According to Pieyre de Mandiargues, it was in the United States, a new country, that Burri had been struck by the deterioration of industrial materials and machines, which, on the scale of a human life, became old rusted and damaged bodies, as one would not have expected of technological objects.

But when we carefully consider the actions that Burri performs on his paintings,[5] his tars and other lacquers, his glued and sewn sack-cloths, we understand that for him it is not so much a matter of "homeless representation," to repeat the expression Greenberg

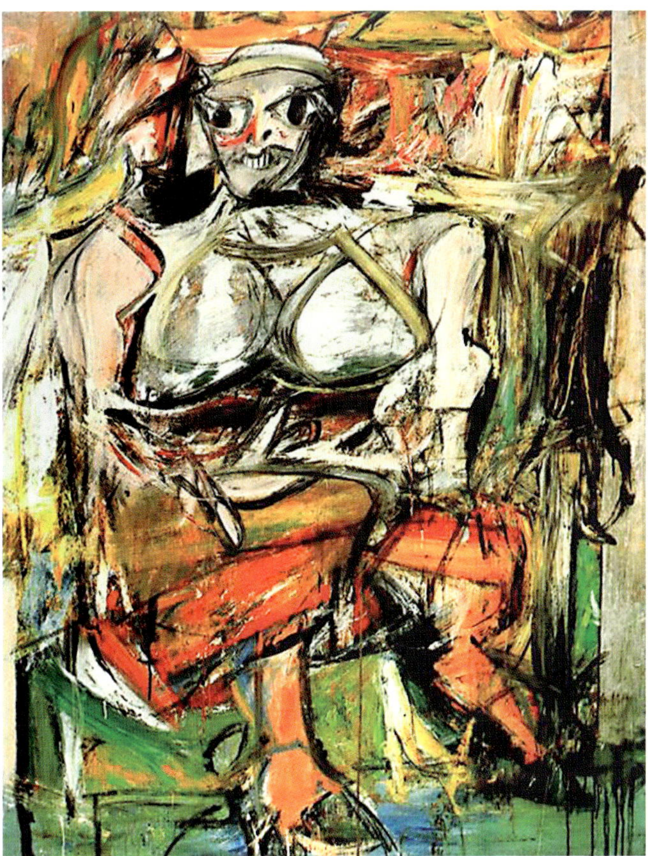

2. Willem de Kooning, *Woman I*, 1950-1952

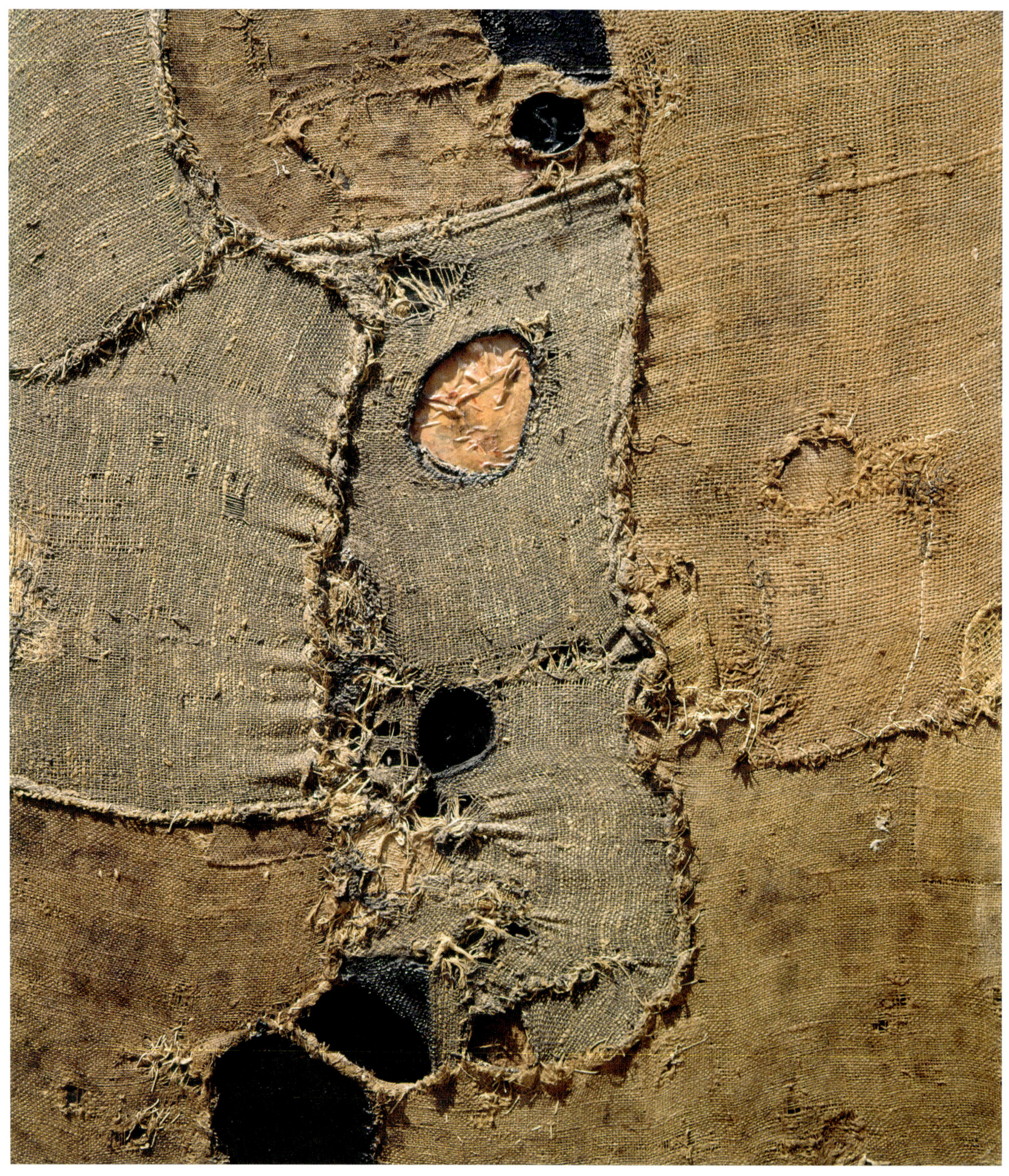

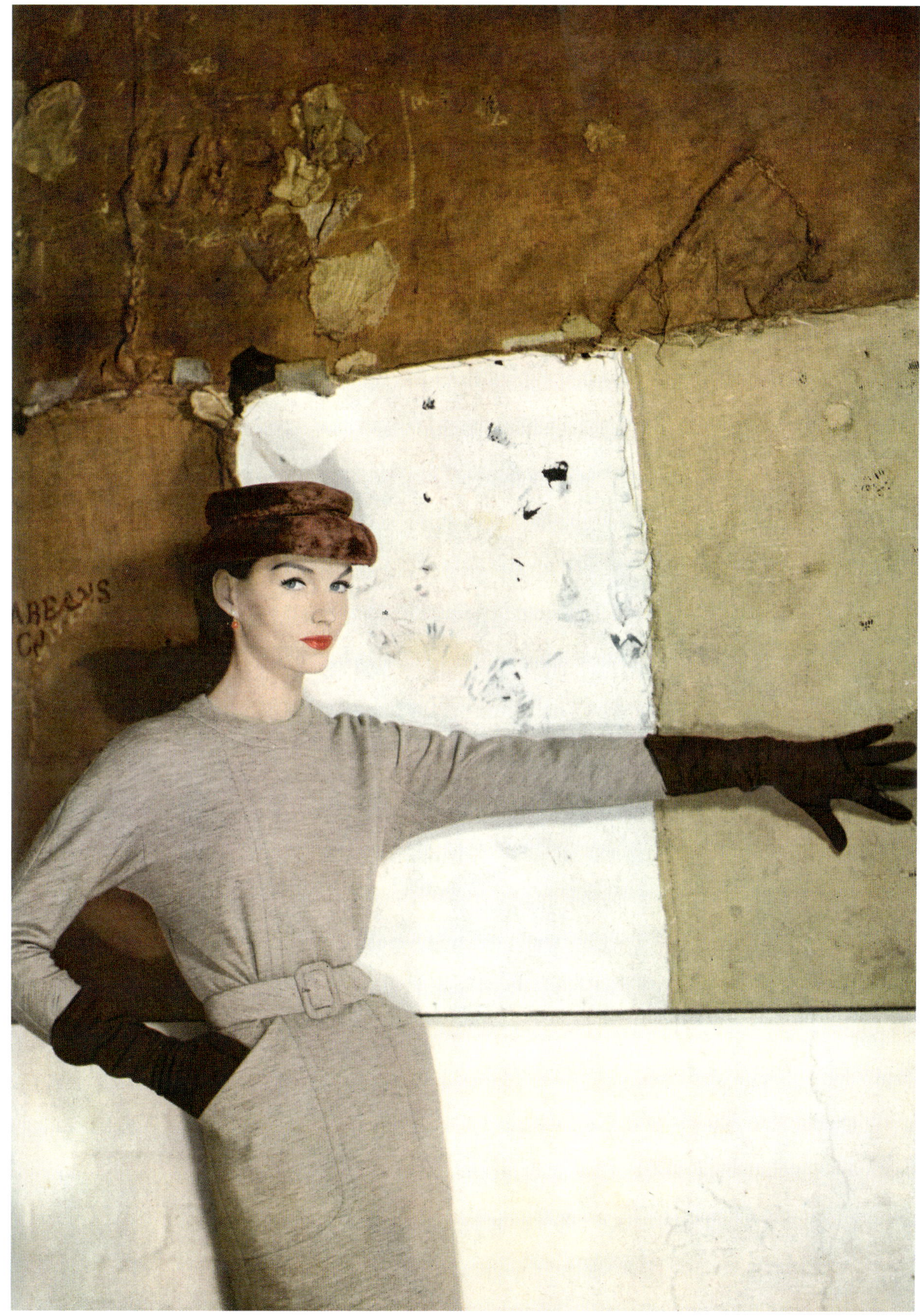

3. Alberto Burri, *Sacco B*, [1953] Città di Castello, Fondazione Palazzo Albizzini Collezione Burri

4. *Grande Sacco*, (1953) New York, Stable Gallery, 1955, from *Harper's Bazaar*, September 1955

used about De Kooning, in the sense of wanting to depict or to show the recognizable impression of a body, as of making gestures that are addressed to (and suggest) a body, transitively, just as Fontana's chisel marks or notches did not represent space but created it, made it happen. What takes place is the institution or inauguration of a body, not its representation. I felt something similar when with my own eyes I saw Jannis Kounellis create bodies in his studio in Umbertide by the at once simple and ritual gesture of sewing and tying clothes. Similarly, a *Sacco* by Burri designates a body, makes it exist, through action. The sewing and sticking, the holes and the tears constitute its visible articulations, in the way one utters and articulates a word, a phrase, of language to transmit a mental image whose reality imposes itself on the listener. A *Sacco* can also be experienced as a garment in which a body can be projected, as shown by Louise Dahl-Wolfe's photograph of a fashion model whose body language and measurements merge into *Grande Sacco* (1953), exhibited at the Stable Gallery in New York in May 1955 (fig. 4). Ettore Sottsass has even shown that jute sacking could be fetishized by the display of precious colored fragments functioning as relics on large non-specific expanses, as in friezes, mosaics, and even Klimt's paintings.[6]

In short, by an analogy between microcosm and macrocosm, Burri's matter paintings in the years 1950–60 also refer to cultivating land. Those Harlequin suits, evoking a form of polyculture in which the pieces sewn together seem to correspond to fields of different crops, are above all a symbolic catalogue of cultivation activities. Just as Fontana's *Nature* pieces refer to gestation, origin and fertilization through the gestural language of penetration and churning, so, in Burri's work, the piercing of surfaces and the ripping open and arrangement of materials with each other literally make forms grow as if under the influence of an organic life force.

5. Alberto Burri, *Ferro D*, 1958
Private collection

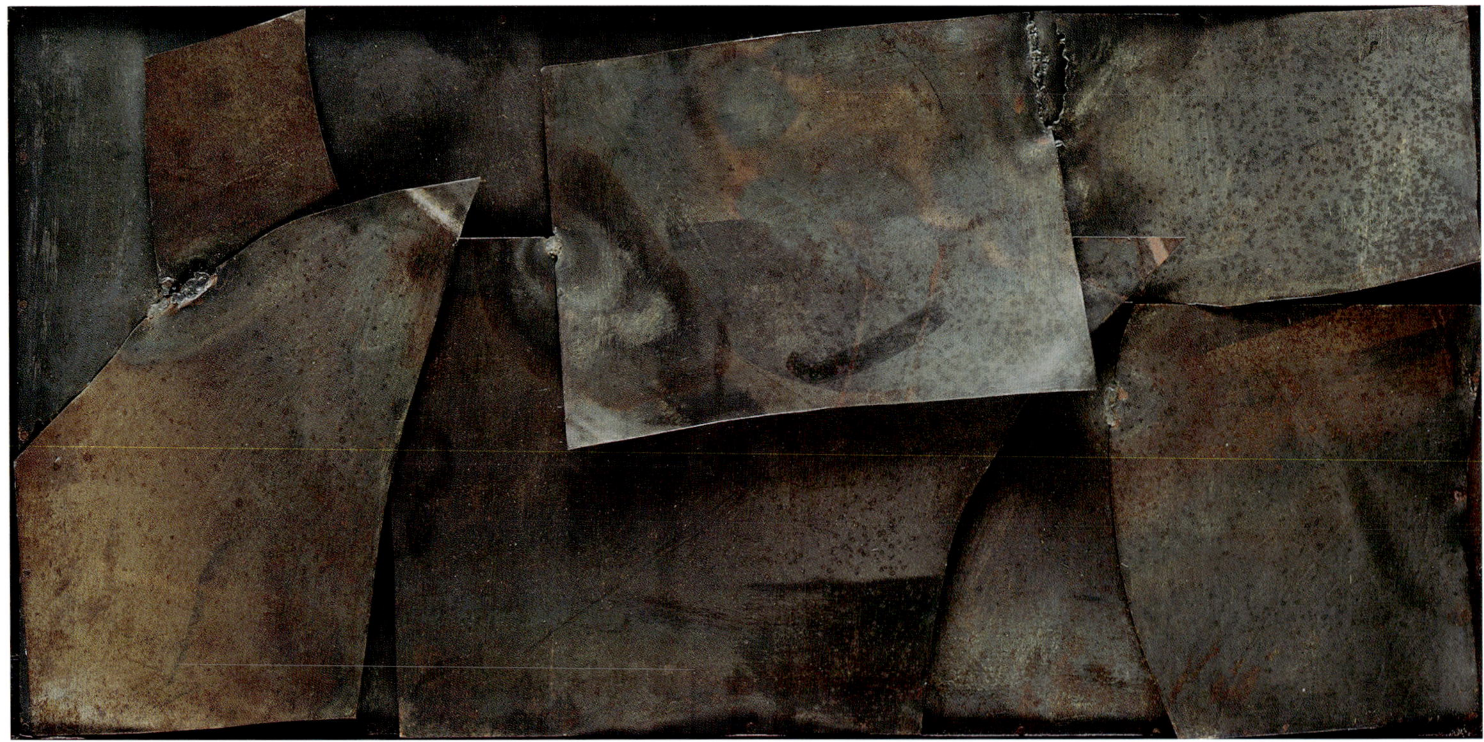

6. Alberto Burri, *Catrame*, [1949] Città di Castello, Fondazione Palazzo Albizzini Collezione Burri

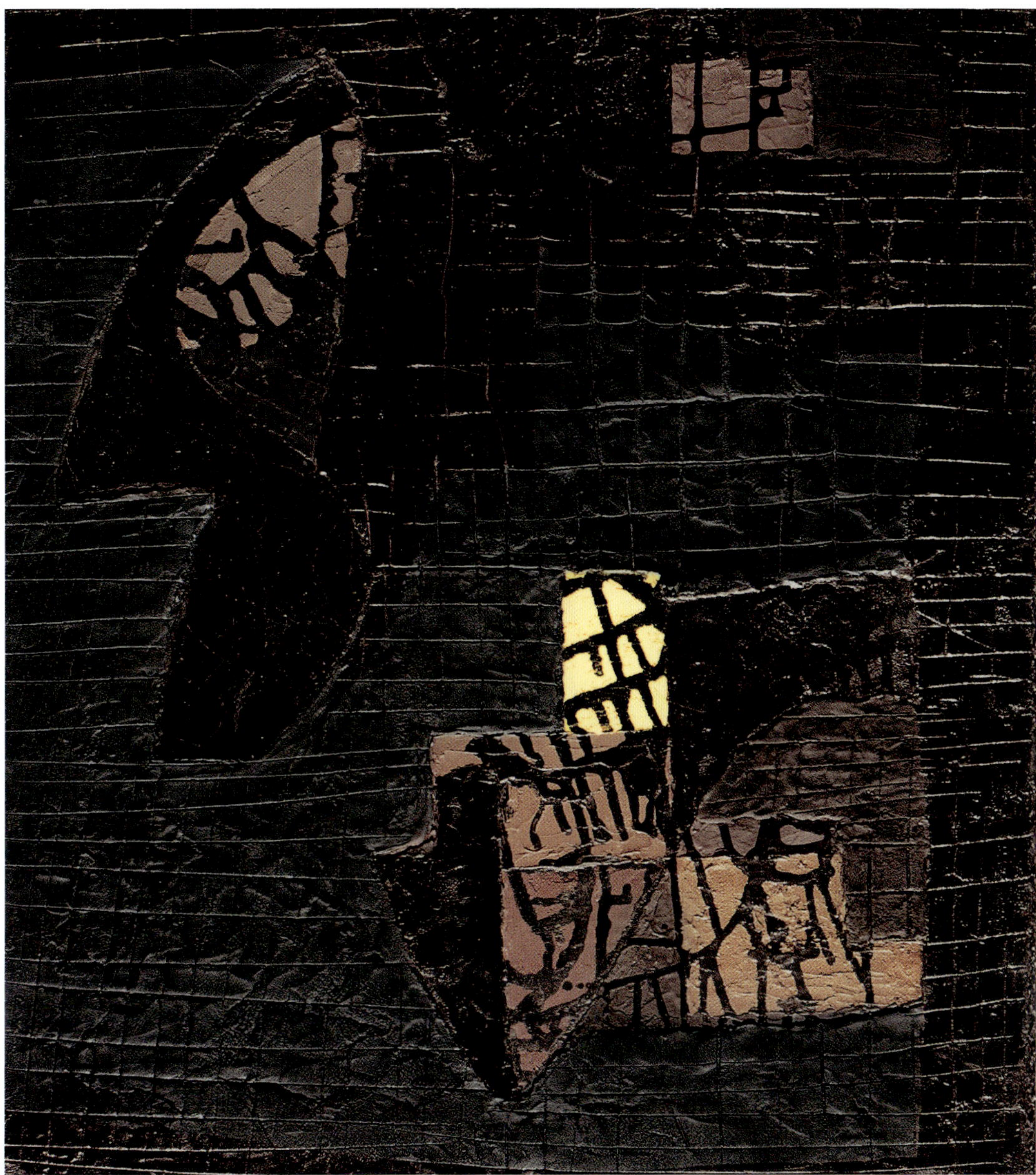

The Chemistry of Materials and the Ecosystem of the Work

In a previous article[7] I have shown the parallel between Burri's procedure and that of the artists of French Nouveau Réalisme in terms of the use of materials drawn from industry and of products used in the consumer society that was being established in the 1960s. A parallel, but also clear differences. Burri was never a devotee of quantity, accumulations, or mechanization. "Matter has the floor," wrote Pierre Restany (1930–2003), the founder of Nouveau Réalisme, in *Cimaise* in 1962, on the subject of Alberto Burri's work. But he added that the latter showed great "restraint with regard to matter." He let it express itself "mezzo voce," almost imperceptibly, in his works. He sensitized the viewer "to this or that quality of fabric grain, the ink stencilling of a figure or a letter, the veins and knots in wood, the sharp edges of metal blades."[8] (fig. 5)

Burri's matterism dates in part from his stay in Paris during the winter of 1948, where he was able to visit Miró's studio and watch Dubuffet using tar. He exhibited from 1949 at the Salon des Réalités Nouvelles and Christian Zervos reproduced one of Burri's *Catrami* in his journal *Cahiers d'Art* in 1950.[9] (fig. 6) In 1956, he exhibited with César at the Galerie Rive

Droite. In 1972, in his preface to the catalogue of the Alberto Burri exhibition at the Musée National d'Art Moderne in Paris, Jean Leymarie rightly referred to Burri's "successive materializations." This artist did indeed conduct countless experiments with and on the most varied materials, abandoning jute sacking for industrial coverings, tars, lacquers, cements, cellulose coatings, panels of cork or insulation, and other metal constructions.

In the exhibition *BURRI la pittura, irriducibile presenza*, presented at the Fondazione Giorgio Cini in Venice in 2019, Bruno Corà showed the performative and experimental nature of the artist's work with industrially produced materials. He had a fascination for the *fleurs du mal*—the flowers of evil—which flourish on rusty, burnt, stained, even rotten materials. A certain artificiality arising from combustion of wooden assemblages burnt with a blowtorch and of smoke-impregnated, hardened rags, or of plastics or materials such as that charred remnant of a zip from a woman's undergarment, paradoxically create a second nature, as wild as nature itself. This second nature is the proof that time has done its work and that the artist can "recycle" the industrial world. But I have borrowed the expression *fleurs du mal* from Baudelaire because Burri, like Niki de Saint-Phalle, Jacques Brown, and Rebecca Horn, in particular, bore the mark of his exposure to toxic fumes, when conducting his experiments, in his very flesh, and had permanent lesions in his lungs.

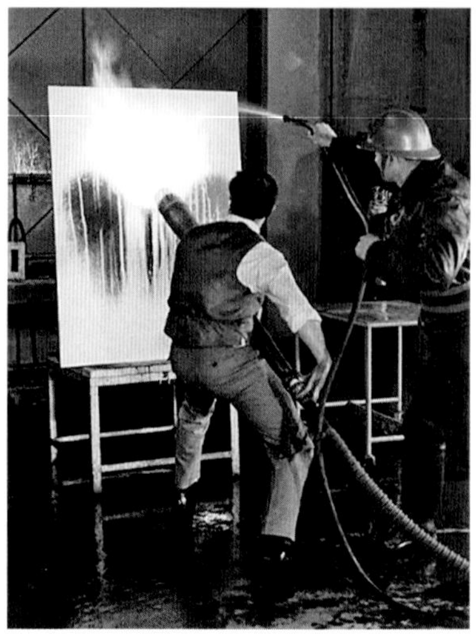
7. Yves Klein at work on a *Peinture de Feu*, late 1950s

Burri's experimental art joins the combustions of Yves Klein (fig. 7) and Bernard Aubertin, the bubbles of David Medalla's *Cloud Canyons*, what Jack Burnham called Hans Haacke's thermal and aquatic "art of systems," or the inflatable sculptures of Zéro or Hans-Walter Müller. The artist takes natural elements and processes, such as air, fire, or later desiccation (for the *Cretti* with their multiple coats of varnish) and makes them his allies, his assistants in the substantive work of painting.

Alberto Burri, born in 1915, belonged to the generation of the critic Roland Barthes (1915–1980), who glorifies plastic in *Mythologies*. Barthes traces "the reverie of man at the sight of the proliferating forms of matter" and declares that "the age-old function of nature is modified: it is no longer the Idea, the pure Substance to be regained or imitated: an artificial Matter, more bountiful than all the natural deposits, is about to replace her, and to determine the very invention of forms."[10] There is no doubt that in his *Plastiche* and in his virgin plastic combustions Burri felt the same magic power of plastic as a inexhaustible matrix of forms. Many materials used by artists of that generation strike us now, like the plastics that became widespread during the Thirty Glorious Years (1944–1974), as ecological aberrations. From this point of view, the modern project has failed, and in renouncing plastic Piero Gilardi even came to the conclusion that artists had to give up producing tangible works, as he did for many years.

However, Alberto Burri's last major artistic adventure was indeed the *Cretti*. It was then that he reconnected with the notion of a ground, a field whose thicknesses evolve as if they were living and whose planned drying process is an unstable equilibrium between the artist's expectations and the qualities and powers of matter. As if providing the basis for an awareness of the uncertain equilibrium between the human (and art) world and the environment.

Cretti: Painting as a New Pact with Nature

The exhibition *Rivisitazione: Burri incontra Piero della Francesca* (Sansepolcro, 2014–15) began by recalling the jute sacks which made it possible to transport the provisions supplied by the UNRRA to the destitute after the war, in 1949. As Bruno Corà recalls, Burri seized on

8. Alberto Burri,
Rosso Plastica, [1961]
Private collection

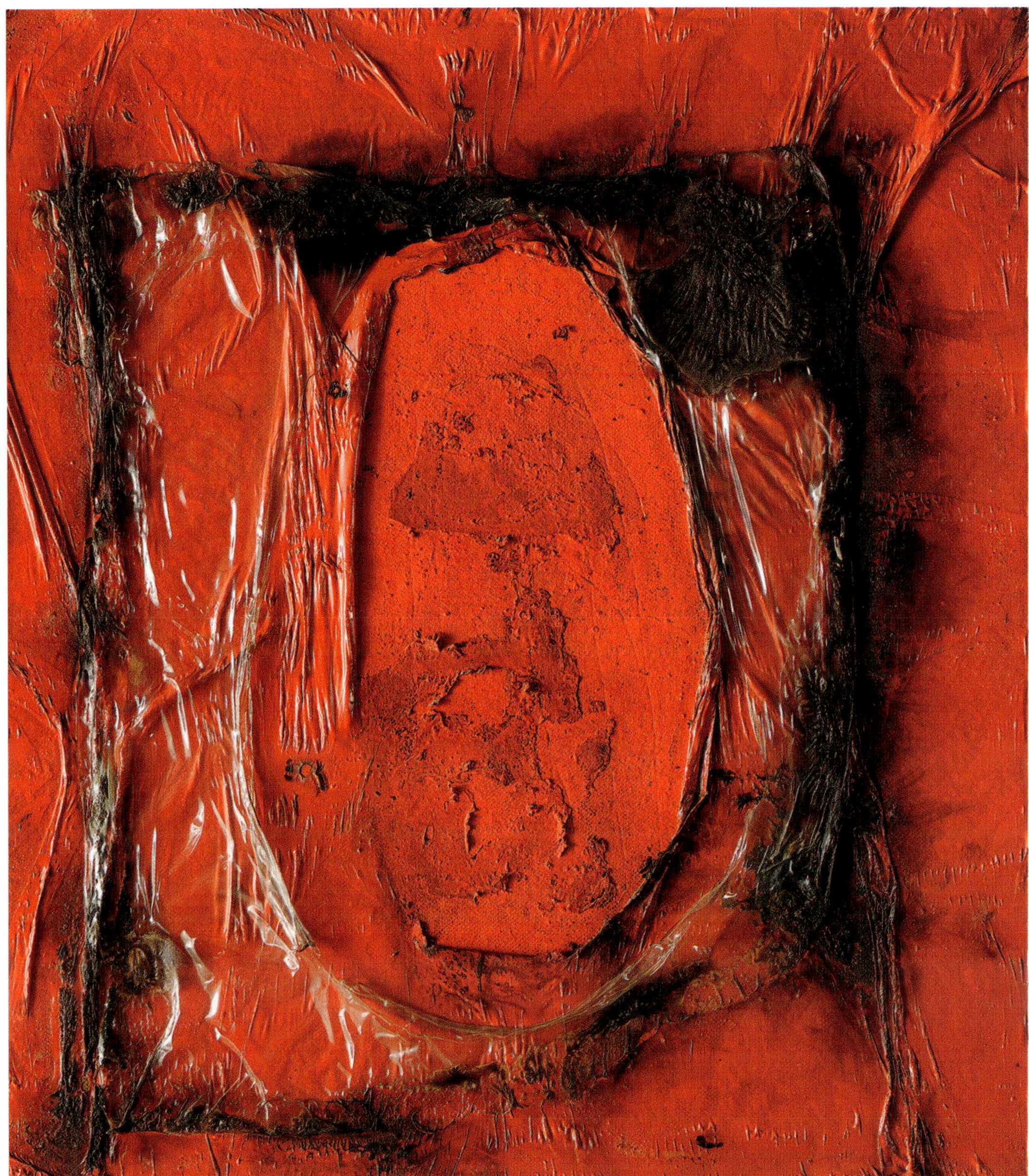

this humble fabric to reset painting from scratch. In doing so, he rediscovered the Franciscan tradition of a type of Italian painting that transfigures simple reality. The sack, a symbol of poverty and fragility, was raised to the dignity of history painting. But nowadays, by a kind of reversal due to the destructive power of time, it is the painting of Giotto, Piero and Masaccio that appears at once fragile and noble: noble because their art is revered, fragile because just as jute sacking material frays and degrades, the skin of a painting cracks.

In 1973 Burri initiated a new series of works, the Cretti, which bear only a superficial formal relationship to the black curved lines on a white ground of Jean Dubuffet's *Hourloupe* cycle (fig. 10), as they are obtained using a subtle and almost traditional technique of planned ageing of the varnishes applied in successive coats. The parallel between *Grande Bianco Cretto* (1974) (fig. 11) and Piero della Francesca's *Polyptych of the Misericordia* (between 1446 and 1462) shows the same semicircular format, confirming that Burri wanted to compare himself to the Quattrocento master.[11] The characteristic texture of the craquelures is at once a tribute to the materials science of the Italian masters, a kind of cry of distress in the face of the deterioration of works, and the expression of a desire to rescue them and

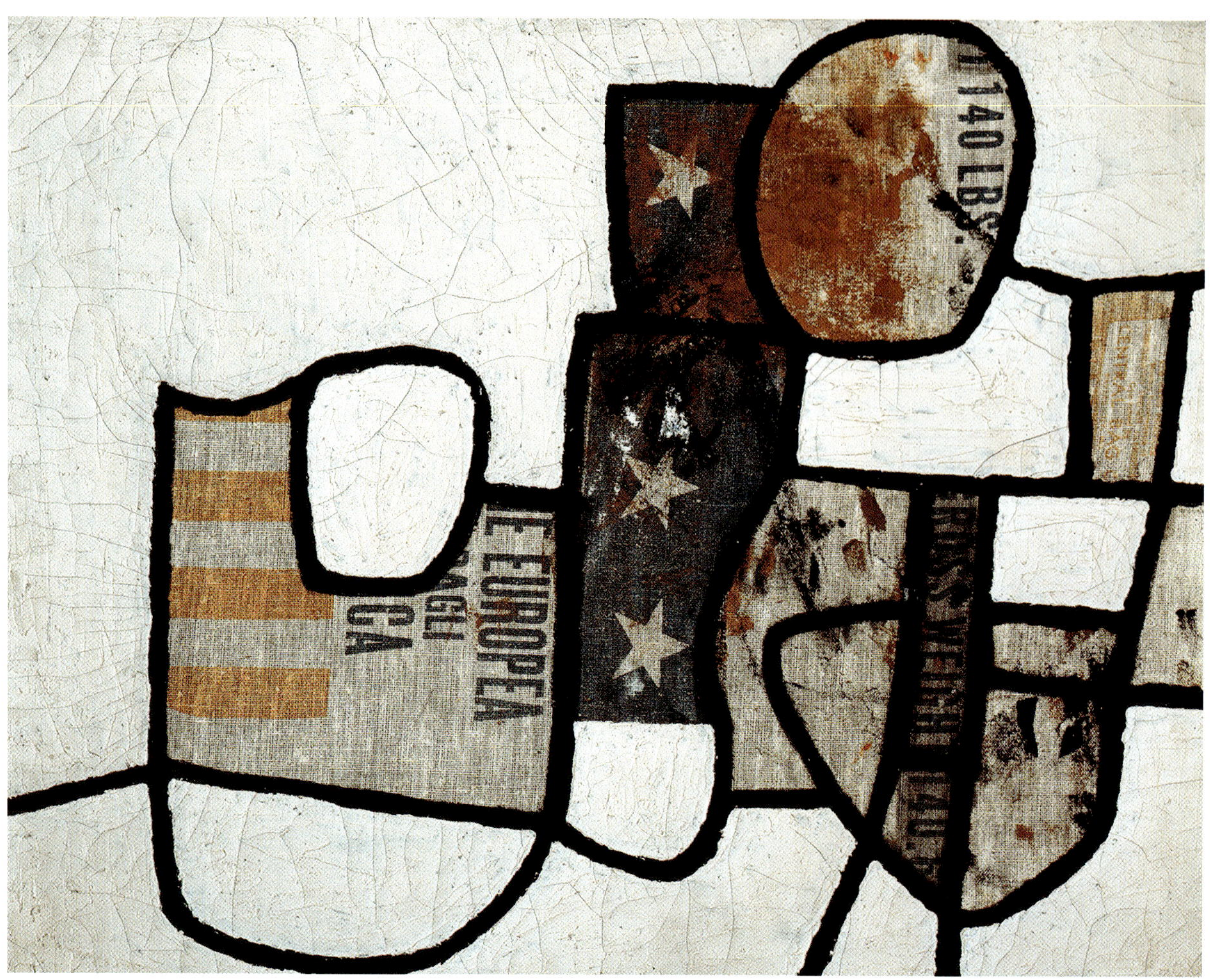

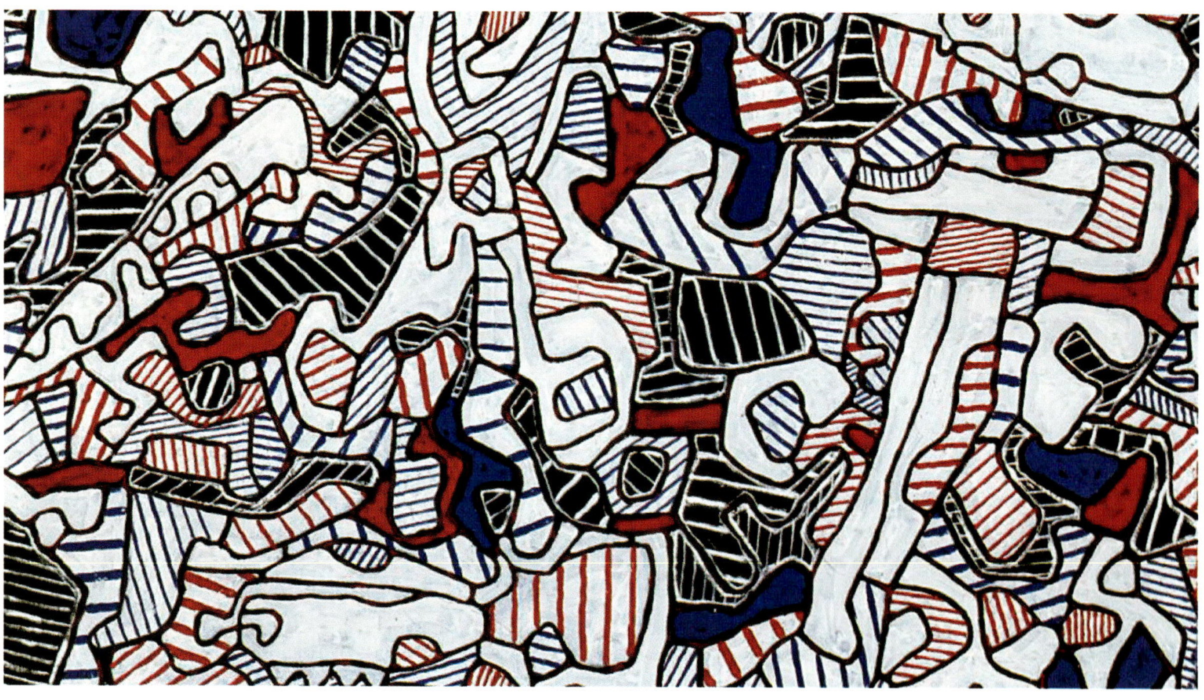

9. Alberto Burri, *SZ1*, 1949
Città di Castello, Fondazione Palazzo Albizzini Collezione Burri

10. Jean Dubuffet, *L'Hourloupe*, 1966

11. Alberto Burri,
Grande Bianco Cretto, 1974
Private collection

fix them for eternity. The *Cretti* series is the most poignant as regards awareness of the declining state of masterpieces, which paradoxically gives them their tragic beauty, and the will to assert the act of art as something that, if not immortal, is at least eternal in the memory of people, who will perpetuate its gestures and traces.

Burri extended this magnificent insight by producing the *Grande Cretto Gibellina* (1985–89) in the open air in Sicily (fig. 12). It will be recalled that after the Sicilian village of Gibellina was destroyed by an earthquake in January 1968 and rebuilt some distance away, Burri suggested covering the ruins of the former village with a cement screed. Wind turbines were later installed on the hills overlooking the *Grande Cretto*. They show the power of nature, which provides modern humans with the energy they need. Yet that same power was the origin of the destruction. The ambivalence of nature: good or bad for humanity, at different times.

In 1945, when he was a prisoner of the Americans in a camp in Texas during World War II, Alberto Burri painted a landscape entitled *Texas* (cat. 1), in which a wooden wind turbine can be seen, making it possible to draw water from the well supplying a farm. A fence, two trees and a path are the only figurative elements in this work, which is rich in painterly matter, where the dense, primitive yellow ochre and red earth is the main subject, whereas human beings seem to be non-existent. Forty years later, when he covered the destroyed village of Gibellina with a layer (*coltre*) of cement, Burri seems at first sight to have been mimicking the massive power of the material that buried the human settlement. Just as the Texas farm in 1945 seemed to be absorbed by the earth, whose colors pervaded it, as well as the strip of sky we can see beyond the horizon, positioned very high in the picture, Gibellina was in a sense fossilized. Like Pompeii and Herculaneum buried by the ashes from the eruption of Vesuvius, it was covered by the earth stirred by telluric forces.

In the immensity of Texas, as in the earth of Sicily, Burri confronts, and confronts us with, a power out of proportion with that of human beings: there is something sublime in both works, even though their scale is completely different. The artist places us face to face with the vast destructive power of matter. But the profound message of Burri's work is that the memory of what has been destroyed can be preserved through the technological implementation of a more resistant material, which human ingenuity adds to nature using components of nature itself: cement. In the painterly earth-matter of *Texas*, Burri includes some human signs which give meaning to the world, and in *Grande Cretto* the village is reborn in form-matter: the blocks of cement conform to the groupings of houses and the street layout as they were before January 1968, and their grid, thus reconstituted, looks like the craquelure of a gigantic painting.

So as a provisional conclusion, it seems to me that we can now appreciate the fact that alongside his undeniable desire to be modern and use the chemistry of his time and the materials provided by industry, Alberto Burri reached the point of looking for what I will call a kind of new pact between the artist and nature, a pact based on taking account of the different timescales of human beings and their environment and, at the same time, on a mutual "taming" process. The artist has reversed the destructive force of nature, turning it into a creative force. While Burri is quite obviously a great informalist artist and the pre-

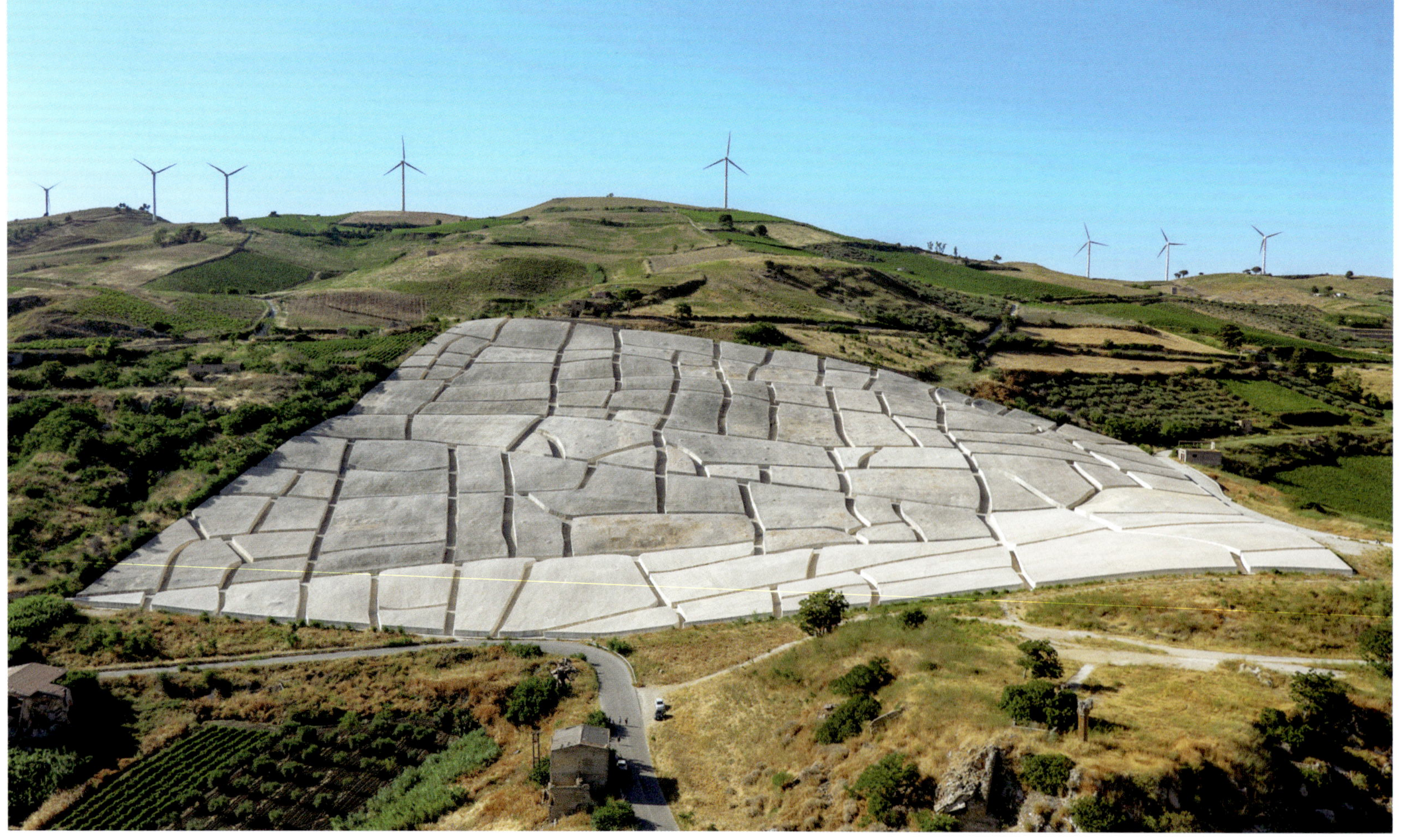

12. Alberto Burri, *Grande Cretto Gibellina*, 1985–2015

12. Alberto Burri,
Cellotex EOR, [1985]
Private collection

cursor, in this domain, of a new genre of works seeking that unstable equilibrium I have just defined, this is not because he opposes the objectification of forms. Indeed, Restany correctly saw that the implementation of matter in Burri always takes place in the framework of a "geometric structural pattern," or at least in a "geometric spirit," and that he uses "color as a covering that serves to mask the extroversion of matter."[12] Maurizio Calvesi also rightly states that Burri felt concerned with the "traditional values" of painting and that his use of sacks as a medium is "one last and successful attempt at reanimation" of the art of painting.[13] And Daniel Abadie offers a dialectic treatment of the life of forms versus the life of matter in Burri's work: "The clear emergence of geometric forms—in the *Cellotex* works, for example—is accompanied by a relative erasure of matter effects, while their conspicuousness, whether in the *Sacchi* or in the *Cretti*, relegates deliberate organization of forms to the background."[14] If Burri can be seen as a major informalist artist and a pioneer in this domain, in my view it is because he treats the work not as an object, but as an ecosystem in which he manages to create phenomena analogous to those produced in nature. Burri's art has thus become the laboratory of our contemporaneity.

[1] Clement Greenberg, "After Abstract Expressionism," *Art International* 6, no. 8 (October 1962): 24–32.
[2] Françoise Choay, "Par-delà l'image et le symbole: Alberto Burri," *Art International* 5, nos. 5–6 (June–July 1961): 30–33.
[3] Michel Tapié, foreword to *Burri peintures, César sculptures* (Paris: Galerie Rive Droite, 1956), n.p.
[4] André Pieyre de Mandiargues, "Burri: la ferraille et la fleur," *XXe siècle* 12 (May–June 1959), 51–56.
[5] As in the photo feature which accompanies the article by Milton Gendel, "Burri Makes a Picture," *Art News* (December 1954), where he can be seen working on the floor like Pollock.
[6] Ettore Sottsass, "Tele di sacco più preziose di Klimt," *Domus* 292 (March 1954), 52. One might also think of what could be called the "glorious bodies" of the informalist painting of Toti Scialoja and Afro.
[7] See Thierry Dufrêne, "Alberto Burri: Materialità e Nouveau Réalisme francese," in Bruno Corà, ed., *Burri. Lo spazio di materia. Tra Europa e USA* (Città di Castello: Fondazione Burri, Palazzo Albizzini, 2016), 92.
[8] Pierre Restany, "Un art brut soumis à l'esprit de géométrie: Alberto Burri," *Cimaise* 59 (May–June 1962): 12–25.
[9] Christian Zervos, "Quelques jeunes," *Cahiers d'Art*, 25th year, no. 1 (1950), 246, ill.
[10] Roland Barthes, *Mythologies*, trans. Annette Lavers (New York: Noonday Press, 1972), 97, 99.
[11] See Pietro Bellasi, "Dagli strepiti dei materiali ai silenzi della materia: Jean Tinguely, Yves Klein, Alexander Calder, Alberto Burri," in Corà, *Burri: Lo spazio di materia*, 100–109.
[12] Restany, "Un art brut," 22.
[13] Maurizio Calvesi, *Alberto Burri* (New York: Harry Abrams, 1975), 8.
[14] Daniel Abadie, "Burri: La violence et la grâce," in *Alberto Burri: Cretti e Cellotex* (Città di Castello: Rubini e Petruzzi, 1984), n.p.

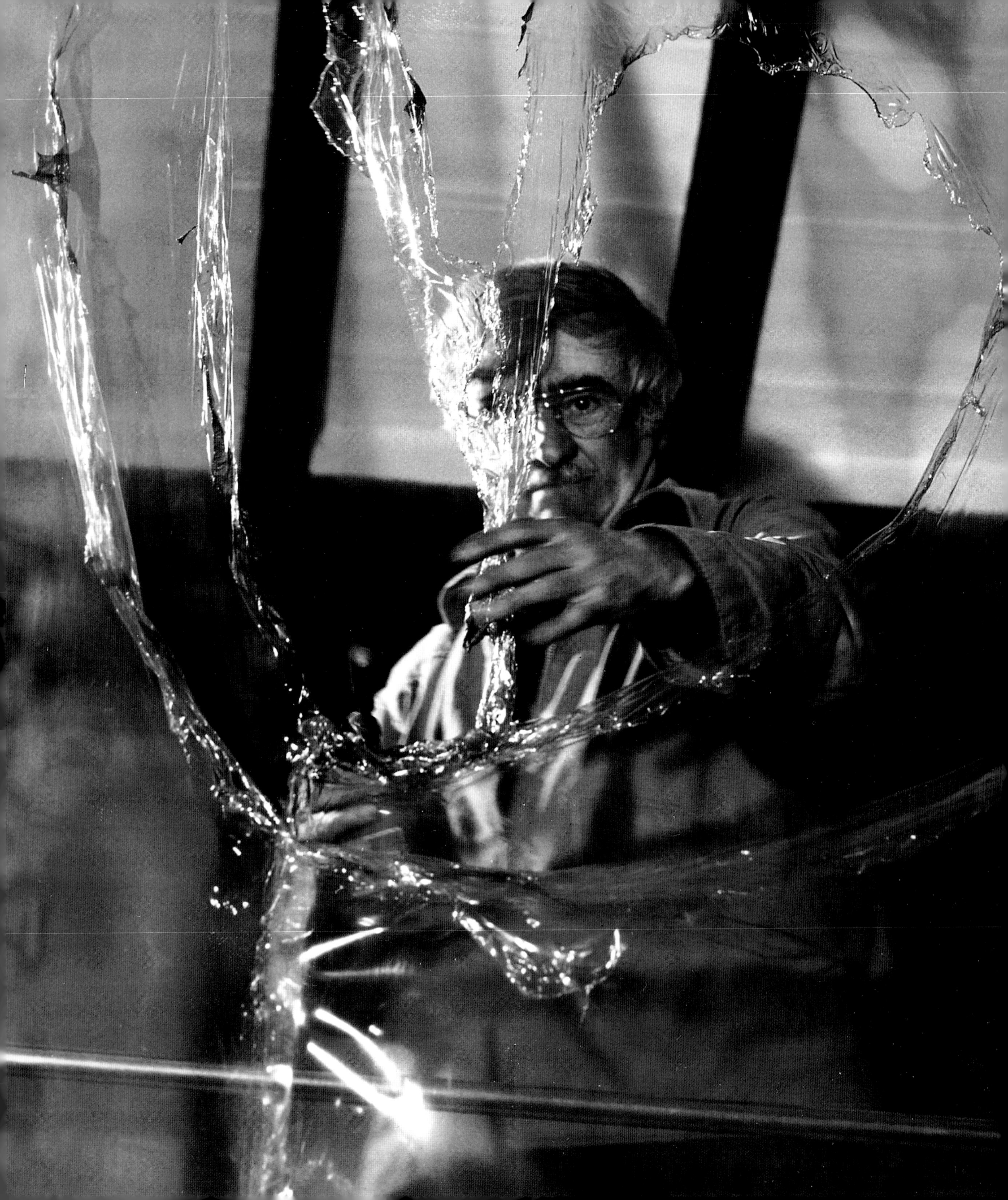

Alberto Burri, Joseph Beuys, and Post-War Art in Italy and Germany

Petra Richter

The Silence of Alberto Burri and the Speech of Joseph Beuys

On 3 April 1980, at the invitation of the curator Italo Tomassoni, the Italian painter Alberto Burri (1915–1995) and the German sculptor, installation, and action artist Joseph Beuys (1921–1986) (fig. 1) met for the first time in the Sala della Cannoniera of the Rocca Paolina in Perugia. The confrontation of their different artistic positions promised a rich discussion about the function of art, but the exchange of ideas that had been planned by Tomassoni did not turn out as he had envisaged. While Beuys eloquently presented his progressive message to the audience, Burri remained silent. For Burri, the message of his artistic works was conveyed through their physical existence and this could not be translated into words and phrases: "my painting is a reality that is part of myself, a reality that I cannot reveal in words."[1] In Burri's view, only in the medium of art, through engagement with the fundamental principles of painting, sculpture, and materials, did experiences become manifest that could not otherwise be given rational expression and eluded verbal expression.

By contrast, Beuys believed that the very mystery of an image brought "the senses into motion because they want to comprehend"[2] and provoked questions that could subsequently become the subject of verbal discussion. He did not consider both artistic work and verbal expression to have equal value—he attributed differing degrees of power of imagination to each—but was instead concerned with the interrelation of discourse, actions, and the work object. These provide a reflexive level that complements that which is given visual expression and additional aesthetic value in the art works and actions. One testament to this approach were the many blackboards, covered in writing, schematic figures, diagrams, and notes in white chalk, on which he recorded the results of a talk or a discussion. They document the key terms of his sculptural and political imagination and concretely address the notion of a "cultural revolution."[3] Six of these blackboards were also produced in the course of this talk in 1980 and were given to the city of Perugia (fig. 2).[4] Speech served Beuys as a medium of communication with which to convey to the audience his artistic concept of transforming social relations and to highlight to people the potential for self-determination as well as to create an awareness of their capacity for freedom. By contrast, Burri rejected the use of language as a medium for conveying the artistic concept or for extending artistic action into the social realm.

Alberto Burri, Casenove di Morra, Città di Castello, 1976

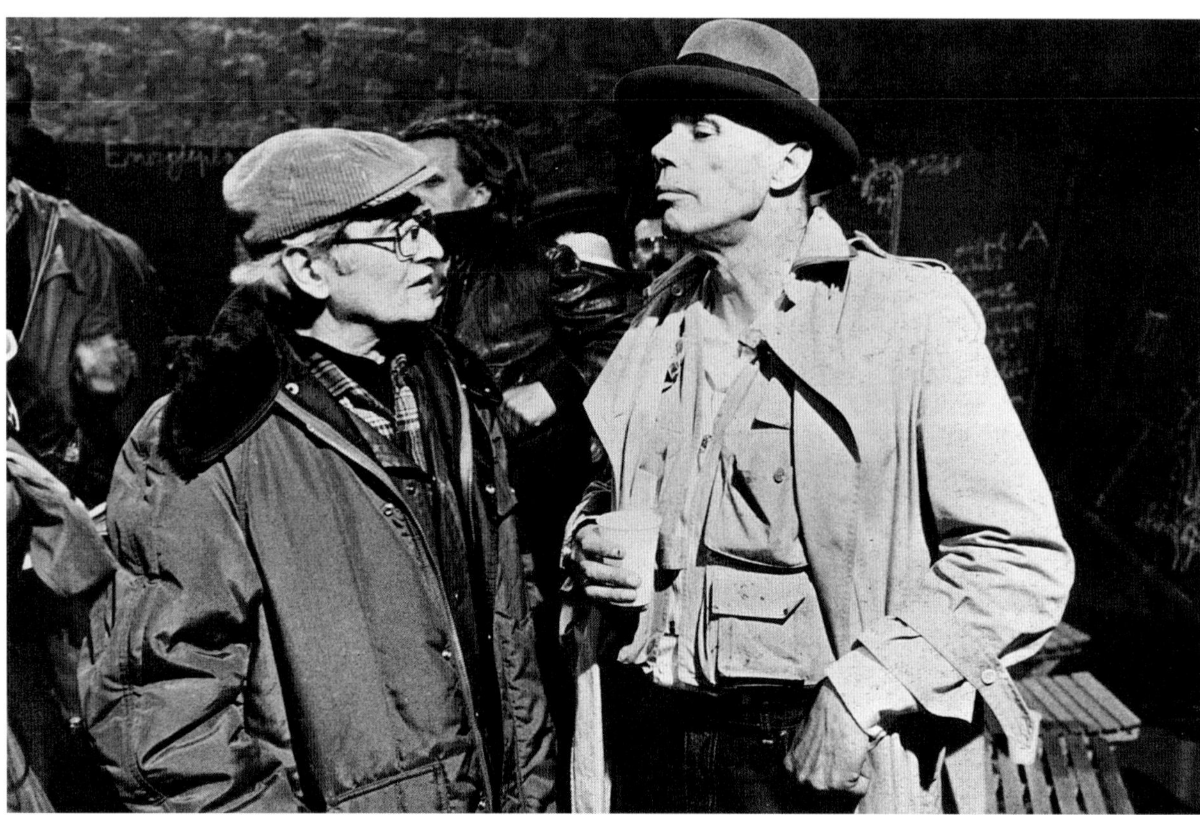

1. Alberto Burri and Joseph Beuys at the Rocca Paolina, Perugia, 1980

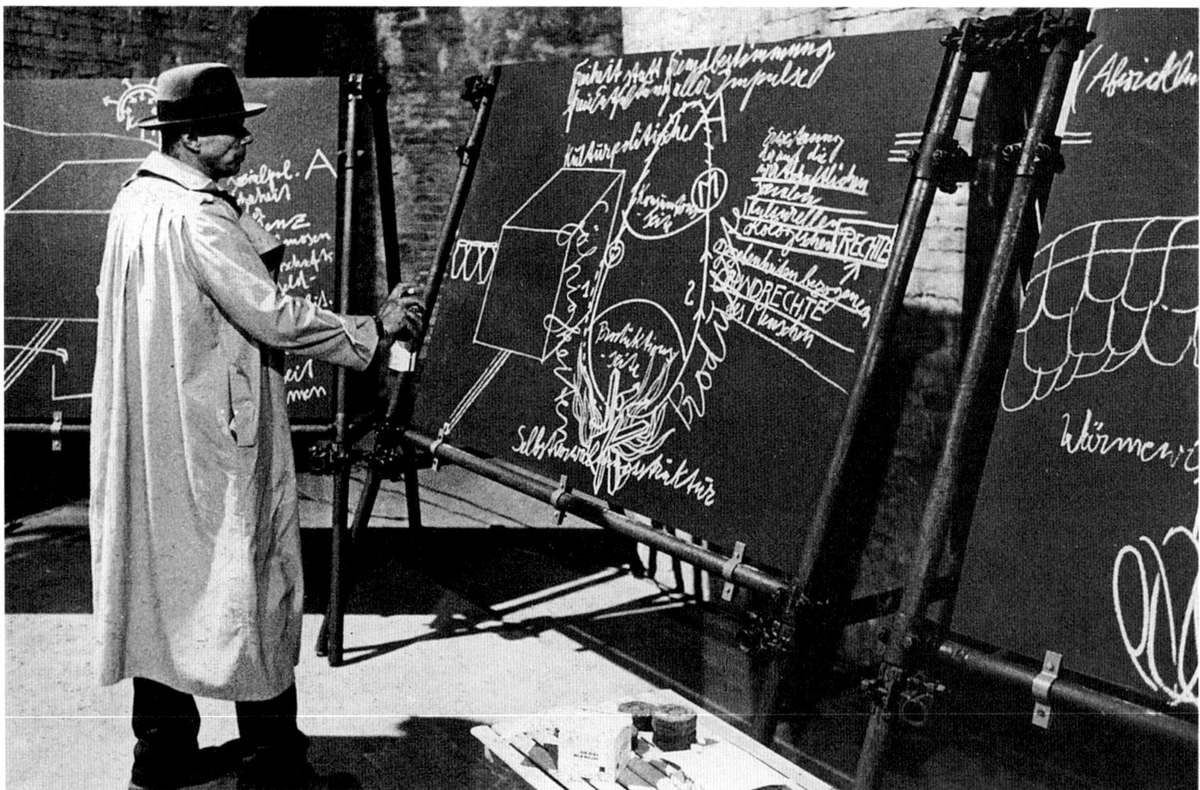

2. Joseph Beuys and his blackboards, Rocca Paolina, Perugia, 1980

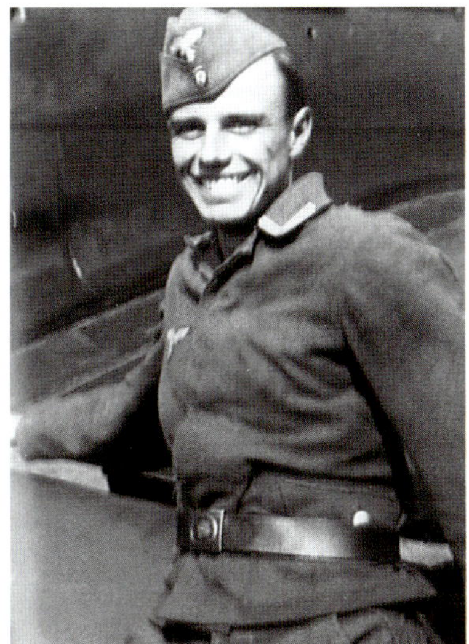

3. Joseph Beuys
in Königgrätz, 1941

4. POW camp, Hereford,
Texas, ca. 1960

Alberto Burri and Joseph Beuys. Two Artists During Fascism and National Socialism

Alberto Burri and Joseph Beuys both belong to a generation shaped by traumatic experiences of war, with which they engaged through aesthetic reflection and specific artistic media. Both artists grew up under dictatorships; like many young people, they complied uncritically with the regimes. Beuys joined the Hitler Youth at twenty years old; Burri, who was a little older,[5] participated in Mussolini's war of aggression in Ethiopia from 1935 to 1936, a war which violated international law. Both men volunteered for military service: Beuys completed training as a radio operator in Posen and Erfurt in 1941 (fig. 3), while Burri began his service as an army doctor in 1940, just five months after passing his university medical exams in Perugia. Mussolini was overthrown in July 1943 and on 8 September 1943 the Italians signed an armistice with the Allied Forces, but Burri had already fallen into American captivity in Tunisia in May the same year. He spent his captivity in a POW camp in Hereford, Texas, until 1946, where—as a result of refusing to cooperate with the Americans—he was subjected to severe detention conditions (fig. 4).[6] It is in this period that he made the existential decision no longer to work as a doctor, but instead to dedicate all his time to painting—and above all to forget the events that had occurred around him.[7]

The trauma he suffered during the years of war also moved Joseph Beuys to become an artist after the war. Radio operator and aerial gunner Beuys, who had been in military service from 1941 to 1945 and was severely injured on several occasions,[8] decided in May 1943, during deployment in southern Italy, "to learn the sculptor's profession after the war." [9]

While the traumatic experiences led the quieter and more distanced Burri to become a silent artist, Beuys reacted with the contrary decision to accord speech extraordinary importance: "my path led through speech, as strange as that is; it did not come from a so-called artistic talent."[10]

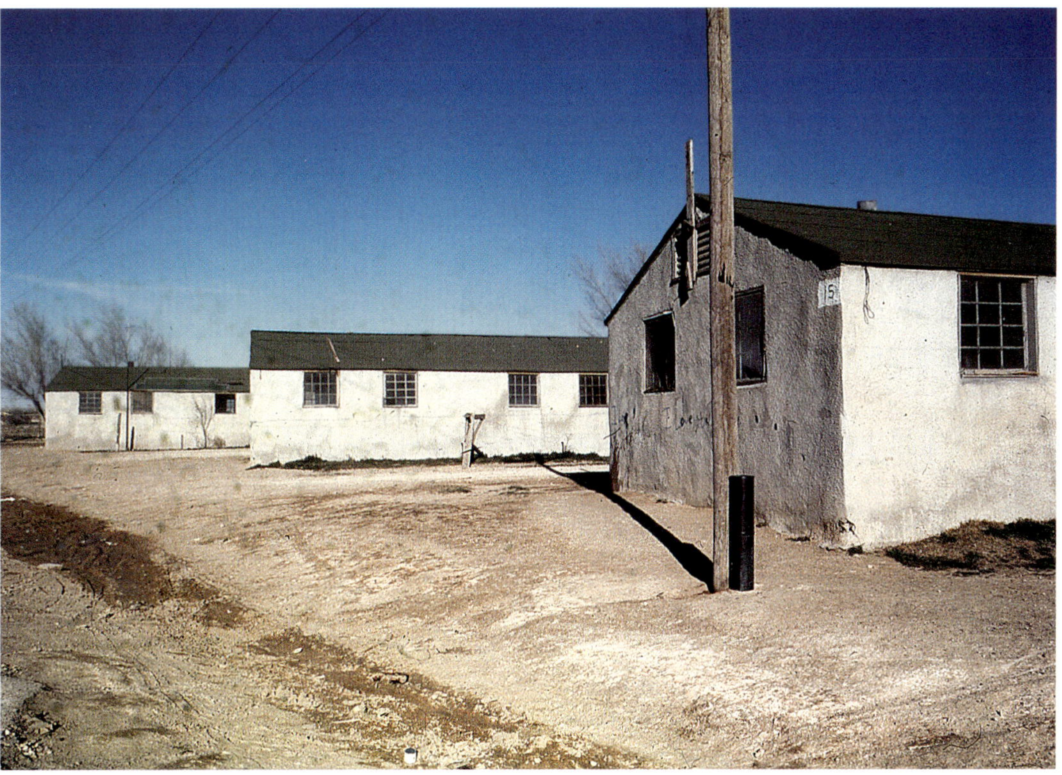

Beuys's eloquence and Burri's silence not only reveal contrary characteristics, but also controversial artistic concepts. Common to both is their definitive contribution to the expansion of artistic methods and materials. They belong to the artists of the post-war era, who, through experimental use of new materials, contributed to the turn away from the panel image and the expansion of art production beyond the traditional forms of painting, drawing or classical sculpture.

Artistic Developments in the Post-War Period in Germany and Italy

Cultural conditions in the post-war period in both Italy and West Germany were characterized by the general individual and systemic effort to distance oneself from the "academic and official forms of expression of Nationalism and Fascism" of the pre-war period[11] and to reappraise the previously vilified—especially by national socialist propaganda—historical and contemporary avantgardes.[12] Focus now lay on the search for a new artistic beginning and a new cultural identity.

Against the background of the intensifying Cold War between the eastern and western powers, abstraction was implemented as a moral and aesthetic victory of the free West,[13] an instrument distinct to totalitarian systems such as the GDR and its state art, Social Realism. While abstraction had long been accepted as a world language of art in international art theoretical discourse, the discussion surrounding non-representational and figurative art as well as the avant-gardist understanding of autonomy and a politically engaged art continued to polarize the cultural-political discourse in Italy and Germany for many years.[14]

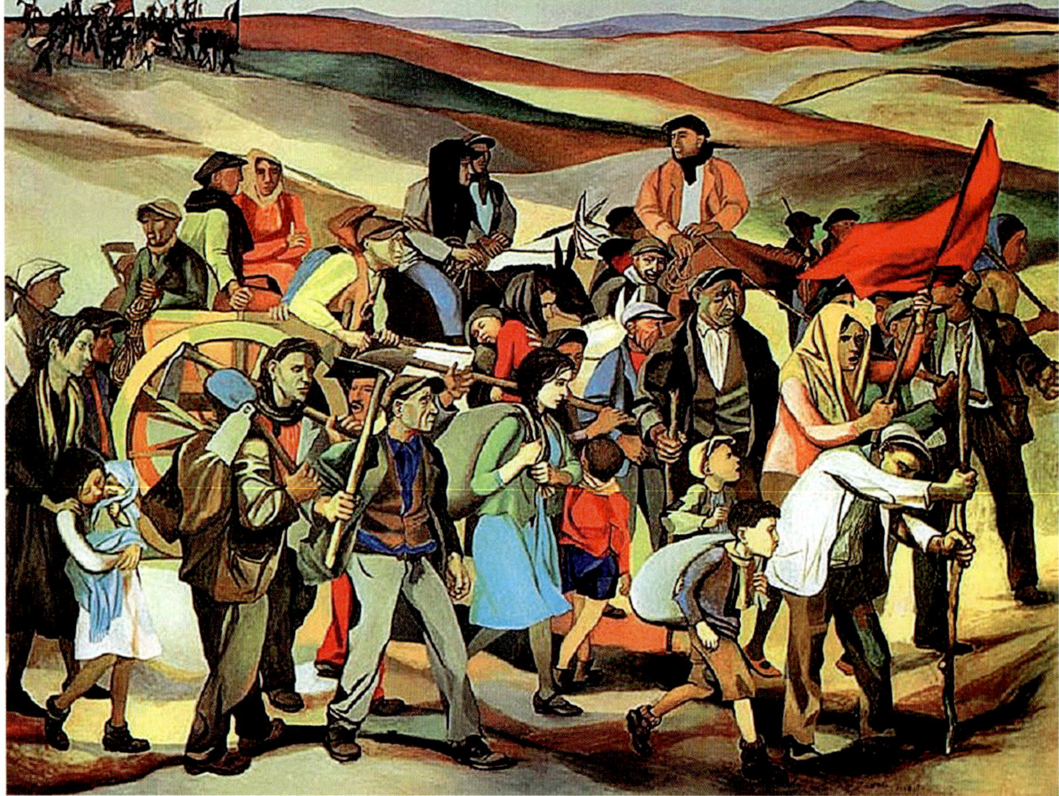

5. Renato Guttuso, *Occupazione delle terre incolte in Sicilia*, 1949

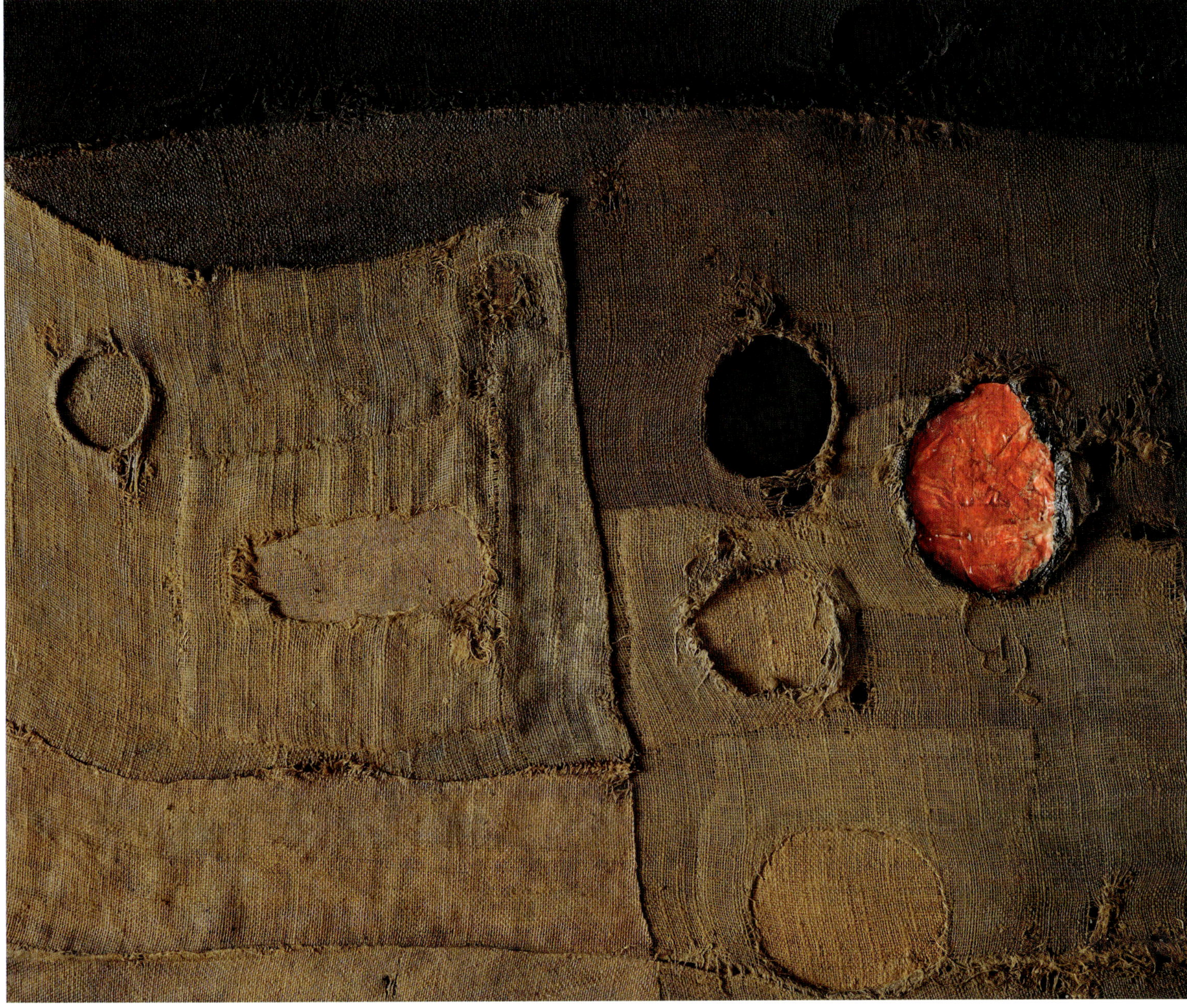

6. Alberto Burri,
Sacco, 1953
Private collection

The Path of Alberto Burri into Abstraction

Alberto Burri, who returned to Italy in 1946 and had experienced neither the German occupation of his country nor the period of the Resistenza, was confronted with an economically backward country and an art stagnating in regionalism but, in the shadow of French informalist painting, on the threshold of a new direction.

Abstractions by the artists' associations, including the Fronte Nuovo delle Arti, the dynamic images of Emilio Vedova (1919–2005) and Toti Scialoja (1914–1998), as well as the punctured and slashed canvases of Lucio Fontana (1899–1965) from his *Concetto spaziale* series begun in 1949 all mark a new artistic beginning. Fontana clearly distanced himself from the politically engaged realistic painting of, for example, Renato Guttuso (1911–1987) (fig. 5). The most significant spokesperson of the cultural policy of the PCI, Guttuso saw more concrete, progressive potential in realistic art than in the positions presented by abstraction.[15] Artists such as Alberto Burri, Emilio Vedova, and

Lucio Fontana together with art historians such as Lionello Venturi, Carlo Giulio Argan, and Palma Bucarelli successfully resisted an art that had subordinated itself to Stalinist party politics and its associated ideologization.

7. Joseph Beuys, *zeige deine Wunde*, 1976

Burri began to paint abstract images in Rome in the late 1940s, proceeding autodidactically after initially attempting figurative paintings during his time as a POW.[16] He had executed his first paintings in Hereford on burlap sacking through want of available materials, but in a composition executed in 1949 he returned to the material as an image medium. He used torn, frayed, rough burlap (*sacchi*) as a painting surface, shaped it into a spatial composition, integrated—in the tradition of the collages of Picasso and Schwitters—Duchamp-style ready-mades, banal materials unworthy of art such as wooden planks, iron, and plastic materials. Burri's first solo exhibition in the L'Obelisco gallery on Via Sistina, Rome, documents his painterly innovations, such as the shift of focus from color material to pure material. As color material and image medium transition from one to the other as creased, crusty, torn, and patched substance they become a poetic image substance that eludes content-related references.

The artist created further innovative forms such as *Muffe*, small images in traditional materials that suggest bacterial growth, or *Gobbi* of 1950, which presents the expansion of the canvas in space, a subject that intrigued Fontana, as well as international artists such as Emil Schumacher, Piero Manzoni, Robert Rauschenberg, Ellsworth Kelly, and Pino Pascali.[17] In 1953 Burri was invited to New York by the director of the Guggenheim Museum, James Johnson Sweeney, to participate in the group exhibition of European artists. An exhibition in the Museum of Modern Art followed in 1955. Beuys was only granted an exhibition in New York in 1979, not least as a result of American criticism of European art, which was viewed as the heir of an idealistic tradition of thought and tending towards transcendentalism.

Burri's series using worn burlap, created from 1949 onwards, is frequently interpreted as an expression of the injuries and defilements that Burri was, as a physician, unable to heal with medical means. In particular the burlap sections that resembled dirty and torn bandages covering the red color of a wound were understood by people, for whom the traumatic memories of the war were still very recent, as a metaphor of the "open wound of the world."[18] Burri's painter friend Scialoja expressed a similar opinion; for him the *Sacchi* were *capolavori*: "instead of painting, he affixed pieces of rough sacking to which he added color, creating things like bloody sores." (fig. 6)[19]

A reference to Burri's American captivity was also read into the integration of the fragment of the American flag in *SZ1*, 1949. Yet, Burri always refuted any suggestion of biographical references and associated iconographical interpretations linked to the events of the war, although an ambivalence between the referential aspects and the autonomy of formal materials remained evident.

Beuys's Artistic Concept of Social Sculpture

While Burri's distancing questioned the possibility of a coherent communication of the meaning of history, reflection of the continued impact of the events of war is evident in Beuys's work and was described by him in those terms. His understanding of the true extent of the war and the national socialist atrocities was expressed in an irreversible shock, which, from the mid-1950s, led to a severe physical and psychological crisis. The "works filled with pain" that he created in this period are testament to the deeply

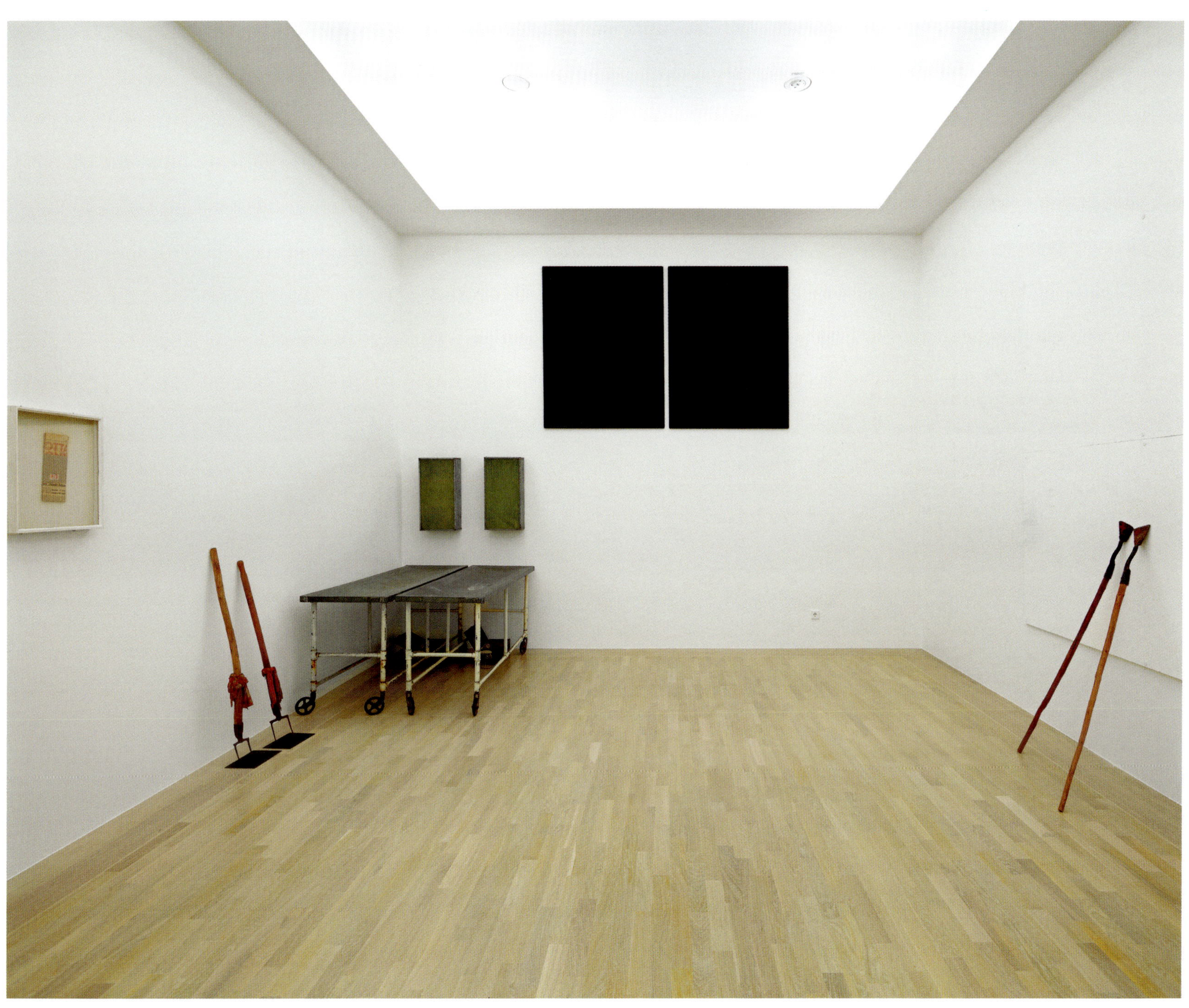

authentic realm of experience this crisis engendered.[20] Only through a complete reorganization of his being, like a shamanistic self-initiation, was he able to redirect this state into a "thoroughgoing process of renewal."[21]

The thought processes he experienced in this phase allowed him to develop the cornerstones of his worldview and his understanding of himself as an artist. His beliefs and mindscape, his scientific interests, extraordinary knowledge of the plant and animal world, are all given expression in poetic drawings, sculptures, and designs. For the rest of his life, these early works served him as a reservoir for exemplifying key terms that he realized in the concept of anthropological art and Social Sculpture in the 1960s.

The existential experiences of traumatic injury of a physical and psychological kind, which came to the fore in Beuys's period of crisis, found expression in his work

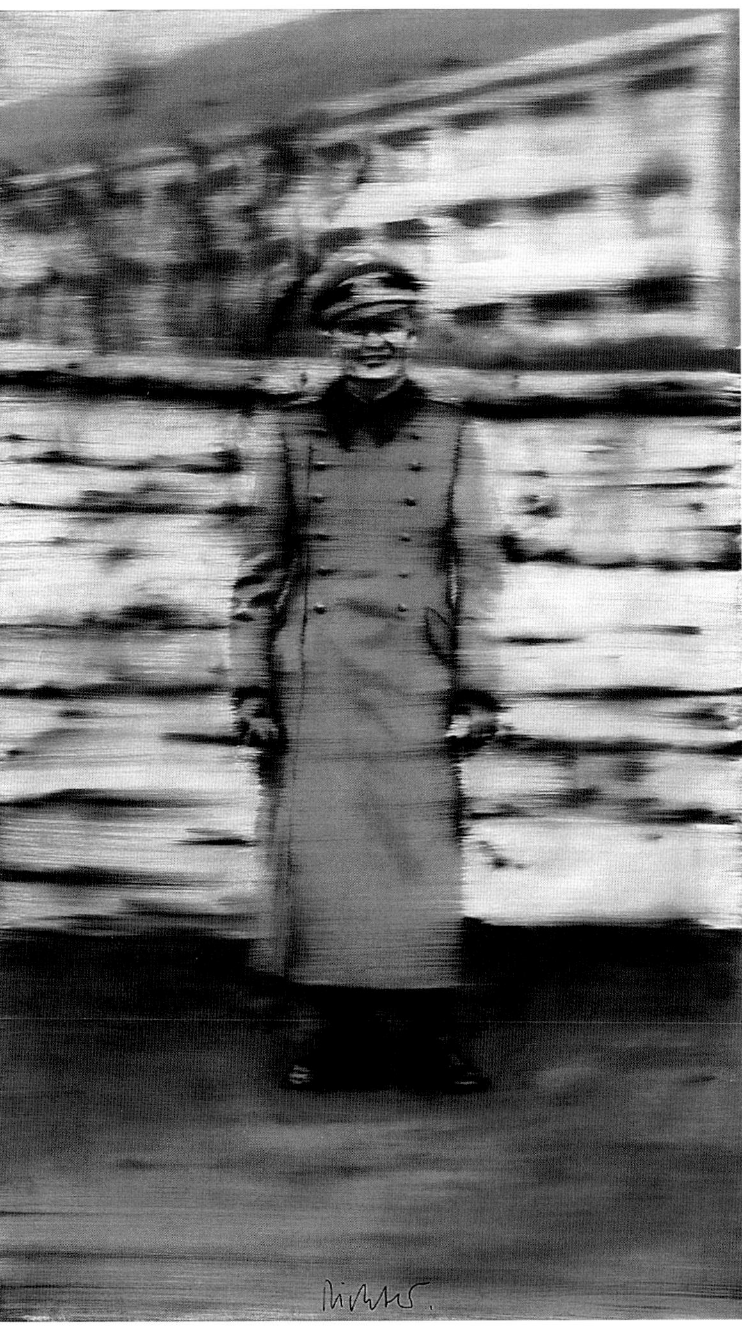

8. Gerhard Richter, *Onkel Rudi*, 1965

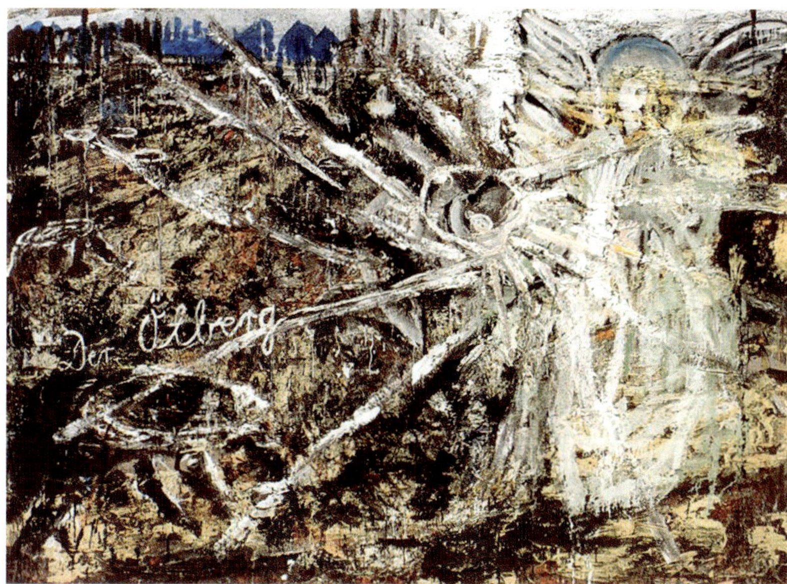

9. Anselm Kiefer, *Der Ölberg*, 1980

at a fictional level. His 1976 installation *zeige deine Wunde* (show your wound) (fig. 7) can be interpreted as an appeal to people to confront unresolved trauma. Acknowledging guilt and critically addressing issues that had been suppressed above all by National Socialism were the first steps to coming to terms with the past. It is out of this process that Beuys developed his therapeutical approach based on the powerful effect of artistic action combined with his programmatic goal of a healing transformation process. The phenomenon of making experiences of the taboo past the subject of artistic engagement is also evident in works by artists such as Georg Baselitz, Gerhard Richter, (fig. 8) and Beuys's former student Anselm Kiefer. (fig. 9). Exhibitions such as *Hommage à Lidice*, 1967, in which, among others, Richter and Beuys participated, thematized the atrocities of the Nazi past; in his work *Onkel Rudi* Richter drew attention to the involvement of his own family in the events of the Third Reich. Through the selection of materials such as lead, straw, hair, ash, as in the work *Unternehmen Seelöwe*, 1975, Kiefer brings national socialist history to the fore and recalls the crimes of that past to the present, as he does in *Margarete Sulamith*, 1981.

Beuys, who taught at the Staatliche Kunstakademie Düsseldorf from 1961, had already begun to expand the traditional definition of art through the examination of new functions and sought to redefine the social relevance of art in the 1960s. He developed—in contrast to the American sculptural concept of a minimal and conceptual art that was conveyed in the teachings of Rudolf Steiner—a definition of art that was expanded to address anthropological issues, in which every form of work is considered an expression of creativity. The impetus of innovation that broke through the boundaries of familiar forms of art expressed itself in the early 1960s through the use of unusual materials such as grease and felt and through a practice of actionism[22] with the aim of opening up areas that went beyond verbal expression and rational knowledge to integrate the spiritual dimension. Faced with utopian energies that were utterly exhausted, Beuys, based on his concept of Social Sculpture, sought ideas for the reformation and democratization of society in order to find strategies to overcome the social problems of the future. In his view, the potential for change could only be guaranteed through a non-violent confrontation of ideas, which had to be carried out in communication with people according to the principles of art.

For all the differences and complexities in the two artists' understanding of the role of art and of the artist, Burri's 1984 work *Grande Cretto Gibellina* (fig. 10) can nevertheless be interpreted as the expression of an idea that is common to both. Burri presents the tragic event of the 1968 earthquake in Gibellina with blocks of white concrete, in which is stored the suffering of the people who once lived here. In this monumental, minimalistic presentation Burri remains formally faithful to his central notion of autonomy, but goes beyond that concept by creating a paradigm for human sympathy and even consolation. It is in their moral goals and values, in seeking to counter suffering with art, that these two artists here come together.

10. Alberto Burri visiting the *Grande Cretto* under construction in Gibellina, May 1987

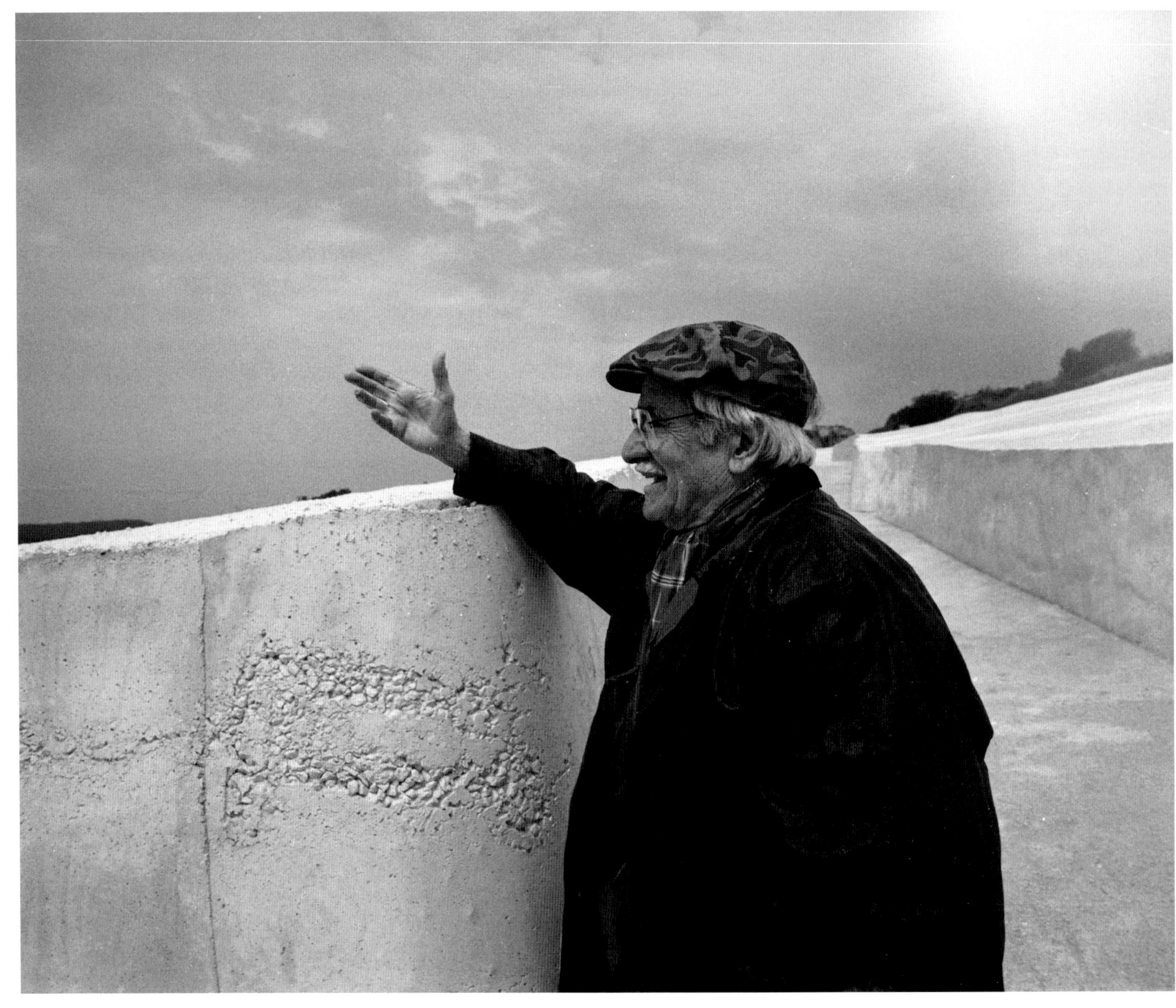

[1] Stefano Zorzi, *Parola di Burri* (Turin: Allemandi, 1995), 11.

[2] Beuys, as cited in Ernst Günter Engelhard, *Joseph Beuys. Werke aus der Sammlung Ströher* (Basel: Kunstmuseum Basel, 1969), 34.

[3] Willi Bongard, "Letter from London," 1977, in Jörg Schellmann, ed., *Joseph Beuys. Die Multiples. Werkverzeichnis der Auflagenobjekte und Druckgraphik* (Munich-New York: Schellmann-Schirmer/Mosel, 1992), 564.

[4] They are still held by the city museum, Palazzo della Penna, in Perugia.

[5] "He was a fascist, as many young men were in his day." Piero Palumbo, *Burri. Una vita*, (Milan: Electa, 2007), 19, 20.

[6] "Fake firing squad executions were staged near the camp to terrorize the undecided," who, like Burri, did not wish to cooperate with the Americans and were therefore deemed "die-hard fascists." They were subjected to inhumane conditions, including starvation. Palumbo, *Burri. Una vita*, 37.

[7] Burri as cited in Palumbo, *Burri. Una vita*, 43.

[8] Beuys's poetically composed life story, his rescue by the Tartars after a plane crash in Crimea in 1944, is an example of working through traumatic experiences. Letters show that Beuys was transported to a German field hospital one day after the crash.

[9] Letter to his parents dated 18 May 1943, in Eva Beuys, ed., *Joseph Beuys. Das Geheimnis der Knospe zarter Hülle. Texte 1941-1986* (Munich: Heiner Bastian-Schirmer/Mosel, 2000), 275. This resolution, which Beuys had in fact already made during his final schoolyears, was now given greater force and was realized upon his return. *Joseph Beuys. Zeichnungen. Aquarelle. Oelbilder. Plastische Bilder aus der Sammlung van der Grinten* (Kleve: Städtisches Museum Haus Koekkoek, 1961), n.p.

[10] Joseph Beuys, "Reden über das eigene Land: Deutschland," (speech, Münchner Podium in den Kammerspielen, Munich, 1985), in Hans Mayer et. al, *Reden über das eigene Land: Deutschland 3* (Munich: Bertelsmann, 1985), 38.

[11] Germano Celant, "In völliger Freiheit. Italienische Kunst 1943-1968," in *Italienische Metamorphosen 1943-1968* (Wolfsburg: Kunstmuseum Wolfsburg, 1995), 4.

[12] In contrast to Germany, artists in Italy such as Renato Guttuso, Lucio Fontana, Emilio Vedova, and Filippo Tommaso Marinetti had in 1938 successfully thwarted the Fascist attempt to carry out an Operation "Degenerate Art." Enrico Crispolti, "Zur italienischen Kunst der 1940er bis 1970er Jahre," in *Deutschland – Italien. Aufbruch aus Diktatur und Krieg*, ed. by Wolfgang Storch and Klaudia Ruschkowski (Dresden: Sandstein, 2013), 132, 133.

[13] The fact that the first documenta exhibition curated by Werner Haftmann, a former SA officer, in 1955 was conducted under exclusion of Jewish and previously persecuted artists and thus once again subjected to ideological co-optation has only been the subject of public discussion in recent decades.

[14] "The debate between the figurative and the abstract artists accompanied the chronicles of the post-war period like a never-ending leitmotif." Palumbo, *Burri. Una vita*, 46.

[15] Wolfgang Holler, "Dynamisierung des Kunstbegriffs – Italien 1940-1960," in Carla Schulz-Hoffmann, ed., *Mythos Italien. Wintermärchen Deutschland. Die italienische Moderne und ihr Dialog mit Deutschland* (Munich: Prestel, 1988), 79.

[16] Beuys began his art studies in 1947 at the Staatliche Kunstakademie in Düsseldorf under Josef Enseling and continued it from 1949 under Ewald Mataré.

[17] Carolyn Christov-Bakargiev, "Alberto Burri: Oberfläche in Gefahr," in *Burri 1915-1955. Retrospektive* (Milan: Electa, 1997), 25.

[18] Werner Haftmann, "Utopie und Angst," in Hans-Gerhard evers, ed., *Zeugnisse der Angst in der modernen Kunst, Ausstellung zum Darmstädter Gespräch* (Darmstadt: Heiner Knell, 1963), 93.

19 Palumbo, *Burri. Una vita*, 64.

[20] Wolfgang Zumdick, "Ganz begreifen werden wir uns nie," in Harald Kunde, ed., *Intuition! Dimensionen des Frühwerks von Joseph Beuys* (forthcoming).

[21] Joseph Beuys, as cited in Götz Adriani, Winfried Konnertz, and Karin Thomas, *Joseph Beuys. Leben und Werk* (Cologne: DuMont, 1980), 66–67.

[22] While European informalism still characterized the context of aesthetic reception, Beuys, inspired by the activities of Fluxus artists, organized the first Fluxus festival — Festum Fluxorum. Fluxus. Musik und Antimusik. Das Instrumentelle Theater — at the Kunstakademie in 1963, and invited international artists.

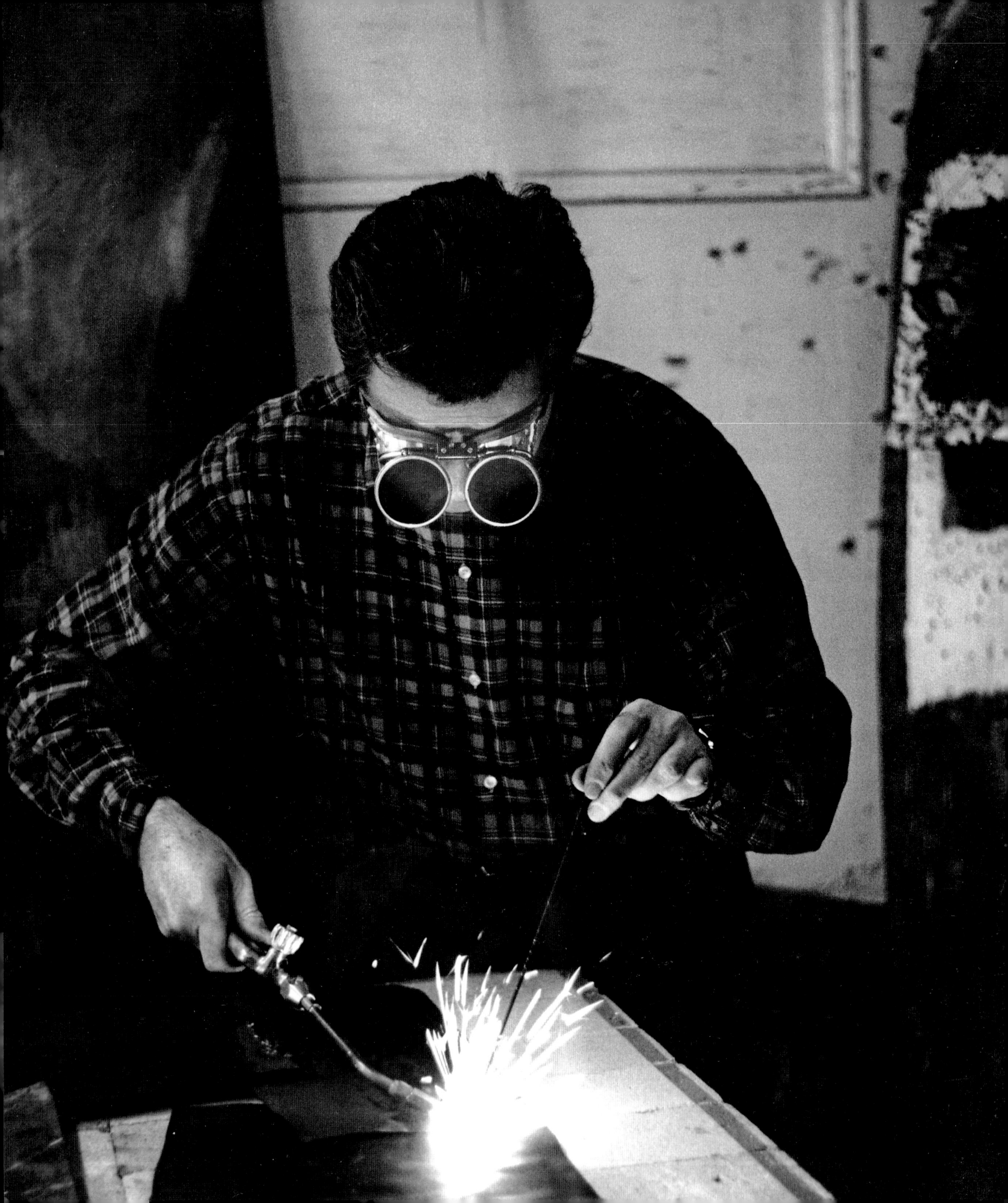

Burri and Material Poetry

Bruno Corà
and Mario Diacono

Bruno Corà Along with Leonardo Sinisgalli (fig. 3) and Libero De Libero, (fig. 5) along with Emilio Villa (fig. 4) and Giuseppe Ungaretti, along with Cesare Vivaldi, you belong to the small group of poets who have written on art in Italy from the post-war period onwards, tackling the work of artists such as Burri, Fontana, Scarpitta, and then Kounellis and others, whose work has built upon that of those masters. Can you map out which aspects inspired your writing in Burri's works, whose radical pronouncements marked the entire 1950s and a large part of the decades that followed?

Mario Diacono In the 1950s and '60s, European abstract expressionism (which came about and was known as informalism) and that of the USA displayed a linguistic radicalism in the expression of art that, in contrast, was relatively absent in literary works. In the post-war period painting launched a new avant-garde, while the language of advanced literature seemed not to go beyond surrealism and Joyce; this obviously because, in different ways in Italy, Germany, Russia, and Spain, avant-garde expressions had gradually been ostracized or marginalized. From the heights of the perspective of the 21st century, and also given their international diffusion promoted by the international art market, I believe in fact that the works of the artists who have given rise to the two mo(ve)ments, art informel and abstract expressionism, no longer appear as formally and clearly separate, as was seen in their age, but as a strongly interconnected yet methodologically separate continuum of events and thoughts of and on the essence of art. In around the mid-1950s, Allen Ginsberg in the USA, Samuel Beckett in France, and Emilio Villa in Italy are writers and poets who enact an analogous linguistic expressionism in literature. Burri's *Sacchi*, *Ferri*, *Plastiche* and *Legni* represented the most resolute and advanced outcomes of the innovation of form and language of the new art in Europe.

BC Can you clarify what the key elements were of poets such as Emilio Villa in the hermeneutic action, considering Burri in particular (but also Fontana, Rotella, Turcato, or Lo Savio and others)?

MD Emilio Villa was Burri's fellow traveler par excellence in his first ten years of work, not only through the activity of the Fondazione Origine and the writings in the *Arti Visive* magazine, but also on account of the quality and innovation in writing with which he developed his critical texts. When, in 1951, comparing Burri to Gorky, he wrote that Burri's practice "is certainly one of the strongest acts, a genetic r aptus/r actus, a source not exactly thinkable, nor dampened by thought, the most unthinkable that painting (that truly suited to being a respond) today can flex and deflect, reflect and combine as a colloidal gelatinous plasmic language," Villa did not so much apply an analogical writing to Burri's painting, rather he rendered the intellectual emotion that it aroused in a critical empathic language. And when in 1955 he published his

Alberto Burri, Via Nera,
Rome, 1959

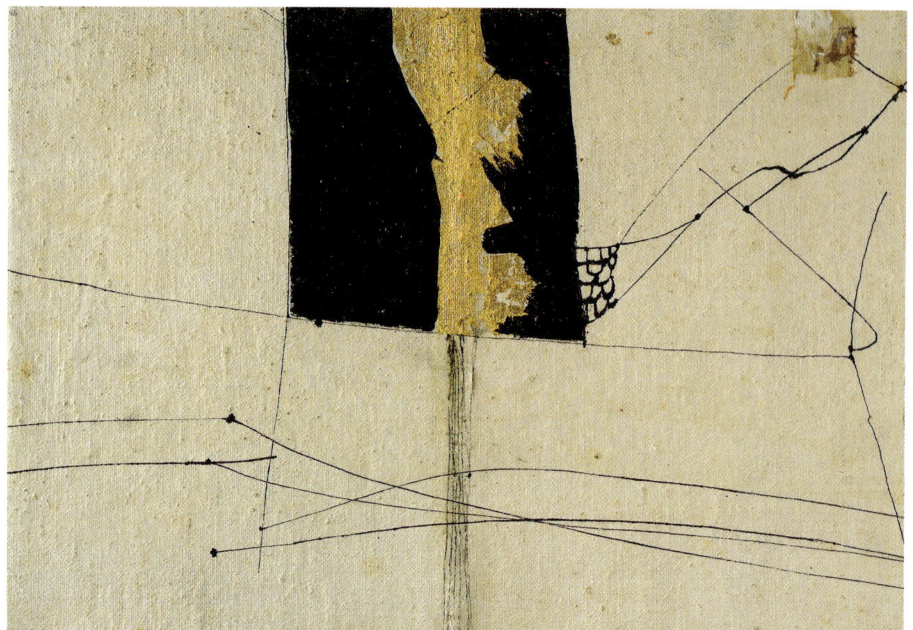

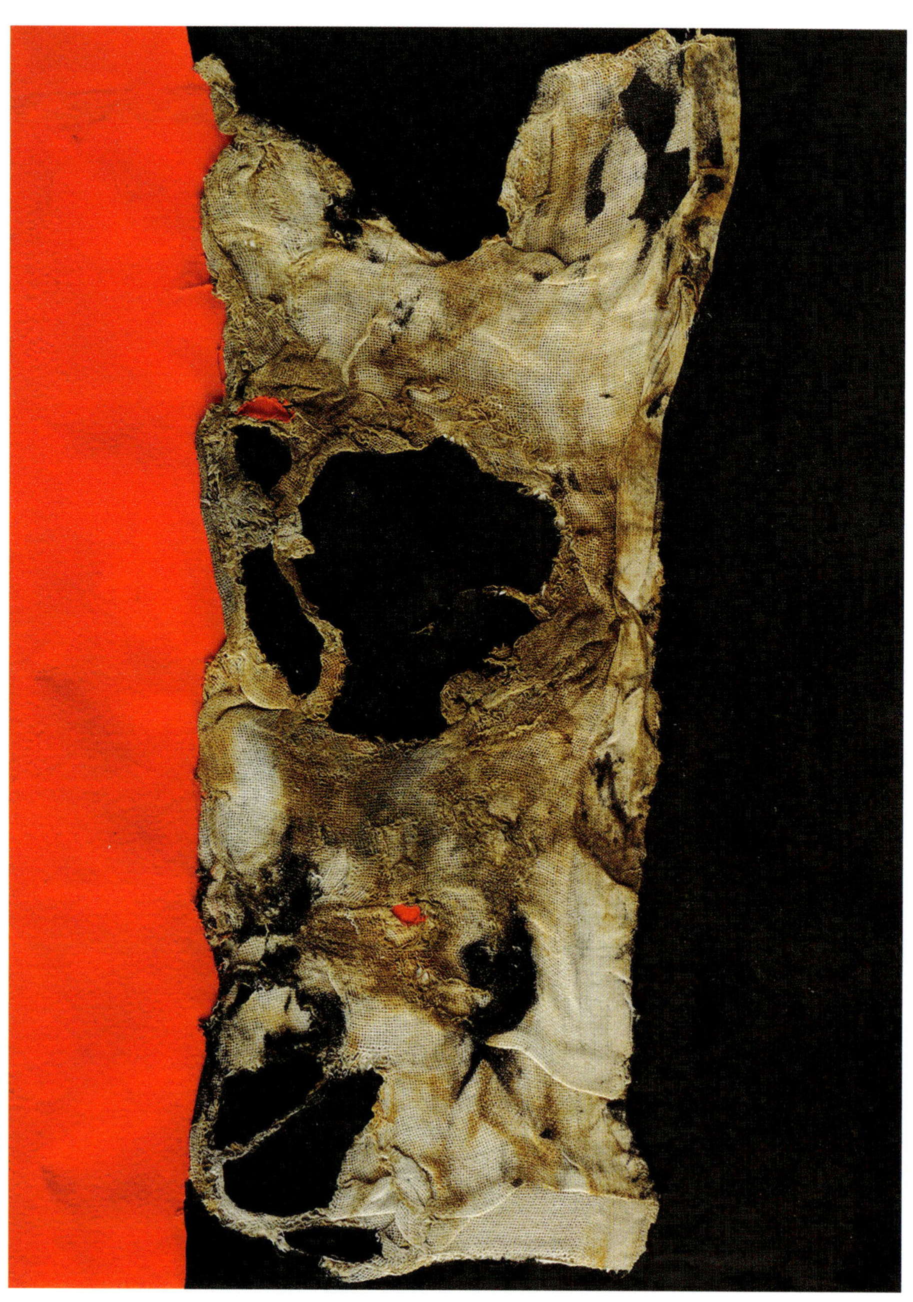

1. Alberto Burri,
Copertina 29, [1953/1954]
Private collection

2. Alberto Burri,
Pagina 23, [1953/1954]
Private collection

3. Leonardo Sinisgalli

4. Emilio Villa

5. Libero De Libero

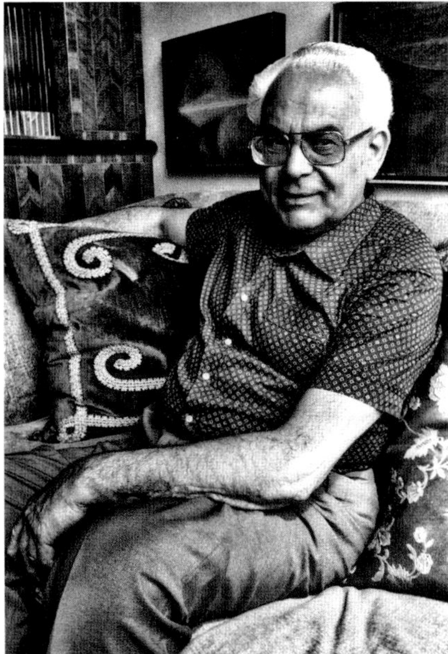

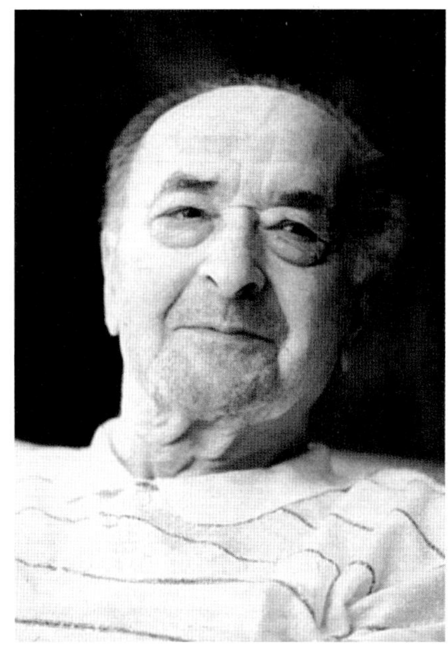

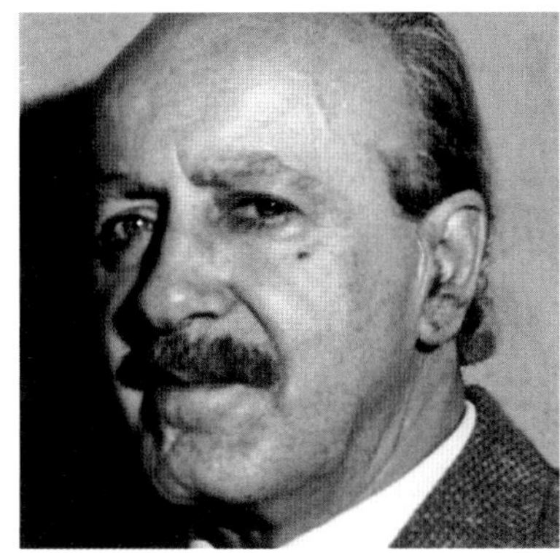

extraordinary book of poems, *17 variazioni su temi proposti per una pura ideologia fonetica* (Seventeen Variations on Proposed Themes for a Pure Phonetic Ideology), Villa's empathy is confirmed and extends into the most audacious bibliographical project of the post-war period: the 99 copies of the book were all to have a dust cover consisting of a small canvas and inside three original works by Burri. For various—and perhaps obvious—reasons, the collaboration with original works by the artist stopped in 1955 with the first ten copies, and was only completed ten years later, when the remaining copies were complemented with a numbered and signed edition with dust covers and graphics by Burri.

BC Your proximity not only to Villa but also to Giuseppe Ungaretti, (fig. 6) of whom you were a collaborator and friend for a long time, prompts me to ask you a similar question to the previous one, since Ungaretti wrote "To Emilio Villa / his friend / Ungaretti." What is the authentic meaning of that dedication by Ungaretti?

MD The dedication appears on a copy of the French translation of Ungaretti's poems by Jean Chuzeville, *Vie d'un homme*, published by Gallimard in 1939. This copy was later given to me by Villa as a gift when I told him that I was working as Ungaretti's secretary. I do not know in which period the book was given to Villa by Ungaretti, but I think before 1950. This specific Villa–Ungaretti connection is interesting because it concerns poems in French, a language that has not only increasingly become the language of election of much of Villa's poetry from the second half of the 1950s onwards but is also significantly present in various of his critical texts, first and foremost on Matta and Capogrossi. I imagine that the meeting indicates that there had been an interaction between the two poets, and that this interaction concerned the importance of French in poetry, particularly in Ungaretti's early poetry: in 1919, in fact, he had published *La guerre in Paris* in 80 copies, a core of poems in French, and in the same year another group of poems in French, *P-L-M / 1914-1919*, had appeared at the end of *Allegria di naufragi* (Merriness of Shipwrecks). However, these French poems, which represent Ungaretti's avant-garde poetics at its peak, were never included in the corpus of his work published after 1920.

BC What, according to the witness accounts, prompted Burri to prefer the language of poets to that of the academicians whom he also frequented, who appreciated his work in so many ways?

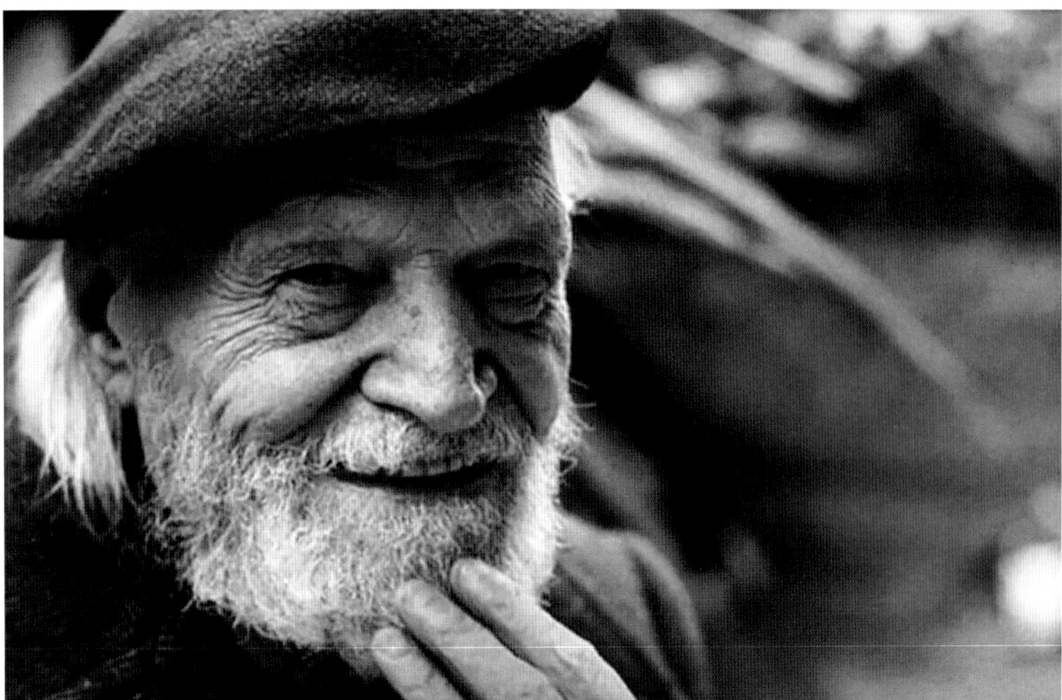

6. Giuseppe Ungaretti

MD I think he appreciated the expressive quality of poetic language more than the analytical quality of critical language. His training as an artist took place totally outside of the academic world, and clearly as an artist Burri perceived that the intensity of expression or expressionism of his abstract and textured works—impossible to describe and comment on in the terms used by an art criticism formed around classical figuration—rather had a consonance with the elusive, hermetic language of poets. On this subject: Ungaretti slept in his studio, and above his bed he had a small painting by Burri that the artist had given him, I believe in 1958 or 1959. They had met, there had immediately been a great empathy, although the painter of that generation that Ungaretti loved most was Fautrier. Ten years later, that empathy remained unchanged and was renewed. For a limited-edition collection of poems by Ungaretti, *Dialogo,* published on the occasion of his eightieth birthday, Burri created an engraving in 59 copies evoking one of his *Combustioni* from the 1950s, and on the copy of the publication that Ungaretti gave to Burri, he wrote as a dedication: "I love Burri, because he is not only today's greatest painter, but he is also the main source of envy for me: he is the first poet of today."

BC On more than one occasion you have already written on the relationship between Burri's painting and that of US artists who undeniably observed him with interest. It would be very interesting if, returning to the topic, you could underline some emblematic episodes of this and, in any event, if you could return to giving a by now historicized overview of the possible repercussions of Burri's painting in US art.

MD As is known, Twombly and Rauschenberg (fig. 7) visited Burri's studio in the early months of 1953; the visits concluded with the exchanging of gifts of small works. In the same year Burri exhibited at the Stable Gallery in New York, where Rauschenberg was in charge of gallery maintenance and would later be responsible for photographing the exhibition. After this first exhibition, in the 1950s Burri repeatedly exhibited in New York: in 1955 again at the Stable and the same year in a group exhibition at the MoMA. In 1960 he was present in the exhibition with which the Guggenheim Museum was inaugurated. His paintings were already in the collections of the two museums, and his work had undoubtedly left its traces in Rauschenberg's

7. Robert Rauschenberg

8. Robert Rauschenberg, *Scatole e feticci*, 1953

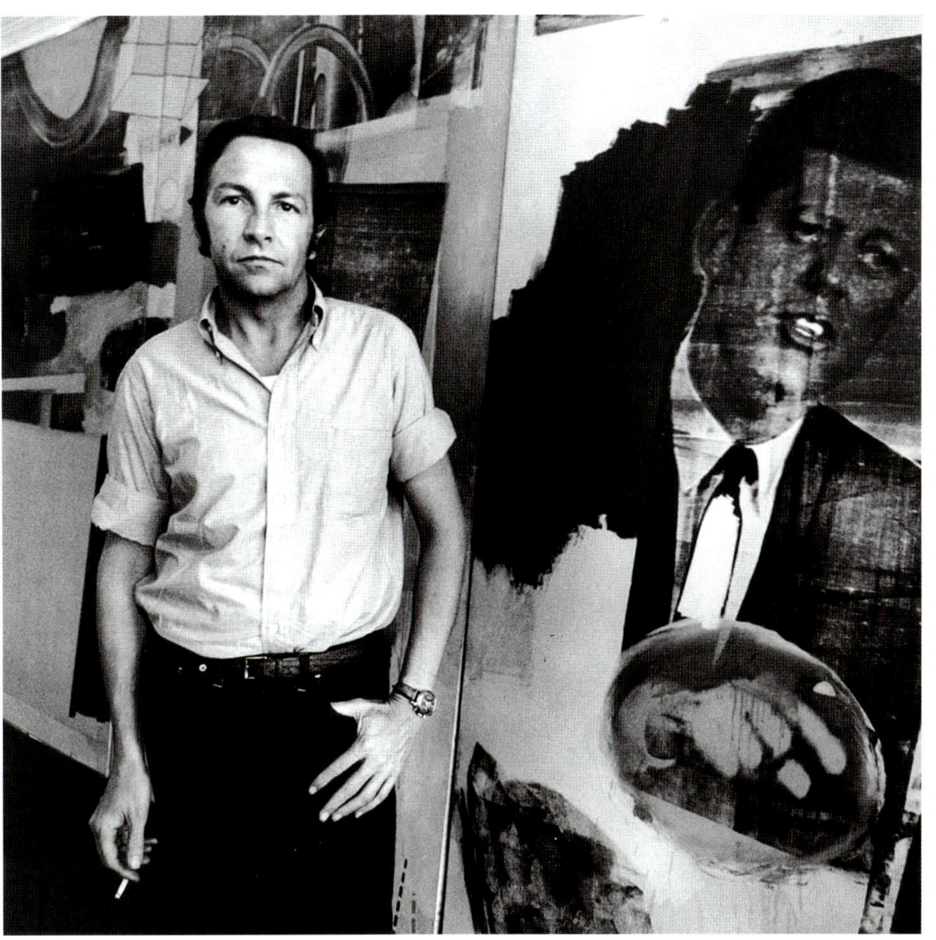

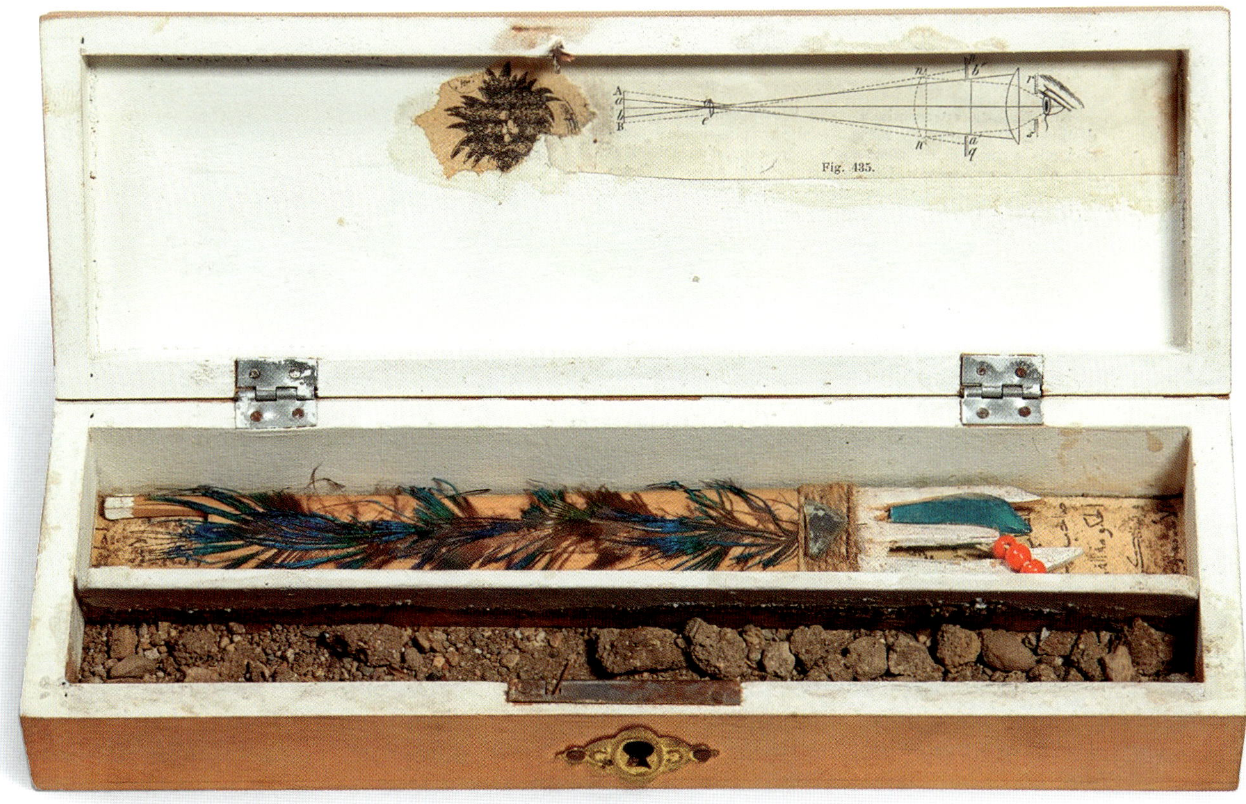

way of treating the surface of the painting and, through Rauschenberg, that of Johns. After 1960, the spirit of his work was undoubtedly present in the works of two new-generation New York artists, Paul Thek and Eva Hesse (fig. 9). The letter that gallery owner Martha Jackson wrote to Burri on 22 February 1960 was therefore prophetic: "With surprise I realize that your work is still very controversial here. The most enthusiastic about it are the young artists, those between the ages of 20 and 30. They say that you and Mondrian are the two artists who inspire American painting at this moment. I think the same. You are decidedly the leader of the artistic revolution that is happening in New York."

BC To what extent could Burri's painting and artistic behavior have encouraged experiences such as those of some artists of arte povera, or individual artists such as Pinot Gallizio, for instance, or Fabio Mauri, and others that will be discussed?

MD As regards Pinot Gallizio (fig. 10) and Fabio Mauri, (fig. 11) Burri undoubtedly represented a model of freedom from the materials, the formats, the very contents of traditional painting. Burri's influence on arte povera, on the other hand, is direct. I would say that the influence that Burri had on Italian painting and sculpture after 1960 was no different from that of Duchamp's ready-mades on US art after 1955. Burri not only indicated to painting and sculpture that the material employed to create a surface and a painting image, a volume and a sculptural image, could be freed from the conventions of traditional media (canvas, brush, oil, wax, bronze, wood, marble), but that the material itself could become image, be the bearer of meaning, if structured intentionally within a form or a concept. It is certainly a possibility that Duchamp's ready-made and Burri's surface-matter, by contaminating each other and combining, governed the entire development of the art that was carried forward between 1955 and 1980.

BC Among the new generations, could you identify some artists who still develop principles that seem to have already moved Burri's painting in his time?

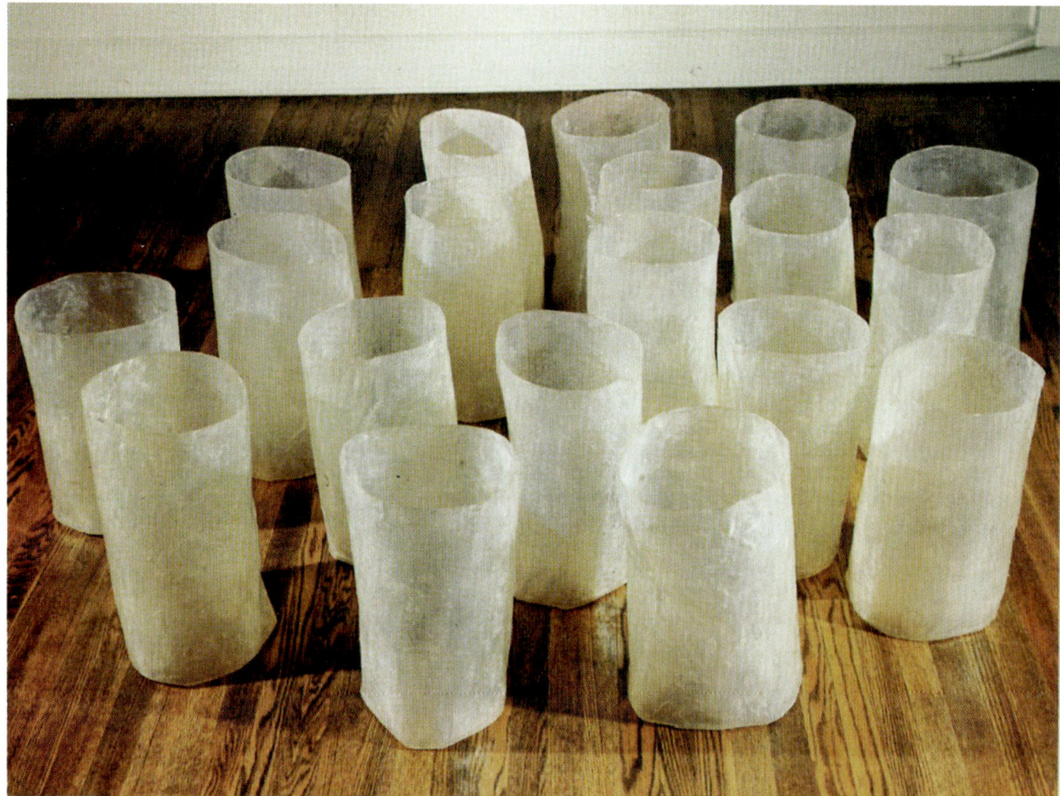

9. Eva Hesse, *Repetition Nineteen III*, 1968

10. Pinot Gallizio, *Rotolo di pittura industriale*, 1950s

11. Fabio Mauri, *The End*, 1970

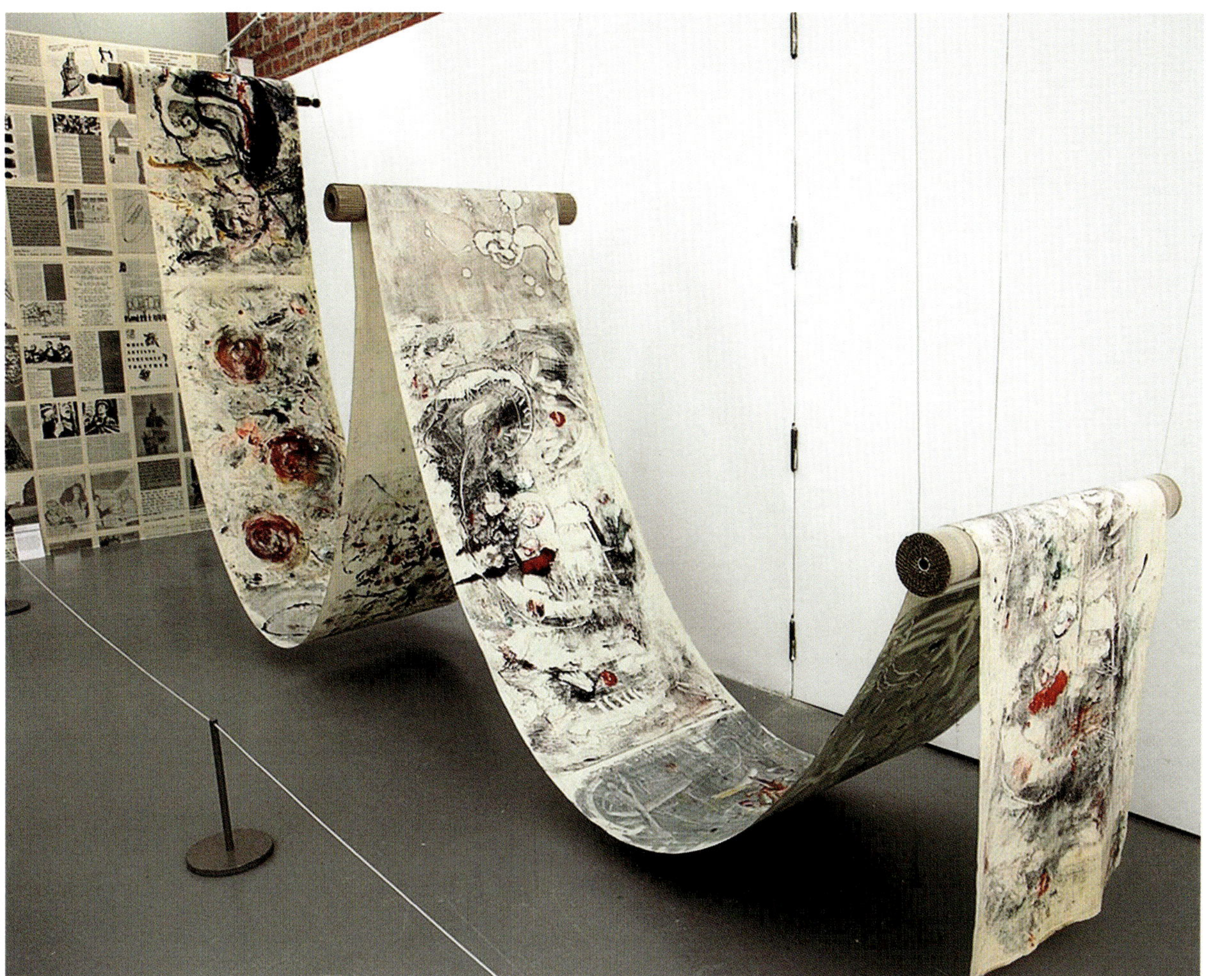

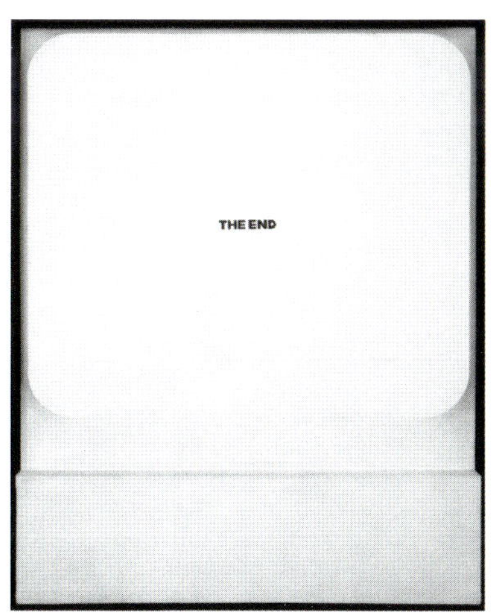

MD To tell the truth, nobody comes to mind. My impression is that the latest, perhaps also the penultimate, generation of artists works without entertaining a sentiment of history. They may appropriate some historical element or other here and there, but their context is the absence of context.

BC If the "silence" of Burri towards his work, that of Marcel Duchamp, and that of Ezra Pound were to be compared, different though they are, could you provide a sense of the peculiarities and the different values of character and strategy?

MD Duchamp's silence, as is known, was the supposed silence of the work: after learning art, he had put it aside and had devoted his energies to chess and to savoir vivre. In reality, as we have seen, he had worked for decades on *Étant donnés: 1. La chute d'eau 2. Le gaz d'éclairage*, (fig. 12) which, I believe, towards the end of the 20th century, had the importance that *Les demoiselles d'Avignon* had had in the early 1900s. Pound's silence was political: I remember that in around 1962 or 1963 Pound visited Ungaretti's house, accompanied by an Italian gentleman whose name I can't remember, but who Ungaretti told me had post-fascist sentiments, to thank him for having signed an appeal by international writers some time earlier for him to be released from the hospital in which he was imprisoned. He stayed there for about an hour. In that time only Ungaretti and Pound's companion spoke; the whole time all Pound said was one word*: Sì*. Burri's silence, in contrast, was over his own work. He wanted the work to speak for itself and of itself; the critical categories that had been applied in art until then were not applicable to his *Sacchi,* and he did not feel the

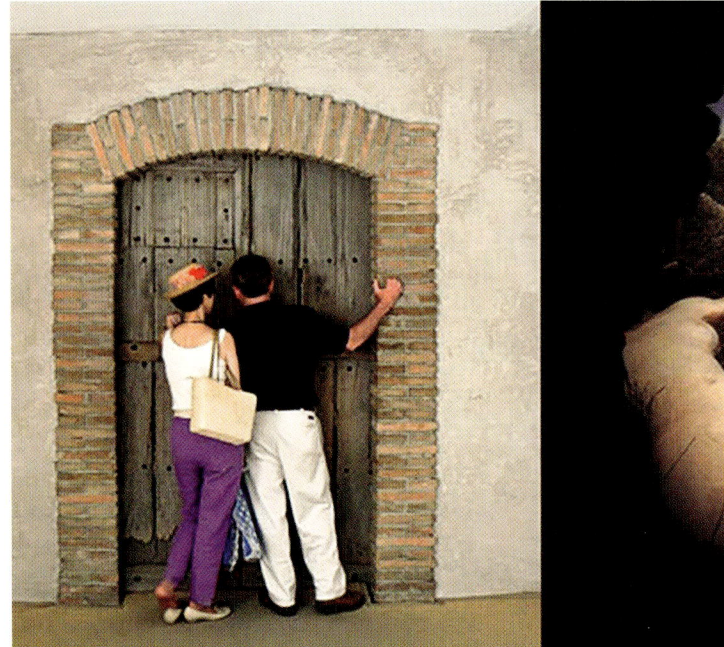

12. Marcel Duchamp, *Étant donnés: 1. La chute d'eau 2. Le gaz d'éclairage*, 1946–1966

13. Afro Basaldella, *Tre sotto chiave*, 1957

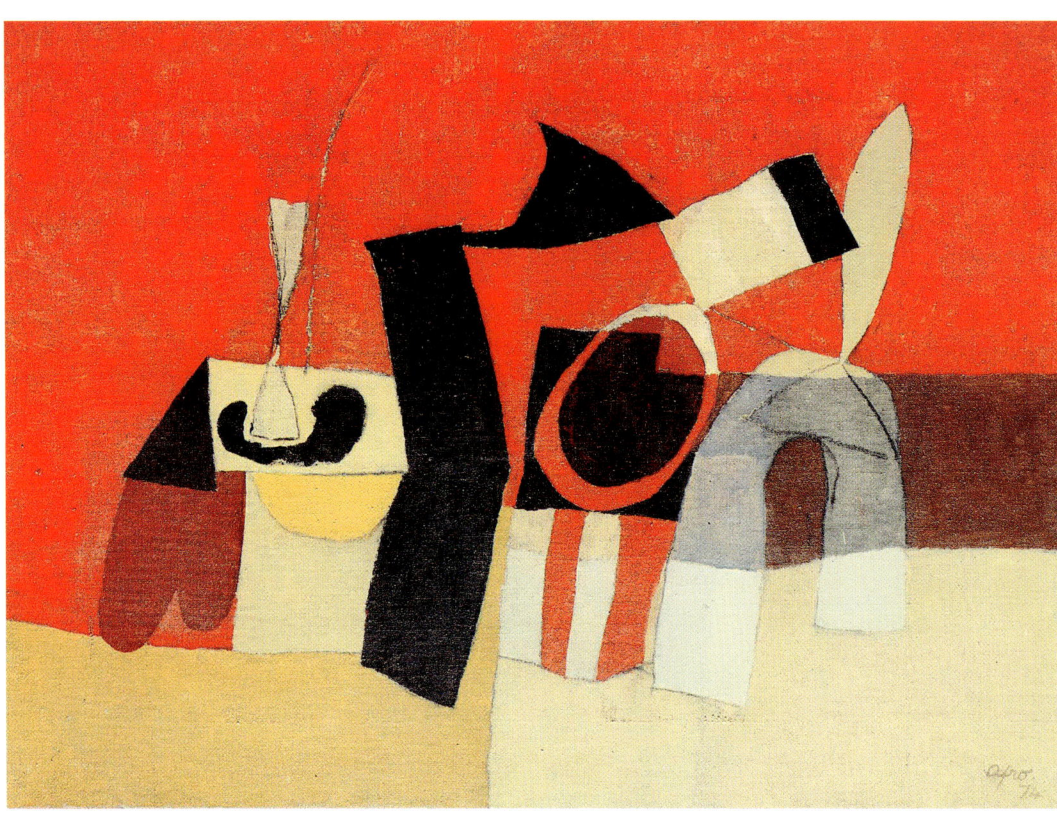

need to propose or invent others. It could be said that his attitude corresponded to the definition—a wordplay on the "I may break but will not bend" saying—that the sculptor Mazzacurati had given for Villa and his texts, "I may break but will not explain" (in Italian, the wordplay is on *piego* and *spiego*).

BC In your view, did an issue exist with the Italian artists in the USA, starting with Burri and Afro, (fig. 13) Vedova and Dorazio, but also Marca-Relli, Scarpitta, (fig. 15) Savelli, up to Pistoletto and Kounellis? (fig. 14) All were considered, but never entirely accepted.

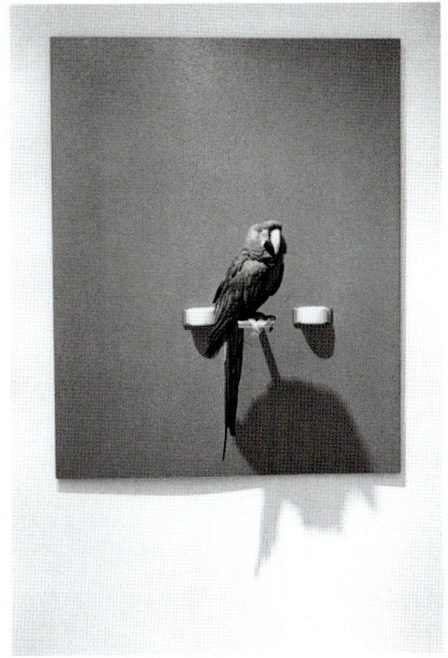

14. Jannis Kounellis, *Senza titolo*, 1967

15. Salvatore Scarpitta, *Senza titolo*, 1958

MD All these artists were represented by galleries in the USA, even if not a great deal of luck on the US market, at least until a while ago. But if you think of the values that the works of Fontana, Manzoni, Boetti, Morandi, and Cattelan have today on the international market—and consider that the artists that you name have almost all had more difficulties in establishing themselves in Italy, where they practically had no market when they were young or at the highest moments of their creativity, than in the United States—it seems to me that for them an issue would exist more with Italy than with the United States. At least until the time when they died or reached an advanced age. I haven't counted them, but I believe there are more contemporary Italian works of art in US museums than there are in Italian ones. Certainly, in Italy those artists met with great critical success, but US post-war criticism was and remains strongly US-centric, with respect not only to Italian but also to European art, with a few exceptions (Bacon, Richter, Kiefer, and Polke, for example). One of the most recurrent remarks that were made in the 1980s on the US neo-expressionists, such ad Salle, Schnabel, and Fischl, was that their art descended more from Europe than from the USA; and until 2014–15, the last time I was there, the only painting by Jean-Michel Basquiat on display at the MoMA was on loan; it wasn't even part of its collection.

BC Which expressions would you use to summarize Burri's aesthetics and practice, and attribute a historical evaluation to him?

MD In a review published in *Tempo Presente* (August 1960) and regarding the 1960 Venice Biennale, I wrote that "the two greatest—and contrasting—metaphysicians are De Chirico and Burri. Burri is the only absolute, the only 'vision' in Italy post-March on Rome." Like De Chirico, Burri marked out a new direction in making art; to the traditional oil painting with which all the greatest visions of art were expressed in the West, from the Flemish to Picasso and Pollock (with the exception of Duchamp's *Large Glass* and of Schwitter's *Merzpictures*), he added industrial technique and materials to create that mental and visual irreality that has always been at the basis of the greatest painting. Even the artists who after Burri have used oil paints on canvas could not fail to take into account his innovation in reinventing the materials of art and in the expressive/expressionist use that he made of them. Other artists simply expanded his vocabulary.

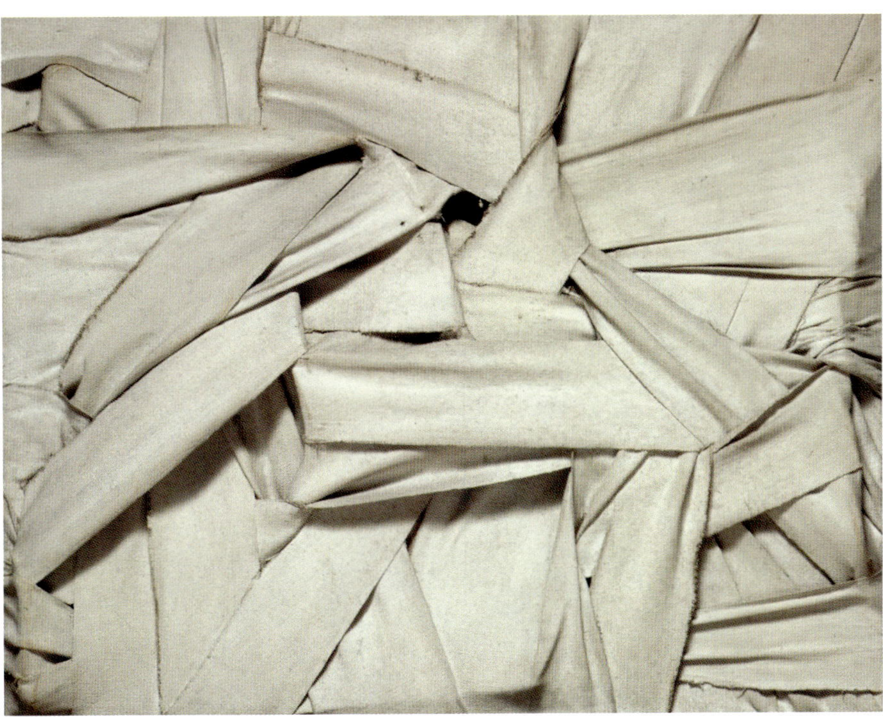

works

1.
Texas, 1945
Oil on canvas
47 × 60.5 cm
Private collection, Rome

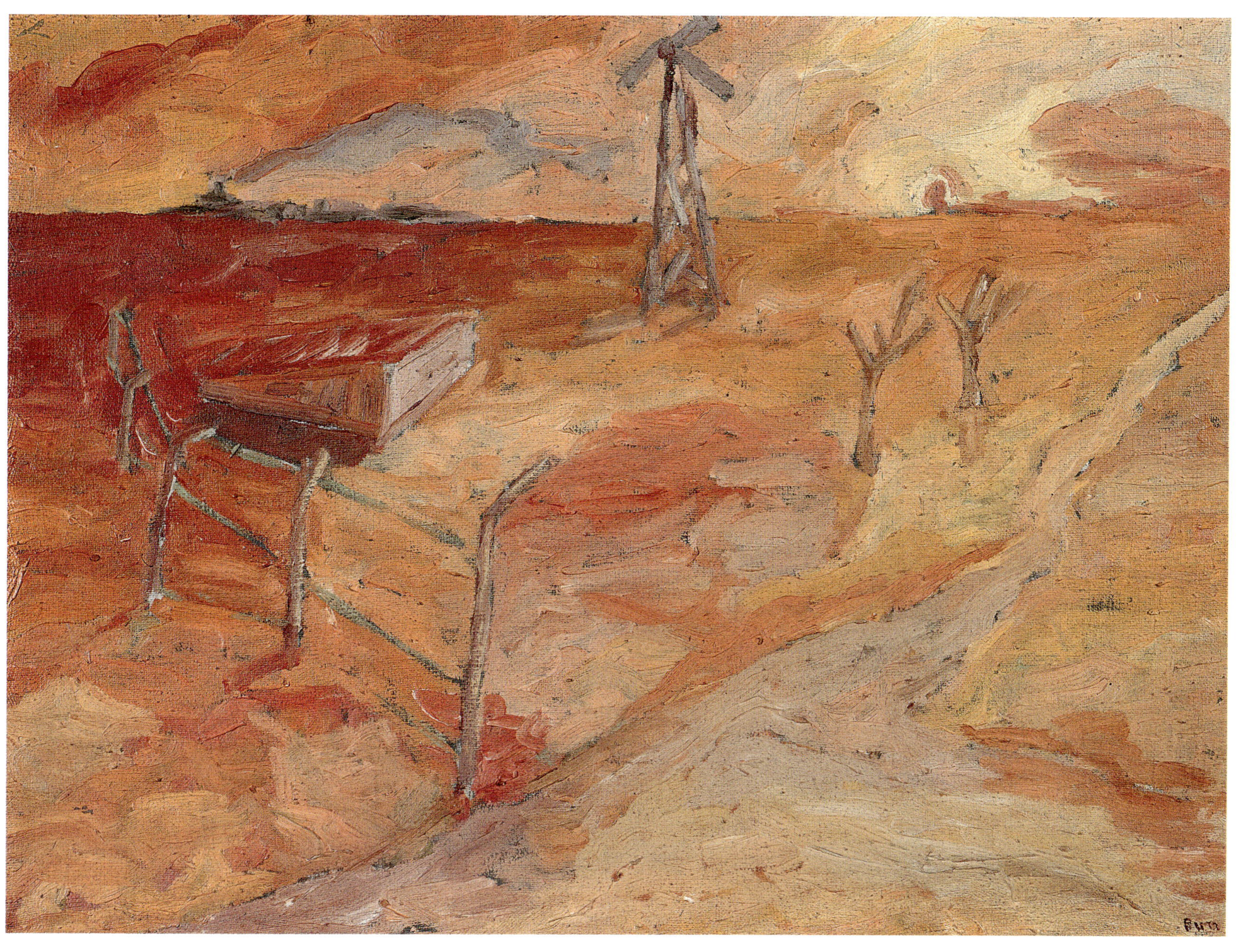

2.
Bianco, [1949]
Oil, enamel, and pumice
on canvas
91 × 111.5 cm
Private collection

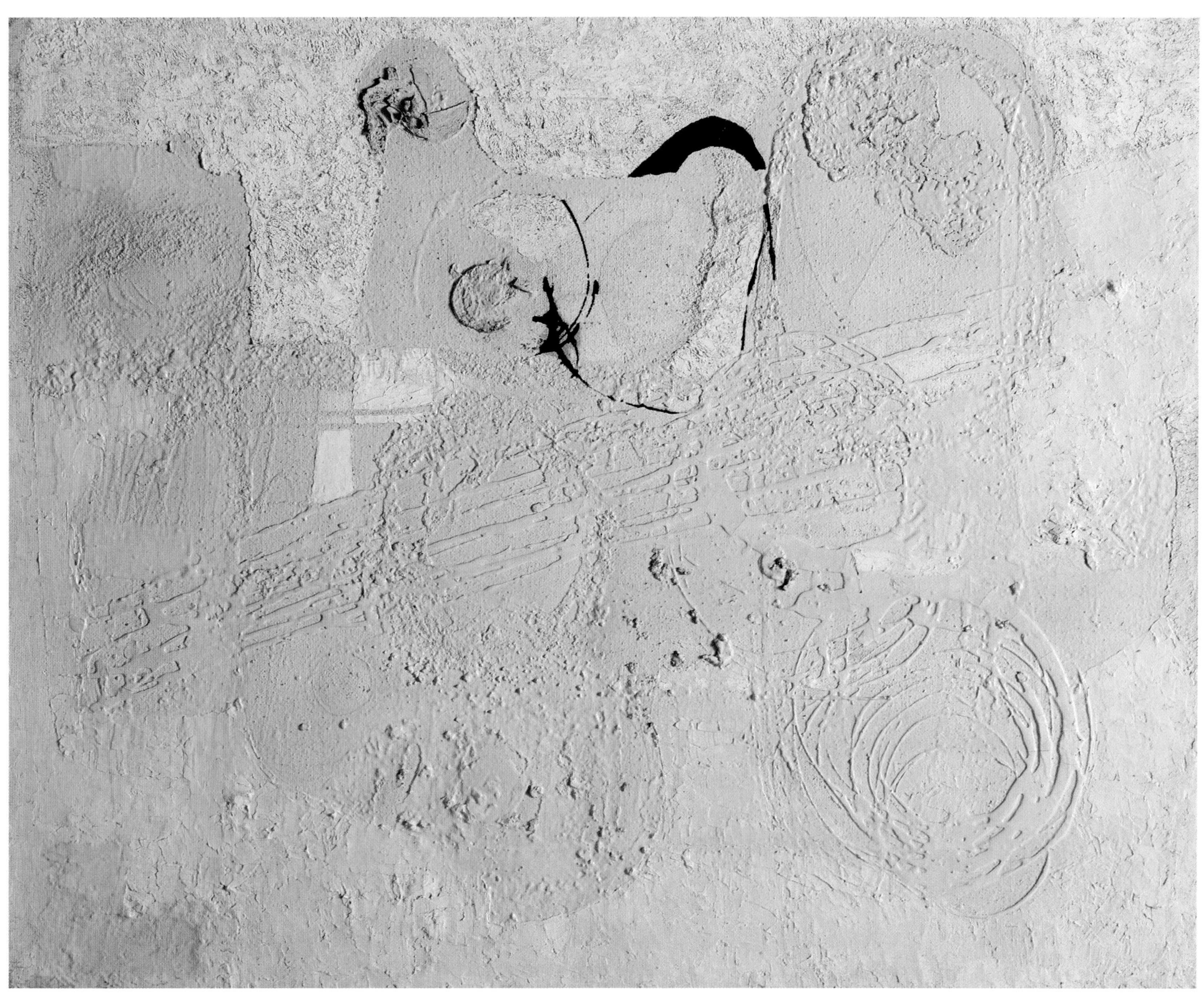

3.
Catrame, [1949]
Tar, oil, and pumice
on canvas
57.5 × 64.5 cm
Private collection

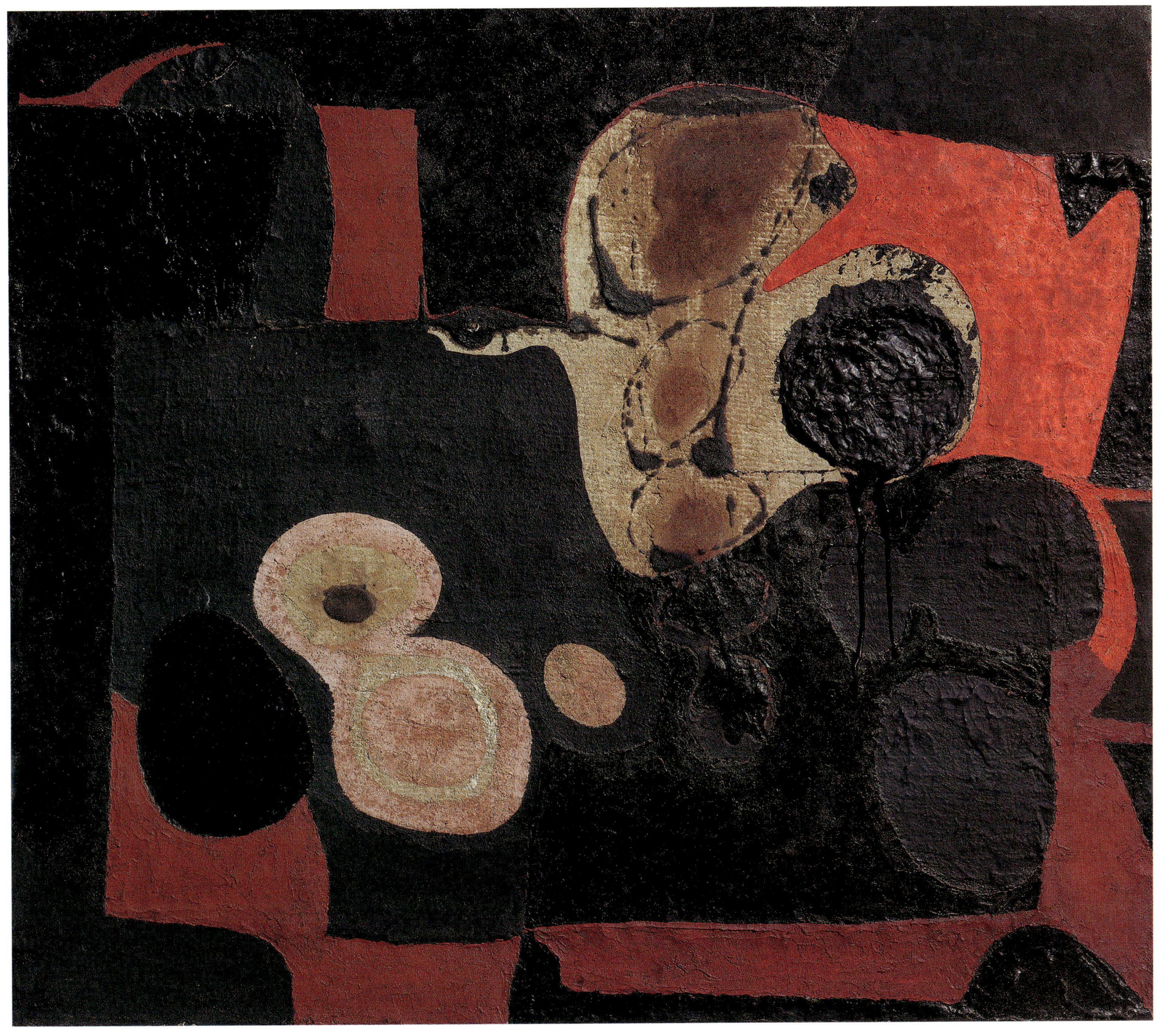

4.
Catrame, [1949]
Tar, oil, pumice, and Vinavil
on board
83 × 47 cm
Private collection

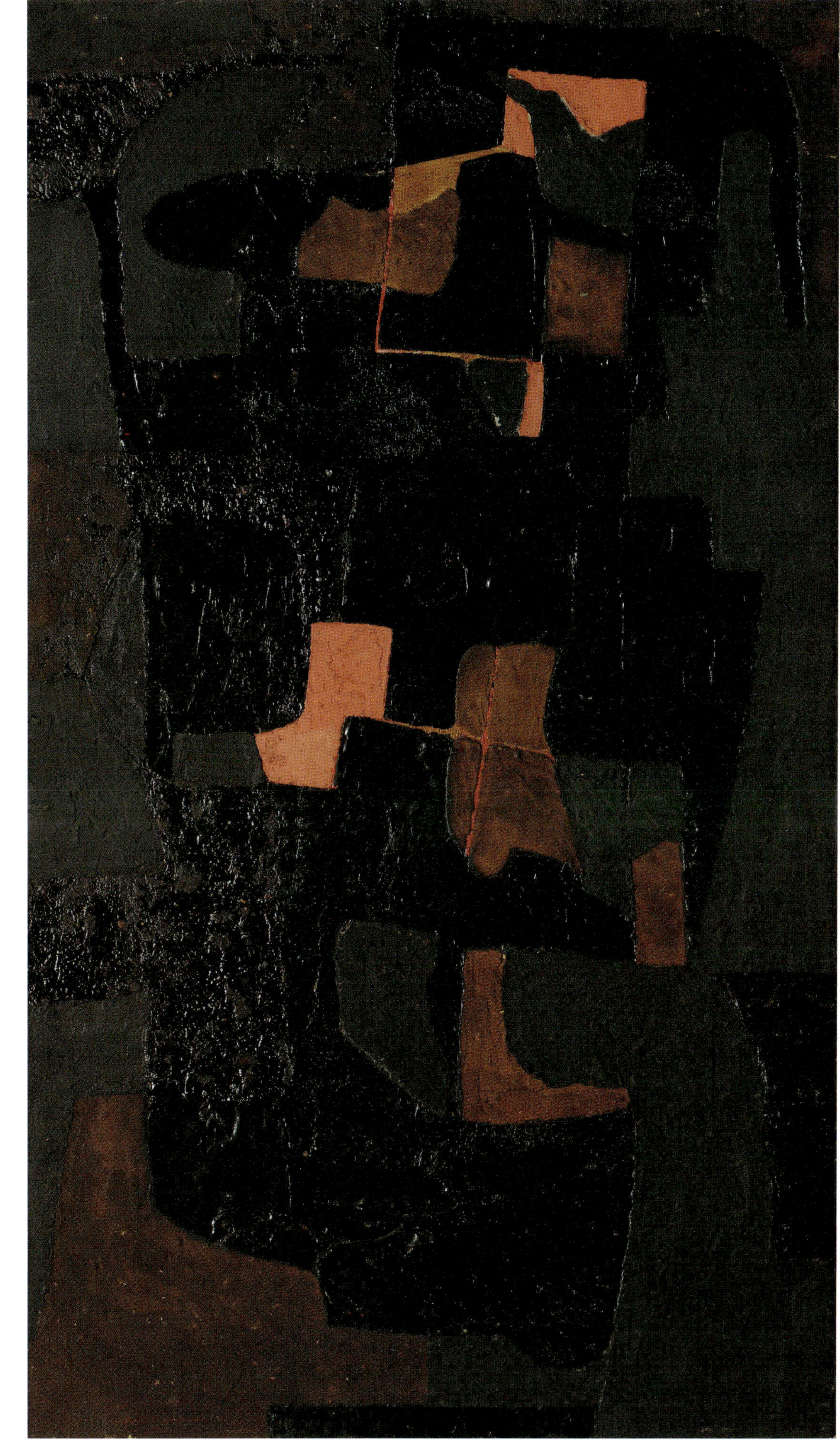

5.
Senza Titolo, [1950]
Oil, wooden segments,
and twine on board
60.5 × 45.5 cm
Private collection

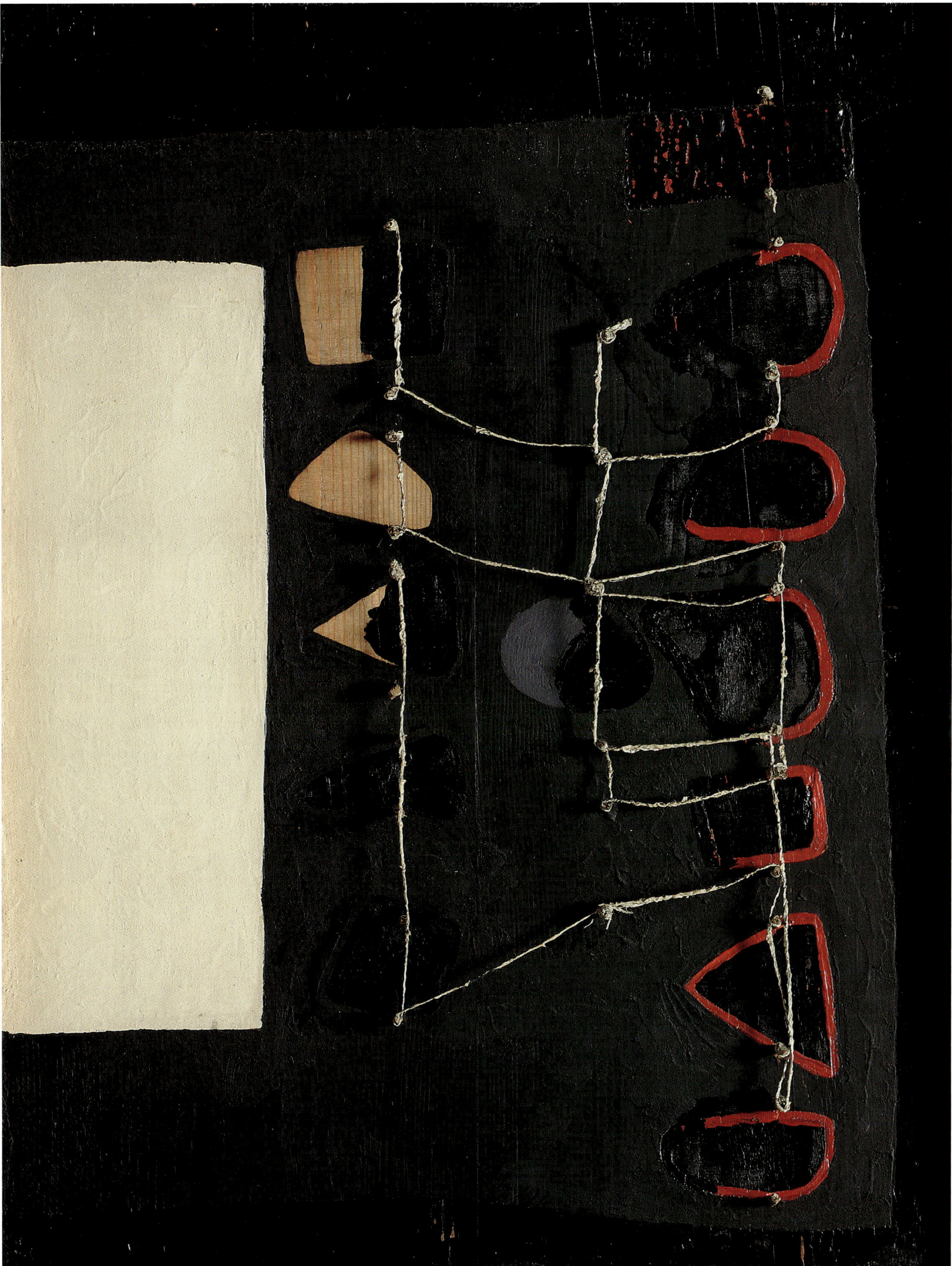

6.
Nero, 1951
Tar, oil, enamel, cardboard, and Vinavil on canvas
52 × 64 cm
Private collection

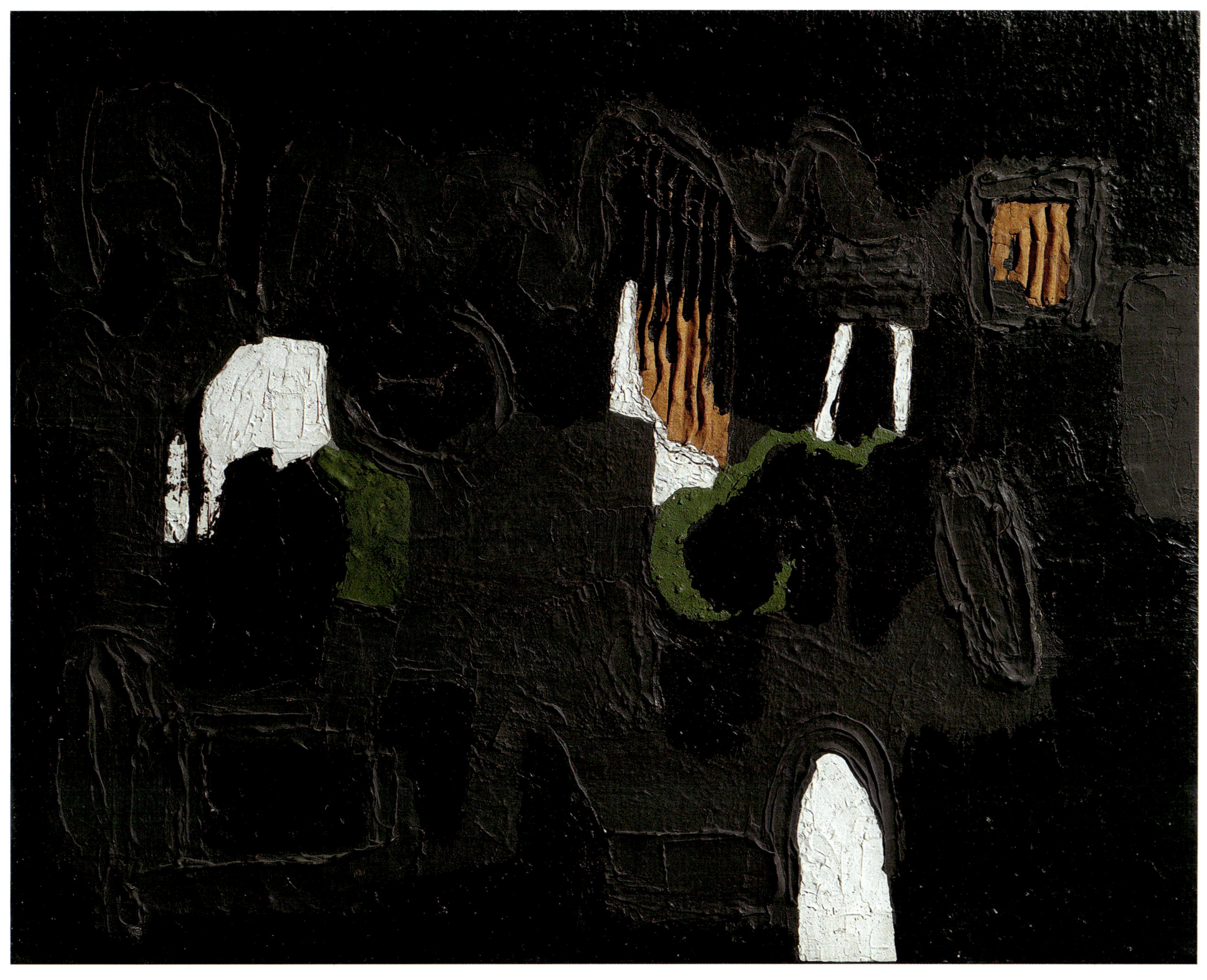

7.
Rosso, 1952
Oil, pumice, and Vinavil
on Cellotex
65 × 59 cm
Private collection

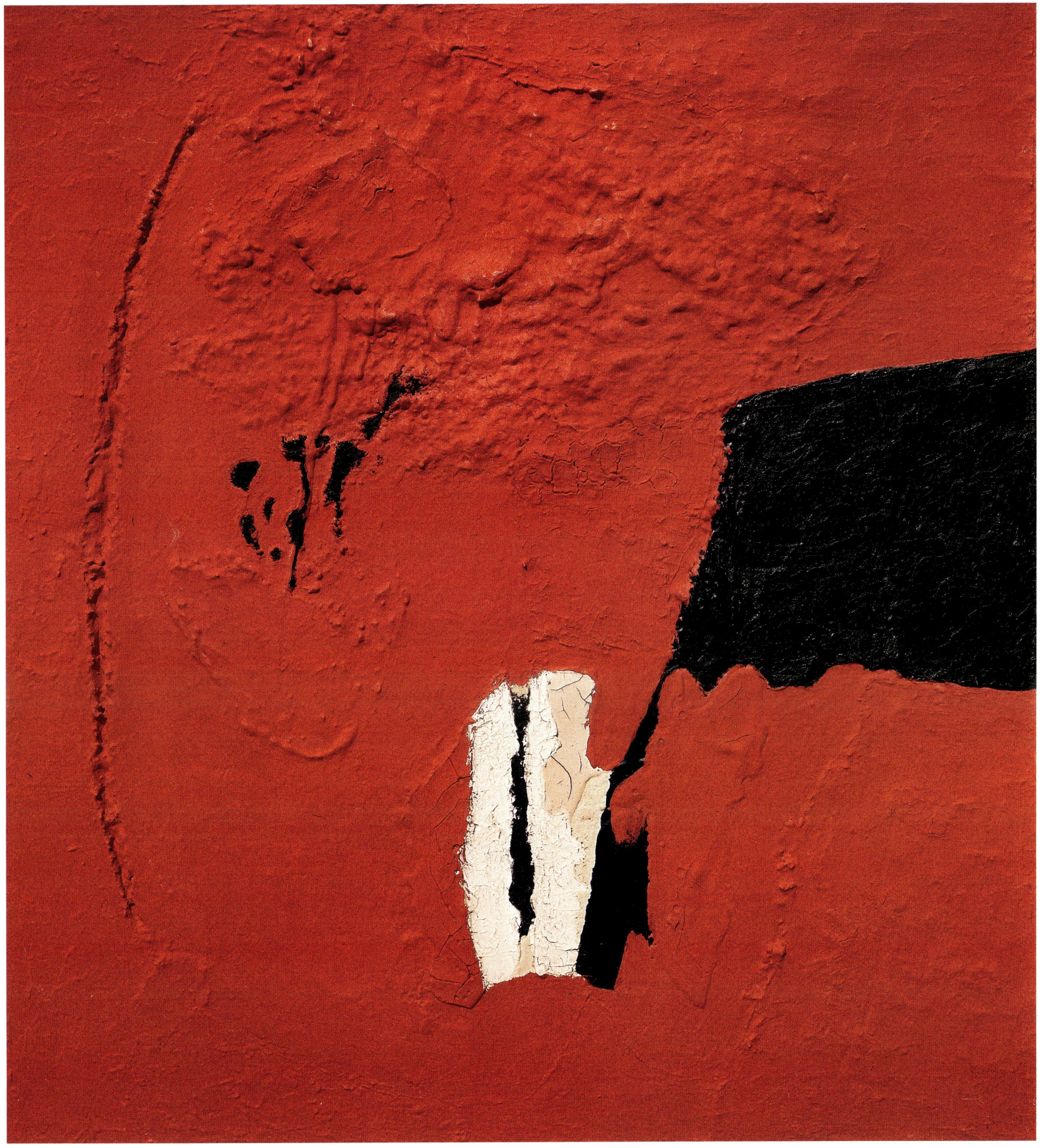

8.
Gobbo Bianco, 1953
Fabric, oil, sawdust, pumice on canvas; metal rod on verso
100.7 × 87 cm
Private collection

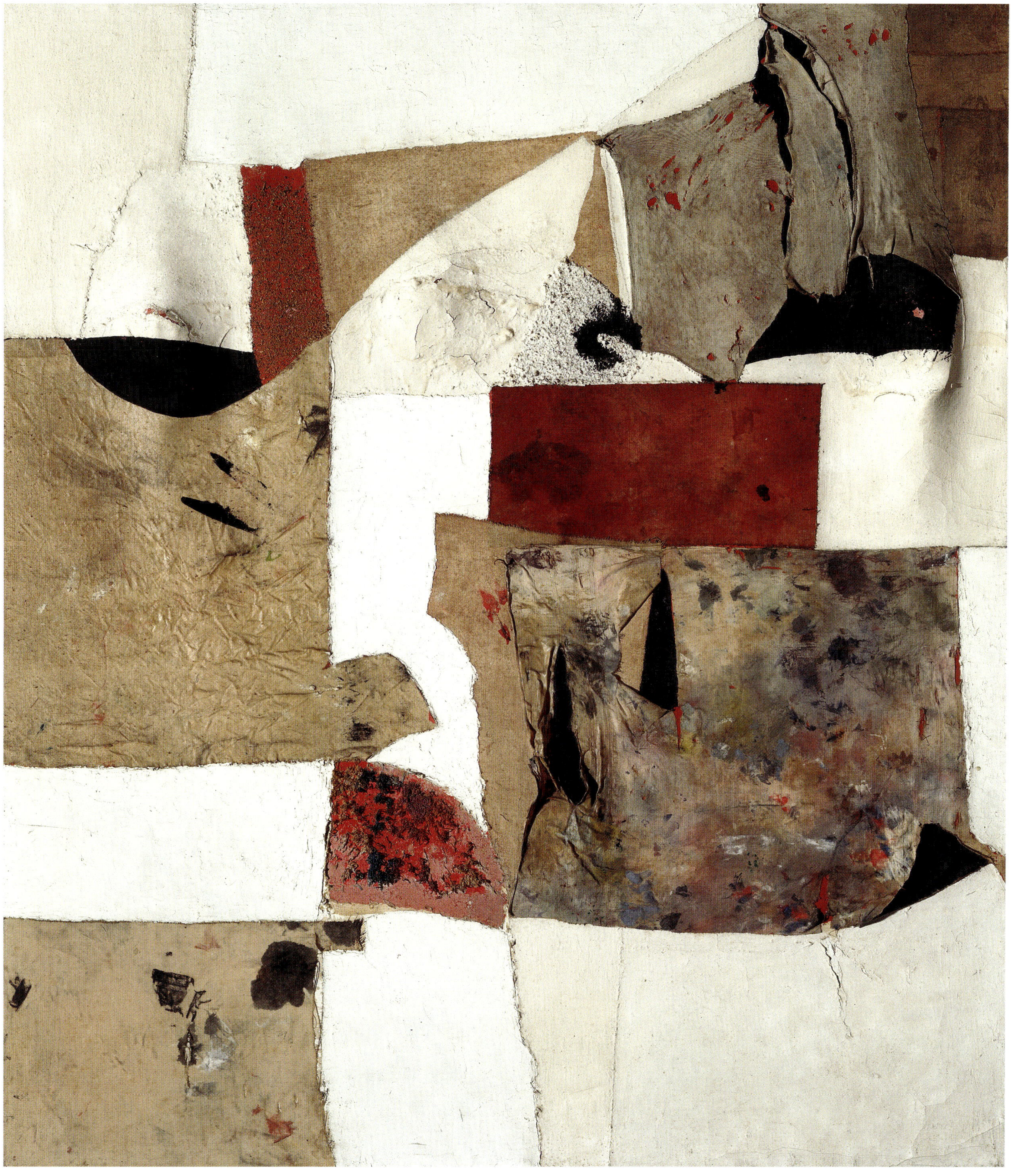

9.
Rosso, 1953
Fabric, oil, and Vinavil
on canvas
76 × 61.5 cm
Private collection

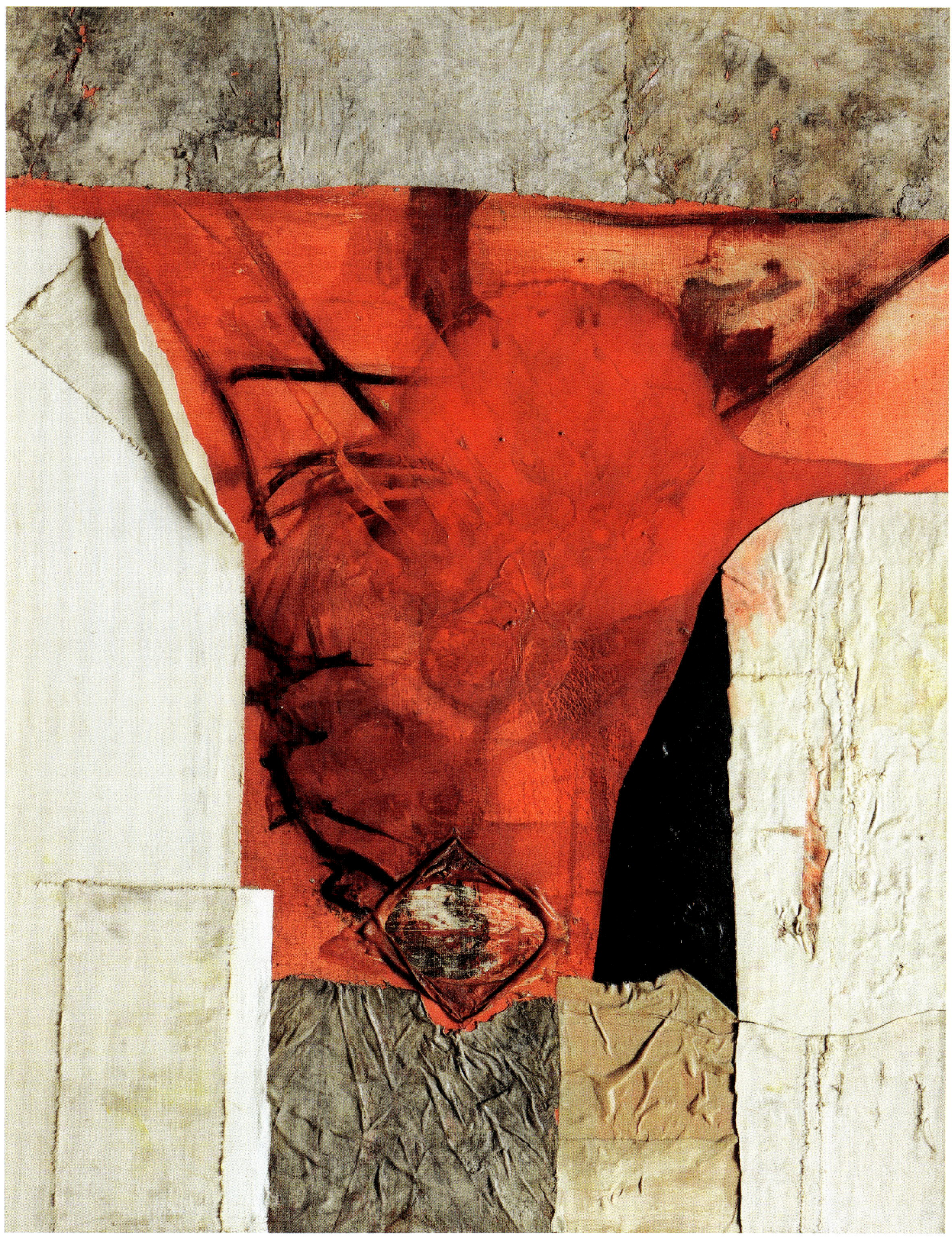

10.
Sacco e Oro, 1953
Burlap and gold on canvas
126 × 111 cm
Private collection

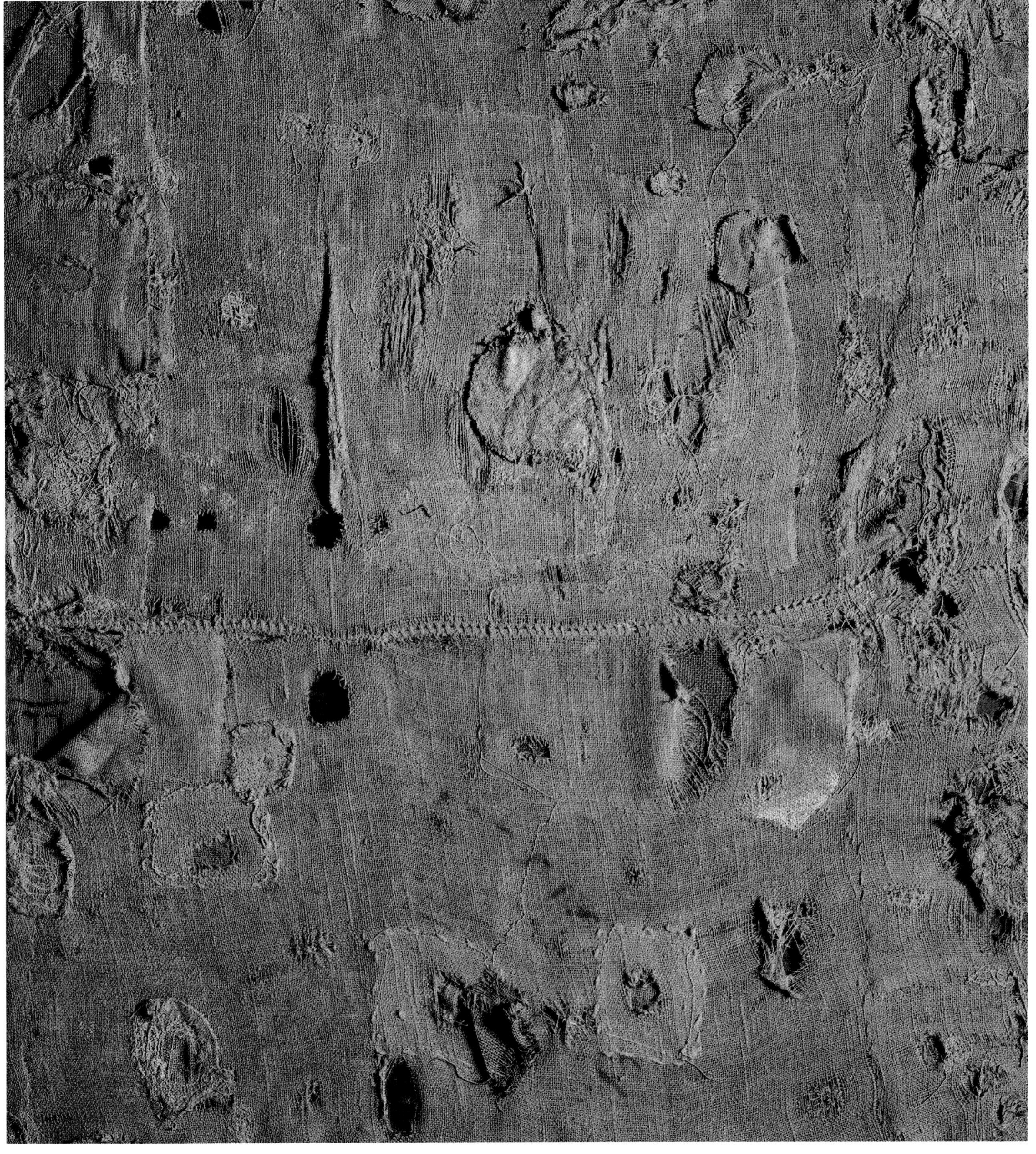

11.
Sacco e Nero, [1954]
Burlap, acrylic, and Vinavil on fabric
130.5 × 150.5 cm
Private collection

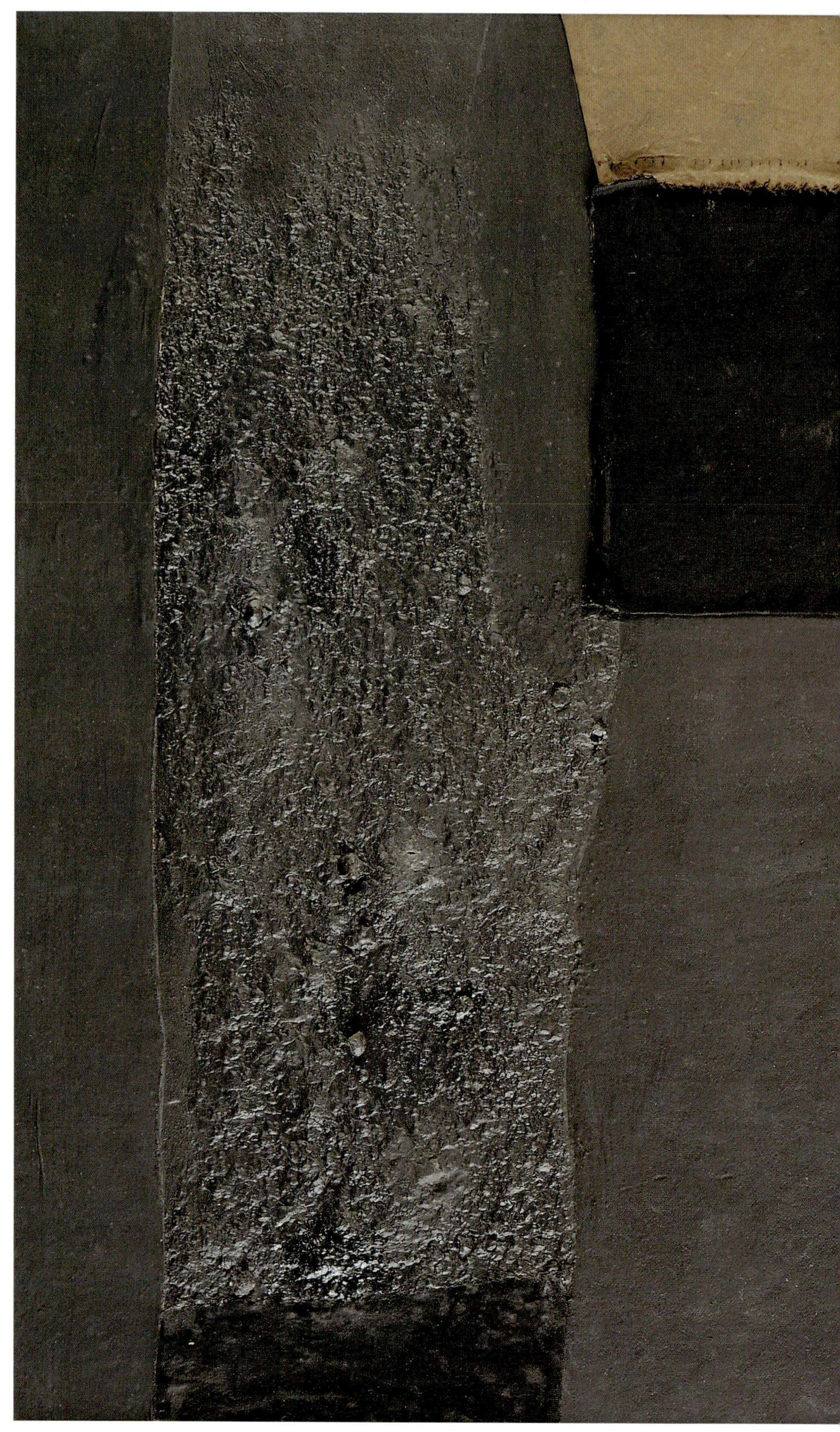

12.
Tutto Nero 2, 1954
Fabric, oil, canvas, pumice,
and Vinavil on Cellotex
99.5 × 149.5 cm
Private collection

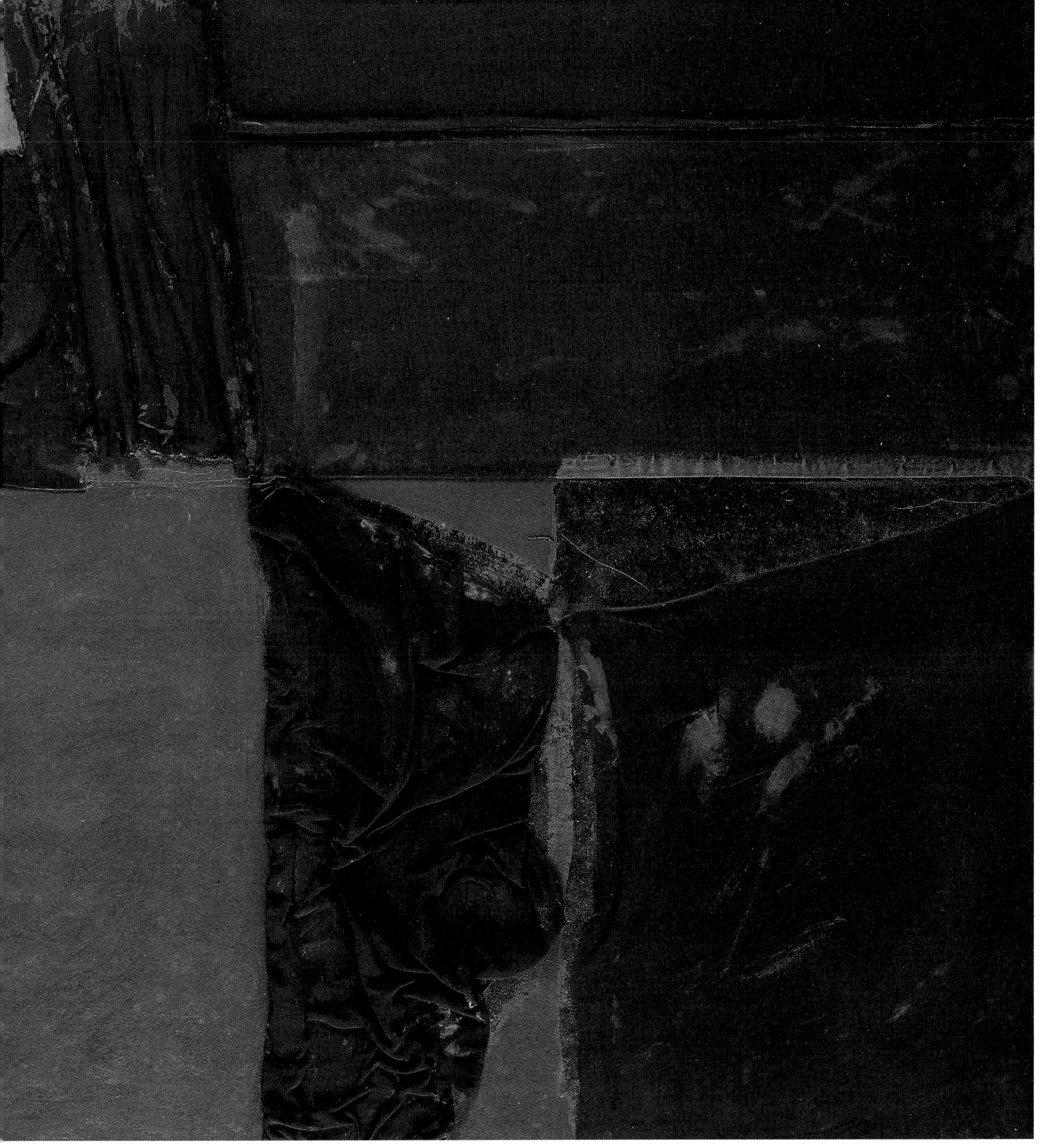

13.
Sacco, 1954
Burlap, gold, oil, and Vinavil on canvas
100 × 88 cm
Mamiano di Traversetolo, Parma, Fondazione Magnani-Rocca

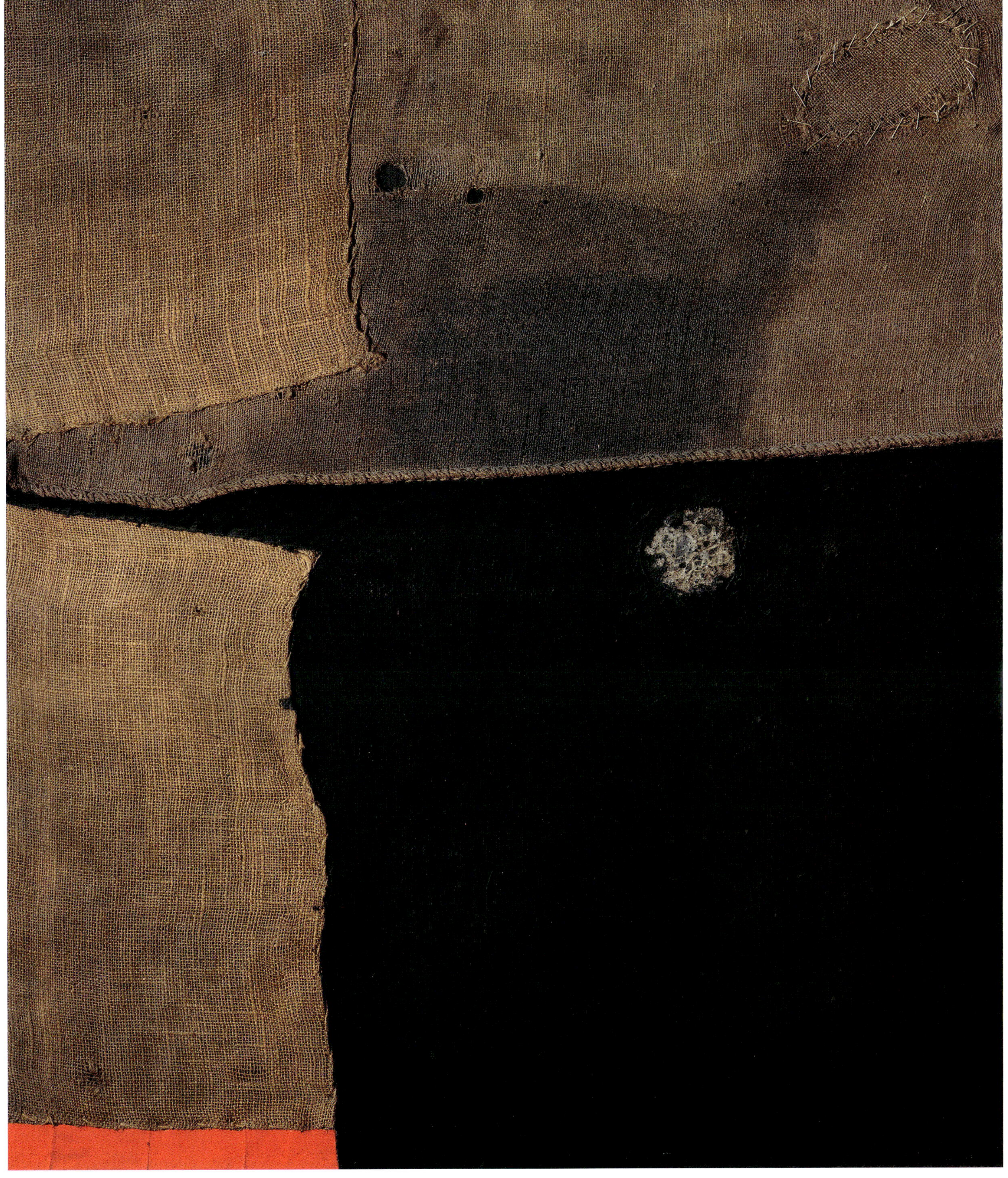

14.
Sacco Nero e Rosso, 1955
Burlap, canvas, fabric, oil, paper, and Vinavil on canvas treated with Vinavil
50 × 86 cm
Private collection

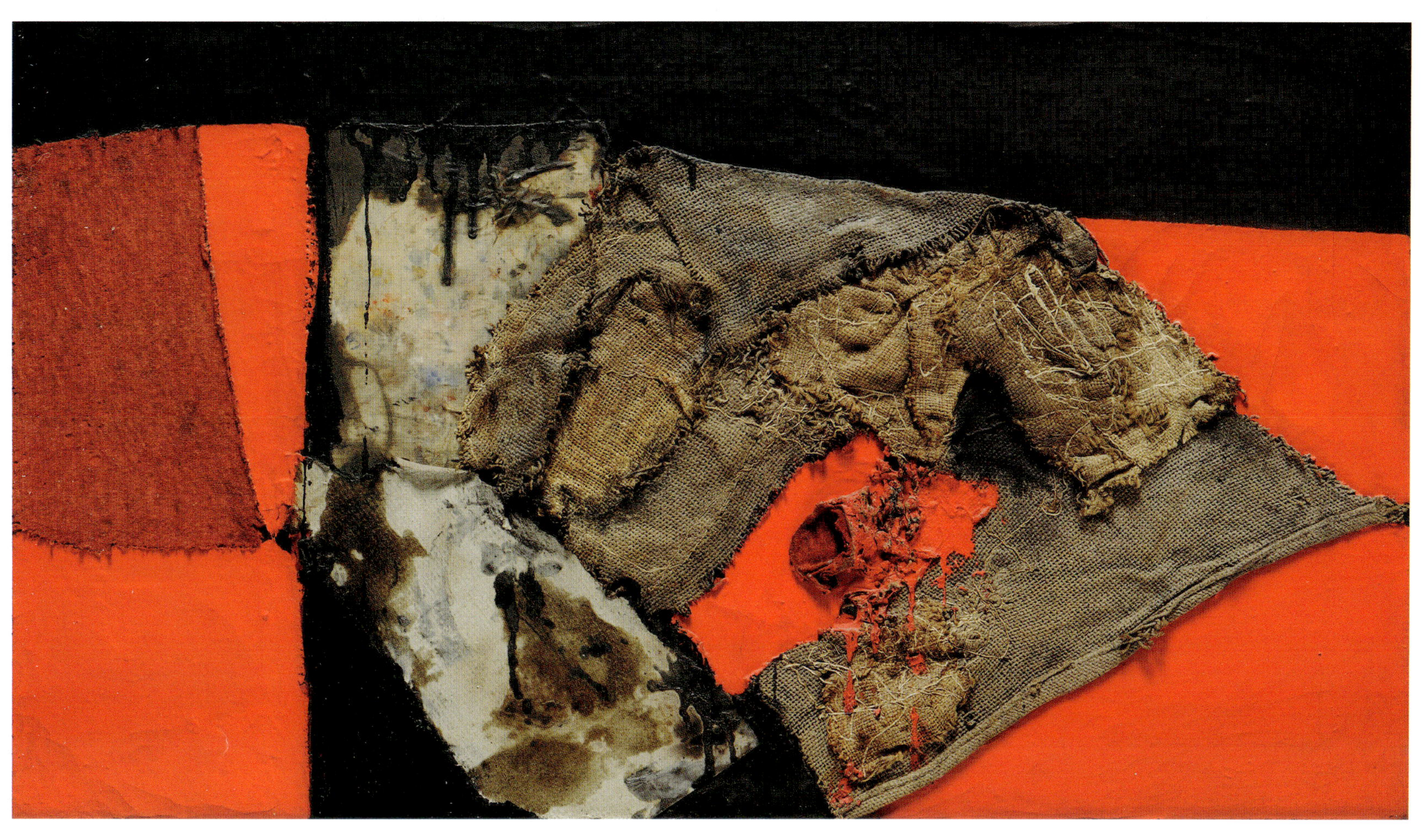

15.
Sacco e Nero, 1955
Burlap, pumice, canvas, oil,
and Vinavil on canvas
67.5 × 108 cm
Private collection

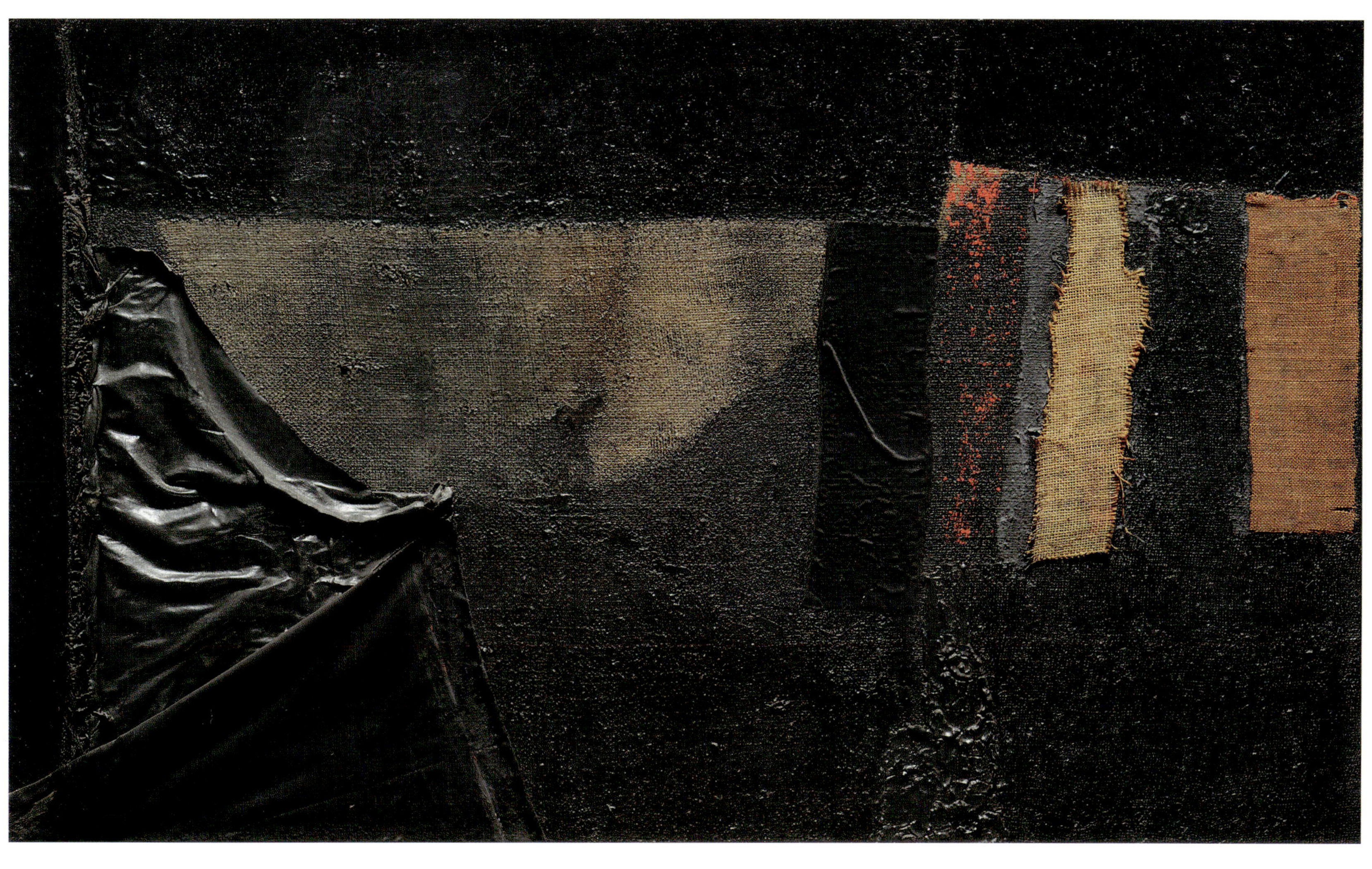

16.
Combustione Sacco, [1956]
Burlap, fabric, oil, Vinavil,
and combustion on canvas
129 × 113 cm
Città di Castello,
Fondazione Palazzo
Albizzini Collezione Burri

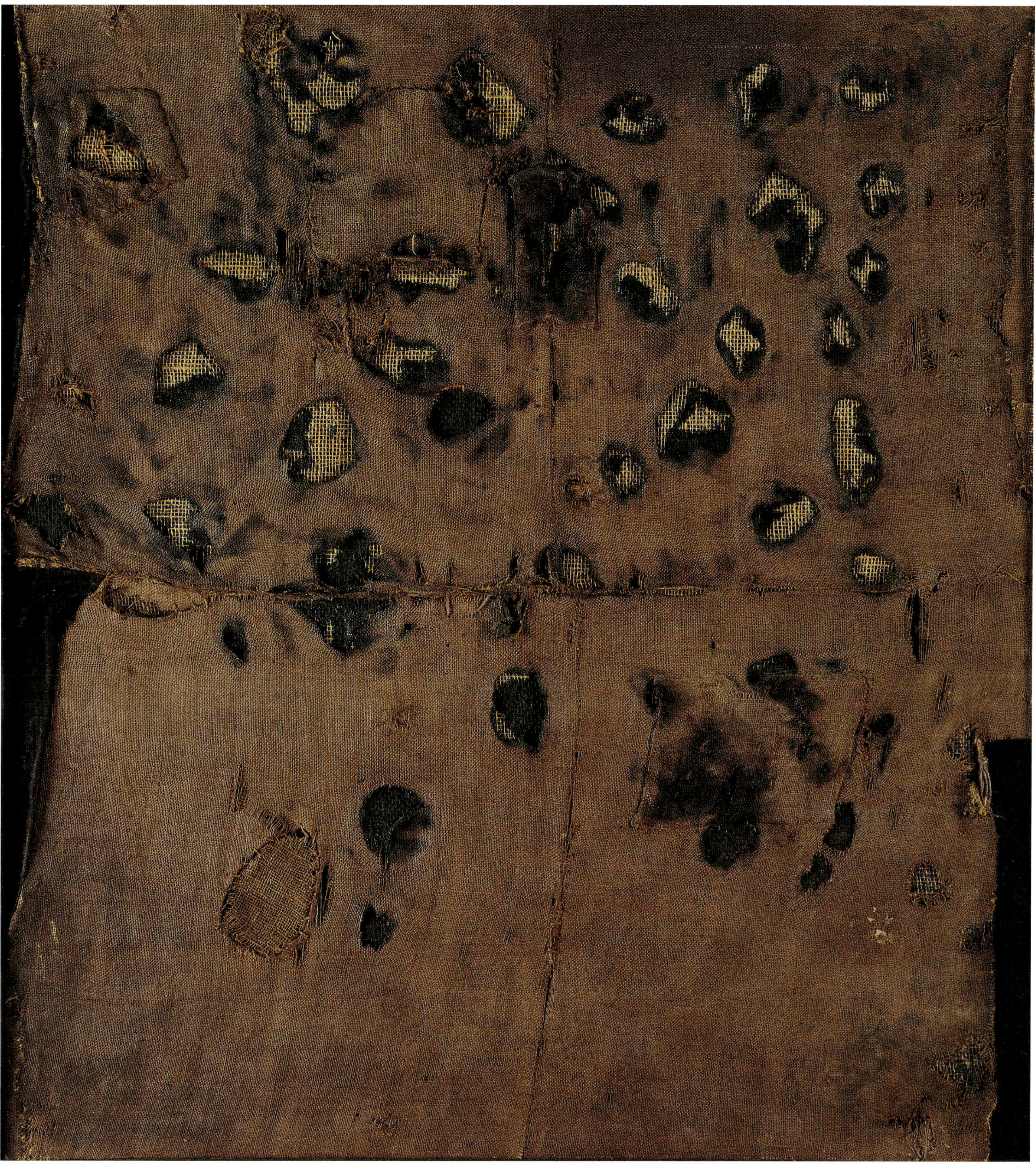

17.
Sacco e Verde, 1956
Burlap, canvas, acrylic,
and oil on canvas
176 × 203 cm
Città di Castello,
Fondazione Palazzo
Albizzini Collezione Burri

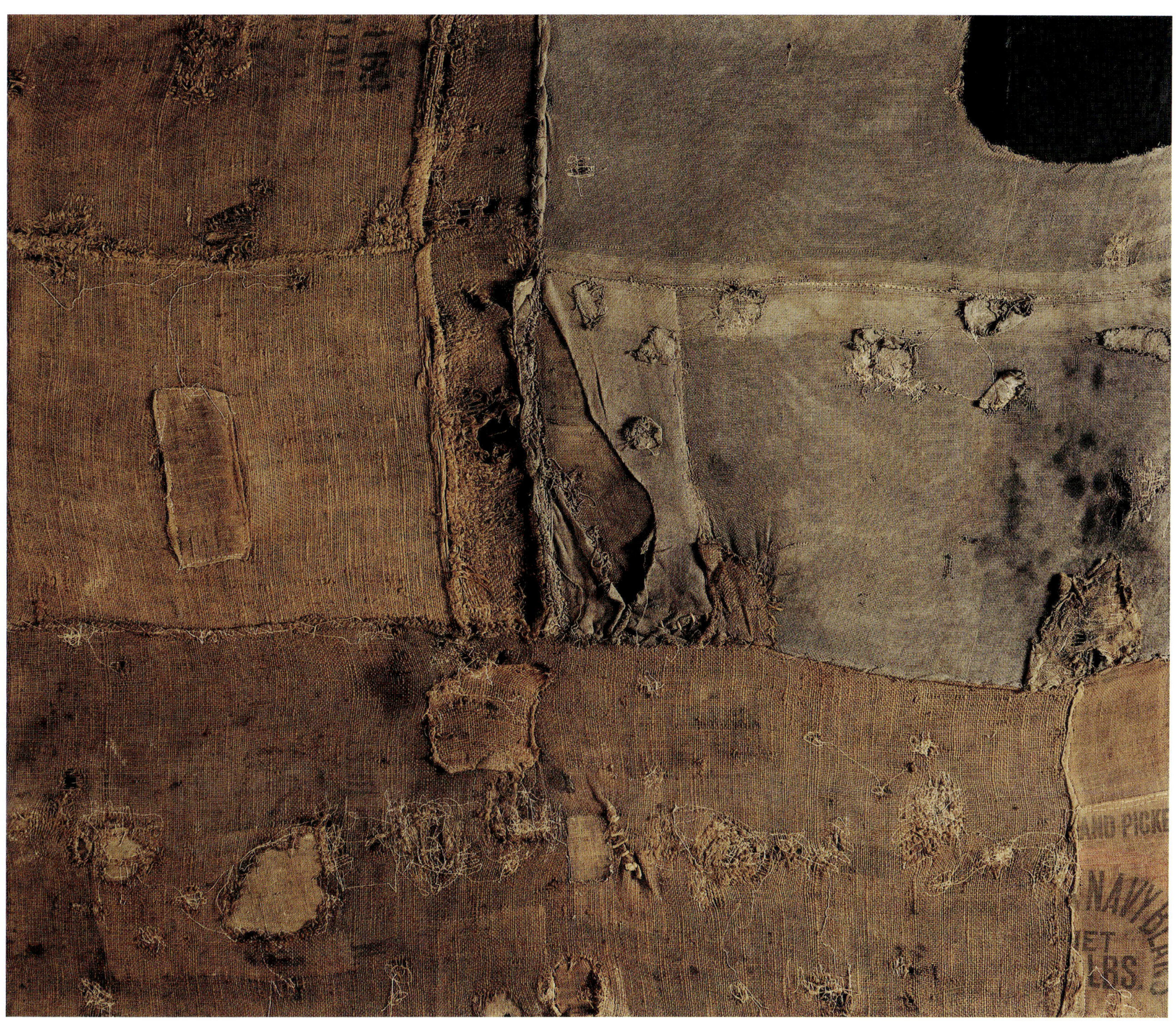
NAVY
LBS.

18.
Tutto Nero, 1956
Fabric, acrylic, Vinavil,
and combustion on canvas
132 × 117 cm
Private collection

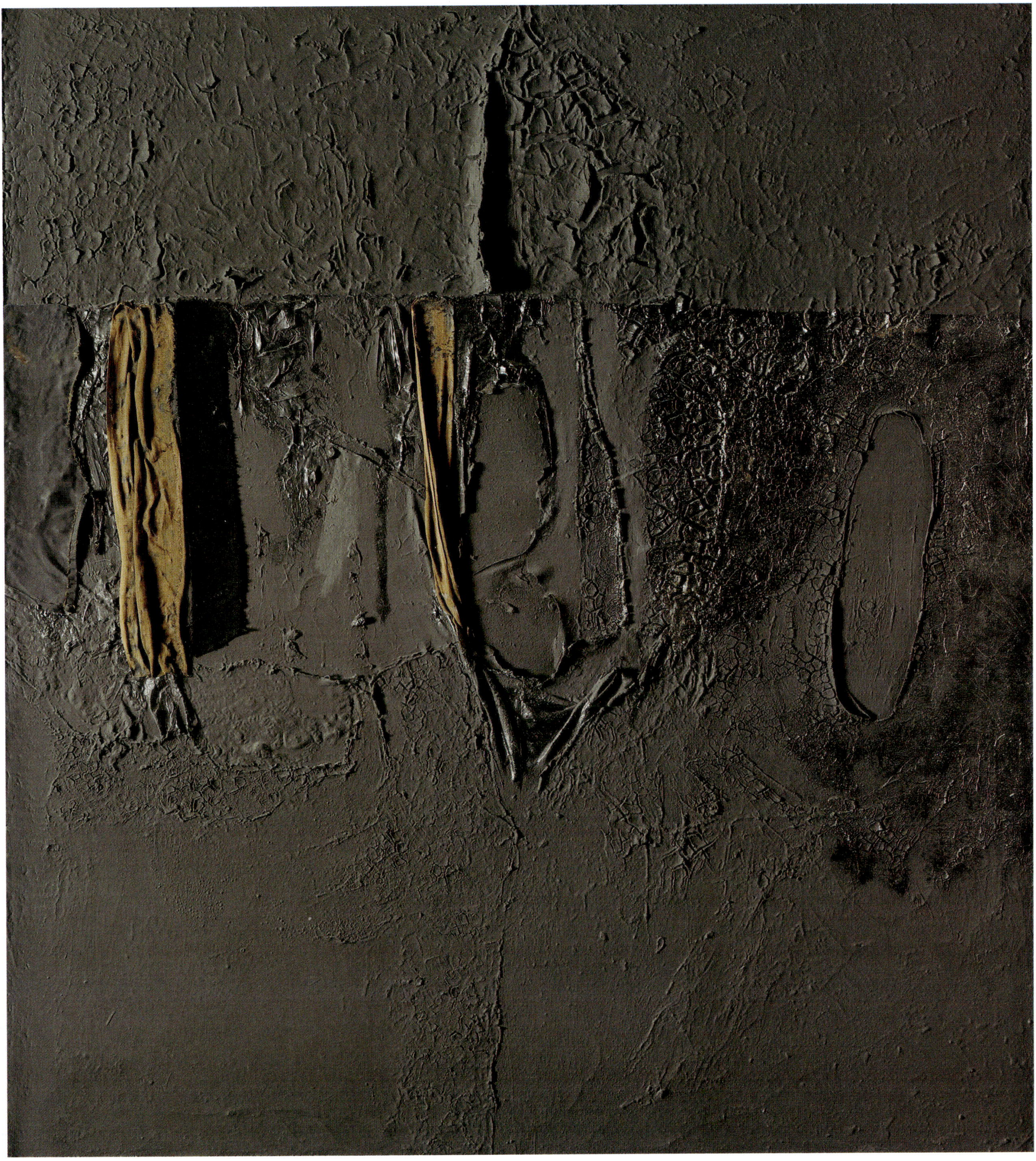

19.
Sacco e Rosso SP 2, [1958]
Burlap, oil, and Vinavil
on canvas
121 × 150.5 cm
Private collection

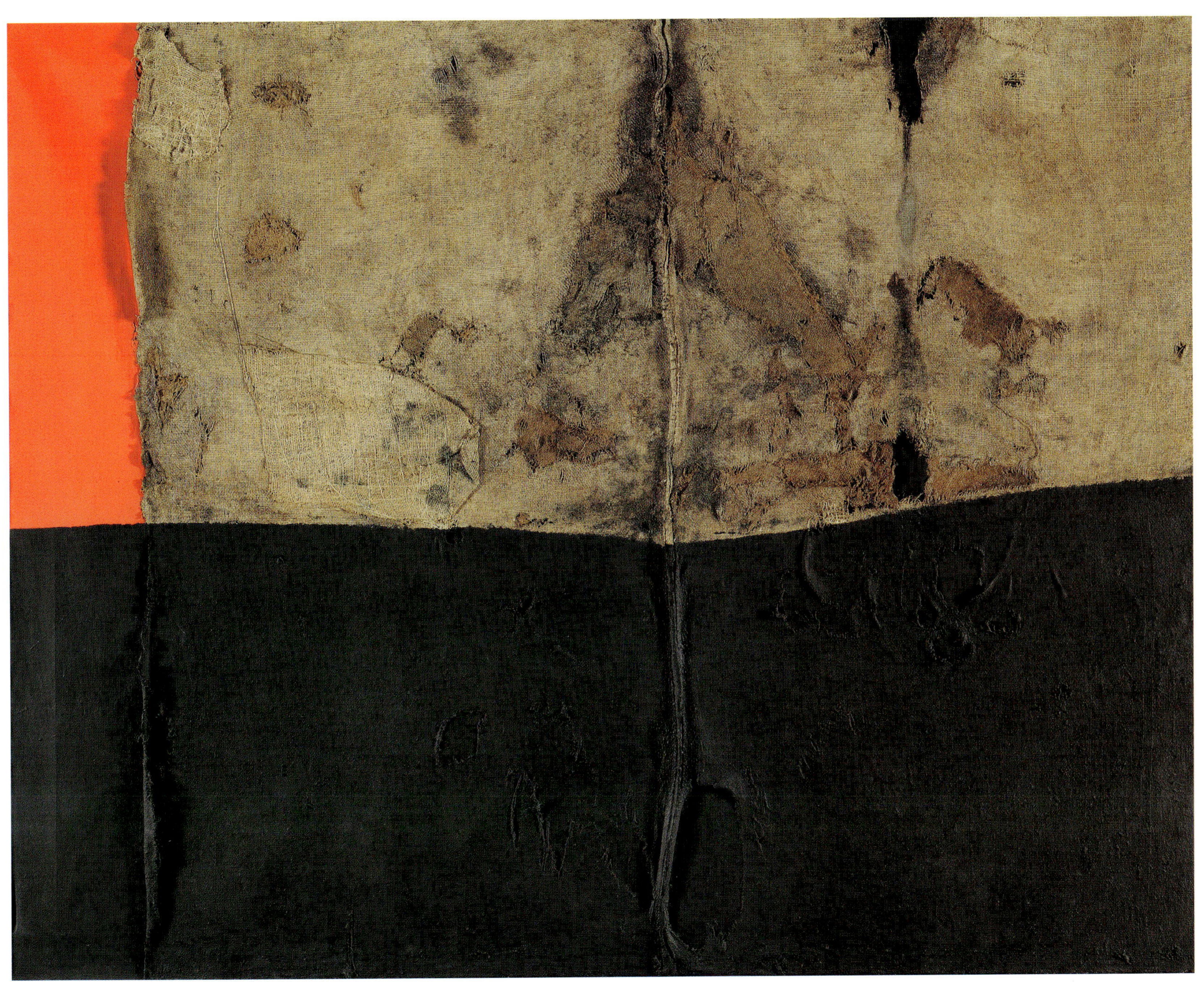

20.
Combustione Plastica, 1958
Plastic, fabric, acrylic,
Vinavil, and combustion
on canvas
98 × 84 cm
Città di Castello,
Fondazione Palazzo
Albizzini Collezione Burri

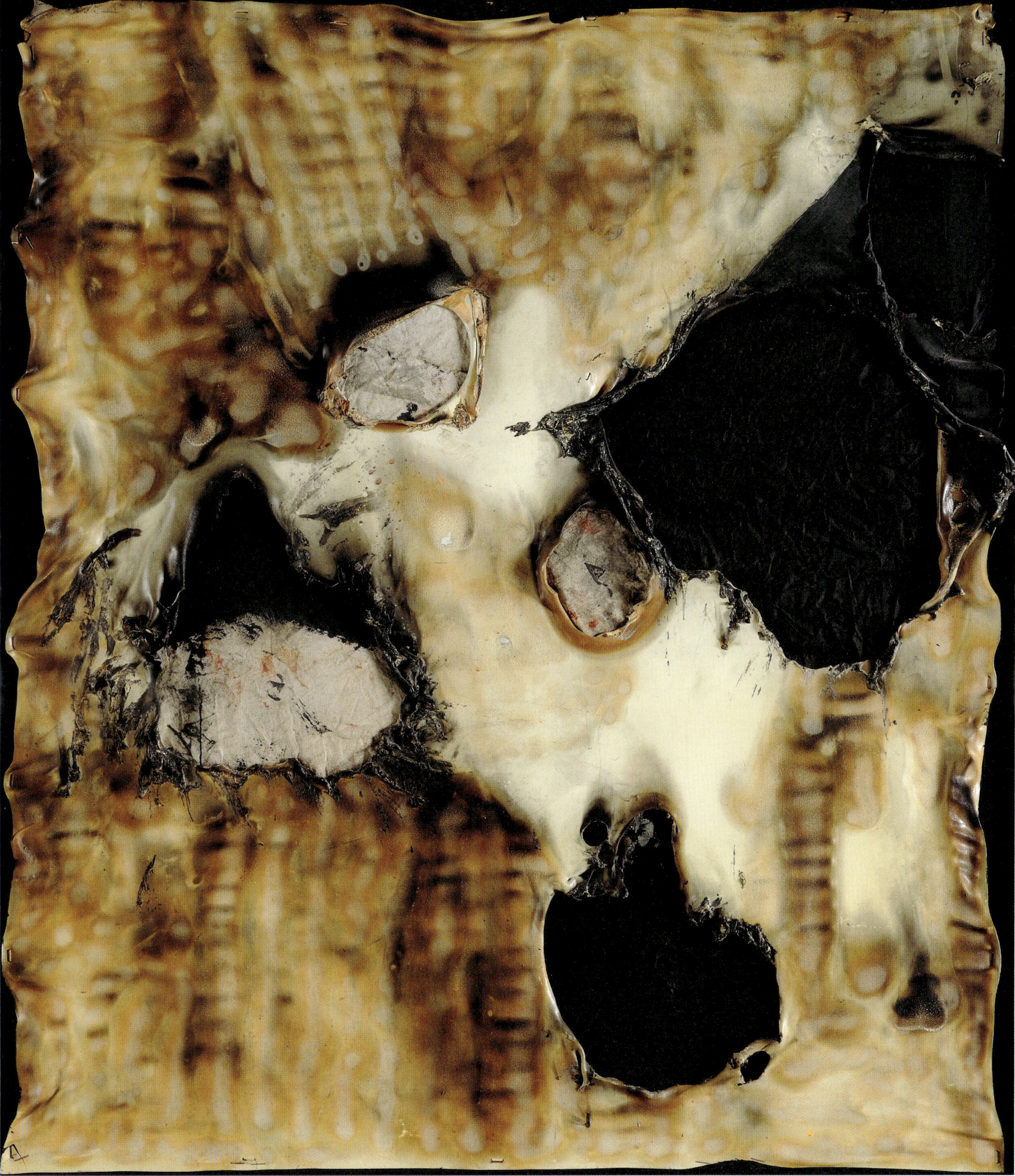

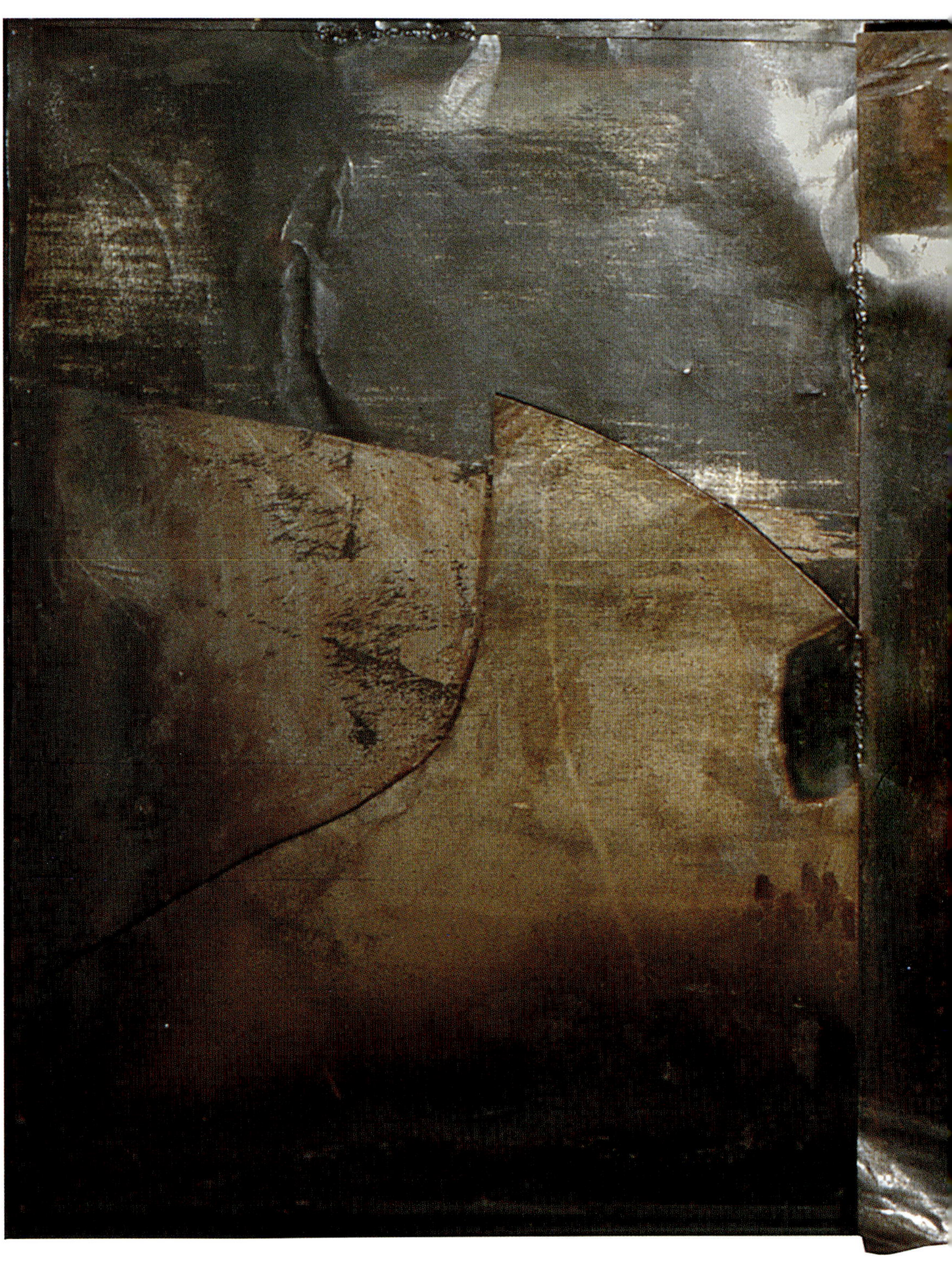

21.
Grande Ferro M5, 1958
Iron
100 × 200 cm
Turin, GAM – Galleria
Civica d'Arte Moderna
e Contemporanea

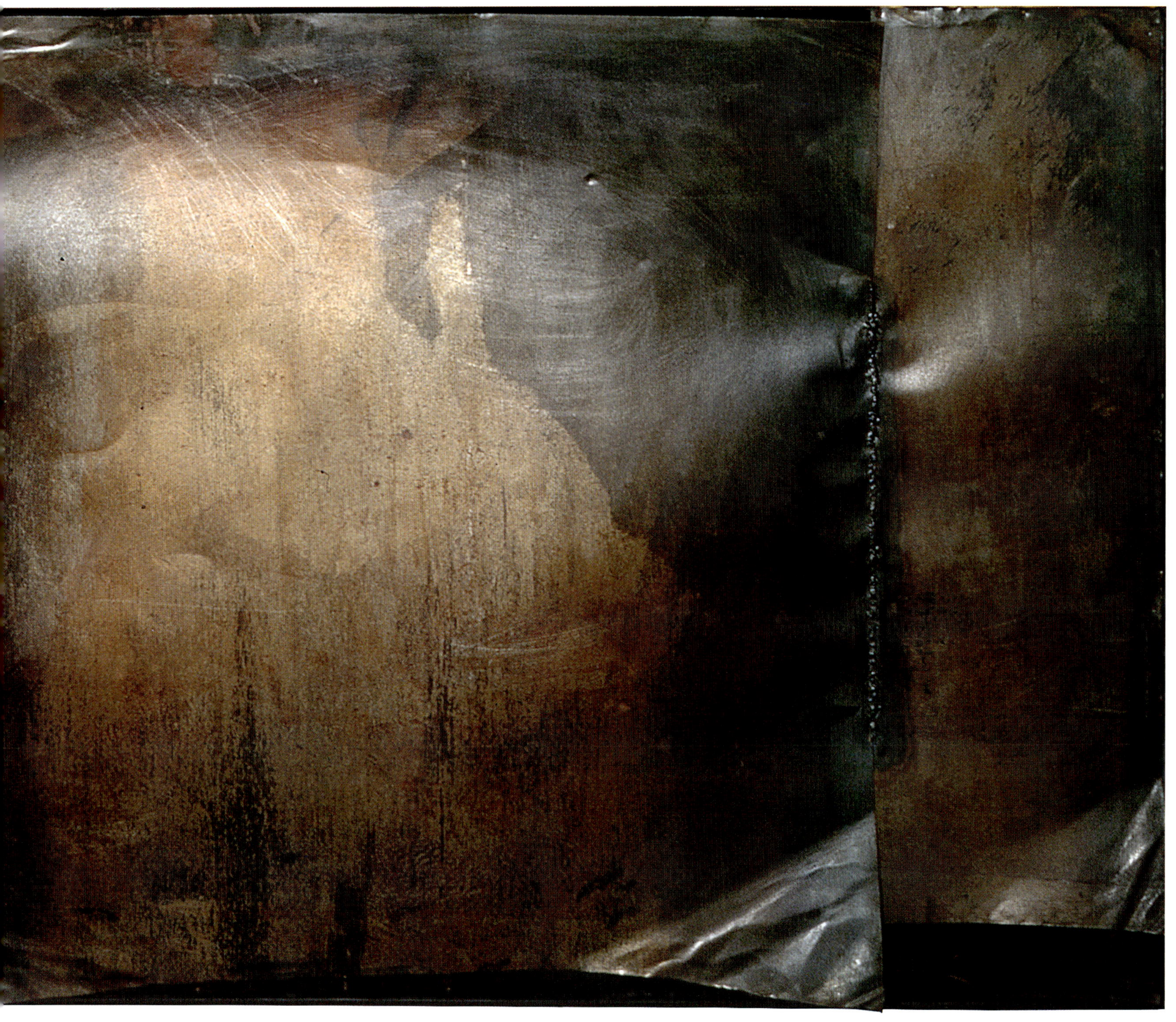

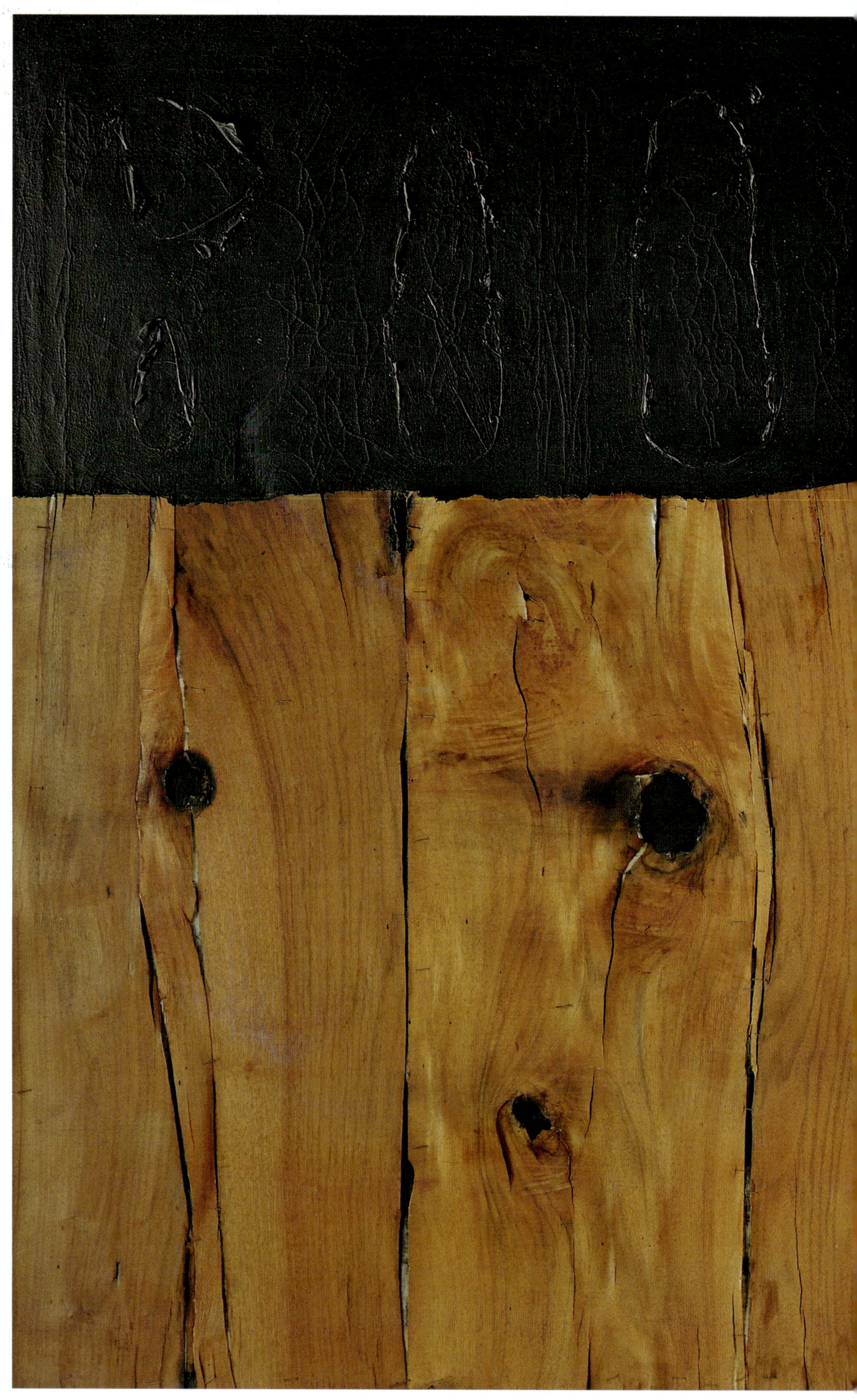

22.
Legno SP, 1958
Wood, canvas, acrylic, combustion, and Vinavil on canvas
129.5 × 200.5 cm
Città di Castello, Fondazione Palazzo Albizzini Collezione Burri

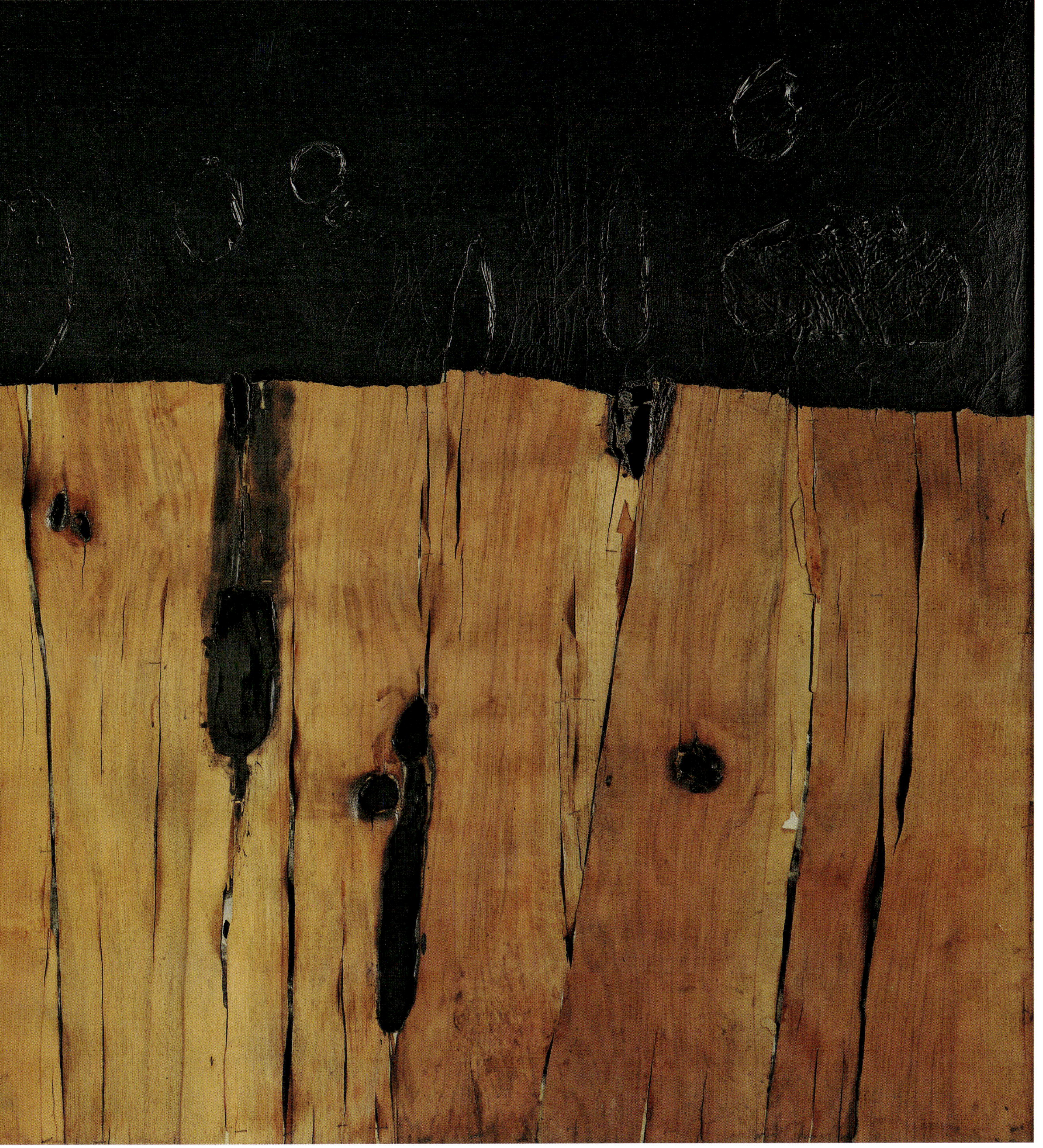

23.
Ferro SP3, [1958/59]
Iron
152.5 × 142.5 cm
Città di Castello,
Fondazione Palazzo
Albizzini Collezione Burri

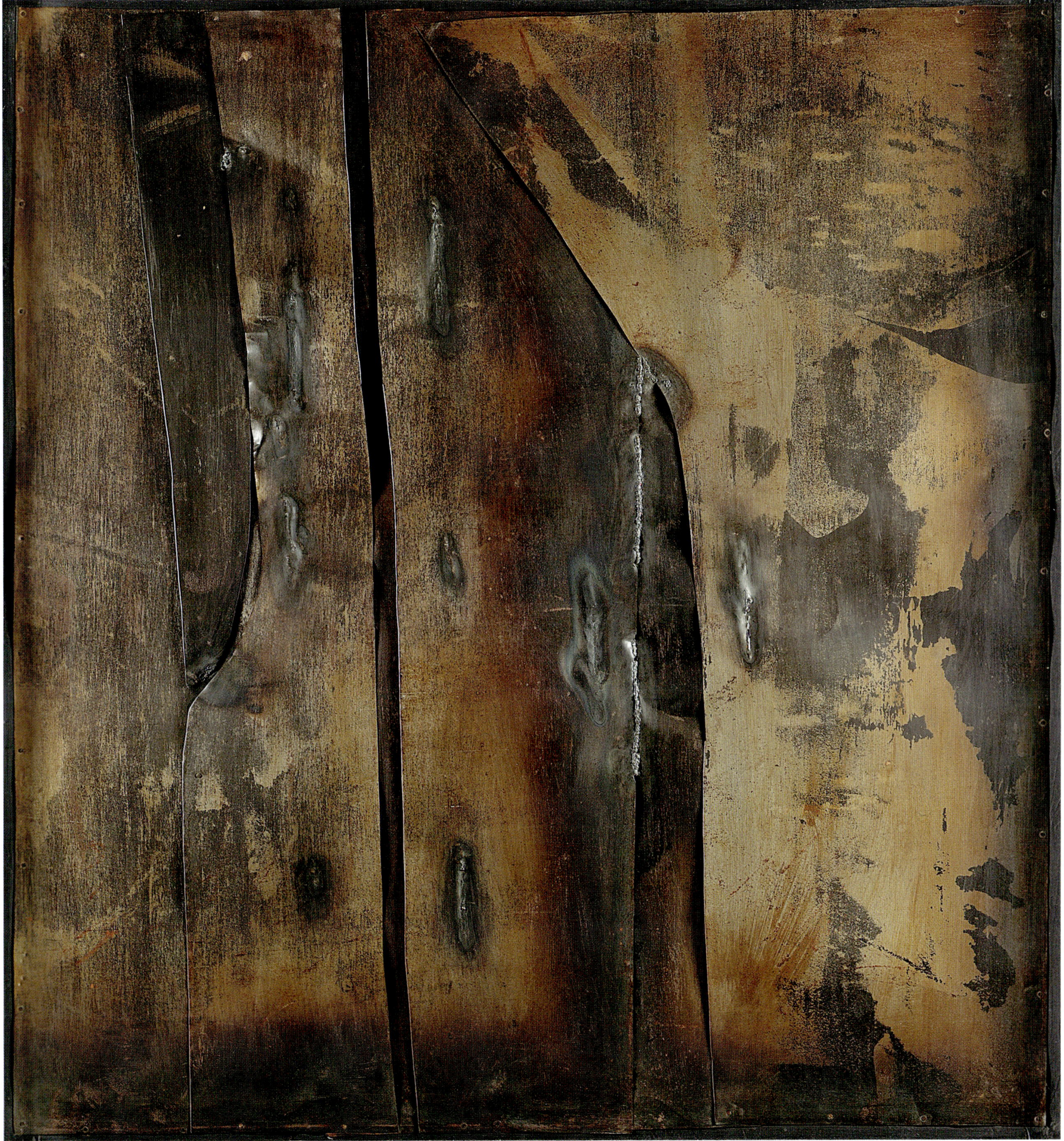

24.
Combustione C7, 1959
Paper, acrylic, Vinavil,
and combustion on canvas
72.3 × 102 cm
Private collection

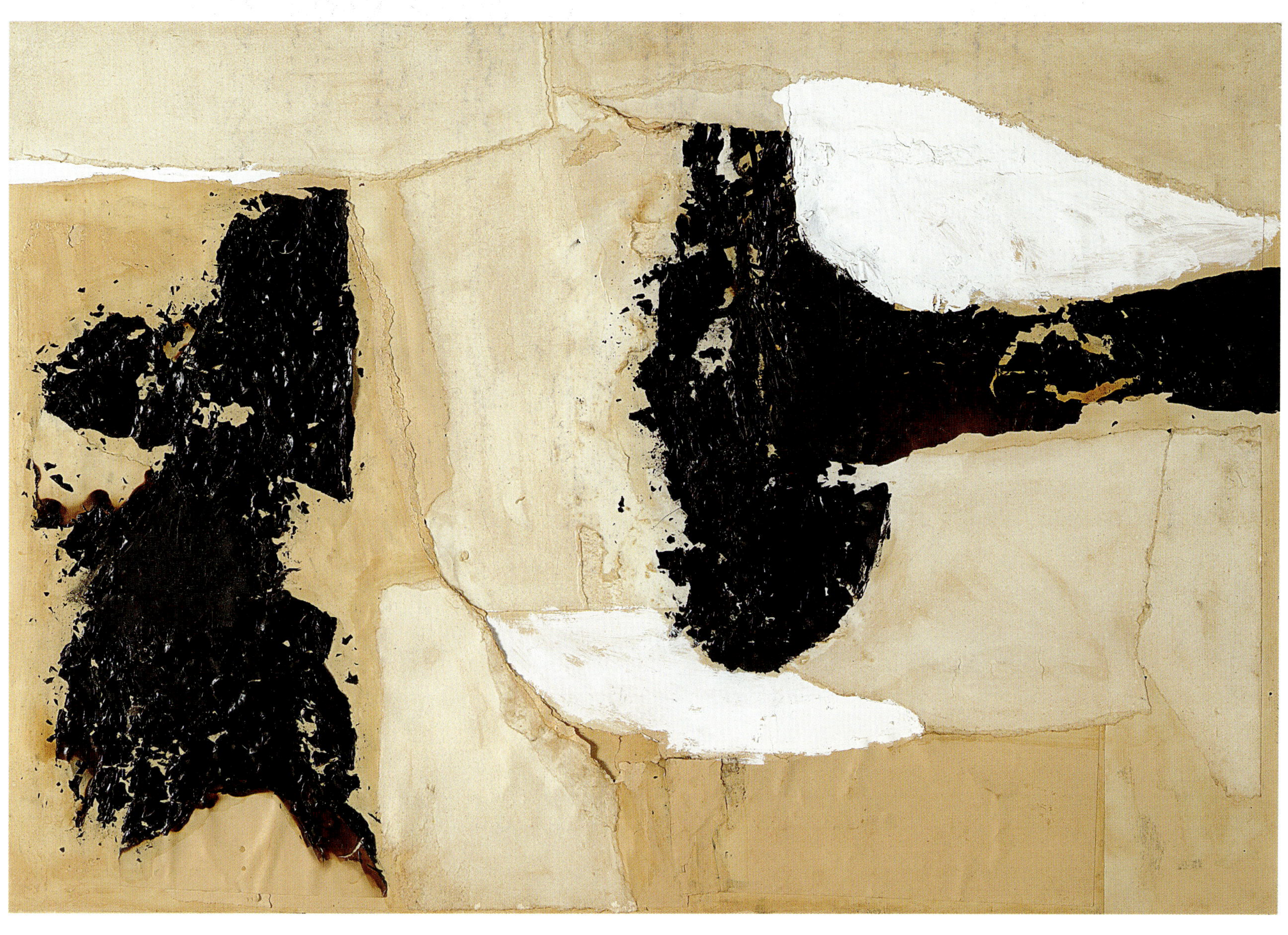

25.
Combustione C8, 1959
Paper, acrylic, Vinavil,
and combustion on canvas
70.5 × 101 cm
Private collection

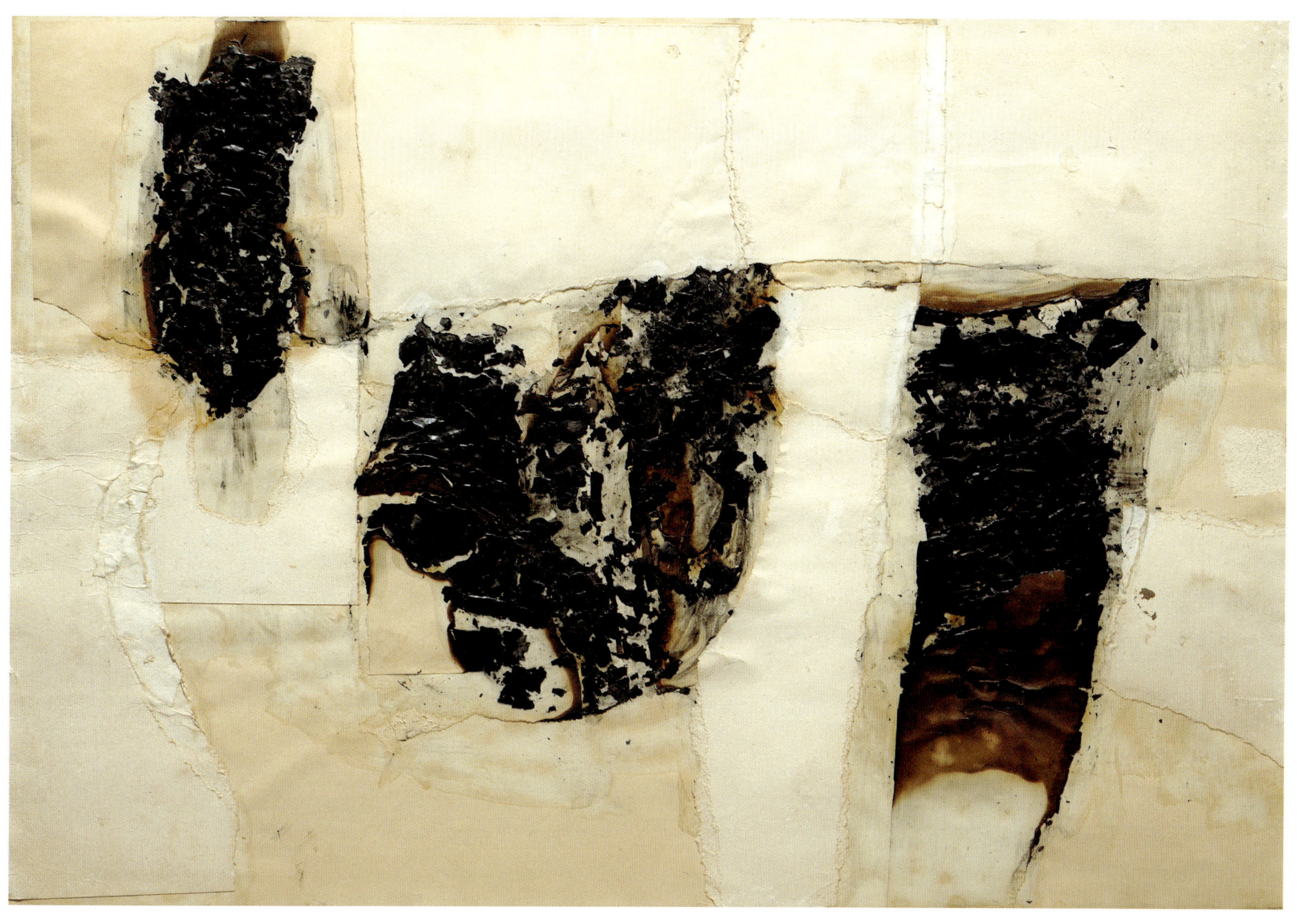

26.
Combustione BA, 1960
Paper, acrylic, Vinavil,
and combustion on canvas
100 × 70 cm
Private collection, Florence –
Courtesy Tornabuoni Arte

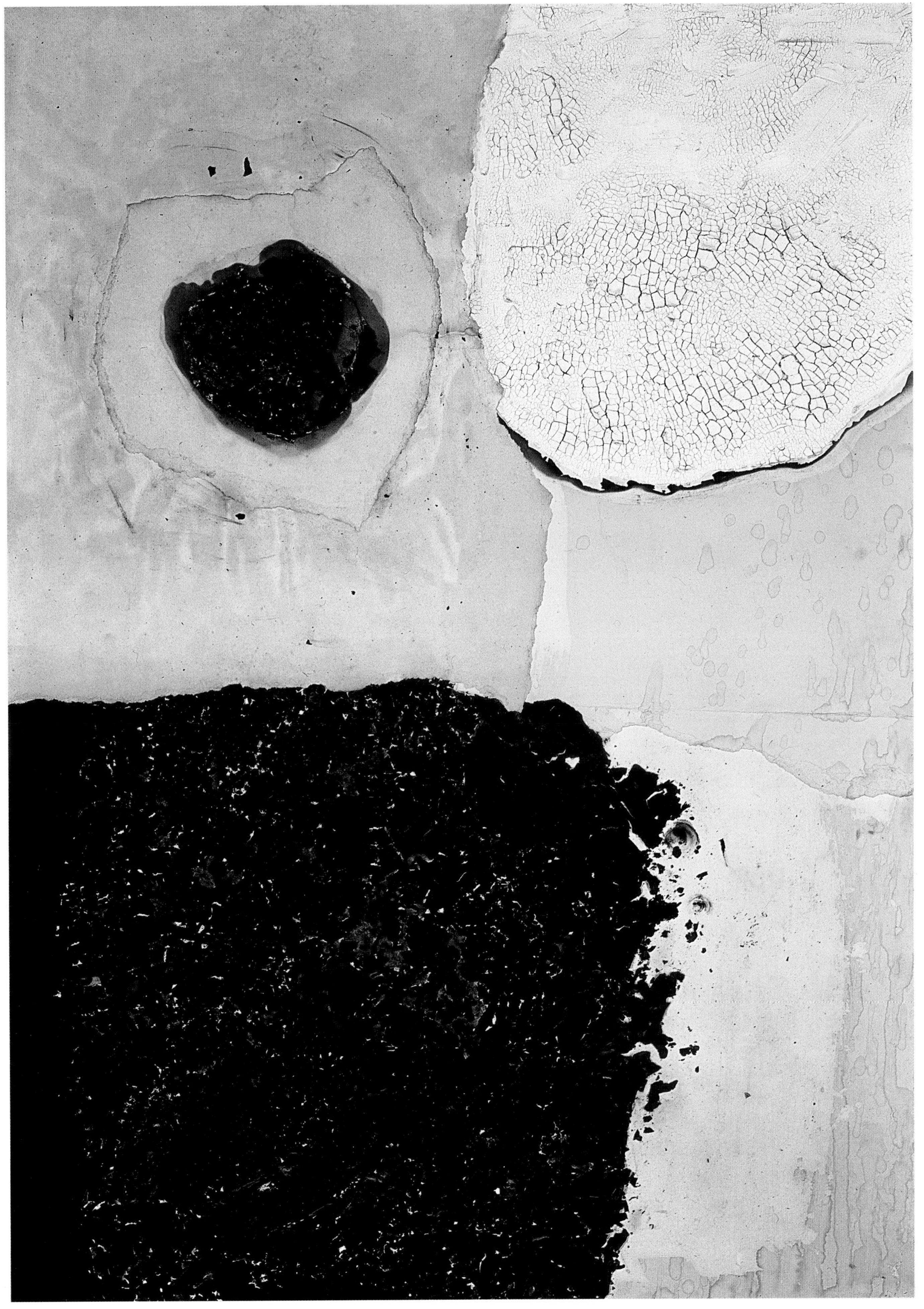

27.
Legno e Rosso, 1960
Wood, acrylic, and Vinavil on canvas
70 × 100 cm
Private collection

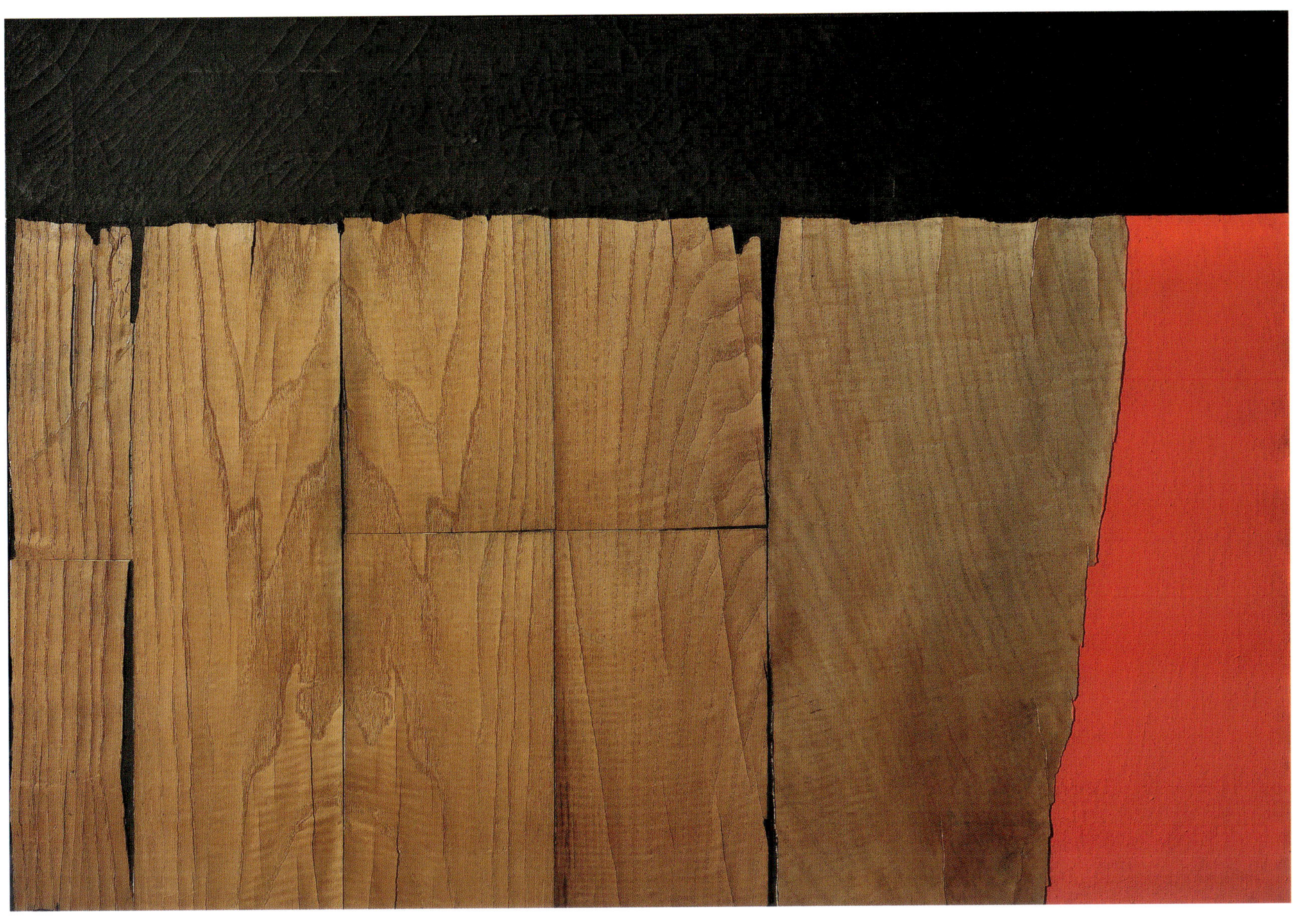

28.
Legno e Nero, 1961
Wood, acrylic, combustion, and Vinavil on wooden framework
168 × 152 cm
Città di Castello, Fondazione Palazzo Albizzini Collezione Burri

29.
Nero, 1961
Plastic, acrylic, sand,
and combustion on canvas
130 × 200.5 cm
Private collection

30.
Rosso Plastica, 1962
Plastic and combustion
on fabric
81.5 × 100 cm
Private collection

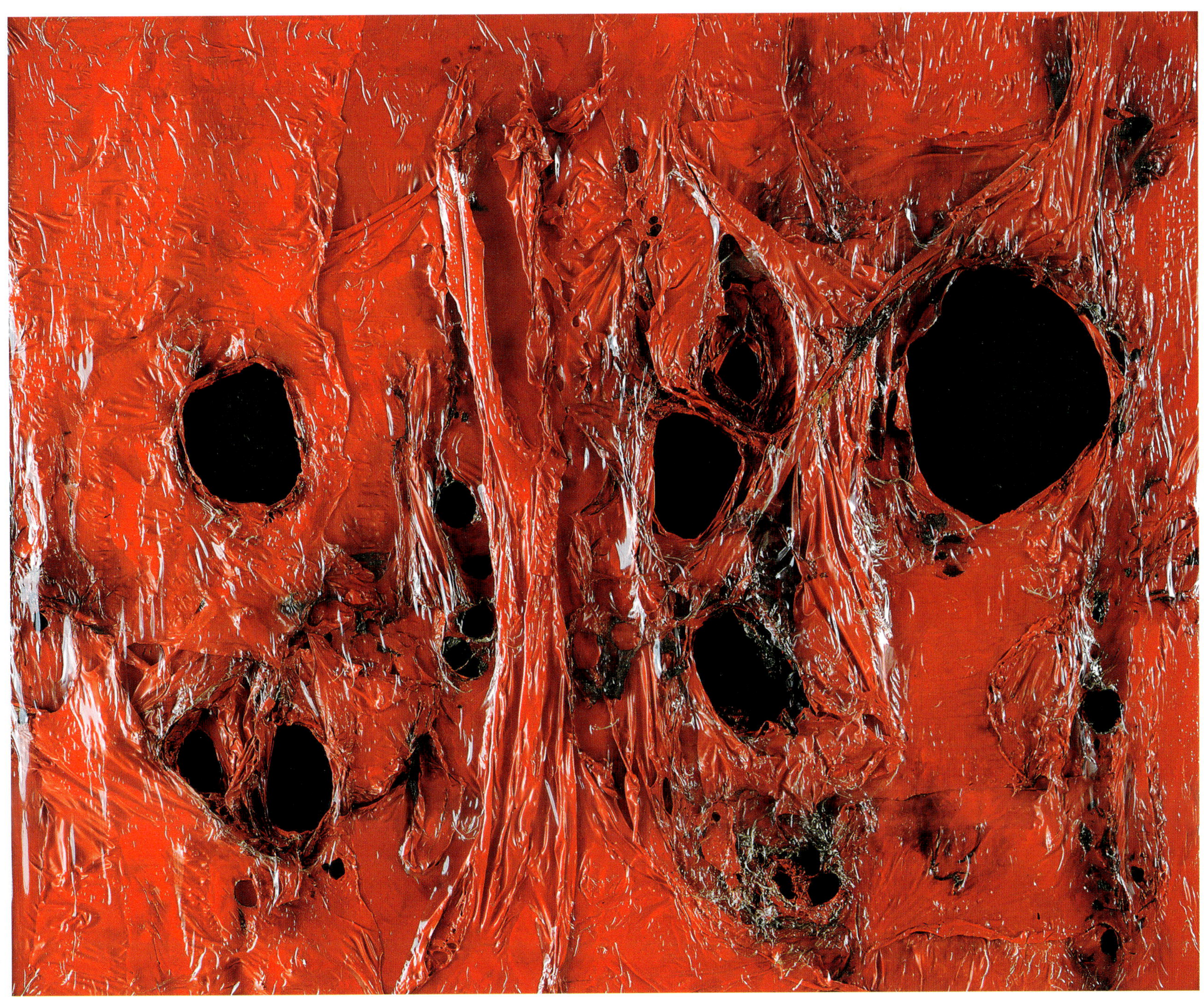

31.
Grande Plastica, [1963]
Plastic and combustion
on aluminum framework
199 × 249 cm
Private collection

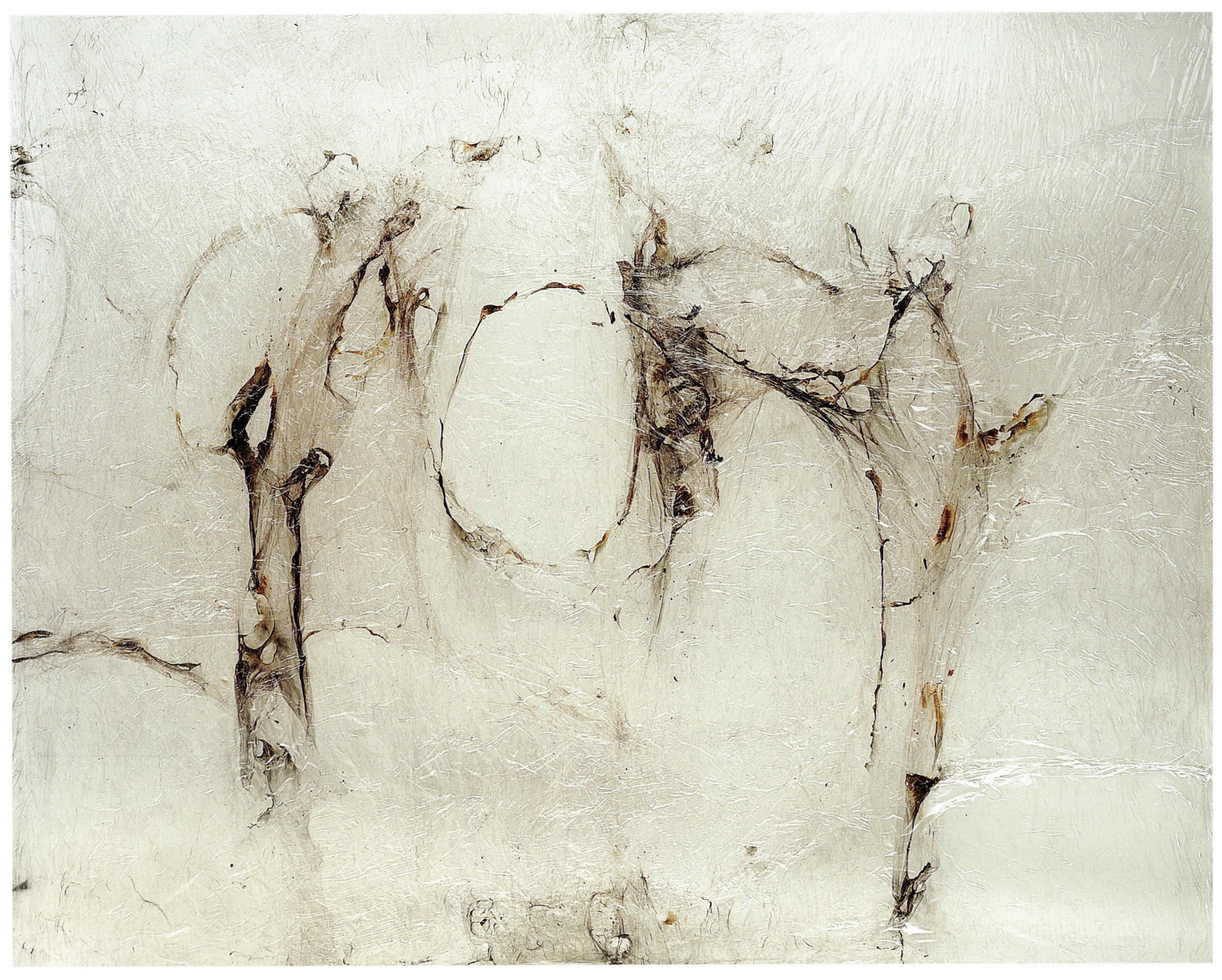

32.
Grande Nero Plastica L.A., 1964
Plastic and combustion
on wooden framework
204 × 199 cm
Private collection

following pages

33.
Plastica Rosso Nero L.A.
(double-sided), 1964
Plastic and combustion
on wooden stretcher
104 × 82 cm each
Private collection

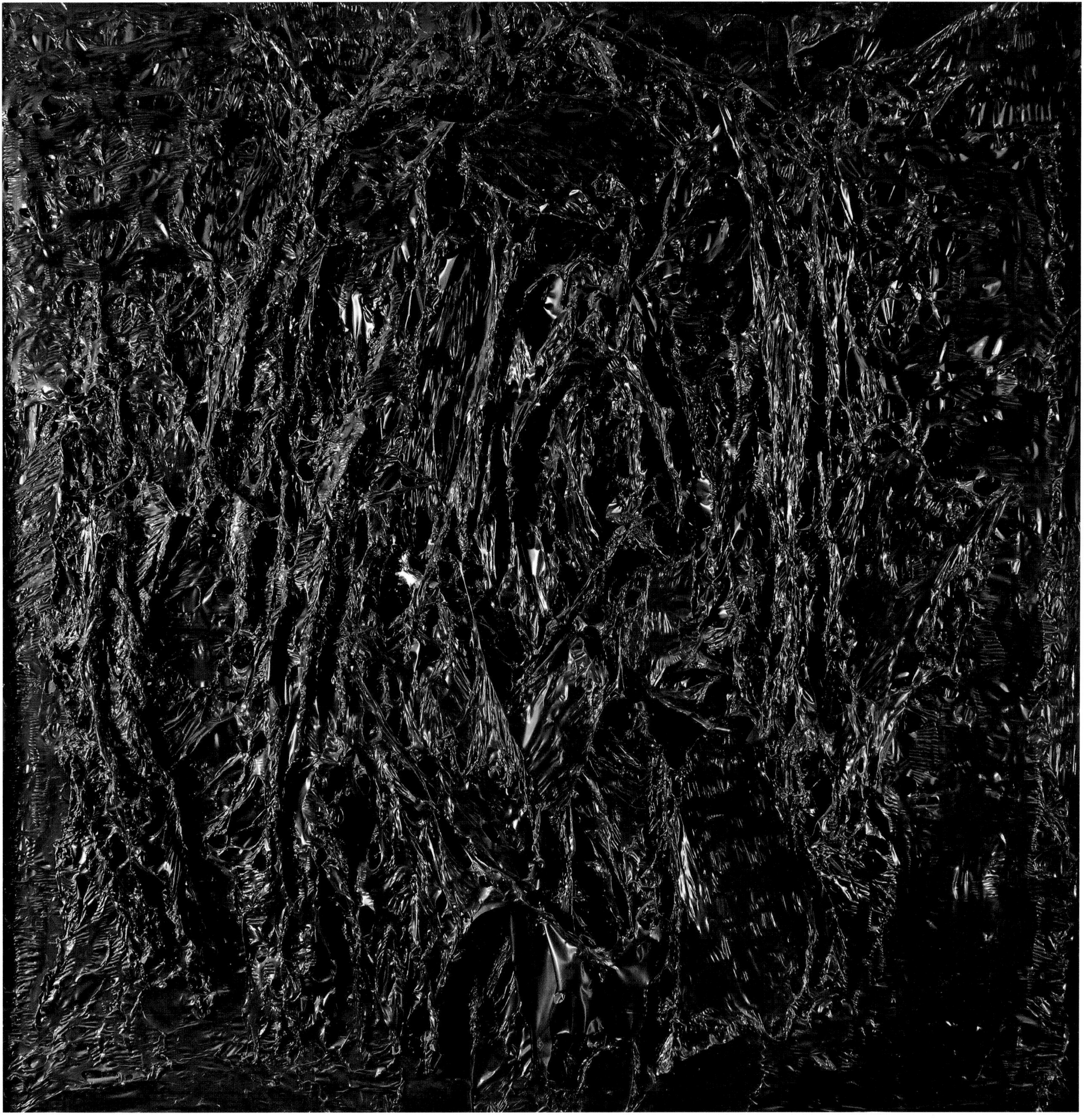

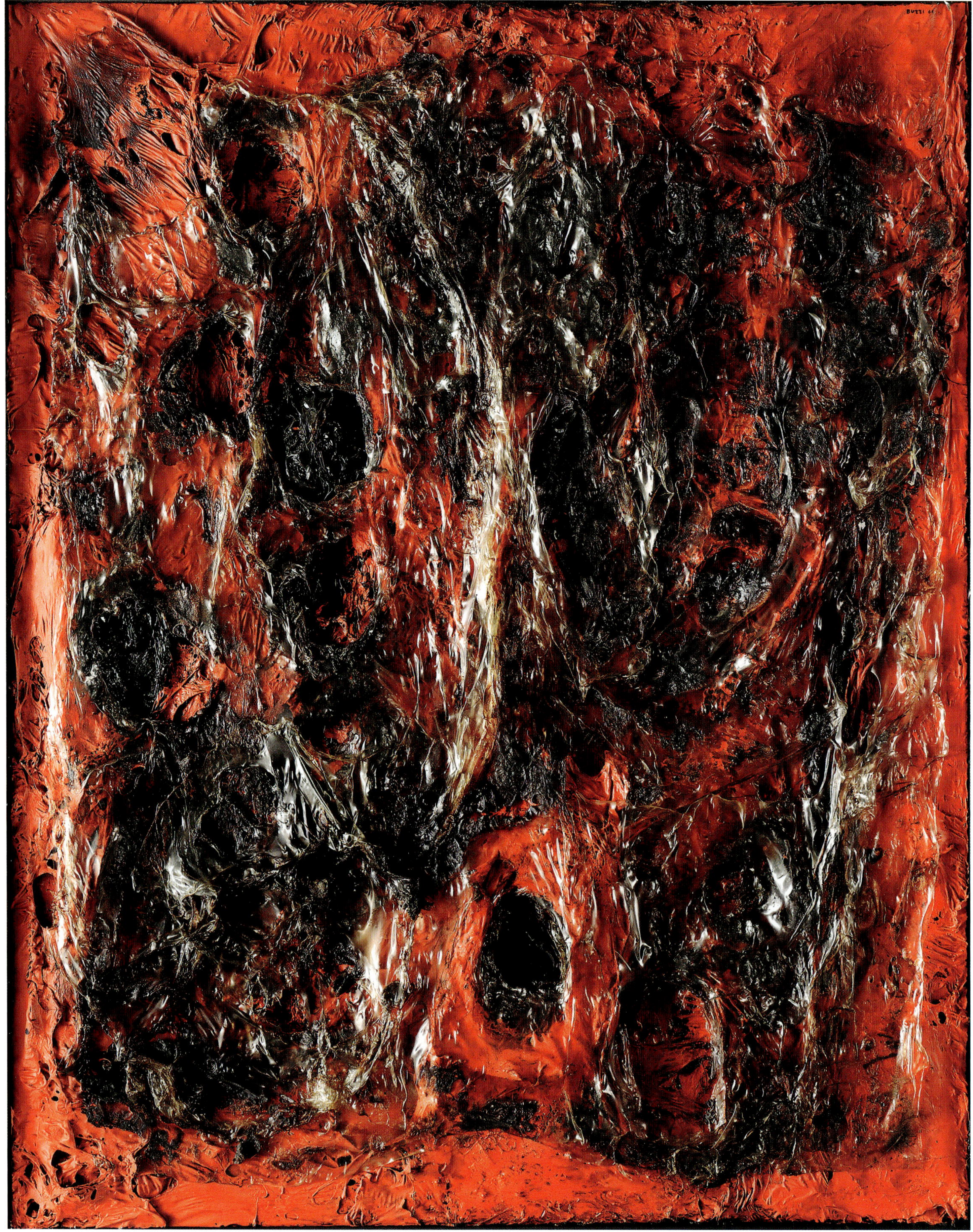

34.
Bianco Plastica B5, 1965
Plastic, acrylic, and
combustion on Cellotex
151.5 × 152 cm
Private collection

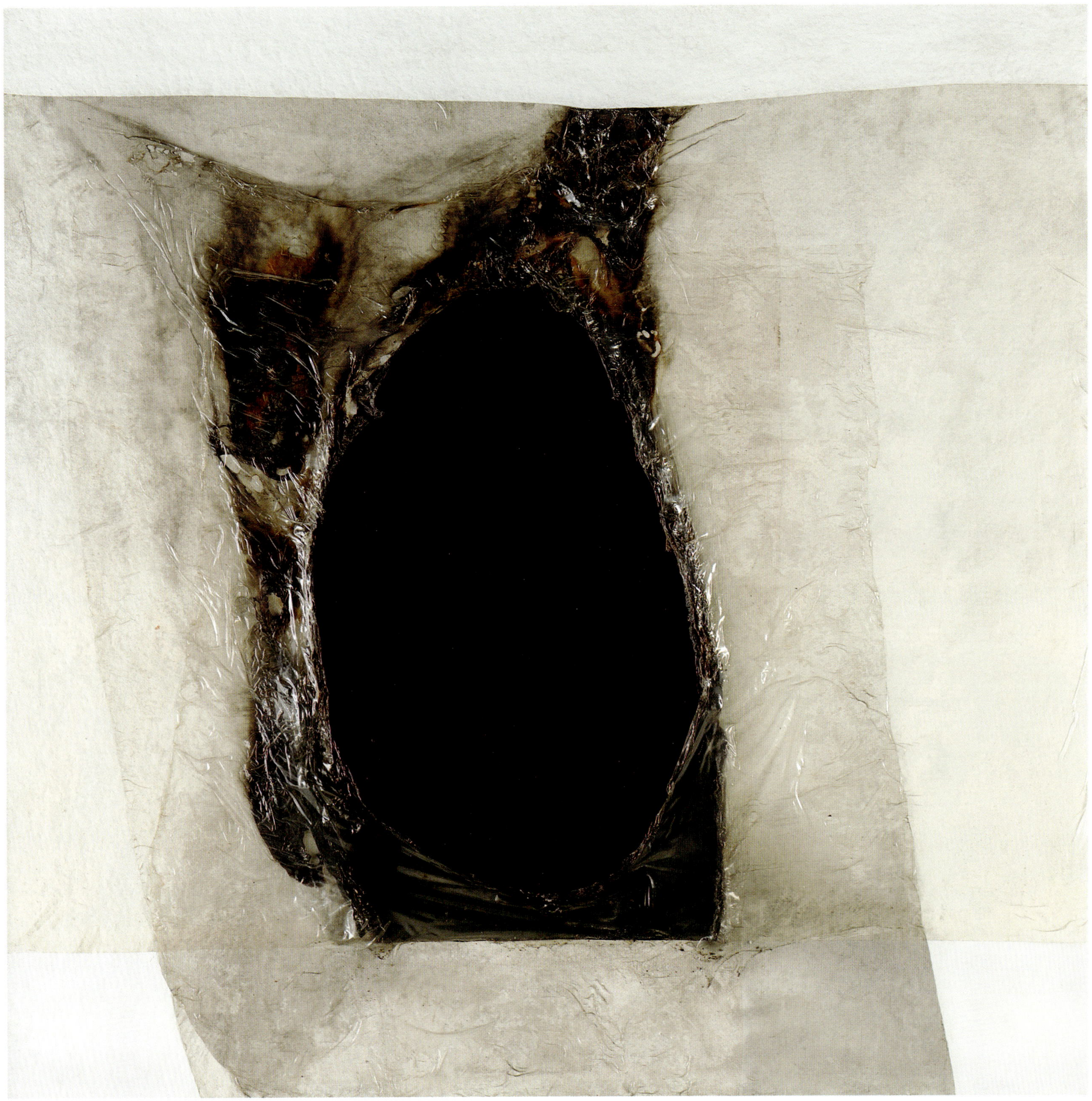

35.
Bianco Plastica, 1967
Plastic, acrylic, and
combustion on Cellotex
156 × 201 cm
Private collection

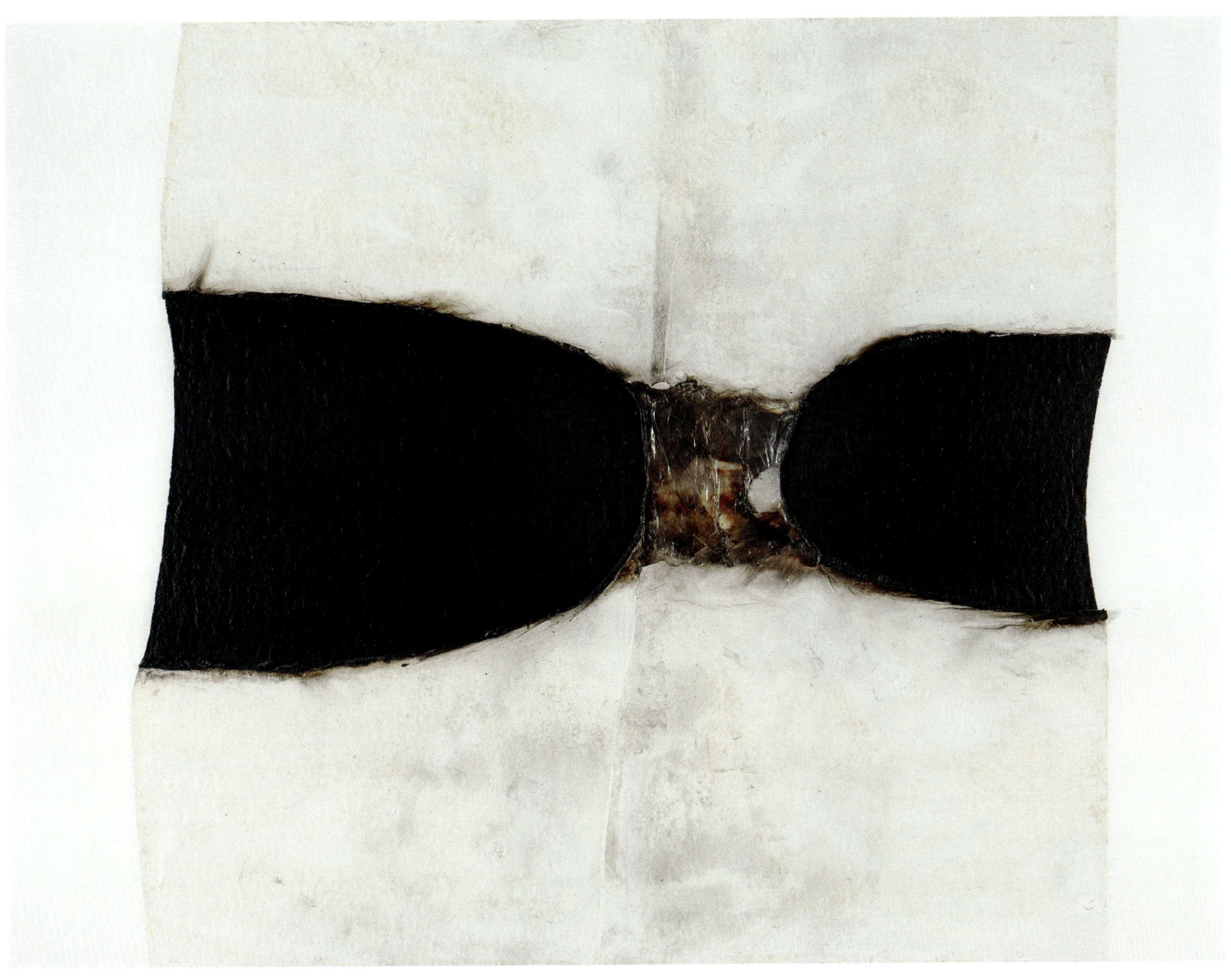

36.
Bianco Nero, 1971
Acrylic-vinyl on Cellotex
75 × 100 cm
Intesa Sanpaolo collection

37.
Bianco Cretto C1, 1973
Acrylic-vinyl on Cellotex
126.5 × 101 cm
Private collection

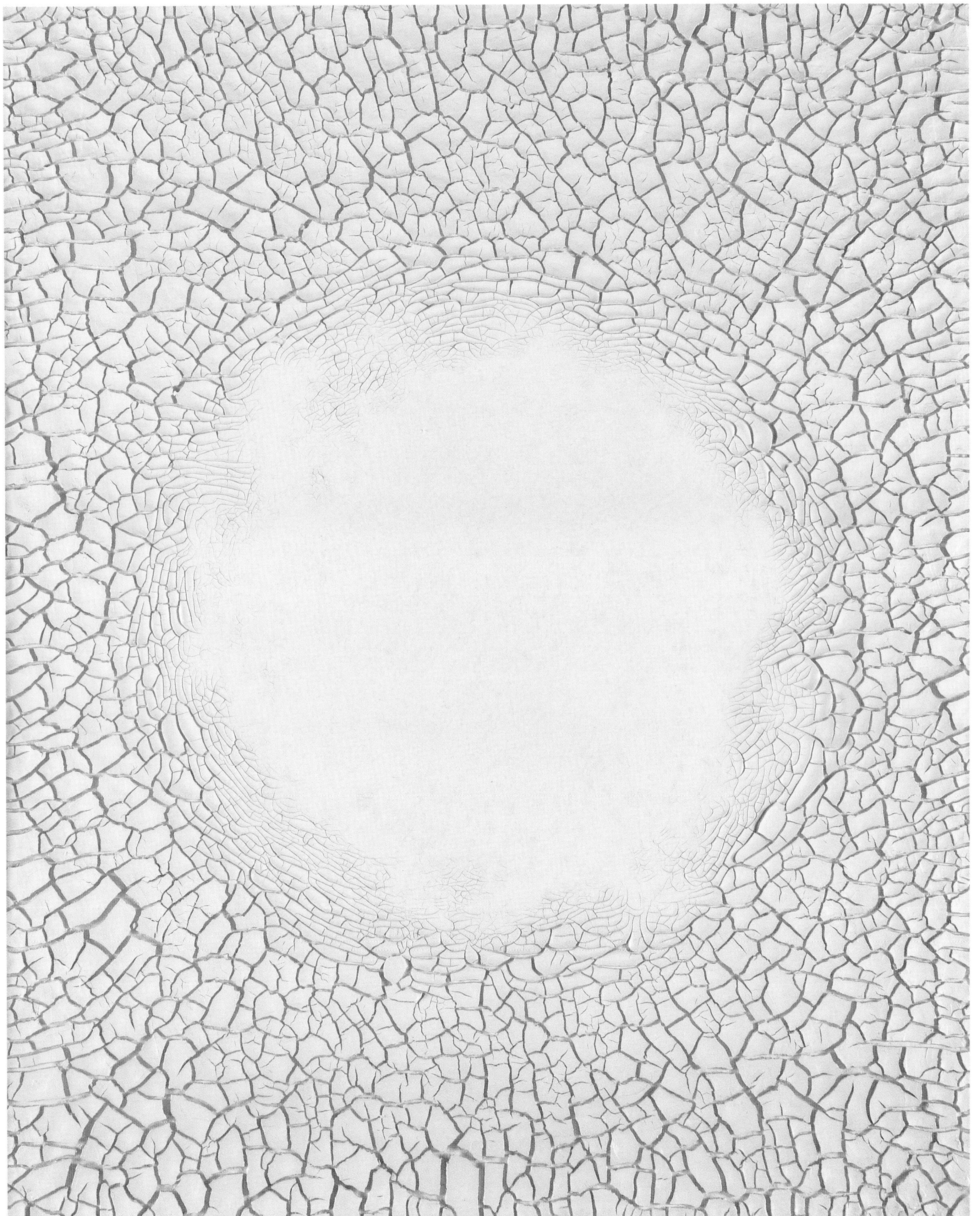

38.
Cretto, [1973]
Acrylic-vinyl on Cellotex
126 × 101 cm
Private collection

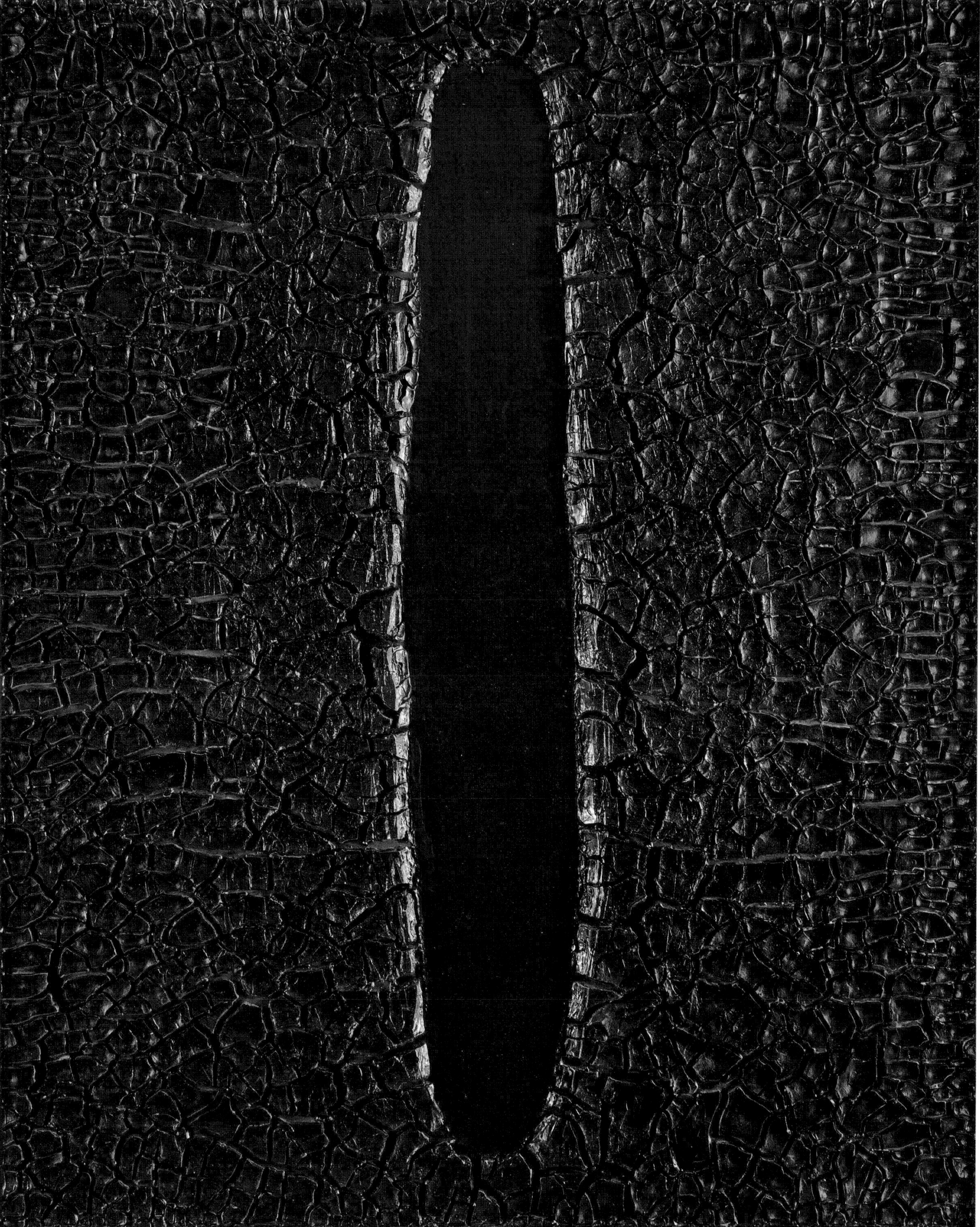

39.
Grande Bianco, 1974
Acrylic-vinyl on Cellotex
126 × 211 cm
Città di Castello,
Fondazione Palazzo
Albizzini Collezione Burri

40.
Nero Cretto, [1974]
Acrylic-vinyl on Cellotex
172 × 152 cm
Private collection

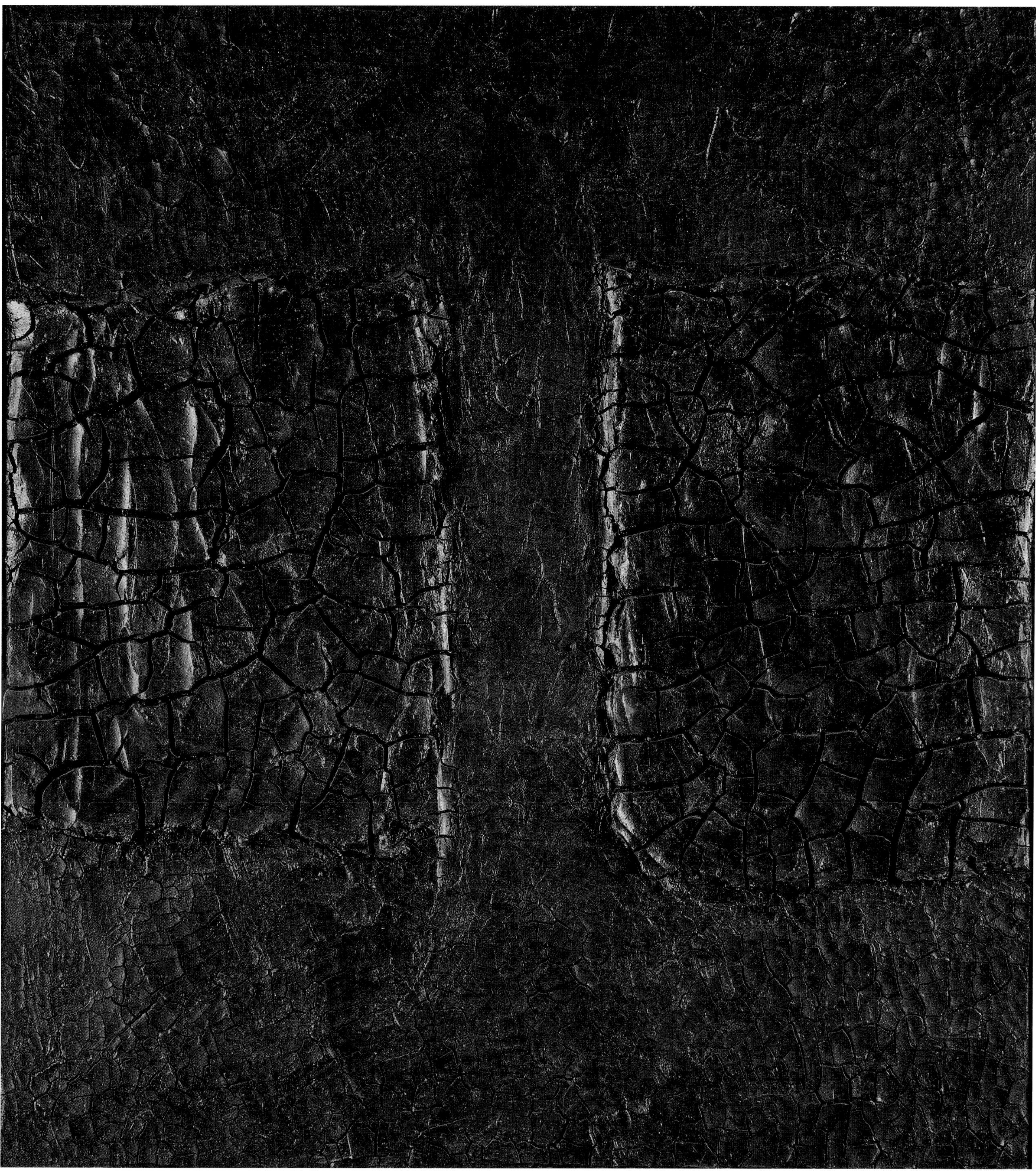

41.
Cretto G2, [1975]
Acrylic-vinyl on Cellotex
172 × 151.5 cm
Private collection

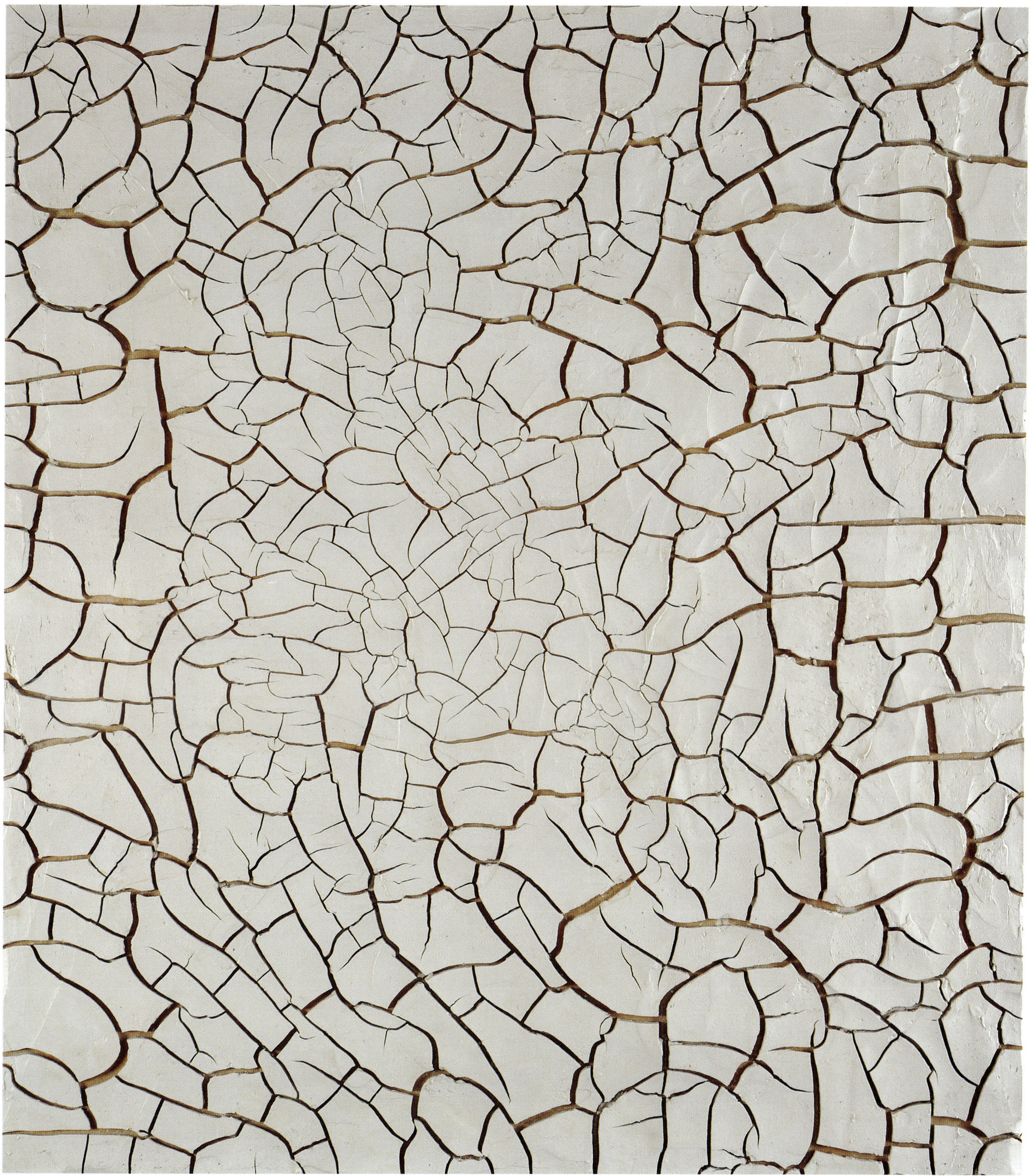

42.
Cellotex, [1975]
Acrylic and Vinavil on Cellotex
150 × 249 cm
Private collection

43.
Cellotex, 1978
Cellotex, acrylic, and Vinavil
126.5 × 211.5 cm
Private collection

44.
Nero e Oro, [1993]
Acrylic, gold leaf, and Cellotex
on canvas
106 × 161.5 cm
Private collection

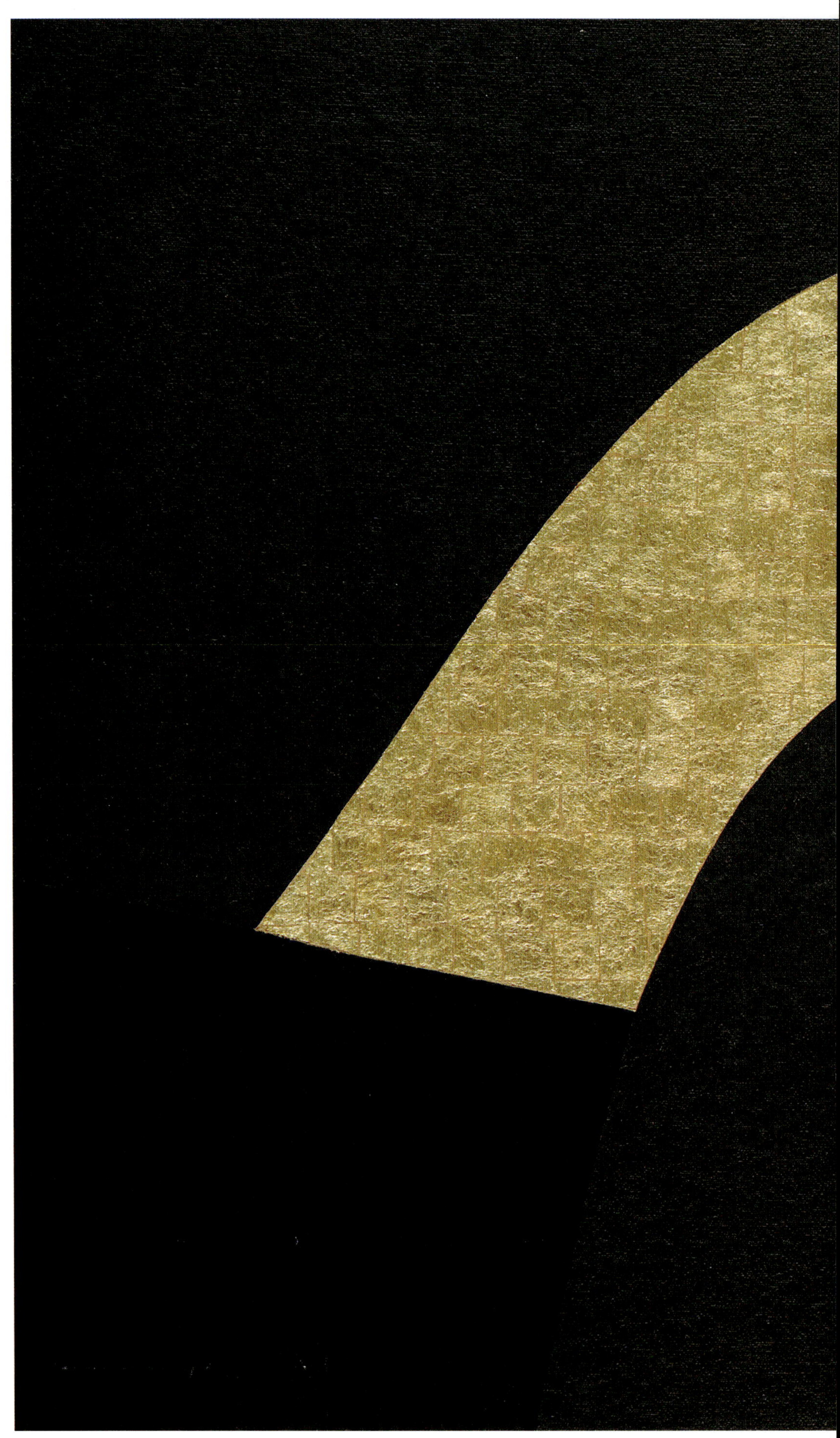

45.
Nero e Oro, [1993]
Acrylic, gold leaf, and Cellotex
on canvas
106 × 161.5 cm
Private collection

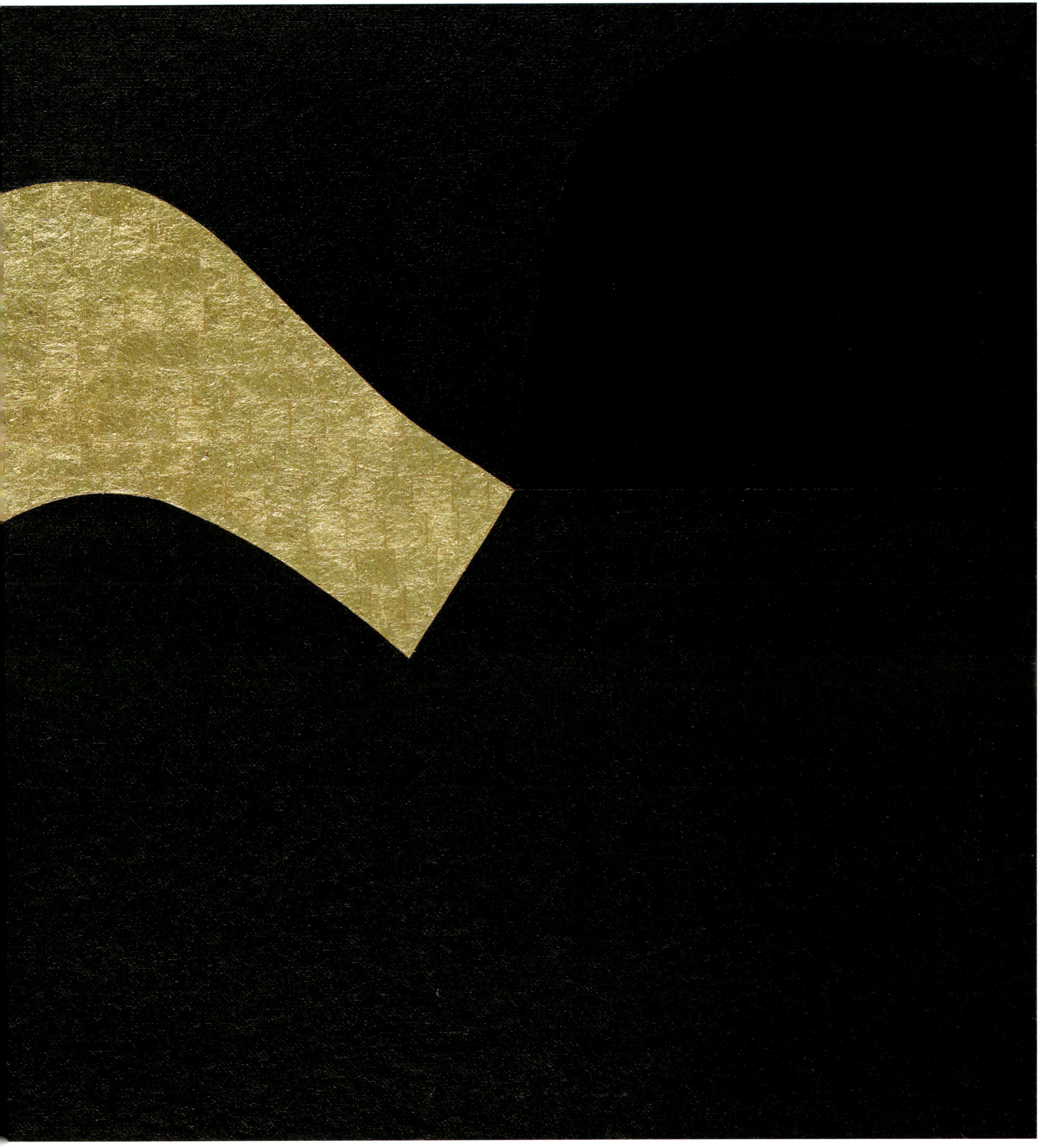

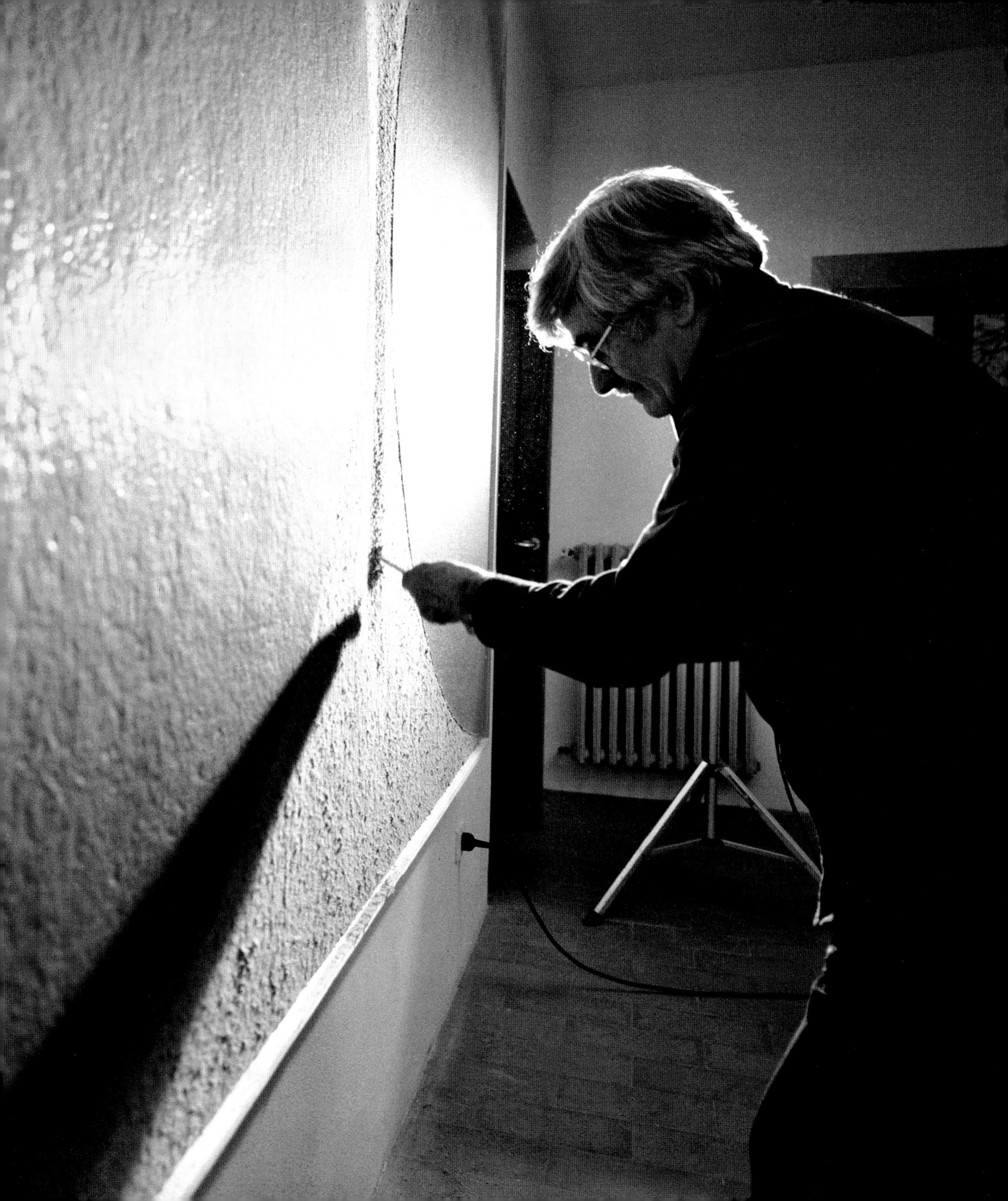

Biographical Chronology

Greta Boninsegni

1915
Alberto Burri is born on 12 March in Città di Castello. His mother, Carolina Torreggiani, is a primary school teacher, while his father, Pietro, is a wine merchant. Vittorio is his younger brother (fig. 1).

1934
After classical studies, he enrolls at the Faculty of Medicine at the University of Perugia.

1935
He enlists as a volunteer for the Ethiopian War (fig. 2) and, with his fellow soldiers of the Volunteer Militia for National Security, he fights in the Amba Aradam highlands in the southeast of the Tigray region.

1940
He gains his degree in medicine and is called up as a physician for the Italian Army.

1942
News arrives that his brother Vittorio, he too a physician involved in World War II, is lost in action in Russia.

1943
During the war he is captured by the British in Tunisia, where he had continued to work as a physician.

1944–45
Handed over to the US Army by the British, he is moved to a prison camp in Hereford, near Amarillo (Texas): he remains there for eighteen months and reaches the decision to give up the medical profession. He begins to paint. In August 1945, a US Army chaplain helps the prisoners to organize an exhibition in the empty officers' barracks. Burri participates in the craftsmanship section with a wooden chess set carved with a razor blade (fig. 4). He creates his first paintings, including *Texas* (1945), which he will send back to Italy at the end of the war via the Red Cross.

1946–47
When the war ends, on his release he embarks on a US merchant ship and in February 1946 arrives at the port of Naples. He returns to Città di Castello. He starts to visit Rome, where he soon moves, as guest of his maternal cousin Annibale Bucchi, a violinist and composer, devoting himself fully to painting. In 1947 becoming acquainted with architect Amedeo Lucchichenti leads to his first solo show at the La Margherita gallery, curated by Gaspero del Corso and Irene Brin, with presentation by the poets Libero De Libero and Leonardo Sinisgalli. Figurative works are displayed in this exhibition, including some executed during his imprisonment in the USA. It is in this extent of time that he comes into contact with sculptor Pericle Fazzini. In this year the Galleria dell'Angelo in Città di Castello hosts another solo exhibition by him. He participates in the 1ª Mostra nazionale di pittura Premio Perugia and, with the work *Pesca a Fano* (1947), is awarded joint second prize with Remo Brindisi and Walter Nativi; the first prize is assigned to Mario Mafai.

1948
He goes to Paris for the first time, where he observes the work of the future protagonists of informal and abstract art. He begins working on the *Catrami*, which he creates with oil, bitumen, sand, Vinavil, and pumice stone applied onto canvas or wood.

1949
In his painting *SZ1* (1949), for the first time he introduces the fabric of a sack of the UNRRA (United Nations Relief and Rehabilitation Administration) bearing the emblems of the US flag. He creates the first *Bianchi*, textured

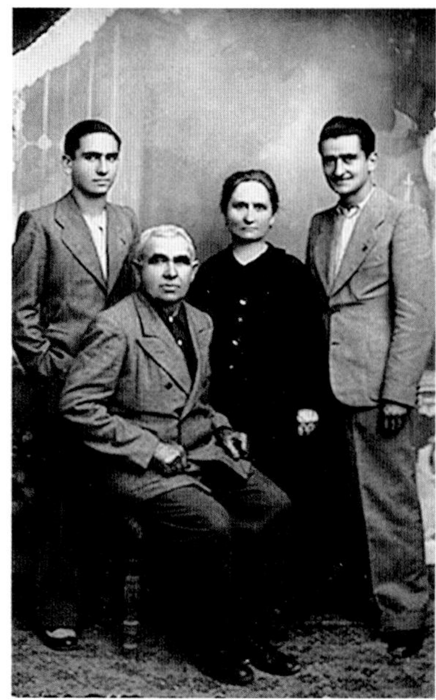

1. Città di Castello, second half of the 1930s. The Burri family: Vittorio, Pietro, Carolina Torreggiani, and Alberto

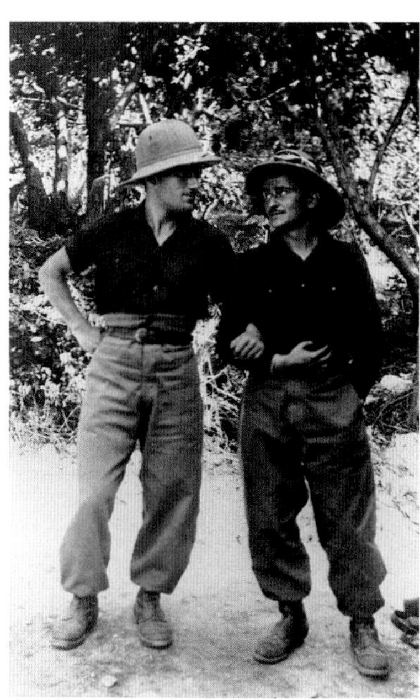

2. During the Ethiopian War, ca. 1935

(*previous pages*)
Casenove di Morra, 1978. Alberto Burri at work

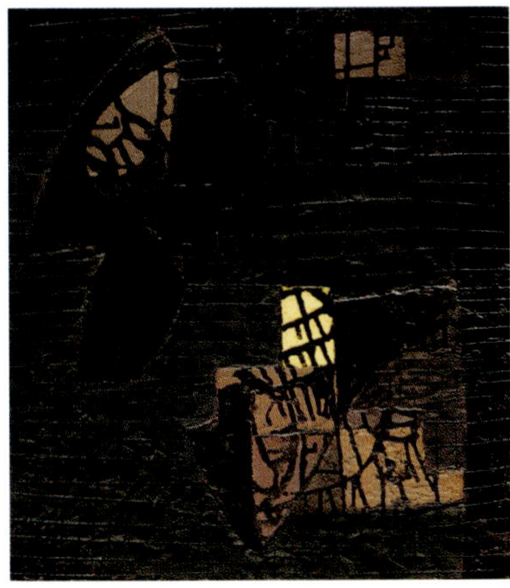

3. *Catrame*, [1949]. Città di Castello, Fondazione Palazzo Albizzini Collezione Burri

4. Chess set made by Alberto Burri while in the Hereford (Texas) prison camp, ca. 1943–45

works characterized by the use of zinc white. He participates in the III Mostra annuale dell'Art Club in Rome at the Galleria Nazionale d'Arte Moderna and at the IV Salon des Réalités Nouvelles at the Musée d'Art Moderne in Paris.

1950

He begins to work on *Muffe* and on protruding paintings, *Gobbi*, for which he uses metal elements to stretch out the canvas from the back. Among these, the *Gobbo* conserved at the Galleria Nazionale d'Arte Moderna in Rome is made differently; in this the sack canvas is pushed outwards by crossed tree branches in the frame. In this year Christian Zervos writes a review of the Italian artistic panorama in *Cahiers d'Art*, and publishes one of Burri's *Catrami*—currently held at the Fondazione Palazzo Albizzini Collezione Burri, in Città di Castello (fig. 3). He creates the first *Sacco* using fragments of an old jute sack. He becomes friendly with Ettore Colla, who introduces him to other collectors.

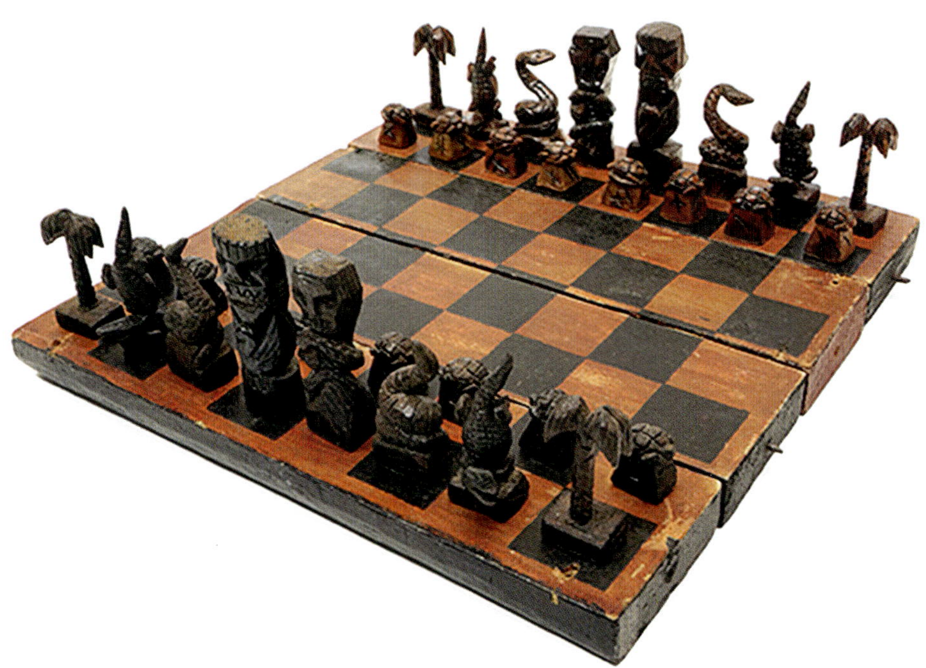

1951

With Colla, Ballocco, and Capogrossi, he participates in the first exhibition, held in Rome, of the Gruppo Origine (an event that lasts just a single evening) as well as in the group's Manifesto. He takes part in the *Arte astratta e concreta in Italia 1951* exhibition at the Galleria Nazionale d'Arte Moderna.

1952

Still in Rome, he moves his studio from Via Mario de' Fiori to Via Margutta, where he creates the first *Grandi Sacchi*. On 3 January the L'Obelisco gallery inaugurates his solo show in Rome of *Neri e Muffe* (fig. 5), which is reviewed in *Il Momento* by Lorenza Trucchi. He participates in the VI Mostra annuale dell'Art Club at the Galleria Nazionale d'Arte Moderna in Rome together with many other artists, including Accardi, Afro, Belli, Cagli, Capogrossi, Consagra, and Dorazio. For the first time the city of Florence hosts a solo show by him.
He takes part in the group exhibition *Omaggio a Leonardo* at the Fondazione Origine in Rome, in which the Gruppo Forma also participates.
In June the XXVI Biennale Internazionale d'Arte is inaugurated, where Burri exhibits *Studio per lo* Strappo (fig. 6), which Lucio Fontana acquires, and *Disegno per Rattoppo*.

1953

The director of the Solomon R. Guggenheim Museum in New York, James Johnson Sweeney, is in Rome visiting Colla, who introduces him to Burri. Sweeney will be the one who promotes him in the USA. The *Alberto Burri Paintings and Collages* exhibition is presented in Chicago at Allan Frumkin's Gallery: this is Burri's first solo show in the USA. In Rome, the poet and art critic Emilio Villa writes the presentation for the artist's solo exhibition at the Fondazione Origine. In the capital the artist also participates in the 82ª Mostra dell'Art Club entitled *Arte Astratta italiana e francese*, at the Galleria

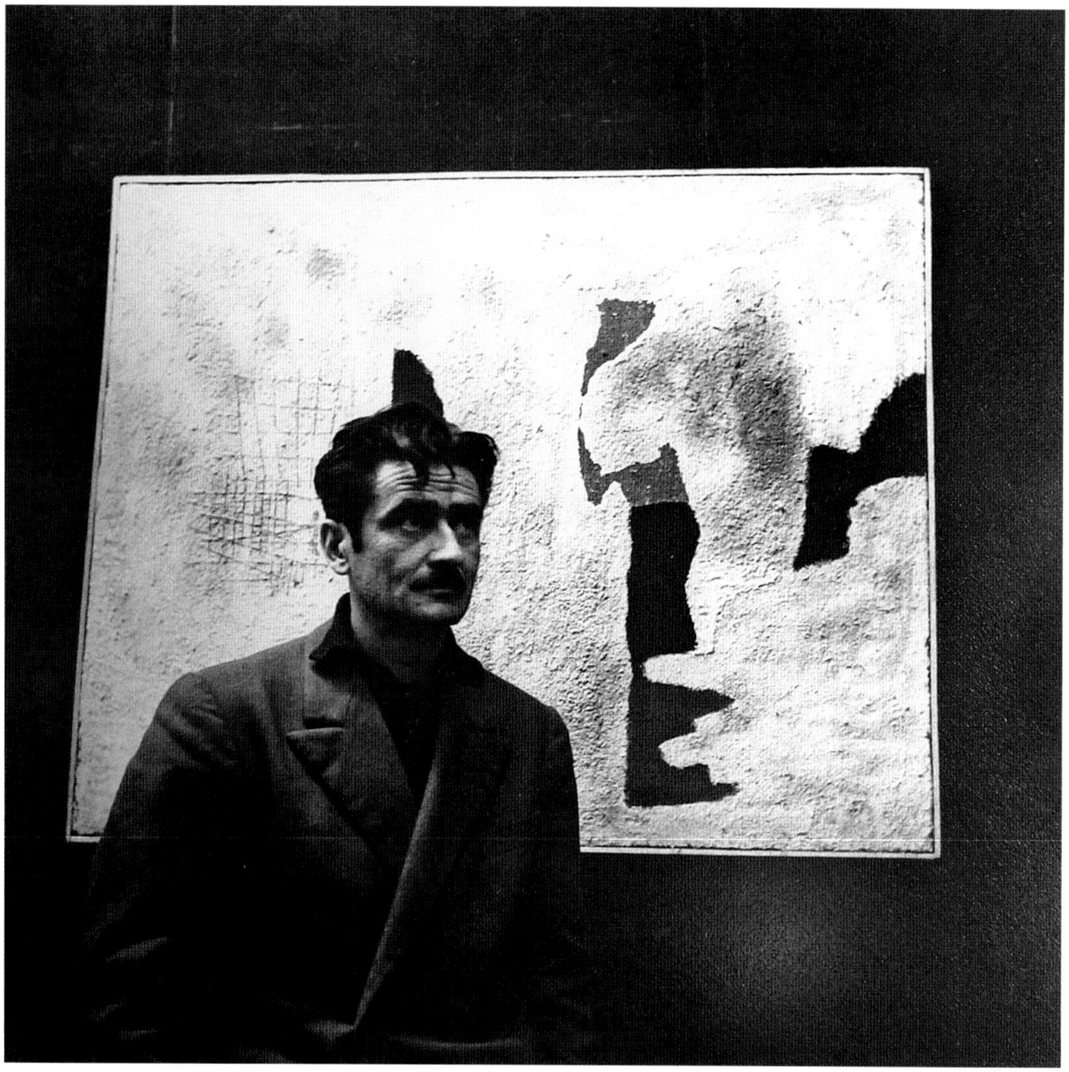

5. Rome, L'Obelisco gallery, 1952. Alberto Burri at the *Neri e Muffe* solo exhibition

Nazionale d'Arte Moderna and, in New York, he takes part in the group exhibition *Twenty Imaginary Views of the American Scene by Twenty Young Italian Artists*. Invited by J. J. Sweeney, at the Solomon R. Guggenheim Museum, to take part in the exhibition *Younger European Painters. A Selection*, he exhibits a *Composizione* (1953), which is later acquired by the same museum and is still part of its collection today. The show travels to other US cities: Minneapolis, Portland, San Francisco, Dallas, Fayetteville, Dayton, Andover, Hanover, South Hadley, and Middletown. At the end of the year, Burri's works are exhibited at Eleanor Ward's Stable Gallery in New York.
Robert Rauschenberg, during his stay in Rome with Cy Twombly, visits Burri in his studio, where he has the opportunity to view the three *Grandi Sacchi* from 1952.

1954

In Rome, Burri moves his studio to Via Salaria and experiments with fire, a new painterly language: he works on the *Combustioni*.
He exhibits in the *New Talent* group exhibition at the Martha Jackson Gallery in New York; the L'Obelisco gallery, in Rome, inaugurates another solo exhibition by him. At the same time, in Chicago, the Frumkin Gallery inaugurates *Alberto Burri. Recent Paintings* (fig. 7). In the summer André Pieyre de Mandiargues publishes a long essay on Burri's work in *La Nouvelle Revue Française*; in the fall Michel Tapié presents him in the *Individualités d'aujourd'hui* exhibition at the Galerie Rive Droite in Paris. In December, in the magazine *Art News*, a long article is published on the maestro's work: *Burri Makes a Picture* written by Milton Gendel with photographs by Josephine Powell.

6. *Studio per lo Strappo*,
[1952]
Milan, Fondazione
Lucio Fontana

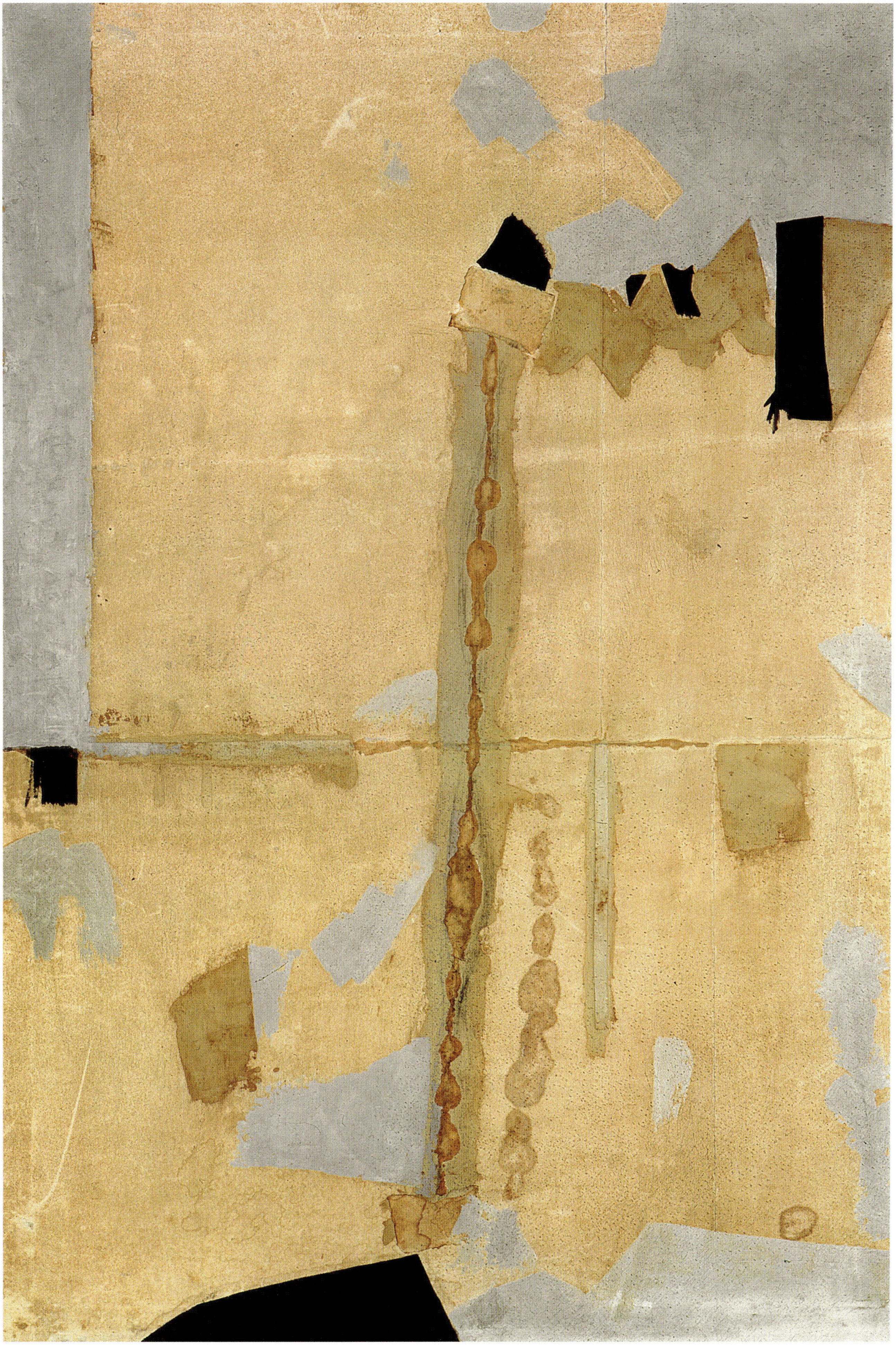

1955

Burri creates a number of *Combustioni*, first on traditional mediums such as paper and wood, subsequently on burnt sacks. He marries Minsa Craig, a US dancer and choreographer. For the first time after his imprisonment, the artist returns to the USA on the occasion of the exhibition curated by Andrew Carnduff Ritchie at The Museum of Modern Art in New York, *The New Decade: 22 European Painters and Sculptors*. The touring exhibition visits Minneapolis, Los Angeles, and San Francisco. At the end of the same month, a solo show is inaugurated in New York by the the Stable Gallery, in collaboration with the Martha Jackson Gallery. This is also the year of the release of the first monograph devoted to Burri, written by J. J. Sweeney, published by L'Obelisco (fig. 8), as well as his first solo exhibition at a US museum venue, curated by James P. Byrnes, *The Collages of Alberto Burri*; the touring exhibition is inaugurated at the Fine Arts Center Colorado Springs and visits other cities in the USA. Burri participates in the Italian section of the 3rd Biennial Exhibition in São Paulo, curated by the Biennale di Venezia at the Museu de Arte Moderna de São Paulo; the relative catalog features an introduction by Umbro Apollonio. The artist exhibits at the Carnegie Institute in Pittsburgh within *The 1955 Pittsburgh International Exhibition of Contemporary Painting*, curated by Gordon Bailey Washburn. He also participates in the VII Quadriennale Nazionale d'Arte in Rome, at Palazzo delle Esposizioni. Despite Burri's success in the US, only this year do the Italian art critics begin to devote more attention to his work.

1956

In June he is present at the XXVIII Biennale Internazionale d'Arte di Venezia and, the following month, participates in the exhibition

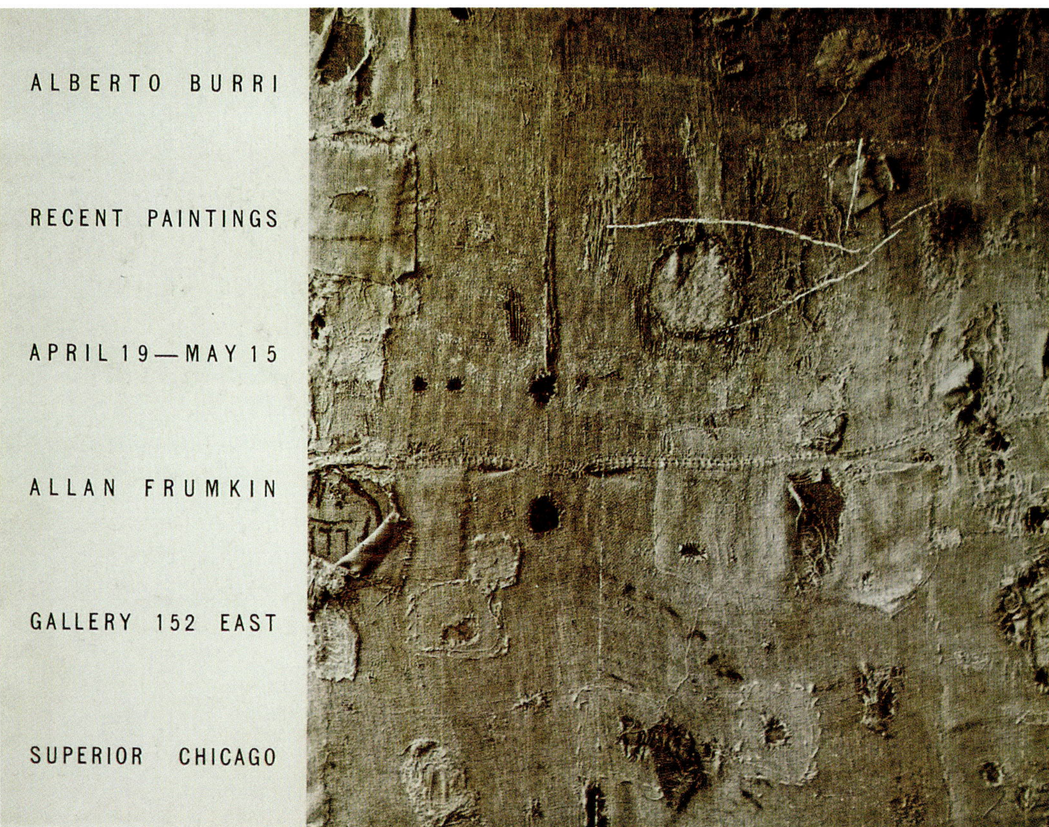

7. *Alberto Burri Recent Paintings* exhibition. Chicago, Frumkin Gallery, 1954. Invitation card

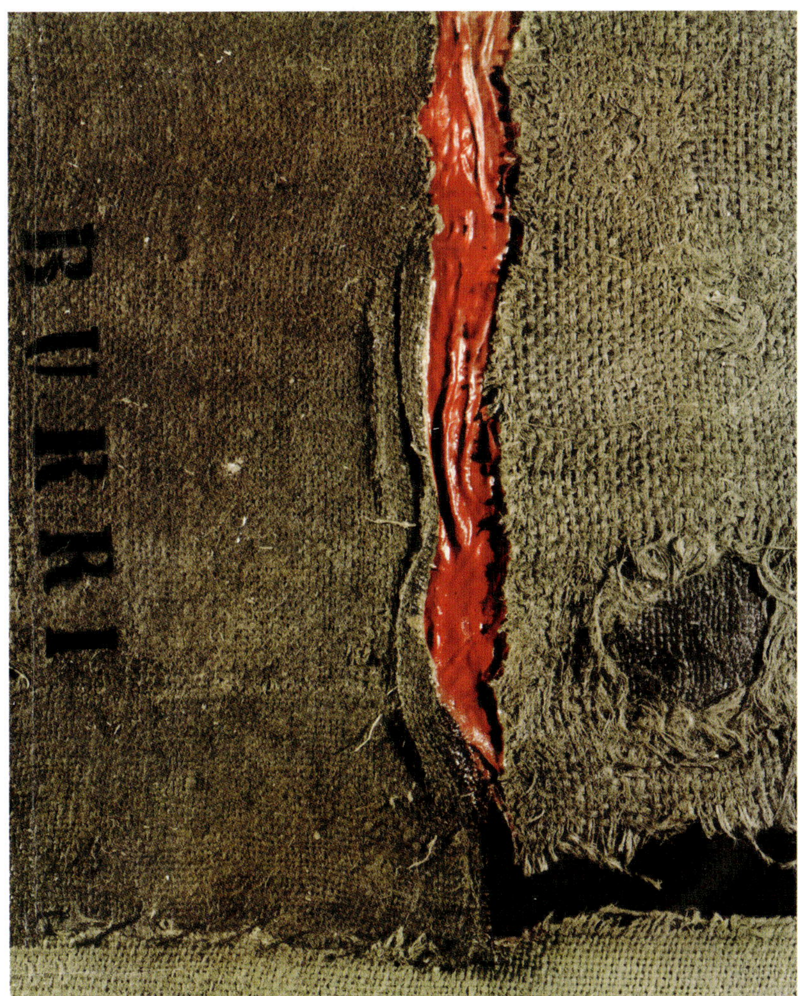

8. James Johnson Sweeney, *Burri*, L'Obelisco, Rome, 1955. Cover

Carnegie Institute.
Pittsburgh, Pennsylvania,
U.S.A.

At the Pittsburgh Bicentennial International held in the Art Galleries of the Carnegie Institute A.D. 1958
Third Prize was awarded to
Alberto Burri
for his painting entitled Grande Legno 2-58
In attestation whereof the members of the Jury of Award have hereunto affixed their signatures.

President of Jury.

9. Certificate of conferment of the award. Pittsburgh, Carnegie Institute, 1958

hosted at the Städtisches Museum in Leverkusen, curated by Lionello Venturi. Again in Venice, the Galleria del Cavallino directed by Carlo Cardazzo hosts Burri's solo show, accompanied by a catalog featuring text by J. J. Sweeney. The *Burri peintures, César sculptures* exhibition curated by Michel Tapié is held at the Galerie Rive Droite in Paris. The artist begins working on the *Legni*.

1957

His solo exhibitions follow in rapid succession: at the Galleria del Naviglio in Milan, directed by Carlo Cardazzo; at the L'Obelisco gallery in Rome; at the Galleria La Loggia in Bologna, and at the Galleria La Bussola in Turin. Burri also participates in group exhibitions: at the La Tartaruga gallery in Rome; the Brooklyn Museum in New York; the Galleria Blu in Milan; the Solomon R. Guggenheim Museum in New York; the Palazzo delle Arti in Turin, and the Galleria La Salita in Rome, to mention just a few. The most significant exhibition of this year, again under the aegis of J. J. Sweeney, is however *Paintings by Alberto Burri* at the Museum of Art Carnegie Institute, a show that travelled to three other US cities. Burri experiments with working with iron sheets.

1958

In Rome, the Galleria La Salita presents the exhibition *Burri*. His works are displayed at various sites, including: the Kunsthalle in Basel, the Statens Museum for Kunst in Copenhagen on the occasion of the exhibition *Moderne Italiensks Maleri,* and the Städtisches Museum Morsbroich in Leverkusen. The artist is again invited at the XXIX Biennale Internazionale d'Arte in Venice. He exhibits the first *Ferri* in Milan in a solo show at the Galleria Blu. He participates in *The 1958 Pittsburgh Bicentennial International Exhibition of Contemporary Painting and Sculpture*, organized by the Carnegie Institute in Pittsburgh, where he wins third prize (on the

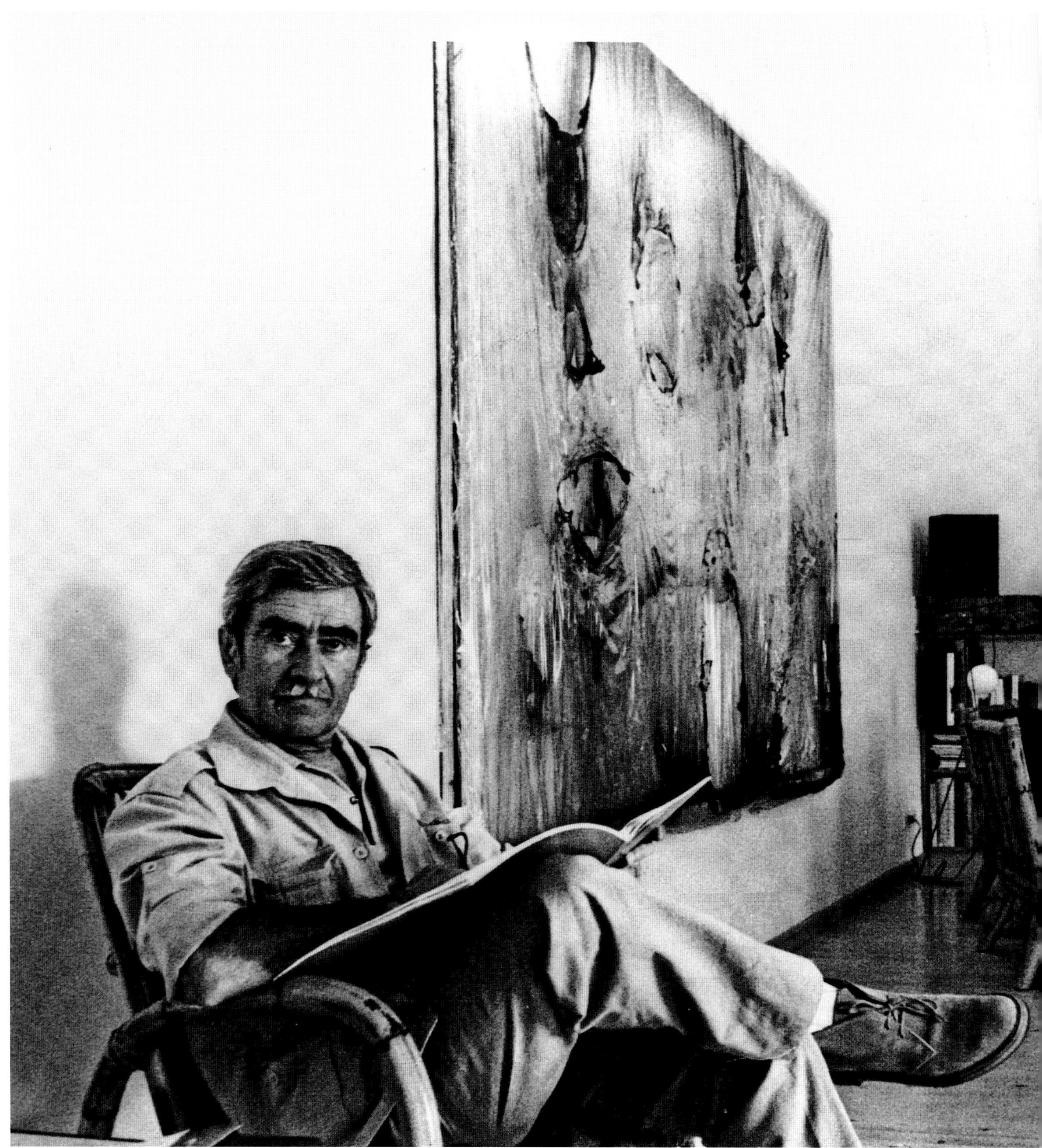

10. Grottarossa, Rome, ca. 1965. Alberto Burri in his house

certificate, among the members of the jury, the signature of Marcel Duchamp is recognizable) (fig. 9).

1959

The Galerie Marie-Suzanne Feigel in Basel inaugurates a solo show by him and the Palais des Beaux-Arts in Brussels devotes an extensive retrospective to Burri, presented by Giulio Carlo Argan. The artist participates in various group exhibitions in the USA. Paul Wember curates his third retrospective at the Museum Haus Lange in Krefeld, which then travels to the Museum am Ostwall in Dortmund. At the same time, several solo exhibitions are also devoted to him in Italy. His work arrives in Japan, to the Salon Syrokia in Tokyo, to then travel from Sendai to Osaka. Burri is invited to exhibit in the second edition of documenta in Kassel. In Vienna, Wember again presents him in a solo show at the Wiener Secession building. Palazzo Grassi in Venice inaugurates the exhibition *Vitalità nell'arte*, where his works are also displayed; the touring exhibition is subsequently hosted in Recklinghausen and Amsterdam. He participates in the 5th Biennial Exhibition in São Paulo.

1960

He moves to Grottarossa (fig. 10), on the outskirts of Rome. His work becomes the subject of a documentary by Giovanni Carandente, which is screened in Italian movie theaters. He holds a solo exhibition at the Martha Jackson Gallery in New York and at the Hanover Gallery in London, where he is presented by Herbert Read. In Munich he participates in the *Neue Malerei. Form Struktur Bedeutung* group exhibition held at the Städtische Galerie im Lenbachhaus. For the first time he has his own room at the XXX Biennale Internazionale d'Arte Venezia and wins the AICA Prize. He takes part in group

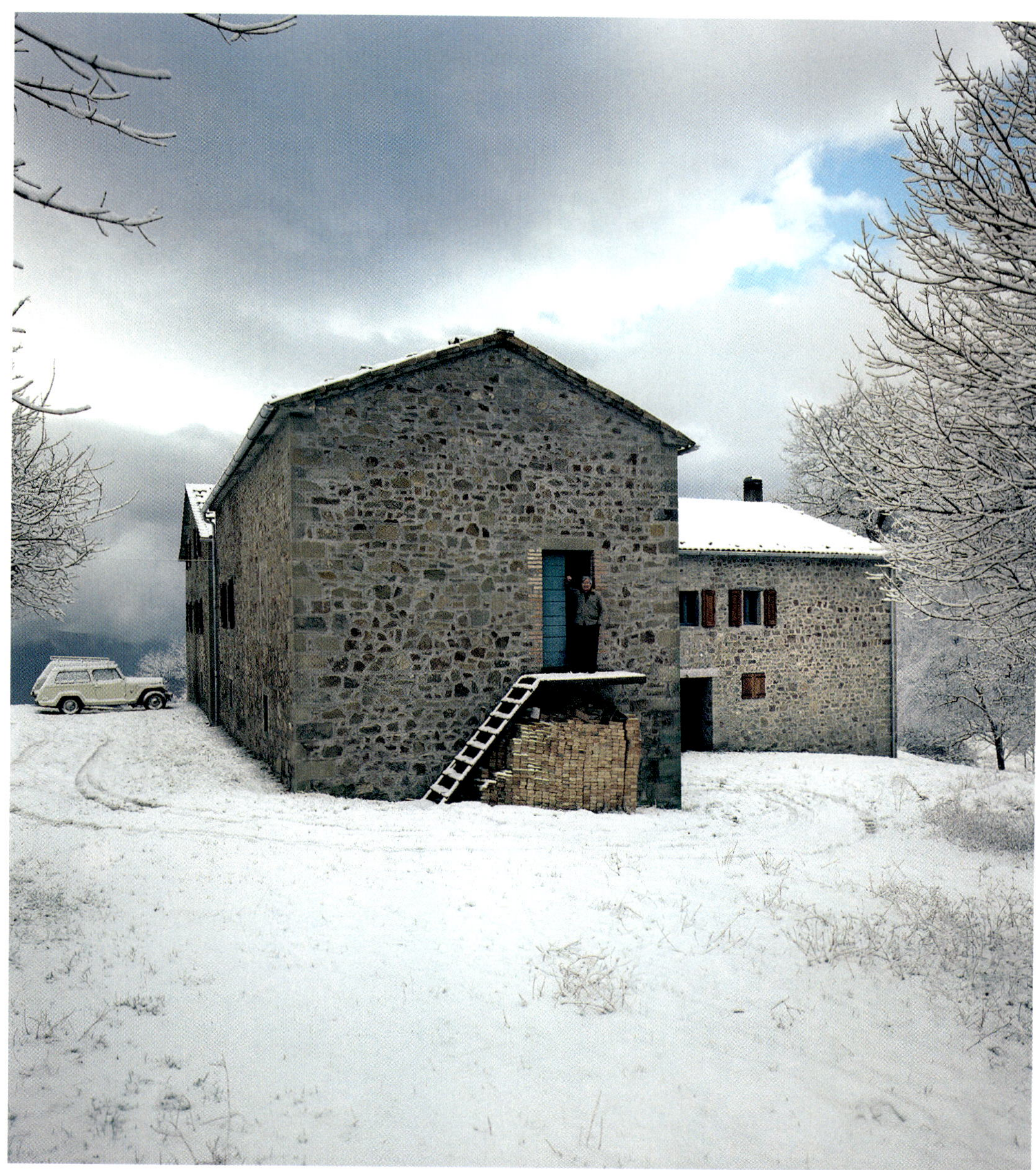

11. Alberto Burri at Casenove di Morra, 1977

exhibitions in the USA and Italy, as well as in Lucerne on the occasion of *Italienische Maler der Gegenwart*. He exhibits in solo shows at the Museo Nacional de Bellas Artes in Buenos Aires and at the Galerie Änne Abels in Cologne.

1961

Two monographs are published, *Burri. Un saggio e tre note* by Enrico Crispolti and *I Ferri di Burri* by Maria Drudi Gambillo and Giuseppe Marchiori. The La Medusa gallery in Rome inaugurates an anthological exhibition on the maestro. He participates, with the award-winning artists from the previous year at the Biennale di Venezia, in the US touring exhibition devoted to them, *Venice Biennale Prize, Winners 1960*. The solo exhibition *Burri* is held at the Galerie de France in Paris. He is present at the 6th Biennial Exhibition in Tokyo, later hosted in seven other Japanese cities. He takes part in the group exhibition *Peintres d'aujourd'hui France-Italie*, at the Galleria Civica d'Arte Moderna in Turin, and in the important review inaugurated at The Museum of Modern Art in New York, *The Art of Assemblage*, curated by William C. Seitz, which subsequently travels to Dallas and San Francisco. He renews his presence at the Carnegie Prize in Pittsburgh.

1962

He purchases an old farmhouse in the Apennines between Umbria and Tuscany, not far from Città di Castello; Casenove becomes both his residence and his studio (fig. 11), but

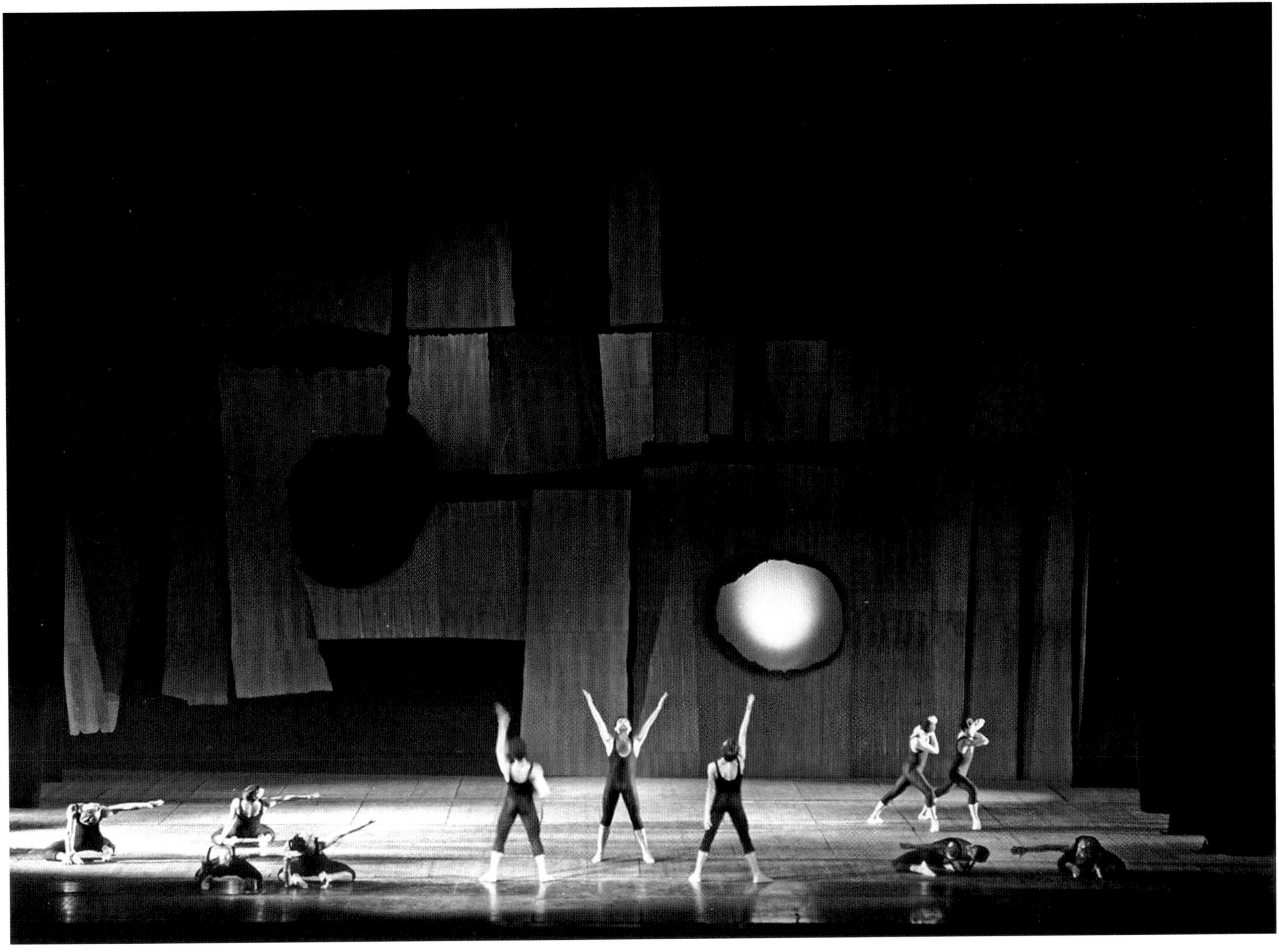

12. Milan, Teatro alla Scala, 1963. Set design for Morton Gould's ballet *Spirituals*

also the ideal place for hunting and sharing this passion with his closest friends. Pierre Restany publishes an article devoted to Burri's work in the magazine *Cimaise*. Antonio Bandera and Enrico Crispolti are the curators of an extensive anthological retrospective of Burri's oeuvre held in summer in the 16th-century castle in L'Aquila, as part of *Alternative Attuali*. The artist creates *Plastiche*, which are displayed at the Galleria Marlborough in Rome and introduced in the catalog by Cesare Brandi.

1963

He purchases a house in Los Angeles, on one of the hills that characterize the city, and will live there over the winter months until 1991. He designs the sets for the ballet *Spirituals* (fig. 12) by US composer Morton Gould for the Teatro alla Scala in Milan. He is part of the group exhibition organized in Turin by the Galleria Notizie, directed by Luciano Pistoi. He participates in the Settimo premio biennale di pittura e scultura Amedeo Modigliani – Città di Livorno, in *The Aspetti della ricerca informale in Italia fino al 1957* exhibition accompanied by a catalog edited by Maurizio Calvesi and Dario Durbé; he partakes in an exhibition held in Darmstadt and curated by Bernd Krimmel, *Zeugnisse der Angst in der Modernen Kunst*. This is the year of his participation in the Australian touring group exhibition *Contemporary Italian Paintings*. The Marlborough in London pays homage to him with the a show, *Alberto Burri*, which the

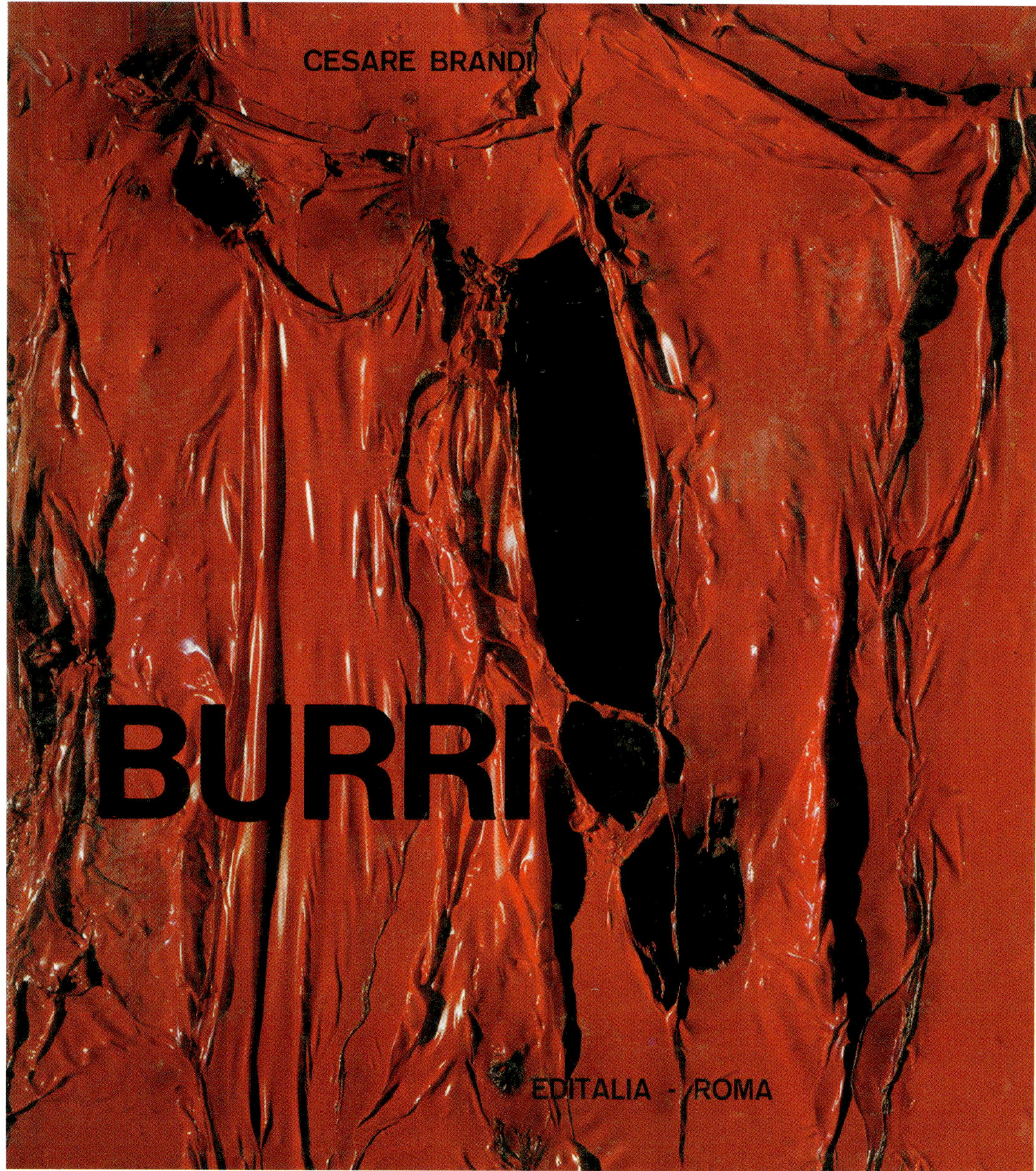

13. Cesare Brandi, *Burri*, Editalia, Rome, 1963. Cover

following year is held at the Marlborough–Gerson Gallery in New York. The Museum of Fine Arts in Houston, directed by J. J. Sweeney, organizes an anthological exhibition that will be hosted by the cities of Buffalo, Minneapolis, San Francisco, and Pasadena in 1964. As part of the "Maestri del XX secolo" series, the publisher Editalia releases the monograph *Burri* by Cesare Brandi, also in an edition in English (fig. 13).

1964

The Galleria Blu in Milan exhibits some of his *Plastiche*. Burri takes part in *Painting & Sculpture of a Decade 54–64*, held at the Tate Gallery in London, and *Vier Italienische Maler, Burri, Capogrossi, Dorazio, Fontana*, a touring exhibition that from the Kestner Gesellschaft in Hannover will also reach Rome, among other cities. The artist exhibits at the XXXII Biennale Internazionale d'Arte di Venezia as well as in Kassel, on the occasion of documenta III. He is present at the *1964 Pittsburgh International Exhibition of Contemporary Painting and Sculpture* and, in Valdagno, wins the Marzotto Prize, the exhibition of which subsequently visits Baden-Baden, London, Humlebæk, Amsterdam, and Paris.

1965

The year begins with the solo exhibition *Plastiche di Burri* at the Galleria La Bussola in Turin. Some of his works are displayed in the

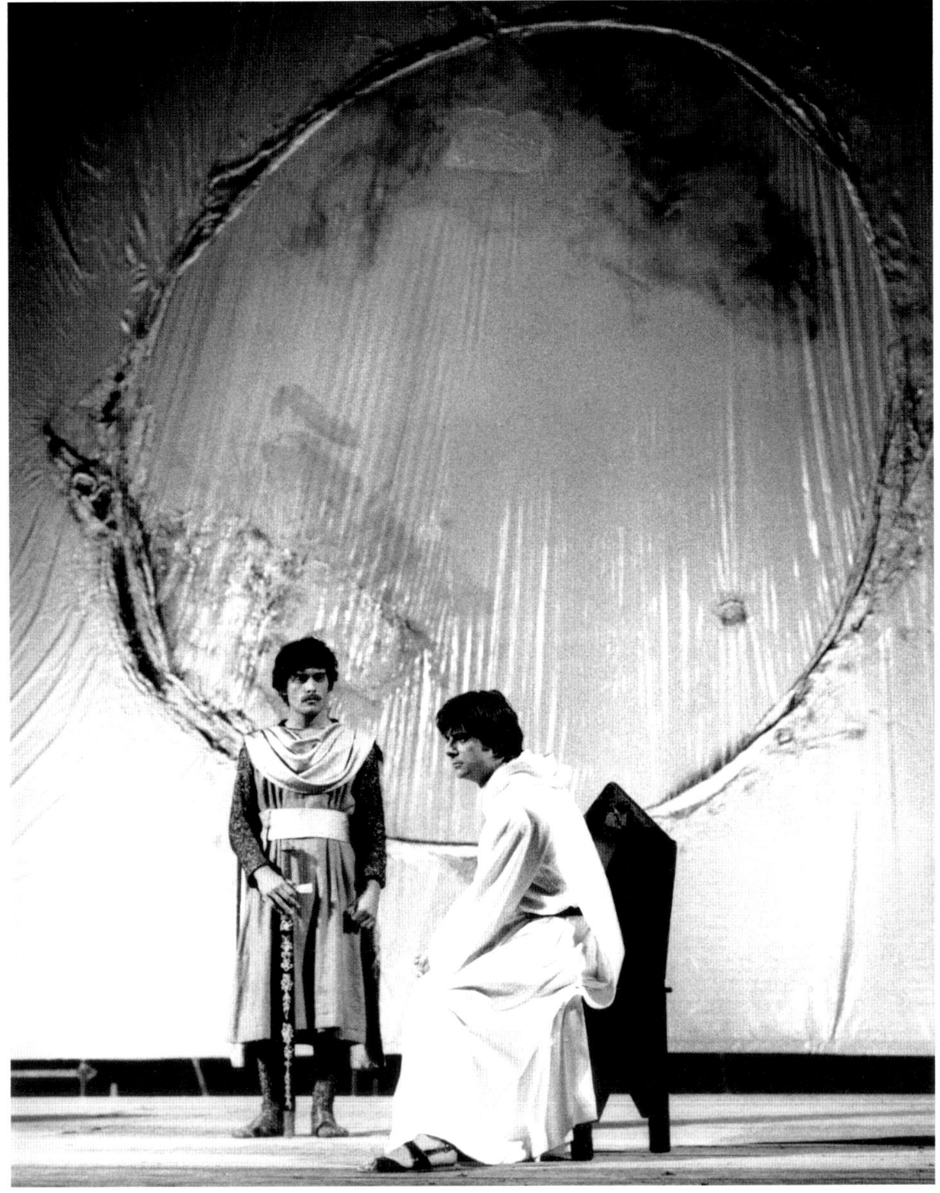

14. San Miniato al Tedesco, 3 August 1969. Set design for Ignazio Silone's play *L'Avventura d'un povero cristiano*, Act II

Italienische Malerei Heute exhibition at the Städtische Galerie im Lenbachhaus in Munich. Burri exhibits at both the IV Biennale internazionale di Scultura in Marina di Carrara and at the 8th Biennial Exhibition in São Paulo, within *Artistas Italianos de Hoje*. Werner Haftmann devotes an in-depth analysis to his oeuvre in the volume *Painting in the Twentieth Century*.

1966

Maurizio Calvesi publishes his studies on Burri in *Le due avanguardie. Dal futurismo alla Pop Art*; *Rapporto 60. Le arti oggi in Italia* by Maurizio Fagiolo dell'Arco is also published. Burri takes part in the *Aspekte 1944-65* group exhibition at the Galerie Beyeler in Basel and in *Aspetti dell'arte italiana contemporanea*, a touring exhibition curated by Palma Bucarelli. Vittorio Rubiu presents the artist's eleven *Plastiche* in the solo exhibition *Alberto Burri* displayed within the XXXIII Esposizione Biennale Internazionale d'Arte Venezia. Together with Lucio Fontana, he participates in the exhibition inaugurated at Wells College in Aurora (New York), touring in ten other US cities.

1967

He participates in the huge retrospective curated by Bernd Krimmel at the Kunsthalle of Darmstadt. There follows his participation in the *Dix ans d'art vivant 1945-1955* exhibition held at the Fondation Maeght in Saint-Paul-de-Vence. The Galleria Comunale d'Arte Contemporanea di Arezzo organizes the group exhibition *Burri, Cagli, Fontana, Guttuso, Moreni, Morlotti. Sei pittori italiani dagli anni quaranta ad oggi.* Another solo show is hosted at the Museum Boijmans Van Beuningen in Rotterdam. Burri is once again invited by the Carnegie Institute to take part in *The 1967 Pittsburgh International Exhibition of Contemporary Painting and Sculpture*. In Rome, the La Tartaruga gallery pays homage to him with a solo exhibition.

1968

1968 is another year of intense exhibition activity, opening with the individual exhibition organized by the Galleria Blu, *Opere recenti di Burri*. Other group shows follow: *Burri – Fontana – Yves Klein – Manzoni* (Galleria Notizie, Turin); *Recent Italian Painting & Sculpture* (The Jewish Museum, New York); *Malerei des zwanzigsten Jahrhunderts* (Kunstsammlung Nordrhein-Westfalen, Düsseldorf); *Collagen* (Kunstgewerbemuseum, Zurich). Burri also takes part in the XXXIV Biennale Internazionale d'Arte a Venezia and in *Cento opere d'arte italiana dal Futurismo ad oggi* at the Galleria Nazionale d'Arte Moderna in Rome. Pierre Restany publishes *Les Nouveaux Réalistes*

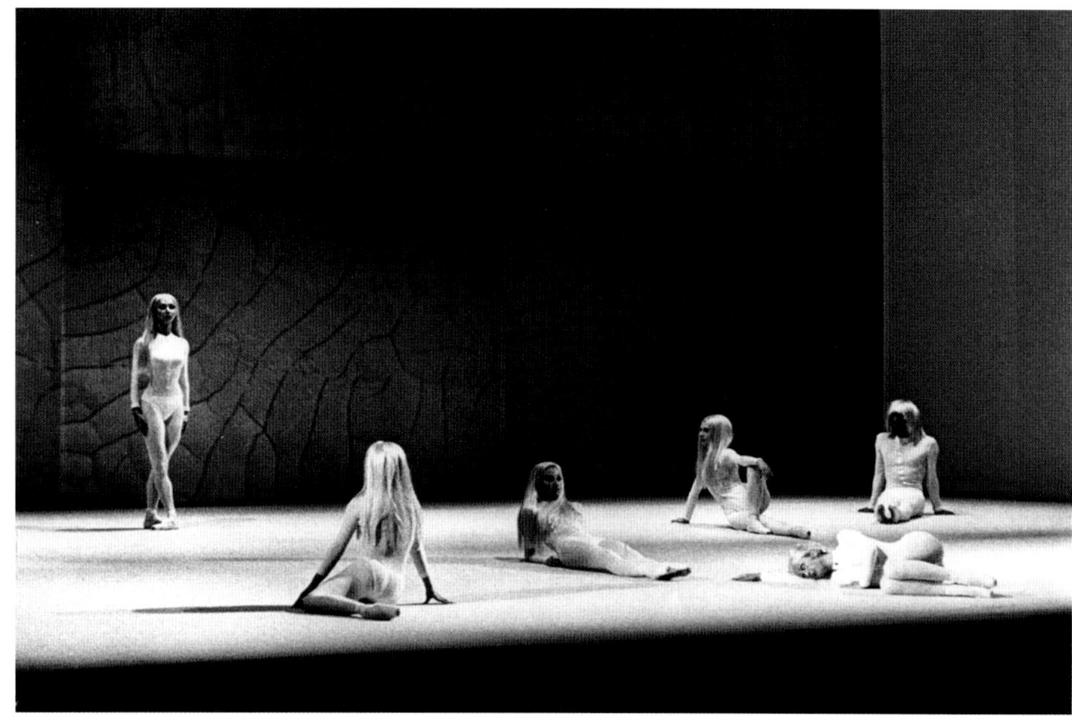

15. Rome, Teatro dell'Opera, 12 June 1973. Set design for the ballet *November Steps*

16. Casenove di Morra, ca. 1973. Alberto Burri at work

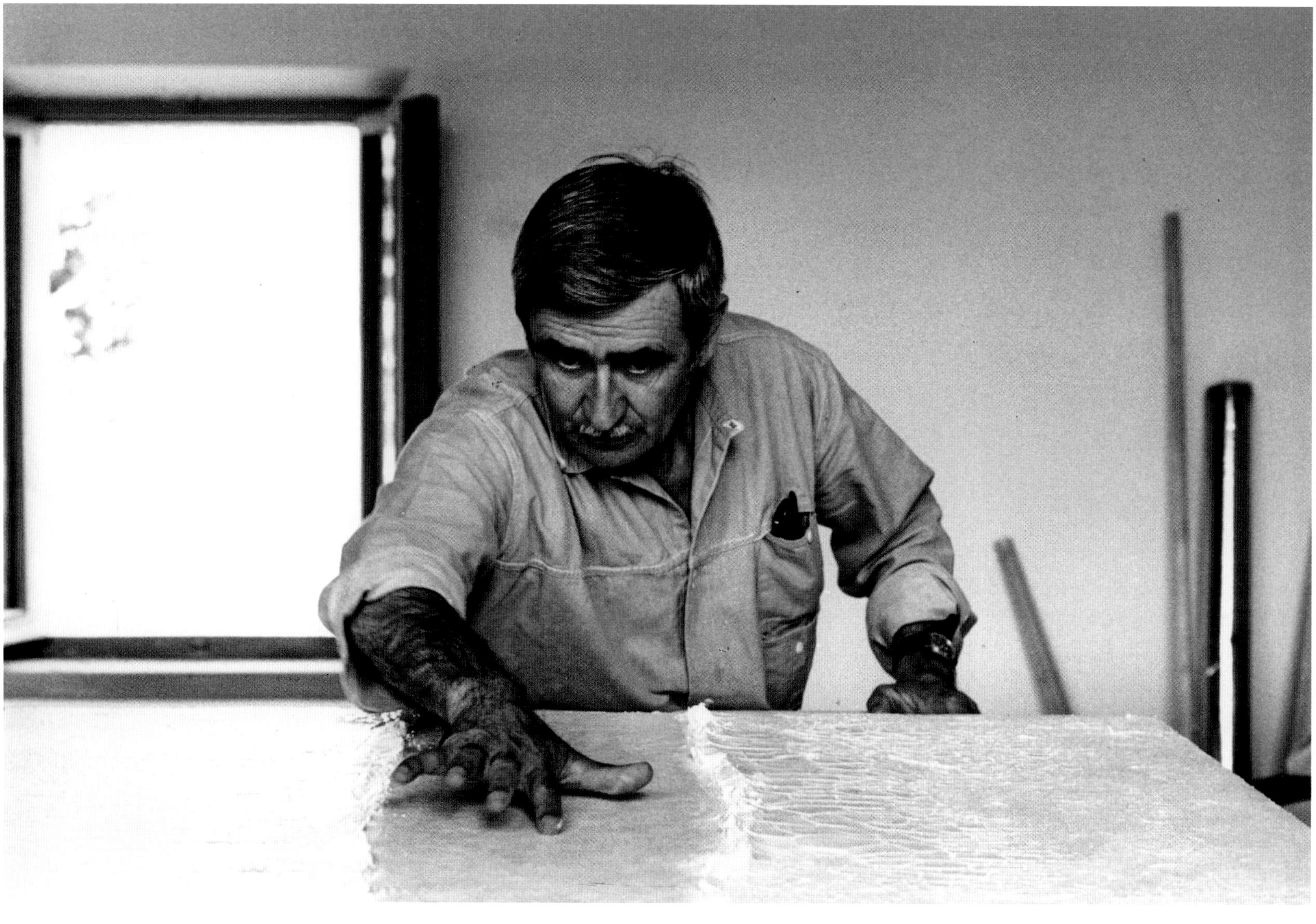

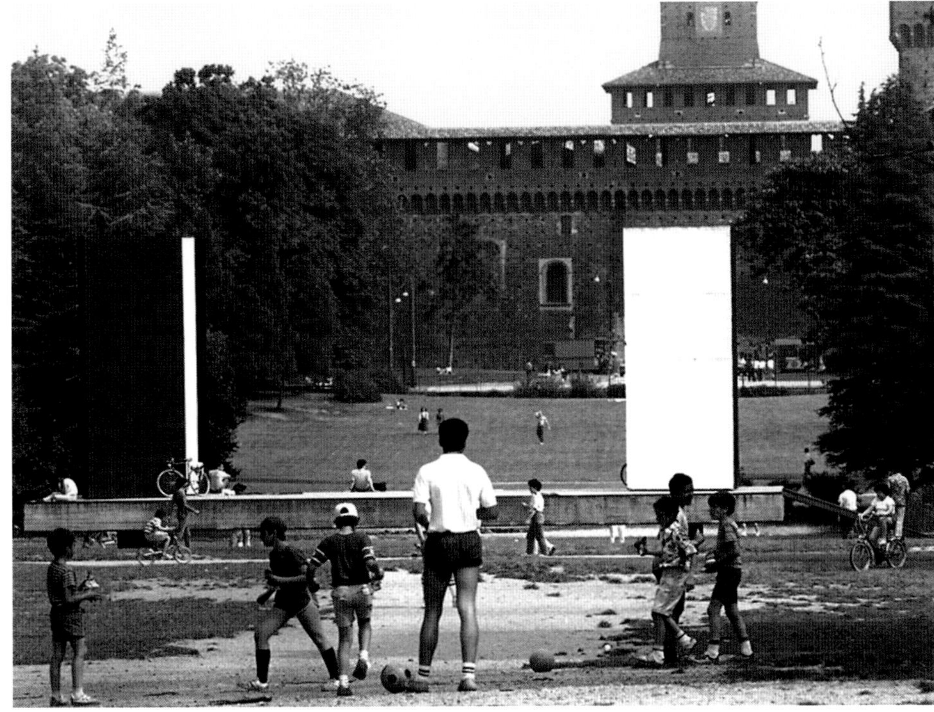

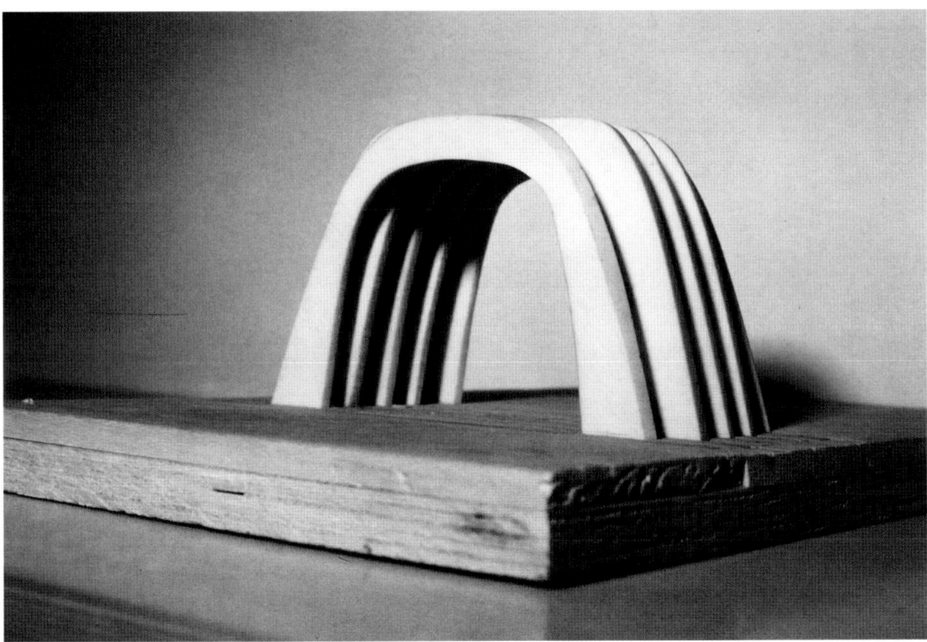

17. Milan, Parco Sempione, 1984. *Teatro Continuo*, 1973

18. *Teatro Scultura Progetto Arcevia*, [1975], model

where, considering the origins of this artistic movement, refers to the textured works of Burri, Dubuffet, Tàpies, and Fautrier.

1969

On the occasion of the XXIII Festa del Teatro in San Miniato al Tedesco, near Pisa, Burri creates the set designs for Ignazio Silone's play *L'Avventura di un povero cristiano* (fig. 14). Burri exhibits solo at the Galleria Sanluca in Bologna, introduced by Francesco Arcangeli. A new documentary on Burri is made by Franco Simongini for the Italian channel RAI.

1970

Burri participates in the Expo in Osaka, where he receives an award for contributing decisively to the success of the initiative with his work. The artist is also included in a group exhibition curated by Giorgio De Marchis and Sandra Pinto and held in Prato, *Due decenni di eventi artistici in Italia: 1950-1970*, and three of his *Plastiche* are displayed at *1970 Pittsburgh International. Exhibition of Contemporary Art*.

1971

Maurizio Calvesi's monograph on Burri is published by Fratelli Fabbri. The group exhibition entitled *Italienische Kunst heute* is held in Vienna, at the Akademie der Bildenden Künste, where a work of his is displayed. He takes part in the touring exhibition *Italian Painting from 1940 to 1960* that is inaugurated at the Western Australian Art Gallery in Perth, subsequently presented in Adelaide, Hobart, Melbourne, Newcastle, Sidney, and Queensland. Two other works are displayed at the Walker Art Gallery in Liverpool on the occasion of the exhibition *New Italian Art 1953–71*. The year closes with the major retrospective curated by Aldo Passoni at the Galleria Civica d'Arte Moderna in Turin.

1972
Burri partakes in Italian and US group exhibitions, and in *Alcoa Collection of Contemporary Art*, inaugurated in Dublin, which travels to fourteen cities in two years. The Musée National d'Art Moderne in Paris devotes an extensive retrospective to him. He exhibits in Rome on the occasion of the X Quadriennale Nazionale d'Arte complemented by a contribution in the catalog by Nello Ponente.

1973
The ballet *November Steps* (fig. 15) is staged at the Teatro dell'Opera in Rome, with music by Tōru Takemitsu, choreographies by Minsa Craig, and scenography by Burri (from a 1972 model). The artist works on his *Cretti* (fig. 16), realized with a mixture of kaolin and polyvinyl acetates; these new works are displayed in an individual exhibition held at the end of the year at the Galleria Sanluca in Bologna. Another solo exhibition is organized in Turin by the Galleria Notizie. On the occasion of the XV Triennale di Milano, within "Contatto arte-città," Burri designs *Teatro Continuo,* an architectural structure—demolished in 1989 and reconstructed in 2015—composed of six rotating screens the vertical axes of which are fixed to a cement base, in turn installed on the ideal axis that crosses Parco Sempione, between the Arco della Pace (arch of peace) and the Castello Sforzesco (fig. 17). On 15 December Burri is honored by the Accademia Nazionale dei Lincei with the Premio Feltrinelli per la Grafica Prize and donates the entire sum for the restoration of Luca Signorelli's frescos decorating the Oratory of San Crescentino at Morra, on the outskirts of Città di Castello.

1974
After exhibiting solo at the Galerie Jacques Benador in Geneva, Burri partakes in *Picasso to Lichtenstein* (Tate Gallery, London); *La ricerca dell'identità* (Palazzo Reale, Milan), and

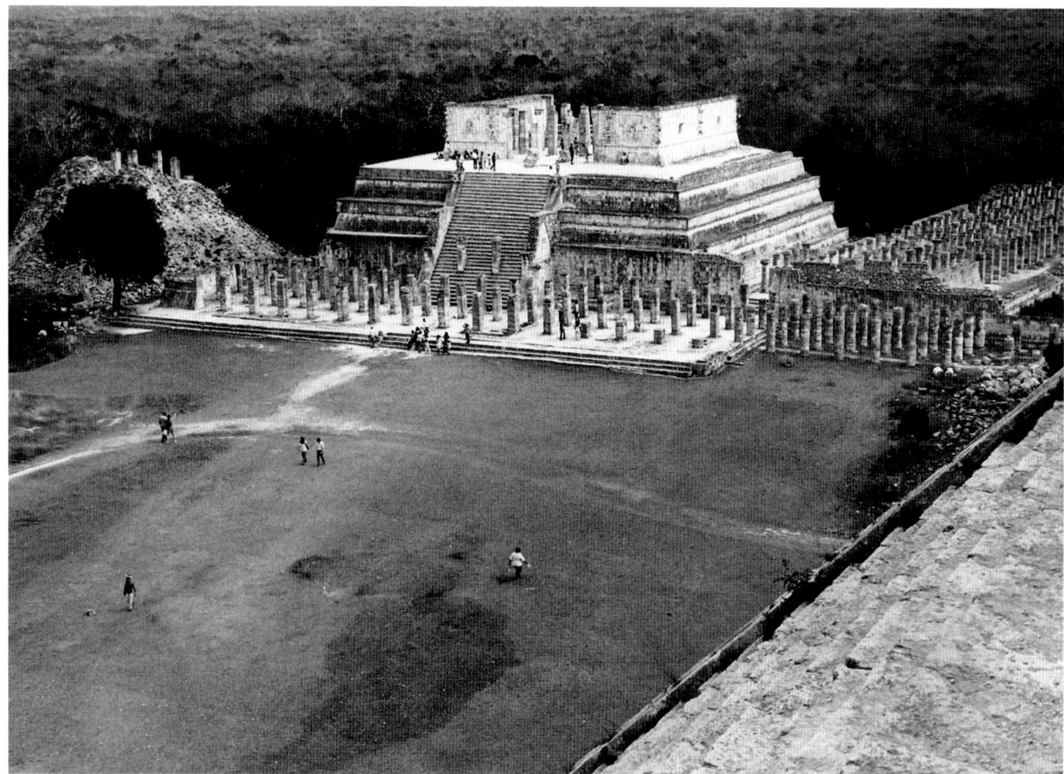

19. Mexico, Yucatán, Chichén Itzá, Templo de los Guerreros. Photograph taken by Alberto Burri, 1975

20. New York, Solomon R. Guggenheim Museum, 1978. Nemo Sarteanesi and Alberto Burri

21. *Grande Cretto Nero Los Angeles*, [1977]. Los Angeles, University of California, Franklin D. Murphy Sculpture Garden

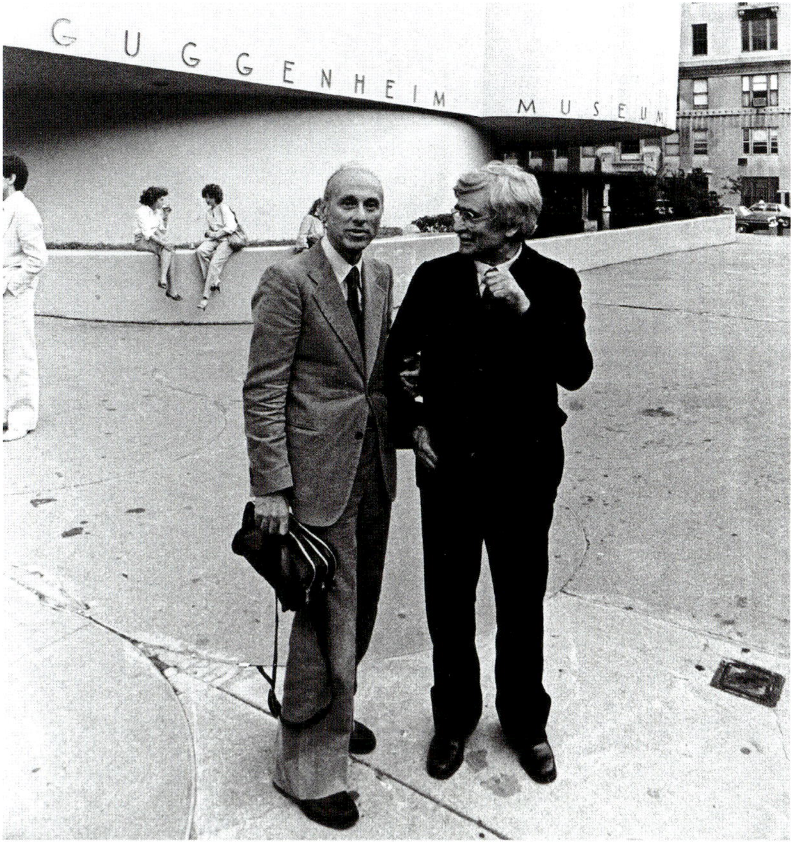

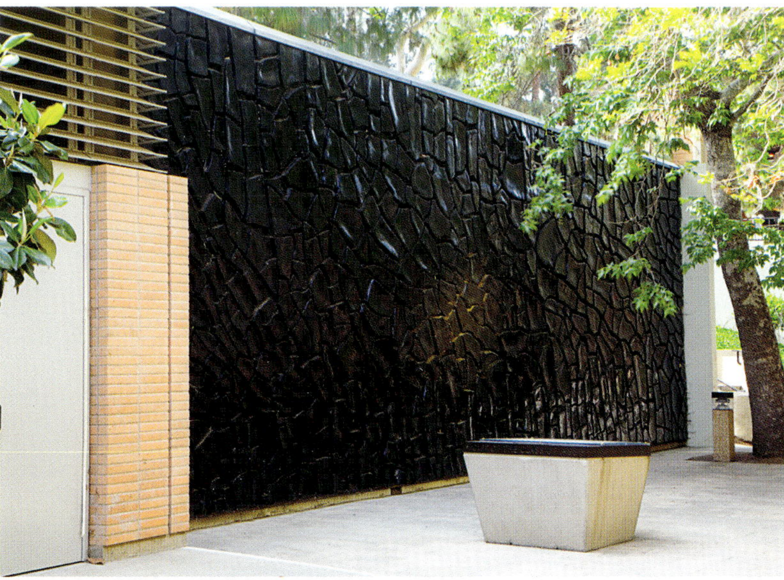

Ghenos, Eros, Thanatos (Galleria de' Foscherari, Bologna) where his work is displayed alongside several artists including Kounellis, De Dominicis, Pascali, Mattiacci, and Zorio.

1975

Burri initiates his first *Cellotex* pictures, created with a wooden compound pressed industrially into panels. He again devotes his energies to activities in the theatrical sphere, producing the curtain and set designs for the three acts of Richard Wagner's *Tristan und Isolde*, which, conducted by Peter Maag and directed by Maria Francesca Siciliani, is scheduled for the start of the following year at the Teatro Regio in Turin; invited to participate in the Operazione Arcevia - Comunità Esistenziale project, from an idea by architect Ico Parisi (alongside Enrico Crispolti and Pierre Restany), he creates the wooden model *Teatro Scultura Progetto Arcevia* (fig. 18) devised to be realized in the open air in the Pre-Apennine hinterland of the Province of Ancona. Cesare Brandi presents Burri in the solo exhibition held in the Sacro Convento di San Francesco in Assisi, where he exhibits ten imposing works. Vittorio Rubiu's monograph is published by Einaudi; this is also the year of his trip to Mexico (fig. 19) and Guatemala.

1976

The Galleria Nazionale d'Arte Moderna in Rome inaugurates the solo show *Alberto Burri*, curated by Bruno Mantura and Giovanna De Feo. At the Palazzo Ducale in Pesaro, Maurizio Calvesi presents *Burri Disegni, tempere e grafiche 1948-1976.* With a *Sacco* from 1956, he participates in the group exhibition *Prospect Retrospect - Europa 1946-1976* at the Städtische Kunsthalle in Düsseldorf. *Scritti sull'arte contemporanea* (vol. I) by Cesare Brandi is published by Einaudi.

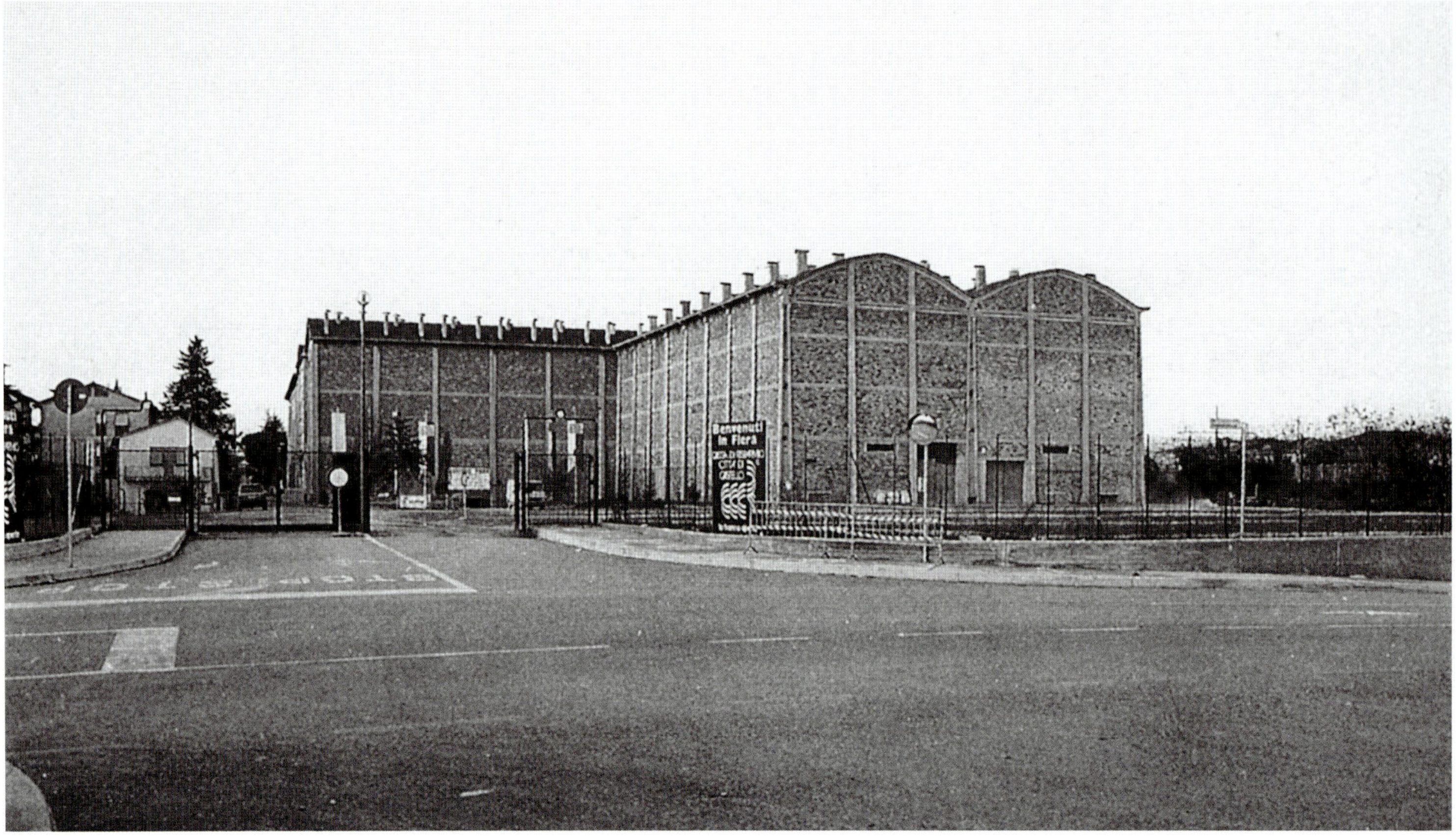

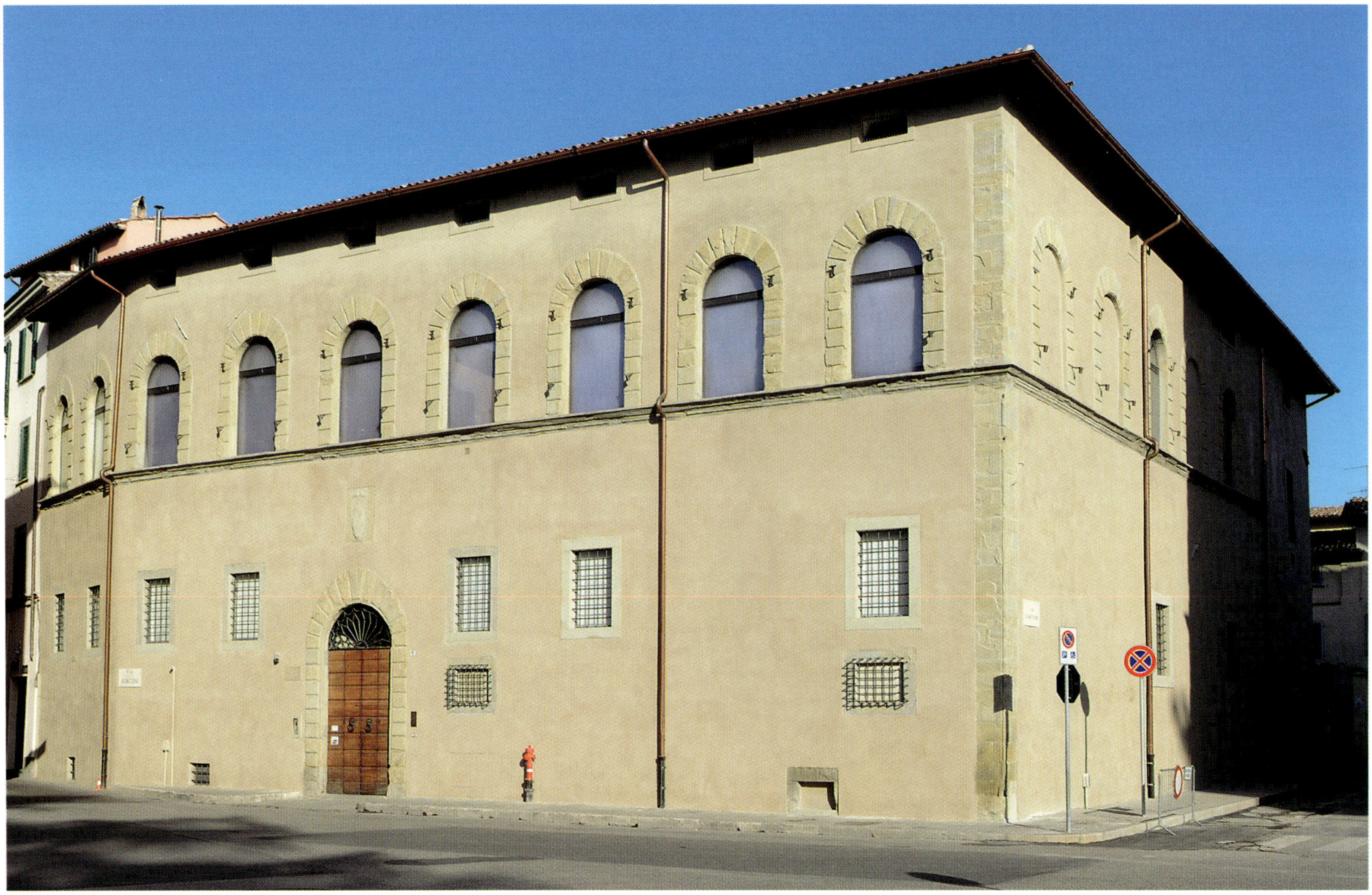

22. Città di Castello, Fattoria Autonoma Tabacchi, exterior of the tobacco drying barns

23. Città di Castello, Palazzo Albizzini, 2015

24. *Grande Cretto Nero Capodimonte*, [1978]. Naples, Museo e Real Bosco di Capodimonte

1977

On 5 February, in Milan, Burri gains special recognition as the "Italian artist of great international renown" at the XIV edizione artistica del Premio Europeo Umberto Biancamano 1975. After the retrospective at the Calouste Gulbenkian Foundation in Lisbon, the Galleria Sanluca in Bologna presents some of his Cellotex pictures to the public. At the Galleria 2RC, first in Milan and then in Rome, Maurizio Calvesi presents *Alberto Burri Opere Grafiche 1973-1977*. The city of Madrid, at Palacio de Velázquez, also devotes an extensive retrospective to him. The most salient event of the year is *Alberto Burri. A Retrospective View 1948–77*, curated by Gerald Nordland, inaugurated in late September at the Frederick S. Wight Art Gallery at the University of the California Los Angeles, which moves to San Antonio and Milwaukee the following year, closing in New York at the Solomon R. Guggenheim Museum (fig. 20). On this occasion, the *Grande Cretto Nero Los Angeles* (fig. 21) is installed in the Franklin D. Murphy Sculpture Garden at the same university. The artist donates this monumental sculpture—measuring 5 meters high by 15 in length and made entirely of ceramics—that becomes part of the permanent collection. The major US retrospective confirms Burri's worldwide success. At the end of the year his graphic works are presented by Richard Kubiak, in Santa Barbara, and three years later they will arrive at the Istituto Italiano di Cultura in New York.

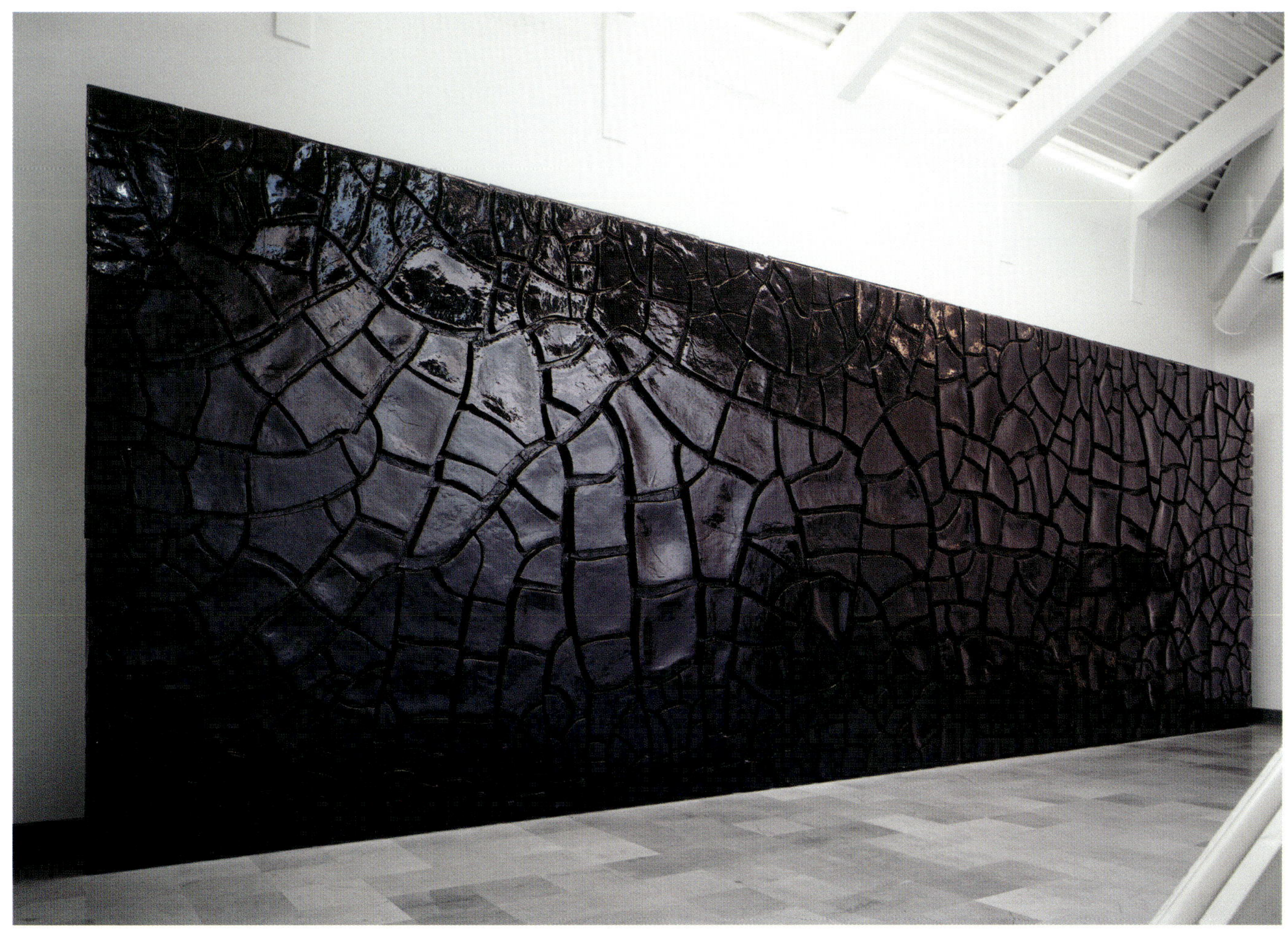

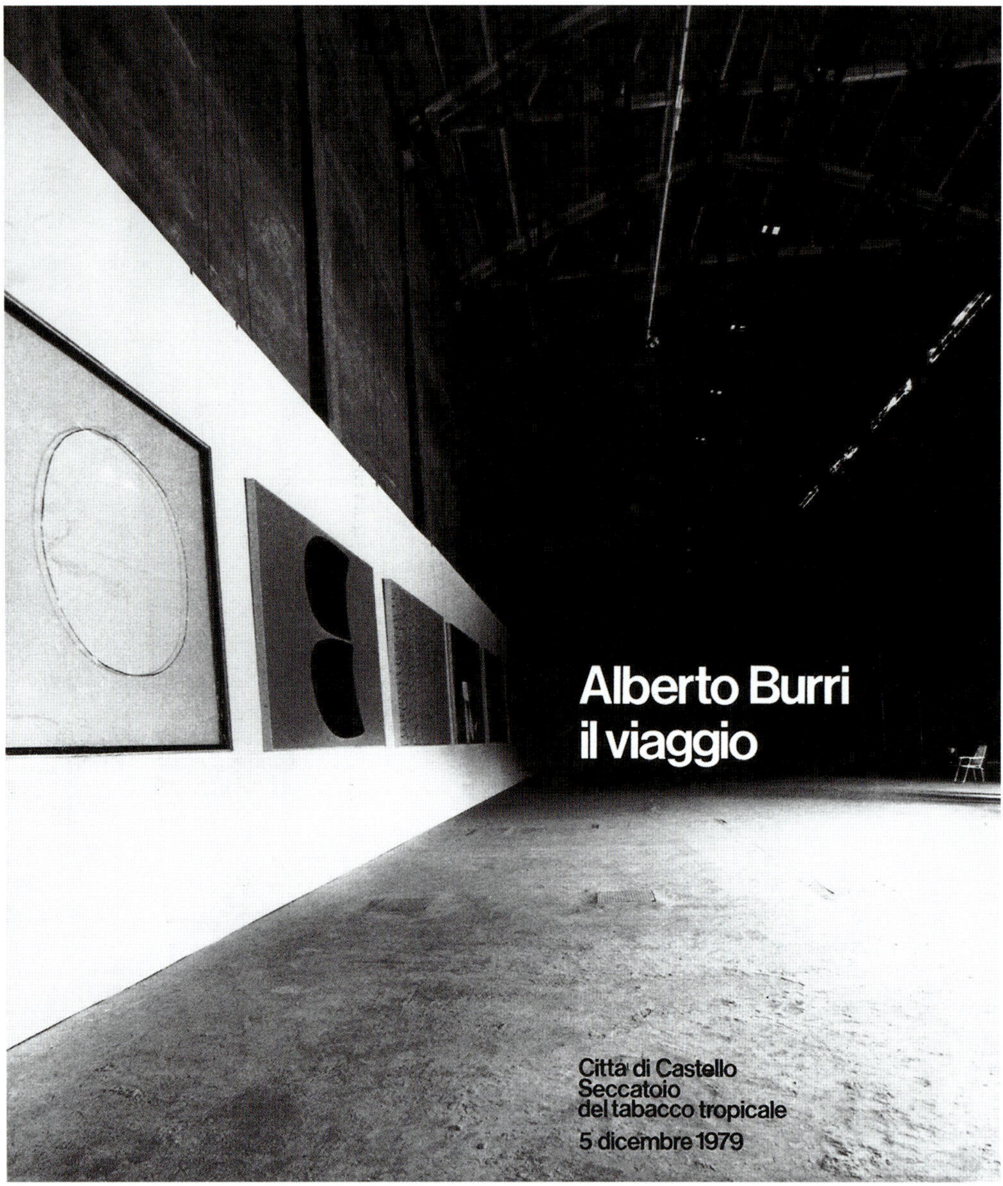

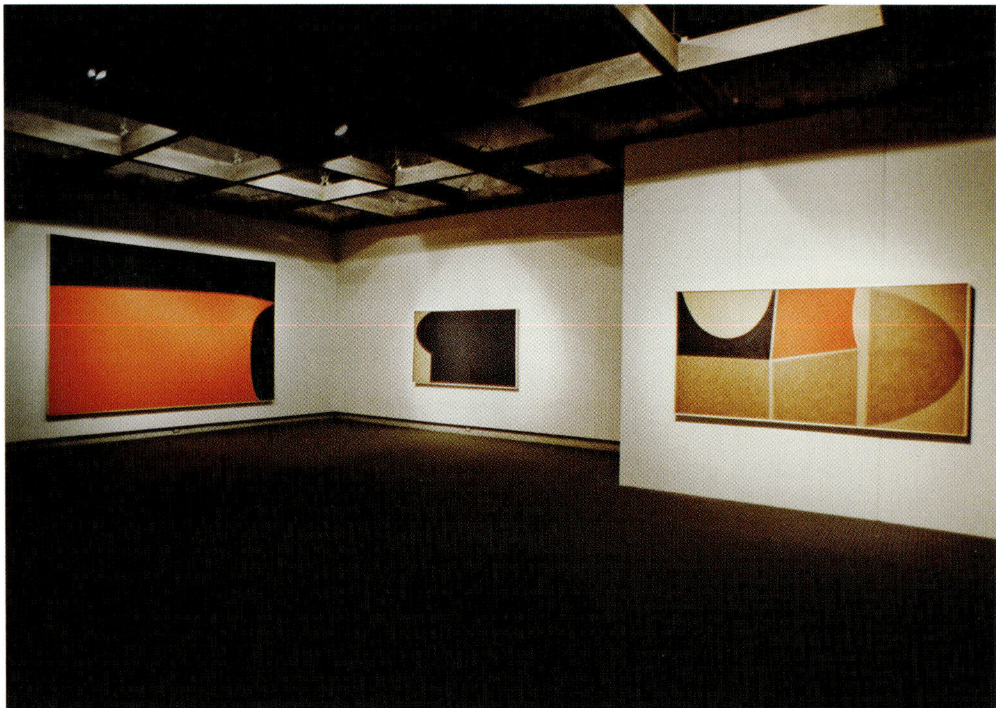

25. *Alberto Burri, il viaggio*, Seccatoio del tabacco tropicale, Città di Castello, 1979. Leaflet of the exhibition

26. Palm Springs, Palm Springs Desert Museum, 1982. View of Alberto Burri's solo exhibition

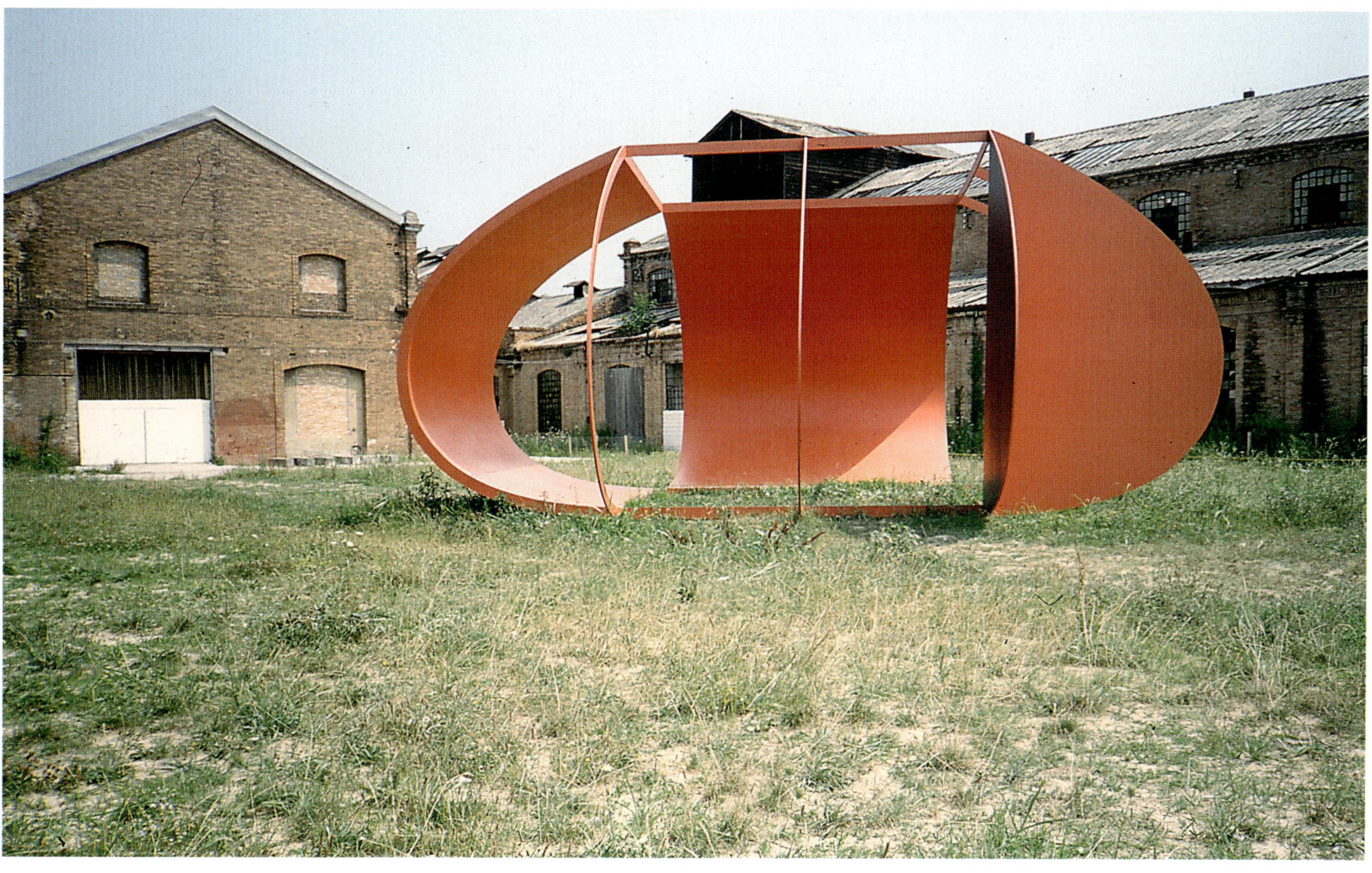

27. Venice, ex Cantieri Navali in the Giudecca district, 1983. *Grande Ferro Sestante*, [1982]

1978

From the Fattoria Autonoma Tabacchi he obtains the license for free use, as a studio, of one of the thirteen barns of the industrial complex for drying tropical tobacco (fig. 22), then disused, built in Città di Castello between the end of the 1950s and the mid-1960s. On 27 February, following the artist's wishes, the Fondazione Palazzo Albizzini Collezione Burri is established in Città di Castello in the Renaissance building belonging to the Albizzini family (fig. 23). In this year Burri exhibits solo in Naples at the Museo di Capodimonte, where, for the first time, his works are displayed within a museum's itinerary of ancient art. For this exhibition, curated by Raffaello Causa and with Giulio Carlo Argan's contribution in the catalog, Burri creates a sculpture, *Grande Cretto Nero Capodimonte* [1978] (fig. 24), similar to the one donated to the University of California, using the same material and of the same dimensions, but this time left to the Naples museum, where it is still housed today. He participates in the Biennale di Venezia.

1979

The Studio Marconi in Milan pays homage to him with *Alberto Burri: Cellotex, Cretti, una scultura, 1978-1979*, a solo show curated by Flavio Caroli and Giorgio Marconi. On the occasion of the exhibition, Caroli's studies are published in the monograph *Burri. La forma e l'informe*. Another solo exhibition is inaugurated at the James Corcoran Gallery in Los Angeles. Burri also partakes in *Italy and Japan. Art in the Last Ten Decades*, an exhibition held in Japan at The National Museum of Art in Osaka. In Città di Castello, the "shed-studio" is opened to critics and the public for the presentation of *il Viaggio* (fig. 25), a cycle of ten interconnected large works devised and created in that location. Conceived for the Staatsgalerie moderner Kunst in Munich, where it will be on display the following year, in Città di Castello the corpus is accompanied by a text by Nemo Sarteanesi, who also contributes to the German catalog, together with Erich Steingräber. The ten paintings inaugurate the season of painting cycles to which the artist will devote himself primarily starting from the late 1970s. This year the restoration work begins on Palazzo Albizzini, which is in a seriously deteriorated state, conducted by architect Alberto Zanmatti with the assistance of Tiziano Sarteanesi, both under the guidance of Burri and Nemo Sarteanesi; the restoration is promoted by Cassa di Risparmio di Città di Castello bank, which owns the building and licenses it for free use to the Fondazione Burri.

1980

On 3 April a meeting is organized between Joseph Beuys and Burri in the Sala della Cannoniera at the Rocca Paolina in Perugia, which inaugurates the exhibition *Beuys/Burri*, conceived and curated by Italo Tomassoni; the sculpture *Grande Ferro*, presented by Burri on that occasion, is now part of the Fondazione Burri permanent collection, in Palazzo Albizzini. On 1st July the National Geographic Society enrolls Burri among its members in recognition of his support in the diffusion of geographical knowledge and the promotion of research and exploration. In September he takes part in the group exhibition held in Florence, curated by Lara Vinca Masini, entitled *Umanesimo, Disumanesimo nell'arte europea 1890-1980*. Burri exhibits solo in Florence also in November, in the spaces of Orsanmichele, within *Alberto Burri Orsanmichele*, curated by Vanni Bramanti; the works on display are nine large Cellotex pictures (now at the Ex Seccatoi del Tabacco, as part of the permanent collection of the Fondazione Burri) and an iron sculpture (donated by the artist to the city of Perugia, now in the Rocca Paolina) characterized by a rotating element on top operated by an adjustable-speed electric motor. Burri is again present in Japan on the occasion of the *Aspetti della scenografia italiana oggi* touring exhibition. In Paris, on 12 December, the President of the French

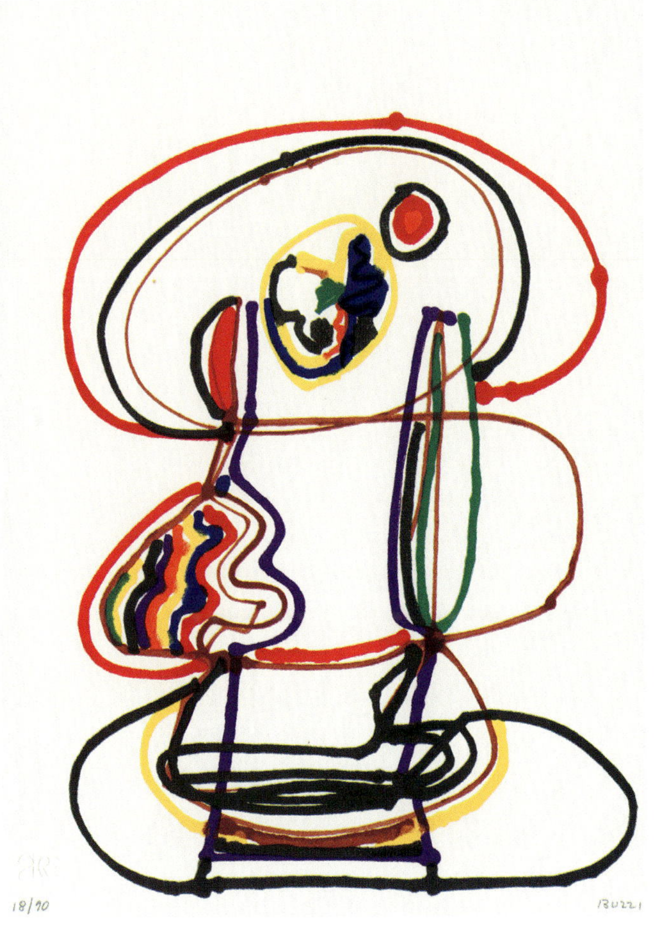

28. *Saffo* (1973–82), lithograph 2 from the series of 10 lithographs included in the book *Saffo* (poems translated poetically by Emilio Villa), Stamperia 2RC, Rome

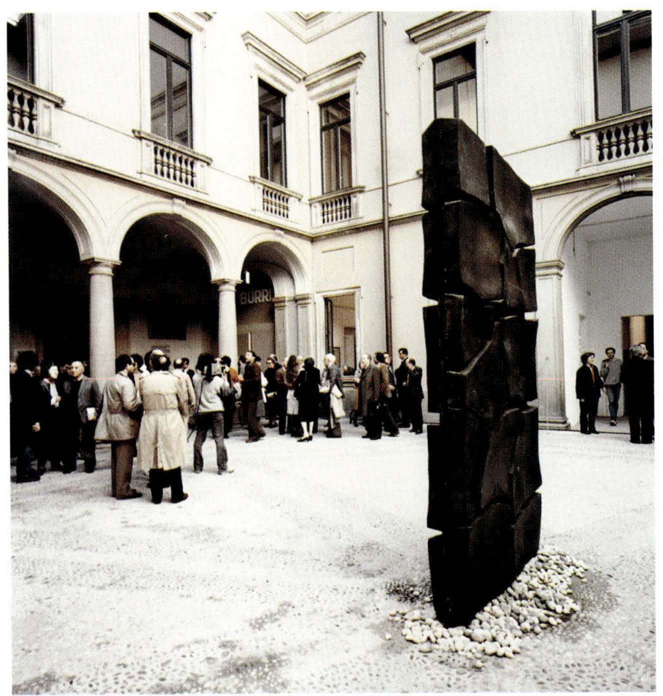

29. Milan, Palazzo Citterio, inauguration of Alberto Burri's solo exhibition, 1984. *Scultura*, [1978]

Republic—as Grand Maître of the Ordre National du Mérite—nominates Alberto Burri to be a Commandeur within the order.

1981

Burri participates in the following group exhibitions: *Linee della ricerca artistica in Italia 1960-1980* (Palazzo delle Esposizioni, Rome); *Paris-Paris, créations en France, 1937-1957* (Centre Georges Pompidou, Paris) curated by Daniel Abadie; *Westkunst. Zeitgenössische Kunst seit 1939* (Museen der Stadt, Cologne). Another exhibition, curated by Cesare Brandi and held at the Palazzo Pubblico in Siena, inaugurates in 1981 with the title *Burri opere grafiche 1959-81.* Solo exhibitions take place at the L'Isola gallery in Rome (*Alberto Burri 1 Scultura 10 Multiplex*) and at the Teatro Rossini in Pesaro (*Alberto Burri. Teatri e scenografie*), presented by Emilio Villa. Burri exhibits also in Düsseldorf within *Schwarz* at the Städtische Kunsthalle and in São Paulo in the 16th Biennial Exhibition.

In Città di Castello his long-standing desire is realized to donate an extensive and carefully chosen selection of his works to his native city and, on 12 December, the anthological collection permanently housed in the historic Palazzo Albizzini is publicly inaugurated. A few days later the solo show *Alberto Burri, Cellotex und Multiplex* is also inaugurated at the Galerie im Taxispalais in Innsbruck, curated by Dieter Ronte, later moving to Salzburg, Vienna, and Klagenfurt.

1982

In California, in Palm Springs, in the exhibition spaces of the Palm Springs Desert Museum (fig. 26), Katherine Plake presents the solo exhibition *Alberto Burri*. The painting cycle *il Viaggio* is displayed in the USA at the Columbus Museum of Art in Ohio, at the Brooklyn Museum in New York and at the San Francisco Museum of Modern Art in California. Burri exhibits solo also in Bologna (Galleria Sanluca) and in Brescia (Galleria d'arte contemporanea La Nuova Città). In Città di Castello, he is honored by the Fattoria Autonoma Tabacchi with the Premio Stelio Pierangeli "for the international prestige given in the field of Art also to the Alta Valle del Tevere." He exhibits in Kassel on the occasion of documenta 7. He is invited to participate in the Japanese touring exhibition *Cento anni d'arte italiana moderna 1880-1980*.

1983

Giulio Carlo Argan presents Burri's cycle *Sestante* at the former shipyards (ex Cantieri Navali) in the Giudecca district (fig. 27). The exhibition features seventeen large Cellotex pictures, with an amazing explosion of colors and an imposing painted steel sculpture installed outside the building. He takes part in a group exhibition curated by Renato Barilli and Franco Solmi, *L'Informale in Italia*, at the Galleria d'Arte Moderna in Bologna. In Rome, and subsequently in Milan, the Galleria 2RC hosts *Alberto Burri. Opere recenti e presentazione del libro "Saffo" Alberto Burri – Emilio Villa* (fig. 28). The artist takes part in the group exhibition *Art contre/against Apartheid* at the Fondation Nationale des Arts Graphiques et Plastiques in Paris; the Special Committee of the United Nations against Apartheid "expresses its great appreciation to Alberto Burri for his precious contribution as an artist to the international campaign for the elimination of apartheid and for the creation of a non-racial democratic society in South Africa."

1984

The monograph by Simonetta Lux *Alberto Burri dalla pittura alla pittura (1983-1944)* is published. *Alberto Burri, Cretti e Cellotex* is inaugurated at the Galerie Sapone in Nice, and complemented by a contribution in the catalog by Daniel Abadie; another show, entitled *Alberto Burri Rosso e Nero* inaugurates at the Galerie des Ponchettes. The sequence of fourteen works,

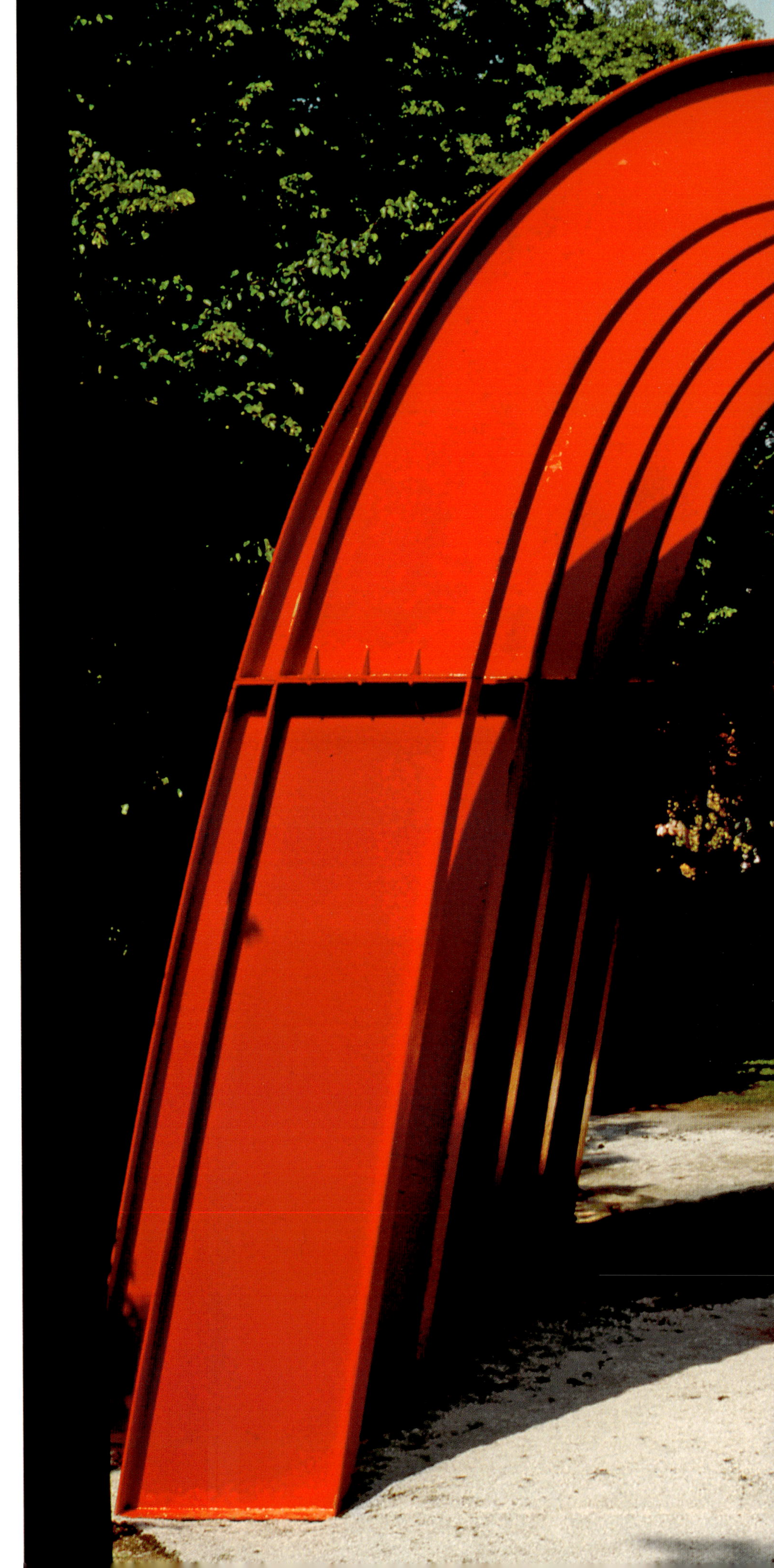

30. Venice, Giardini di Castello, June 1984. Alberto Burri and his *Teatro Scultura*, [1984]

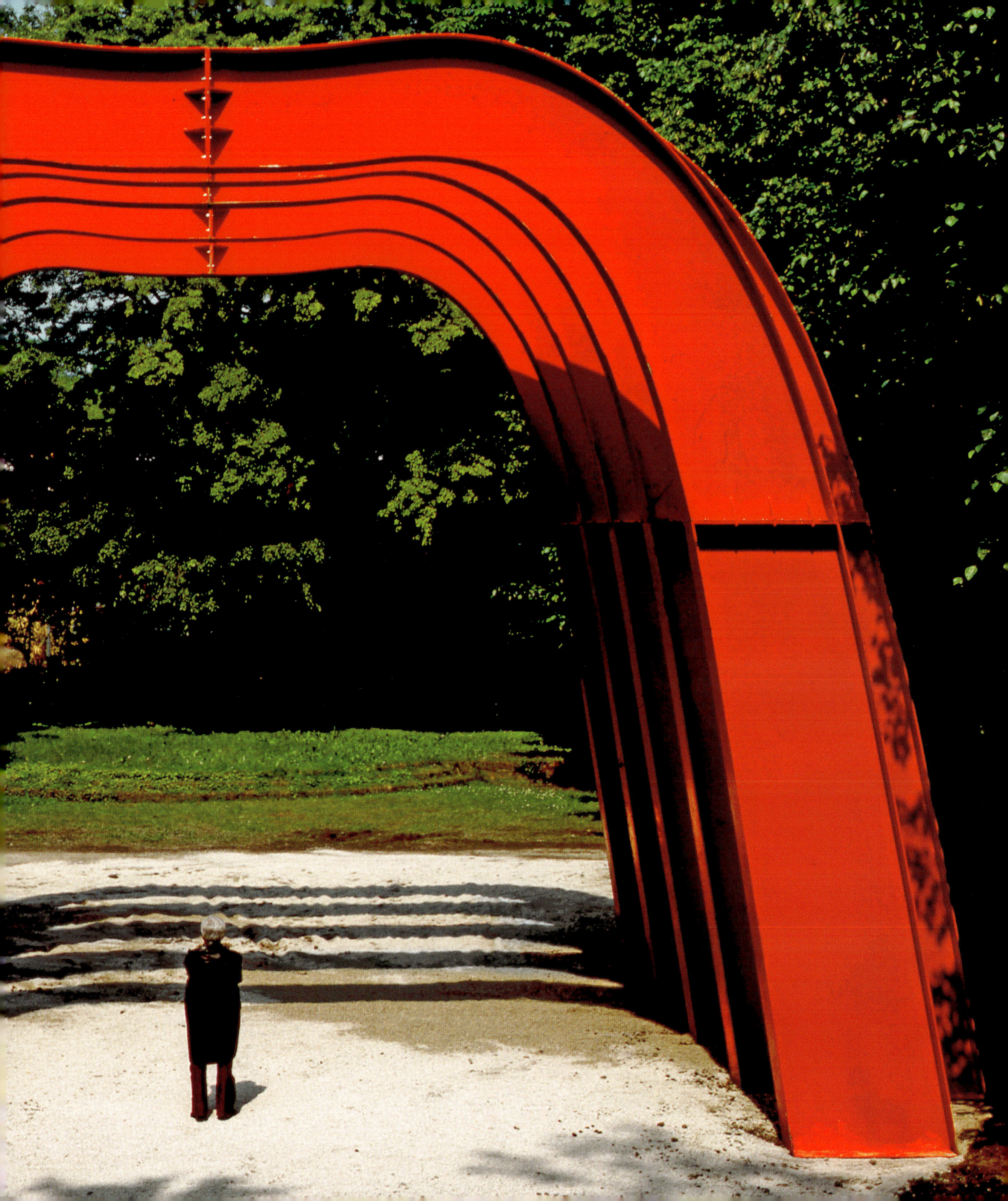

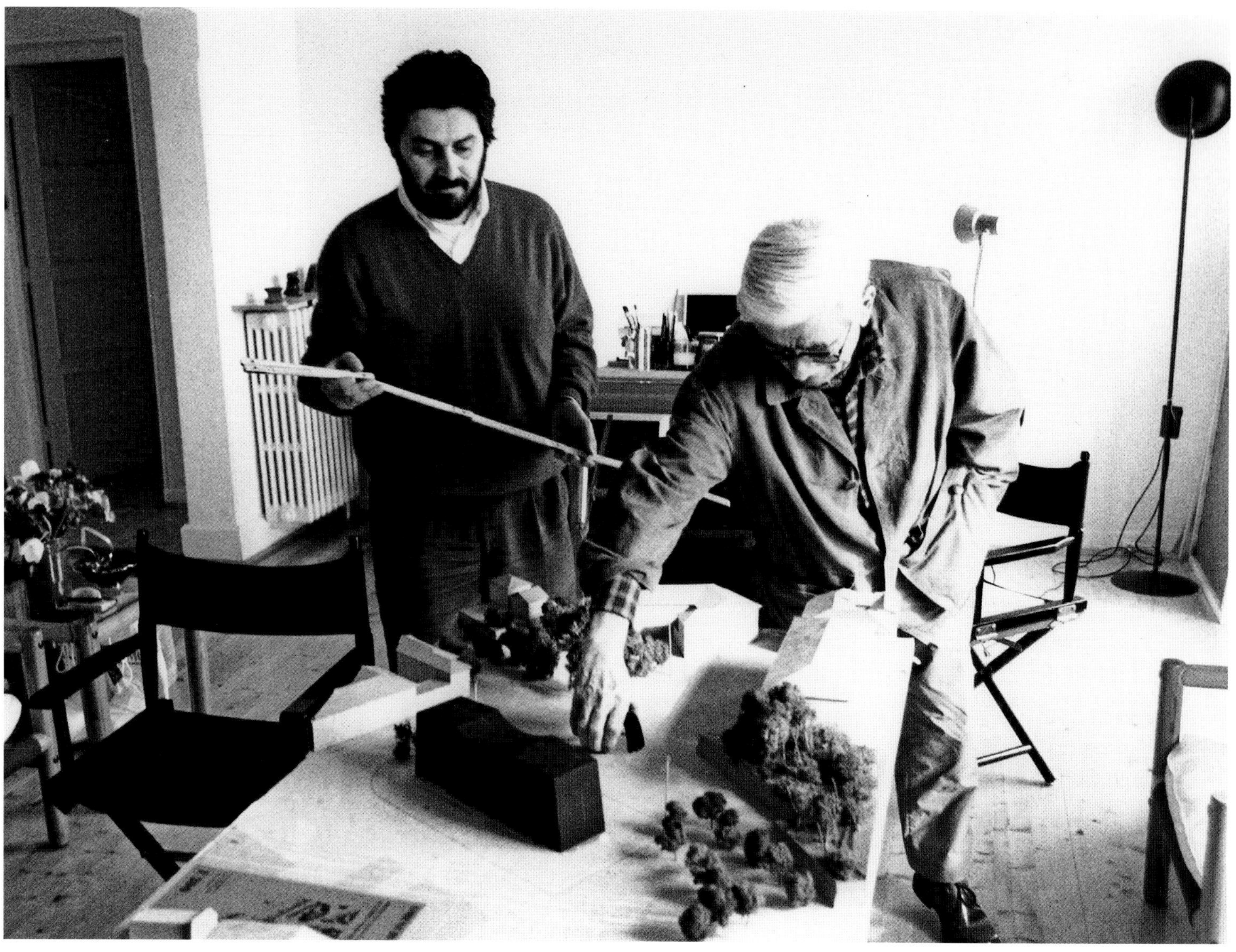

specially created for this venue, is subsequently presented in Toulon. The Pinacoteca di Brera in Milan inaugurates its Palazzo Citterio venue with *Alberto Burri*, one of the vastest retrospectives on Burri's oeuvre, curated by Carlo Pirovano, Carlo Bertelli, and Valentina Maderna (fig. 29). Two works from the 1950s are included in the XLI Esposizione Internazionale d'Arte. La Biennale di Venezia while *Teatro Scultura* (fig. 30), an imposing iron structure painted cadmium red, is installed in the Giardini di Castello; following the maestro's wishes, the work, repainted black, is intended to be permanently placed in the future square redesigned by him in the location of the current Piazza Garibaldi in Città di Castello (fig. 31). He participates with a *Sacco* (1953) in *Ouverture. Arte contemporanea* exhibition, curated by Rudi Fuchs, at the Castello di Rivoli.

At the end of the year *Burri Grafica - piccoli dipinti is* hosted by the Galleria delle Arti of Luigi Amadei in Città di Castello.

1985

Burri exhibits solo within *Alberto Burri Opere recenti* in Bologna, at the Galleria Sanluca; in Toronto three Cellotex pictures are included in the group exhibition *The European Iceberg. Creativity in Germany and Italy Today*, curated by Germano Celant, in the Art Gallery of Ontario. The Kunstverein in Frankfurt presents *Italienische Kunst 1900-1980*, curated by Peter Weiermair. The Galerie Artcurial in Paris pays homage to him with a solo exhibition presented by Jean Leymarie, *Burri, Combustioni, Cretti, Cellotex 1964-1984*. This is the year when the creation begins of the *Grande Cretto Gibellina*

31. Beaulieu-sur-Mer, the artist's dwelling, ca. 1993. Architect Tiziano Sarteanesi and Alberto Burri working on the Piazza Burri project model

32. Gibellina, Trapani, 1985. Start of works for *Grande Cretto Gibellina*

33. Gibellina, Trapani, 1985–2015. *Grande Cretto Gibellina*. Aerial view

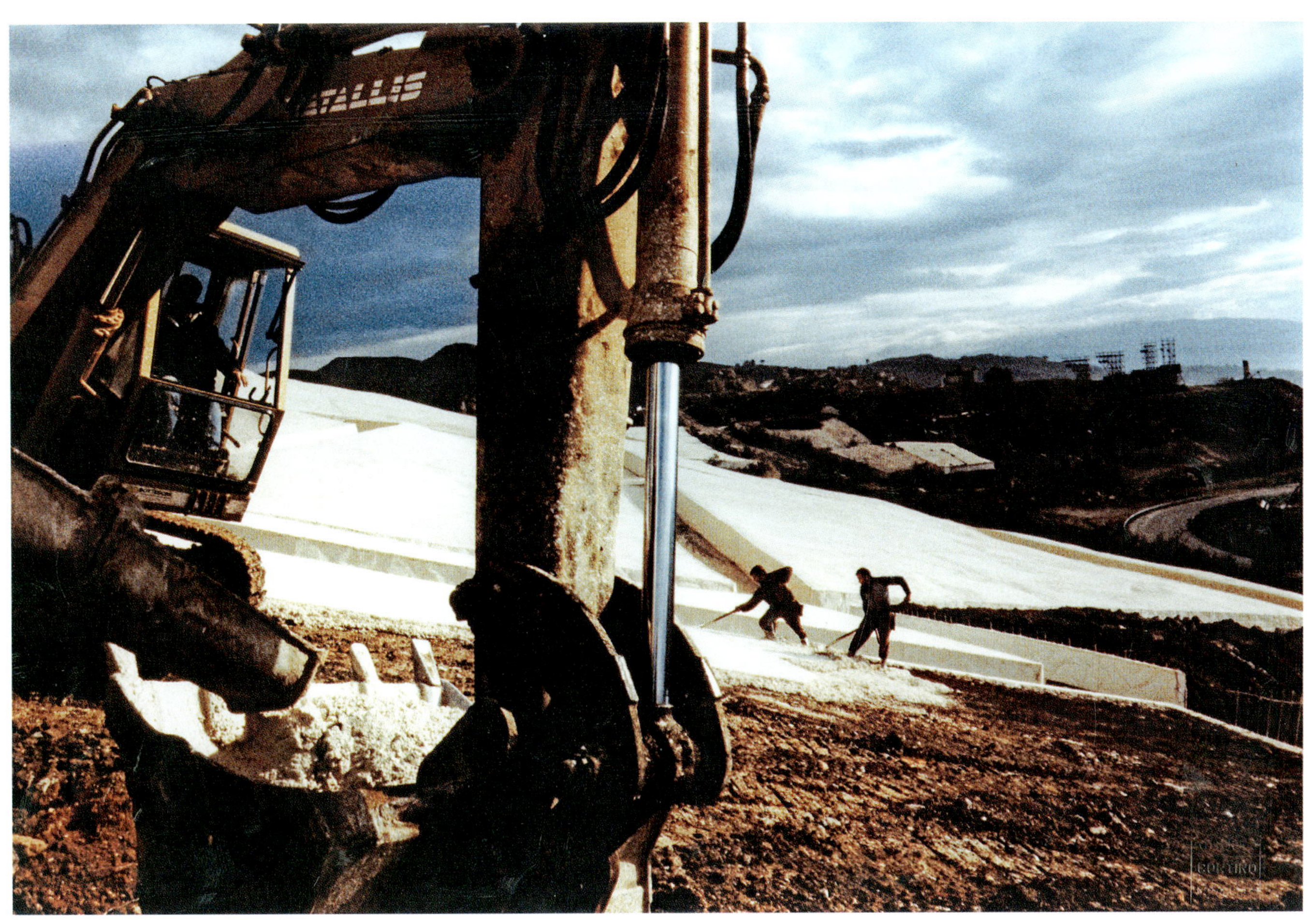

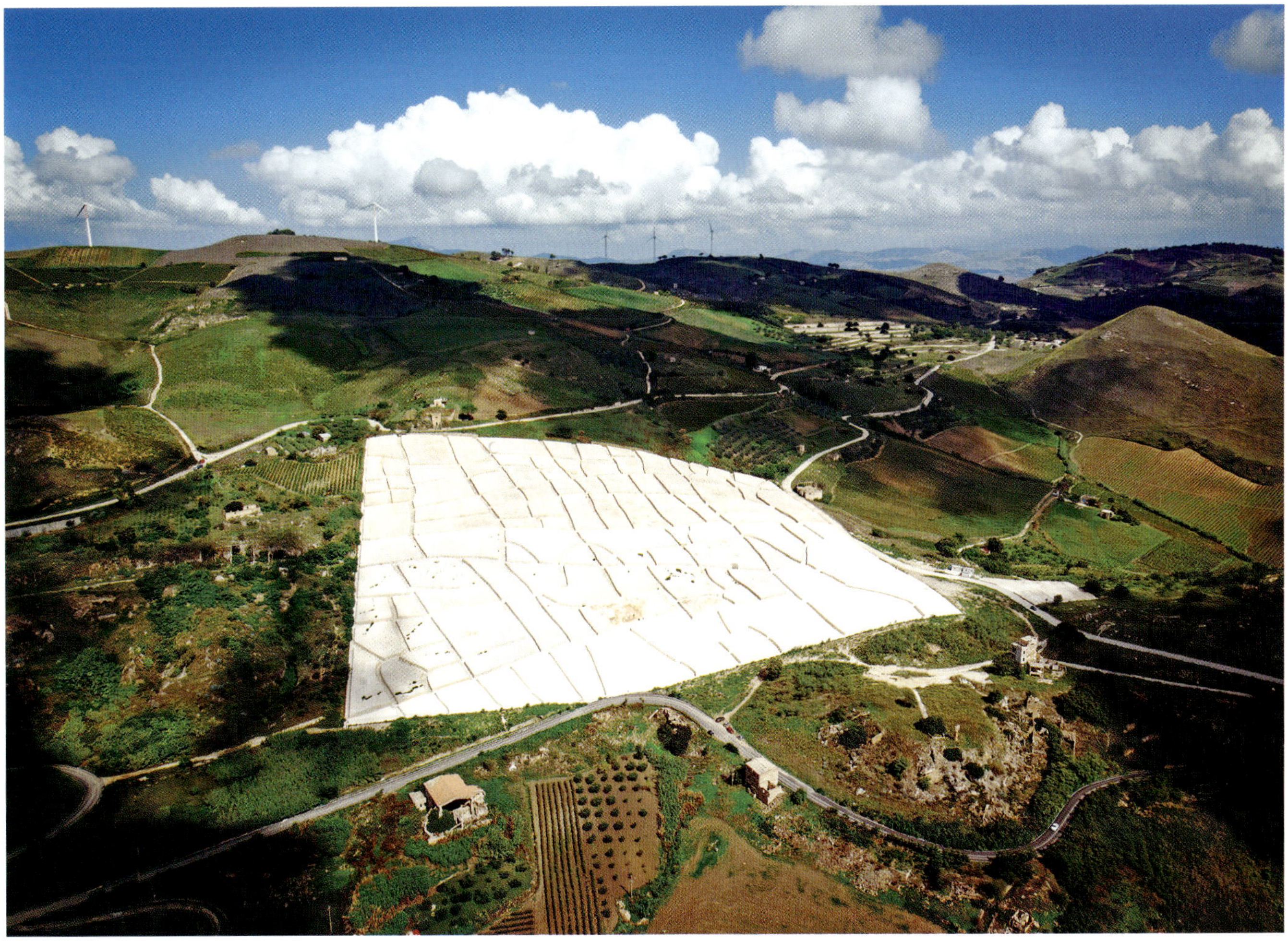

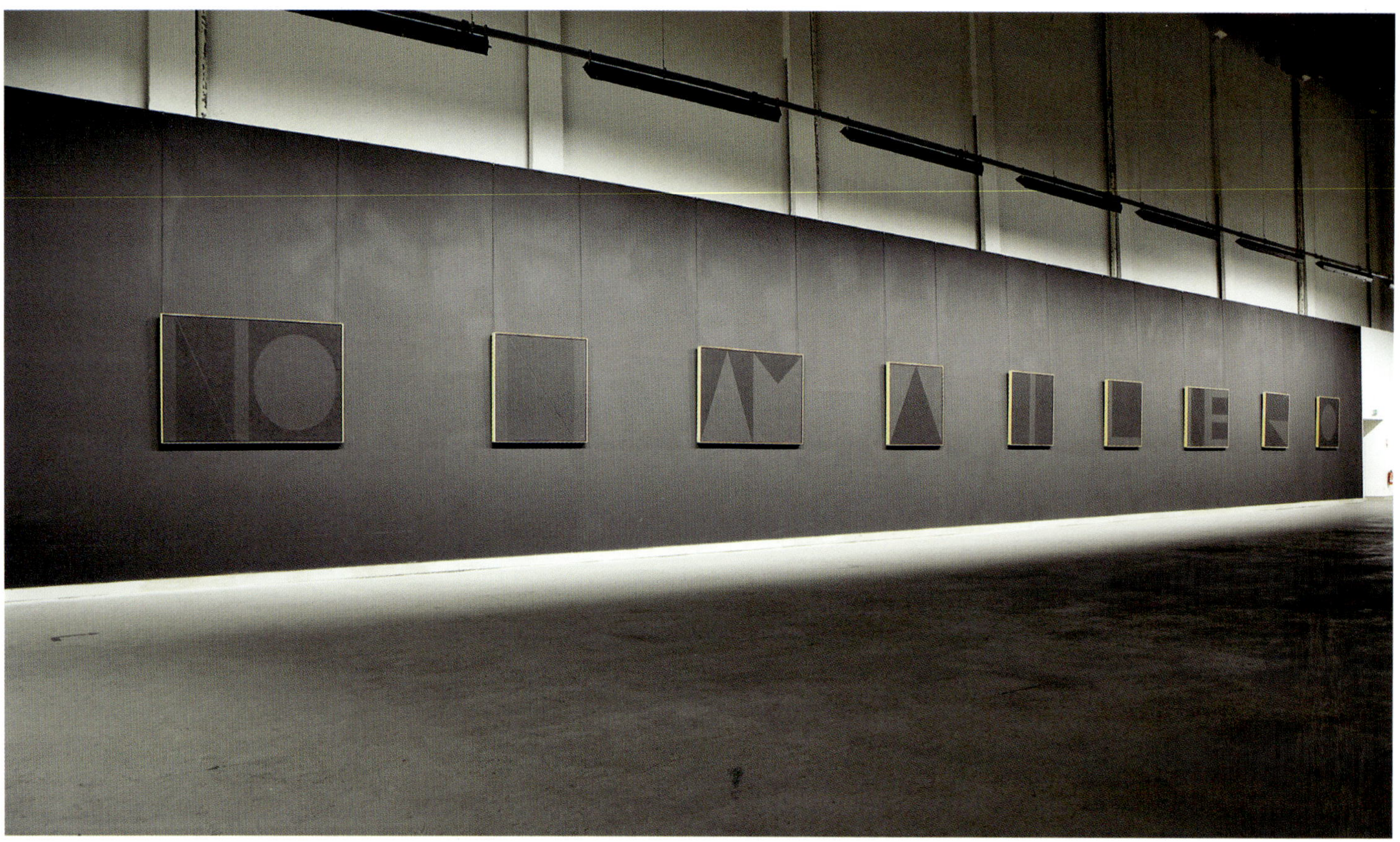

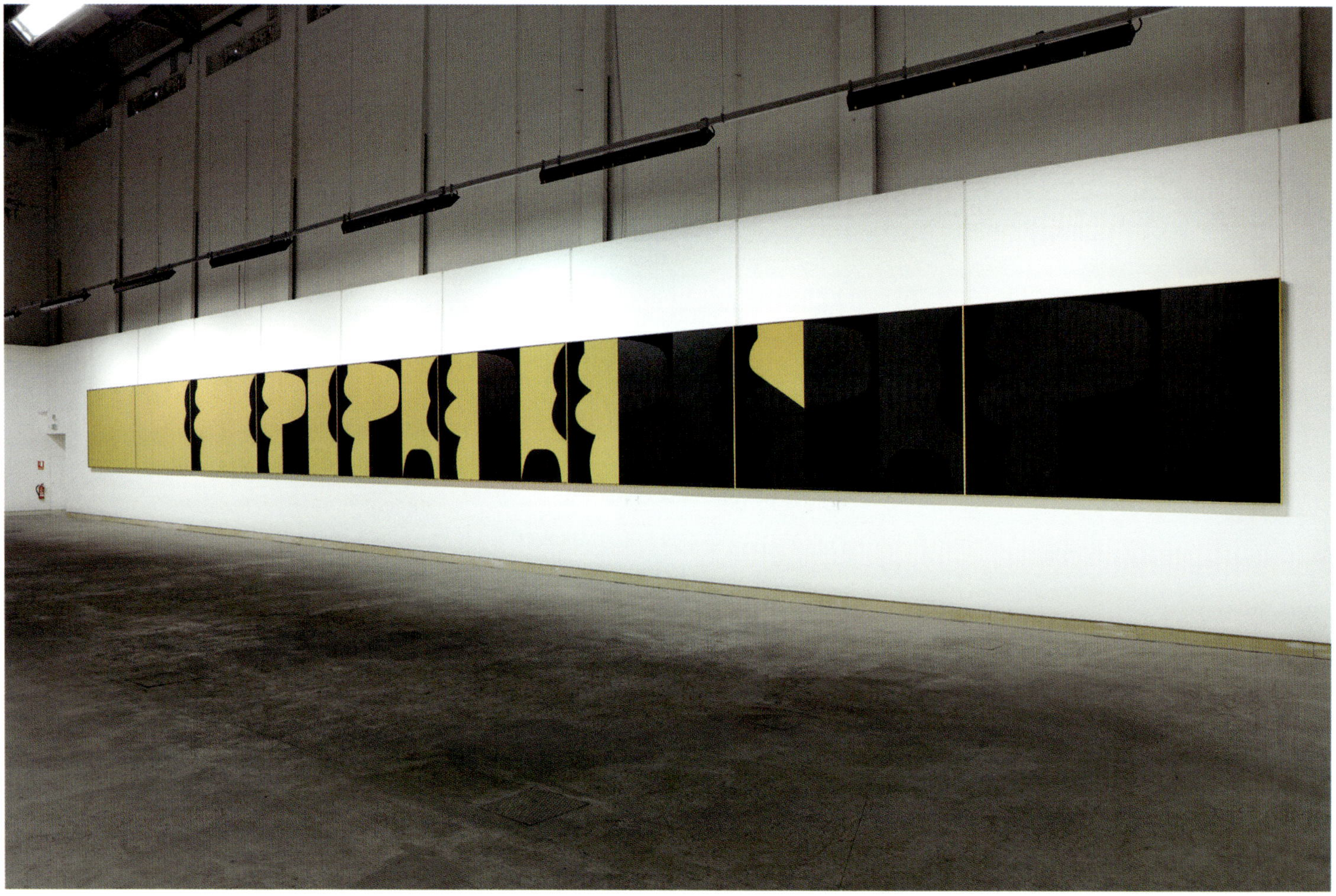

34. *Non Ama il Nero*, 1988. Città di Castello, Ex Seccatoi del Tabacco, Room L

35. *Metamorfotex*, [1991]. Città di Castello, Ex Seccatoi del Tabacco, Room M

(fig. 32), a majestic expanse of white cement that covers the ruins of the Sicilian town of Gibellina, which was razed to the ground by the earthquake that hit the Valle del Belice in 1968; construction works would stall for many years, therefore the project will be completed only in 2015, as part of the celebrations for the centenary of the artist's birth (fig. 33). In this year however, Burri is one of the group of artists included in the *International Paintings Exhibition* at the Hungarian National Gallery in Budapest. Two openings of solo exhibitions take place in Rome: on 3 December the *Annottarsi* cycle is presented at the Galleria Sprovieri, while a few days later *Alberto Burri. Le opere e i giorni/ Lo spazio/ La scena/ Le opere 1969-1985*, curated by Francesco Moschini, is inaugurated at the A.A.M. / Coop. Architettura Arte Moderna.

1986

Burri participates in the group exhibition *Tridente 10. Aspetti di Arte: gli anni Cinquanta, gli anni Sessanta* at the Il Segno gallery in Rome. *Burri 18 paintings 1953–1986* is the title of the exhibition, accompanied by a contribution in the catalog by Gerald Nordland, held at the Di Laurenti Gallery in New York. The artist exhibits on the occasion of the XLII Biennale di Venezia. *Alberto Burri Œuvre Graphique 1959-1985*, a touring anthological exhibition curated by Chiara Sarteanesi and Jean-Marie Lhôte is inaugurated at the Maison de la Culture in Amiens. The artist is conferred the title of Accademico by the Pontificia Insigne Accademia di Belle Arti e Lettere dei Virtuosi al Pantheon for his merits and numbered among the members of the most ancient Italian artistic association. On 10 December the Casa Italiana - Center for Italian Studies Columbia University in New York presents the group exhibition *Italics 1925–1985,* which Palazzo Venezia in Rome will host in 1987.

1987

The former Peroni industrial plant in Rome hosts Burri's *il Viaggio, Sestante,* and *Annottarsi* cycles with a presentation by Maurizio Calvesi. At the same time, again in Rome, Burri exhibits solo within *Burri, Monotex, Multipli, Grande Ferro K* at the Museo Laboratorio of the Università degli Studi La Sapienza. Burri's works are displayed at the Musée d'Art Contemporain in Nîmes within *Italie hors d'Italie*, curated by Johannes Gachnang.

1988

Sixteen Cellotex pictures, entitled *Annottarsi 2*, are displayed in the room devoted to Burri at the XLIII Esposizione Internazionale d'Arte. La Biennale di Venezia. Other works by Burri are on display in *Les Années 50*, a group exhibition held in Paris at the Musée National d'Art Moderne Centre Georges Pompidou. Another cycle is presented within the *Burri S. Vitale* exhibition at the Museo Nazionale di Ravenna in the complex of San Vitale. The artist takes part in the *Stationen der Moderne* group exhibition organized in Berlin by the Berlinische Galerie. The Galleria Sprovieri in Rome exhibits the *Non Ama il Nero* cycle (fig. 34), the *Annottarsi (Up to Nite)* cycle is displayed at The Murray and Isabella Rayburn Foundation in New York, and the *Assegai* cycle is shown in Turin, at the Galleria Eva Menzio.

1989

After the group exhibition curated by Germano Celant and Norman Rosenthal *Italian Art in the 20th Century* (The Royal Academy of Arts, London) and *Arte Italiana. Presenze 1900-1945* (Palazzo Grassi, Venice), there follows a solo show at the Kodama Gallery of Osaka. Burri's works are included in the touring exhibitions *Aspectos da Pintura Italiana do Após - Guerra aos nossos dias* in Brazil and *Orientamenti dell'arte italiana. Roma 1947-1989* in Russia. The artist exhibits solo in Naples at the Galleria Lia Rumma (*Burri 3 Cellotex*), in Vienna at the Istituto Italiano di Cultura (*Wien Modern 89.*

36. *il Viaggio*, 1979. Città di Castello, Ex Seccatoi del Tabacco, Room C

37. Città di Castello, Ex Seccatoi del Tabacco, 1990. Alberto Burri outside his studio

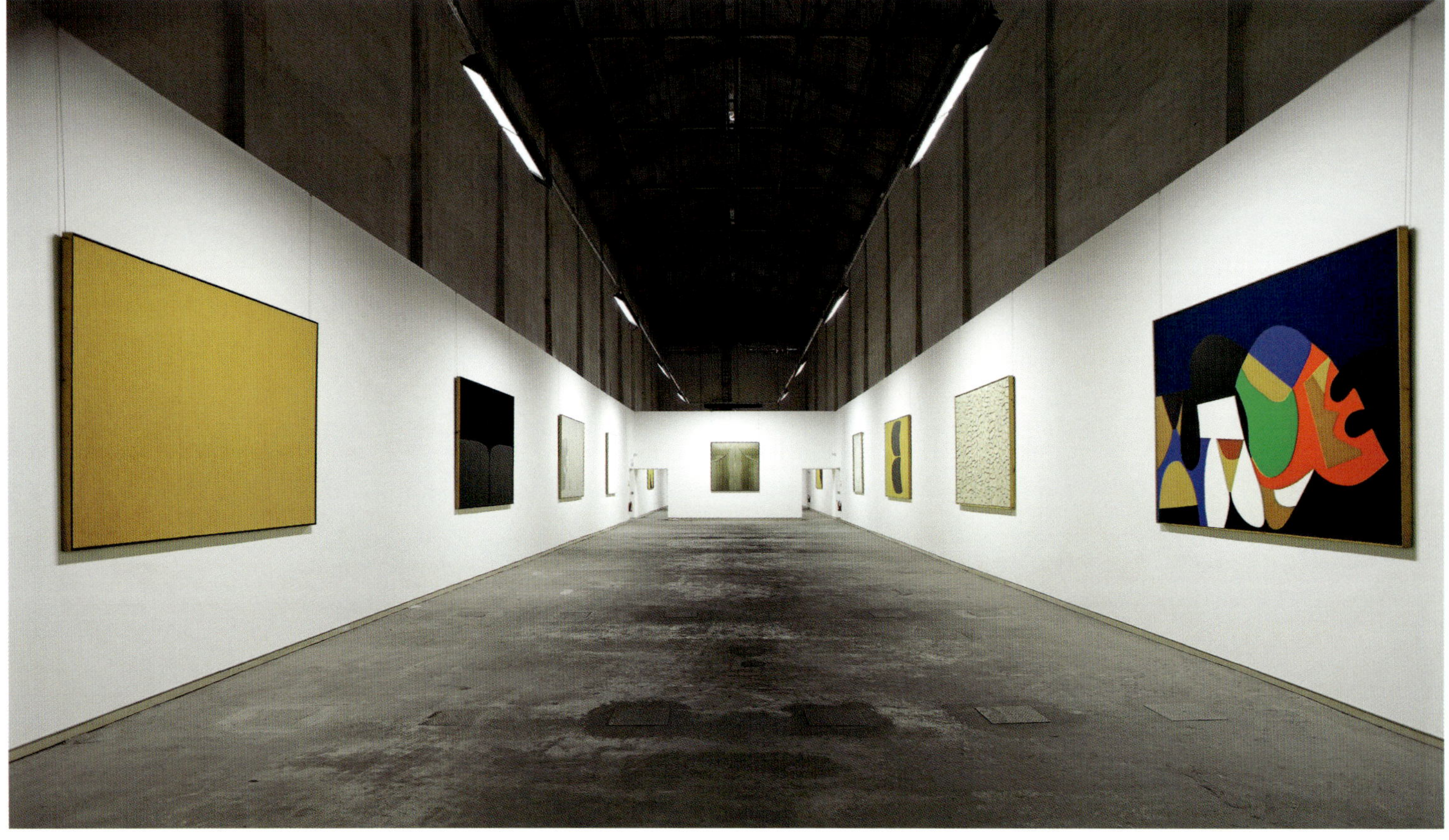

Burri 1984 Rosso e Nero Wien), in Rome at the Galleria Milart (*Burri*), in Città di Castello at the Galleria delle Arti (*Burri 25 grafiche 1 scultura*), and in Nice at the Galerie Sapone (*Burri*). This year, thanks to a donation by the artist, the Fondazione Palazzo Albizzini Collezione Burri acquires the entire industrial complex of the former tobacco drying barns in Città di Castello; work begins on the renovation of the structures to be used as a museum according to a project by architects Tiziano Sarteanesi and Alberto Bacchi, and supervised by Burri.

1990
In New York the Salvatore Ala Gallery hosts the exhibition of the *Palm Springs* cycle. Giuliano Serafini at the Istituto Italiano di Cultura in Athens curates the *Perielio: Burri - Saffo* solo exhibition. In July the second venue of the Fondazione Palazzo Albizzini Collezione Burri is inaugurated at the Ex Seccatoi del Tabacco; these rooms permanently house numerous cycles and two sculptures, while a further three are installed outside. Starting from 2017 in the underground spaces of this center, the following are inaugurated: the entire collection of graphic works, a vast documentary-multimedia section, and an area for temporary exhibitions. On 31 October the Senate of the University of Glasgow awards Burri an Honorary Degree in Letters. He is invited by Germano Celant and Ida Giannelli to take part in the group exhibition *Memoria del Futuro. Arte Italiana desde las primeras vanguardias a la posguerra* that is held at the Centro de Arte Reina Sofía in Madrid. The artist takes part in the *Roma anni '60. Al di là della pittura* exhibition at Palazzo delle Esposizioni in Rome, curated by Maurizio Calvesi and Rosella Siligato.

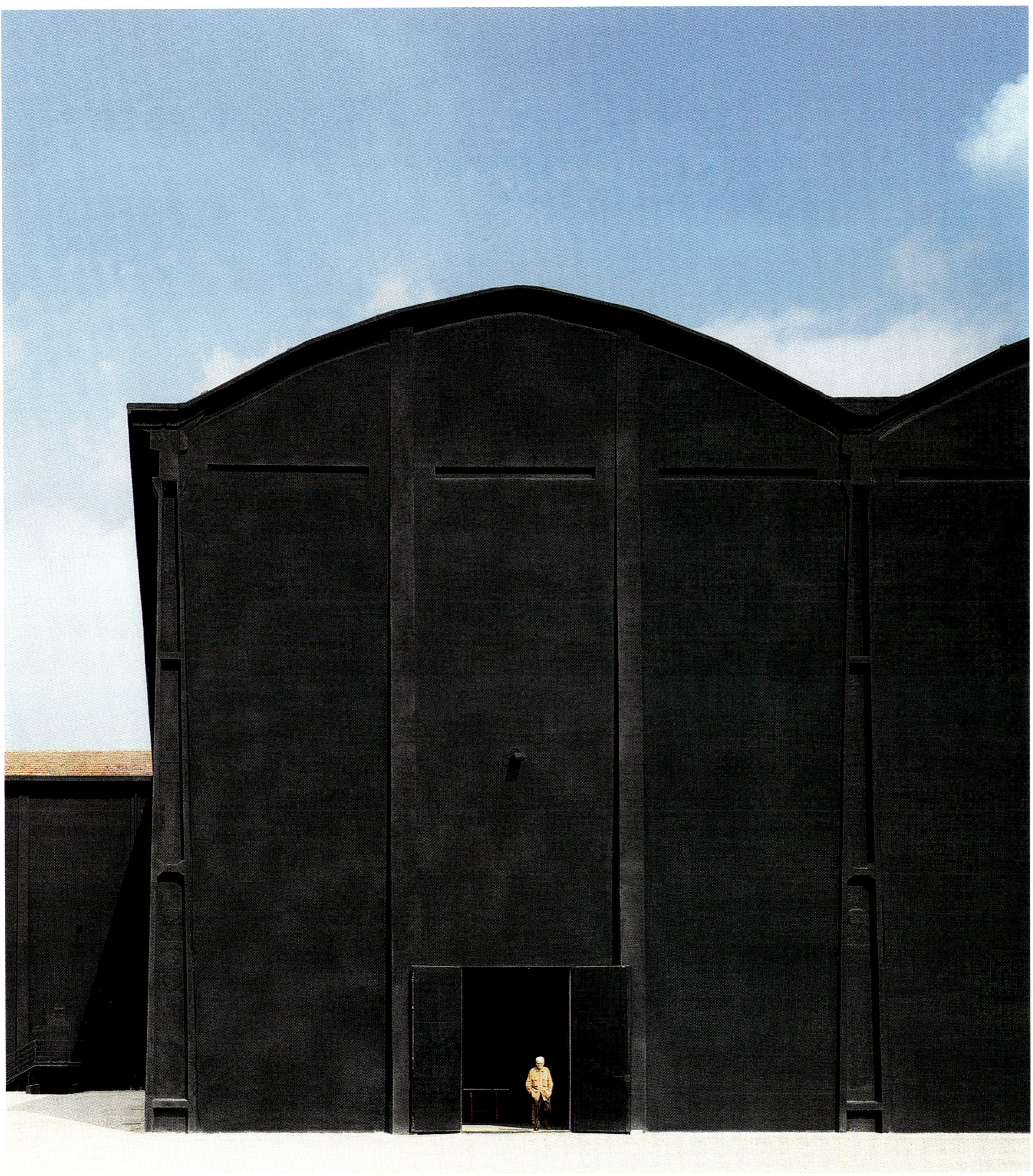

1991

The salient events of the year are the solo shows in Bologna at Palazzo Pepoli Campogrande (subsequently held in Locarno, at the Pinacoteca Comunale Casa Rusca) curated by Carlo Pirovano and *Burri Cellotex 91* in the Castello di Rivoli, presented by Ida Gianelli. A series of three-dimensional prints are on display at Luis and Lea Remba's Mixografia Gallery in Los Angeles, for the exhibition *Alberto Burri Mixoblack*; this is made possible by the Mixografia technique, which the artist accomplishes by working on Cellotex molds with sand and marble powder, with which he defines the forms to be reproduced.
He leaves the house on the hills of Los Angeles and buys one in Beaulieu-sur-Mer in the South of France, along the coast between Monaco and Nice, where he lives during the colder months of the year; he continues to spend his summers in his native city.

1992

The *Metamorfotex* cycle (fig. 35) is inaugurated at the Ex Seccatoi del Tabacco, with the presentation of Nemo Sarteanesi. Burri participates in numerous group exhibitions in Italy and abroad. The Galerie Sapone organizes *Alberto Burri œuvres 1949-1992* at the Grand Palais in Paris, as part of the F.I.A.C. *Alberto Burri pregledna razstava grafike 1962-1981,* a solo show of Burri's graphics curated by Giuliano Serafini is inaugurated at the Galerija Loza in Koper, which subsequently travels to Ljubljana and Fiume.

1993

In Rome Burri is honored with the Premio della Cultura per il 1992 Prize for the Art sector by the Presidenza del Consiglio dei Ministri. He donates *Nero e Oro*, a large work made using ceramics and gold, to the Museo Internazionale della Ceramica in Faenza. In Parma the Galleria d'Arte Niccoli presents *Alberto Burri, la pittura come materia vivente, opere dal 1949 al 1966,* curated by Claudio Cerritelli. The artist is invited in New York by Germano Celant to take part in the group exhibition *Rome–New York 1948–1964* at The Murray and Isabella Rayburn Foundation. *Burri "Grafiche dall'88"* is hosted by the Museo delle Genti d'Abruzzo in Pescara.

1994

The President of the Italian Republic confers on Burri the honorary title of Cavaliere di Gran Croce. *Alberto Burri / Il Polittico di Atene. Architetture con cactus,* a solo exhibition curated by Giuliano Serafini, opens at the National Gallery Alexandros Soutzos Museum in Athens, featuring ten solemn Cellotex pictures; the show is also displayed at the Istituto Italiano di Cultura in Madrid. Burri takes part in a group exhibition curated by Germano Celant, *The Italian Metamorphosis, 1943–1968*, at the Solomon R. Guggenheim Museum in New York. The artist donates the series *Cellotex* (1992), *Oro e Nero* (1993), and *Trittico* (1994), and an individual work, *Bianco e Nero* (1969), to the Galleria degli Uffizi in Florence. In New York the American Academy of Arts and Letters names him an "honorary foreign member" in recognition of his success achieved in the arts.

1995

Burri dies on 13 February in Nice. The many exhibitions showcasing his oeuvre include the XLVI Biennale di Venezia, curated by Jean Clair, and *Roma 1950-59. Il rinnovamento della pittura in Italia* at Palazzo dei Diamanti in Ferrara, curated by Fabrizio D'Amico.

Città di Castello, Ex Seccatoi del Tabacco, 1991. Alberto Burri at work

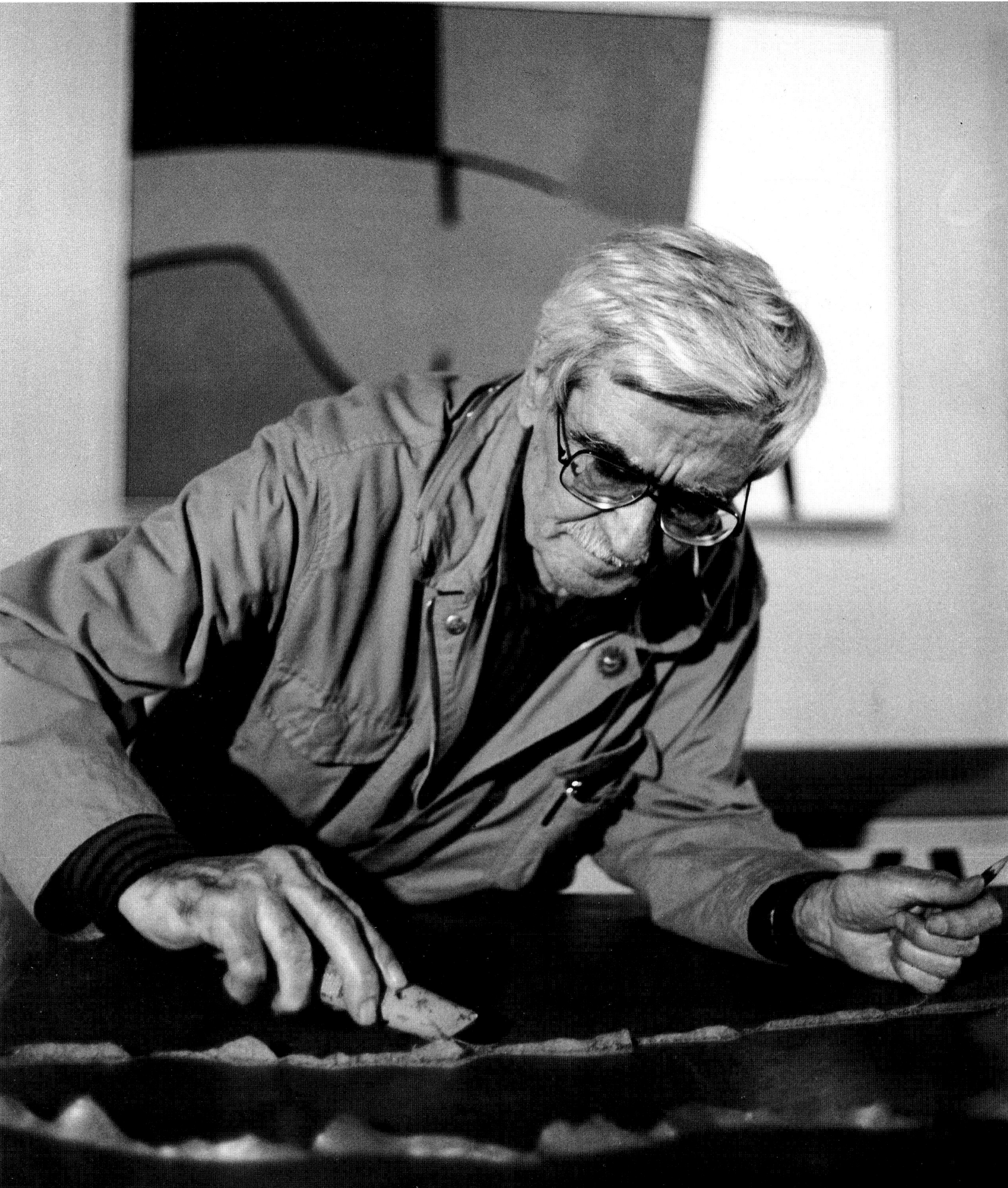

appendix

Selected articles and reviews

Daniel Abadie
Francesco Arcangeli
Giulio Carlo Argan
Carlo Bertelli
Cesare Brandi
Maurizio Calvesi
Enrico Crispolti
Milton Gendel
Eva Menzio
Gerald Nordland
André Pieyre de Mandiargues
Carlo Pirovano
Herbert Read
Pierre Restany
Chiara Sarteanesi
Nemo Sarteanesi
Gabi Scardi
Giuliano Serafini
James Johnson Sweeney
Italo Tomassoni
Lorenza Trucchi
Marco Vallora
Emilio Villa
Marisa Volpi
Allen Stuart Weller
Paul Wember
Alberto Zanmatti
Christian Zervos

1950

Christian Zervos "Quelques jeunes," *Cahiers d'art*, 25th year, no. 1, Paris, 1950.

Il est difficile dans une revue succincte du jeune art italien de le reconnaître au complet. Nous ne ferons que signaler ici son effort pour permettre à nos lecteurs d'avoir une vue générale de ses plans. Il est des artistes que nous avons sans doute oubliés, il en est d'autres dont les reproductions nous sont parvenues trop tard. Les uns et les autres voudront bien nous pardonner leur absence de cette livraison de notre revue, lacune que nous promettons de combler bientôt. Nous n'avons pas cherché ici à classer les talents par familles ou à les grouper sous certains noms génériques. Le temps n'est pas encore venu d'accuser la chaîne de cet art, en en montrant l'un après l'autre les anneaux. En nous réservant donc à plus tard d'indiquer les diverses tendances qui se partagent le jeune art d'Italie et de signaler nos préférences, nous avons rangé les artistes dans l'ordre alphabétique.

1951

Emilio Villa, *Attributi dell'arte odierna 1947/1967*, Feltrinelli, Milan, 1970 (excerpt).

Queste sono alcune fotografie di alcune opere dell'artista italiano (abita a Roma) Alberto Burri. Diciamo pure: pitture, ma esse sono nutrite di un materiale che della pittura conserva soltanto una tragica reminiscenza, quasi come asfittica; un materiale devitalizzato depauperato imputridito consunto e già coartato dal deperimento. Con questo materiale Burri si adopera, da impaziente austero banale chirurgo, quasi di razza alchimista, a rimettere, insieme avanzi detriti cascami di una trepidante realtà, tuttavia ancora bruciante, e quasi storditamente memore (forse, anche, e insieme, evocatrice, evocatoria) del *fluxus sanguinis*, e della vita qualunque (quale?) in esso flusso contenuta, e fluente nello stesso senso (e a volte fluente in direzione contraria o avversa). L'operato di Alberto Burri, il suo tracciato (di fili, di graffi, di tagli, di spaghi) il suo tracciato, il suo campo accidentale, il suo oltraggiato *theatrum* di vita ambigua come la danza di un virus, è da intendere, penso io, come un primo atto: diciamo, atto creazionale, di tipo iniziativo, quindi quasi fosse allegoricamente ritualistico, o, se si vuole (e come vorrebbe il mio vibrante heideggeriano Cyrel Czerna) di tipo esistenziale; di possibilità difensive (apotropaiche) o future: di una futura liberazione dal bene e dal male, dal benemale, dalla tentazione e dall'adempimento. È certo uno degli atti più forti, un *r aptus/r actus* genetico, una sorgenza non proprio pensabile, né dal pensiero attutita, la più impensabile che la pittura (quella veramente atta al responsorio) possa oggi flettere e deflettere, riflettere e coniugare come lingua colloidale plasmica gelatinosa. Io medito su questo pittore che ho perduto venendo in questo nuovo continente, ma che certo ancora opera con rabbia che dovrebbe essere feconda, nel tempo per il dopo, e per il dopo del dopo, fino all'inane e al terribile, come su un audace protagonista. Secondo me, accanto allo statunitense Gorky da qualche anno ormai scomparso nella luce tetra del suo capofitto, come sacrificium, come *pòtmos àpotmos*, Alberto Burri è già da annoverare oggi tra i testimoni della superiore amara iniziativa: del cominciare oggi generando, ma né la vita, né la morte. Non rappresentando, ma facendo.

Questo io dico: che bisogna fare. Ed egli unisce, con la destrezza pura del suo ingegno, scosso e velato, svincolato, tonico, una catena di reliquie corrose, miserabilissime, del tutto scevre di aerazione, del tutto dissociate, cosí dal demone come dall'angelo, *utique utique utique absque numine*, e quasi virilmente disputate e sottratte al nulla numinoso, al nulla divino; e con il mezzo queste reliquie, addossate o innestate in azioni (vuoti, fiati, capogiri, tracciati densi di deposta minaccia e di inerzia provocatoria, stridori dello scomposto che si adagia nel vento fermo, fiati della non-evoluzione o in altre parvenze (non reliquie), matrici morte della viltà dell'obbrobrio della carogneria, materie terrose e laviche, di catastrofe e di energia tellurica, materie di industria e commercio esautorate, senza colore mai, ma in pieno alterco con il colore (sede del "sentimento") tracce di liquami d'infezione vagante) egli tenta di costruire (?) e solidificare (calcificare, nullificare) (calcina sacco asfalto muffa colla merda) una interrogazione gessosa sulla vuota (piaga, sangue) virtú e sul vuoto del mondo. Questa interrogazione è il modo di quella che abbiam detto superiore iniziativa nel pullulio continuo (della piega, dalla piaga, dalla copertura dermica), dal disfacimento cellulare del nulla sorgivo, del nulla cosmoctono: una turbinante offerta di respiro, di cadenze fiatate, con mani e senza nomi, una visitazione palingenica.

1952

Lorenza Trucchi, "Dal casto Omiccioli all'alchimia di Burri," *Il Momento*, 18 January 1952.

[. . .] I "neri" e le "muffe" di Burri meriterebbero un discorso lungo e complesso, un poco fuori dalla critica pittorica: più una ricerca dei rapporti tra arte e psicologia analitica; un inconscio ed abbastanza intelligibile, gioca infatti nell'opera di questo artista e ciò illumina chi osservi la sua opera inquieta ed inquietante. Dal canto nostro non conosciamo personalmente Burri e ci è solo noto che è medico, ma certi avvenimenti, esperienze, passioni hanno causato una tale pittura dove la cultura è del tutto estranea e, semmai, circoscritta soltanto ad essere il buon trampolino od a donare la consapevolezza del "tutto possibile": il resto è di Burri ne è poco se anche infinitamente pericoloso. Tuttavia, ci pare, che non si debba analizzare questi quadri con la freddezza della scienza o la sordità di una tradizione e di principi messi avanti ad ogni costo. Burri va capito così, di getto, e la sua materia, tremenda e splendida, ricca e poverissima, alchimia di colla, biacca, vernici e mistero, sentita quasi fisicamente specialmente ora che ci giunge come una novità imprevista. Del resto qui, dove la scienza ed il calcolo, l'impulso e la freddezza, la sensualità e il nichilismo, sono fusi a tal punto da divenire Babele di sensazioni, conflitti ed incubi, ma anche liberazione, solitudine e poesia: non ci potrebbero aiutare i testi di Jung, né gli alambicchi od i compassi, talora utili per aggirarsi nei cantieri degli astrattisti-architetti, né, tanto meno, la serie degli interrogativi scoraggianti e senza possibilità di risposta convincente, sul cosa voglia fare o dire Burri "mettendo in cornice una tela di sacco rotta e macchiata di colore". Non tentiamo quindi di creare una difesa e, del resto, contro chi ed a favore di chi? Burri ed i suoi, non numerosi, ma fanatici ammiratori, debbono essere talmente convinti da bastare per tutti; ma soltanto desideriamo far osservare agli scettici che non si trovano di fronte a "tappezzerie", a "ironie", a formule pure da integrare pittoricamente, ma a tele nere; bianche, bianche nere, gialle e così via o meglio a materia colorata fuori da ogni classificazione e, nei più dei casi, anche al di sopra di ogni classificazione.

1953

Emilio Villa, *Attributi dell'arte odierna 1947/1967*, Feltrinelli, Milan 1970 (two excerpts).

Nostra dimessa cosmogonia, elegiaca esterrefatta composita, epos per istantanee, tragedie quotidiane, miniatura rapsodica delle grandi formazioni del tempo, avvenute senza traccia o eventuali, il grande sangue, i tracciati del mondo senza requie, la legge che detta lo scrimolo ai frantumi di una visione da mettere su, insieme come materia e come sorpresa, la divagazione profetica delle righe che han modellato le forme degli arcipelaghi e il congegno delle penisole, e lo scheletro delle trote nelle acque dell'Adda.

Nella memoria delle palafitte c'è molto che può diventare materia di una breve e costernata superficie di pittura, ma pittura per modo di dire; e, invece, di quella qualunque altra azione compiuta per rivelare sensi specifici e non confutabili: Burri Alberto coltiva come in vitro, anzi come in lino, queste contrattili anatomie di organismi inespressi, incerti tra una parvenza di materiali biologici fuori uso e un ideale di fulminei universi tra il gigantesco e il minimissimo: una ambiguità spalancata, un desiderio di stringere ricordi di cose che devono chiarirsi; lamentosa cosmogonia supposta con la semplice innocenza di materiali usuali, degli stracci rifiutati dal rione, delle vernici scadenti, delle paste amorfe tra deperimento e cristallizzazione, dei legnami scartati e destinati all'acqua o al fuoco, degli asfalti, delle mucillagini: un modo di rifiuti popolari può farsi analogo e congeniale alle immaginazioni più imponenti: in un punto qualunque del mondo un occhio, vivo e disinteressato come quello che accende la vista di Alberto Burri, può sorprendere e trar fuori lo scatto originato da grembi superiori, dove spira esatto il senso di una nostra epopea laica e popolare; sulla via di scoprire un altro senso della contemplazione e di offrire alla contemplazione nuovi oggetti da essa medesima supposti o desiderati, non siamo forse ancora in una condizione presocratica; ma su questa via siamo, e Burri corre facilmente in testa: i quadri della sua pittura sono da considerare già come paradigmi maturi.

Il pittore, tra incanto e artificio solenne, cancella i colori per condurre i profili della tensione e della costernazione, per illuminare alcune voci, risonanze carpite tra le filiture della meccanica mentale e del suo naturale funzionamento; soli colori il bianco e il nero, rappresentazione della vita e della morte, del giorno e della notte, della volontà e dell'abbandono. Sarà l'ultimo grande sforzo la dialettica del non colore questa specie di insonnia caparbia arcaica futura, come la pietra, come il colore dell'abisso e dell'invisibile, che la pittura di Burri esegue per via allegorica, in una risoluzione allegorica, con il sacco la iuta il nylon le tele la porporina.

Io ricordo la grande invenzione di Burri; l'opaco, l'opacità ardita dopo tutto, pescata nel fondo degli altri colori, e formata in concreazioni molto espressive, l'esistenza del mondo allo stato puro, fatta quasi eleganza, leggerezza pensata all'interno della materia, prima dell'unità e prima delle separazioni: dove le filiture sui crepacci del non manifesto sono frettolosamente, ma con dignitosa abilità, chiuse da suture, opera di un medico destituito dalle sue relazioni sociali, di un medico all'antica; non a caso Alberto Burri è stato un medico, ora trasformato in un chirurgo ben più virtuoso, di rara, precisa libertà; dopo aver girato miracolosamente lungo planimetrie impercettibili di città sepolte nel bitume, o nei labirinti infantili.

Forse si è trovato il mitografo urbano che inventa, in questa sterile sfera che è la pittura, qualche cosa non priva di speranza, e necessaria come il pane, come il lavoro, come i miracoli, come il dramma quotidiano e domenicale, questi quadri un po' imprevisti ogni volta, ogni volta se ne può dire: ecco un'opera che poteva essere fatta soltanto oggi, ecco un'azione che poteva essere compiuta oggi soltanto, non ieri, non domani, con una cicatrice così segnata del tempo soltanto oggi e chissà cosa sarà domani la loro suggestione, forse deperita, forse moltiplicata, sempre però libera dalla magra e scadente eternità museografica, l'inesperta vanità delle avanguardie polimateriche (viziacci), potevano tutt'al piú evocare il senso di improvvisazioni magiche deteriori, o ironie, o proteste automatiche, in questi quadri invece il miracolo c'è: dolcissime o astruse o preziose reminiscenze delle materie quotidiane, investite da una esaltazione concettuale e da una severità oggettiva che stupiscono, come segnale di grandi smarrimenti, e di temi mescolati sottoterra, a filo di terra, e poi rimossi, con il fresco dei bulbi e radici dagli sterri, calcina e zuccheri, miche e vermi: e in questo modo ogni porzione eseguita dal pittore suscita oggetti o racconti o poemi solidificati, che paiono essere rivelazioni, come agitare le tenebre, provocarle; come rigare il crepuscolo con un grido di cristallo, aboliti l'aria, l'acqua, il fuoco, la terra e tutte le idee che spontaneamente si confessino con immagini analoghe. Burri ha elaborato l'assurdo o quasi mistico proponimento di evocare, o mettiamo pure di inventare, i primi principi, i sapori germinali di un organismo assai grande e non sconosciuto, ora, dico, se l'esecutore di un'arte così poca e di risorse così vaghe, quale è la pittura, riesce ad afferrare supposizioni così forti a livello mentale spontaneo, ascoltare pensieri che insorgono da profondità non usuali, e a rendere contenuti maestosi con mezzi addirittura trasandati, consunti, acidi, questo esecutore è un poeta eccezionale, egli ha il gusto e il sentore delle materie in disuso, o senz'altro deteriorate (come il gusto popolare, che è una forte e meravigliosa attrazione, per le materie dei reliquiari cattolici), ma, oltre il gusto, egli pensa, ascolta, elabora una articolata, flessibile e lucida litania, luci di cono pei lividi in pomeriggi di temporale, frammenti e riverberi di una serena bisanzio per tutti, atmosfere laiche, qualità di materie usuali e proletarie difese con amore, nobilitate e composte come da preparare per un superiore galateo, dove la tela e le bende gli avanzi di favolosi imballaggi le fodere e tendine e scatolame e il vinavil e le vernici per le case di tutti e per gli utensili e i veli e gli infiniti bianchi e i neri intensificati e i rammendi e i rattoppi conquistano un pregio solenne, un sentimento compiuto, una illuminazione, una delle allegorie più eccellenti e più concrete che sia possibile conoscere oggi; secondo me, il più elevato tentativo di rappresentare immaginazione vera, al di là della favola, al di là del lirismo e di simili abbandoni, al di là degli ingorghi di ogni genere eccitati dalla letteratura e dalle poetiche.

Allen Stuart Weller, "Chicago,"
Art Digest, vol. 27, no. 9,
1 February 1953.

CHICAGO: The first exhibition in this country of the work of yet another young Italian is to be seen at the Frumkin Gallery, through February 12. The painter is Alberto Burri, and he is apparently one of the few completely non-objective artists now working in Italy. I am assured that his painting is absolutely personal; that, while he is conscious of American non-objectivety, he has developed quite independently of such knowledge, just as he shows no relationship to such an Italian artist as Afro. Yet the curious fact remains that his first experiments as a painter were carried out in Texas, where he was in an American prisoner of war camp. One wonders if there is something in the air! Burri has developed some curious and personal technical devices, and there is no doubt that he has an acute intuitional visual imagination, which at times gives to his work a disturbing excitement. He frequently combines painting and collage. Patches of textiles, contrasting in texture and tone, are stitched and glued into place. In some examples, thin sheets of linen are stretched tight within the frame, then superimposed on an unseen wire structure which pushes the material out into actual three-dimensional forms. Burri likes to use areas of sharply defined white paint on thin white cloth which has been irregularly stained by oil films, just as he likes to use black on black, contrasting shiny and dull surfaces. He employs plaster, sand, metallic paint, resinous glue, and other materials to achieve unusual color and texture effects. At times he exploits heavy areas of pigment which have been allowed to float or move in a viscid manner so that they seem lichenous or like the growth of some kind of fungus. Yet his work is by no means formless. Indeed, he has a sense of delicate balance and his weighing of mass and space is truly architectural at times. A characteristic example is *Composition No. 5*, in which heavy areas of shredded burlap have become permanent plastic elements in a complex pattern of variously woven textiles and areas of flat painted color. Perhaps it is not for nothing that Burri's neighbors in Rome call him "The Tailor."

1954

André Pieyre de Mandiargues, "Burri," *La Nouvelle Revue Française*, year 2, no. 20, Paris, 1 August 1954.

[. . .] Burri, lui, ne court aucun risque de la sorte, et parmi les peintres de cette nouvelle école, proche du surréalisme, qui est la seule à laquelle on puisse le rattacher, il est comme un solitaire, un révolté, dispensateur d'une vision grandiose et noire qui me paraît l'une des plus importantes des temps modernes. Médecin d'abord, c'est en captivité (prison de guerre au Texas) qu'il mit la main à son œuvre plastique. Peut-être faut-il imputer à la sévère ordonnance et aux restrictions en vigueur dans les camps américains le choix des moyens qui lui servent à s'exprimer; peut-être est-ce là facile explication. Le fait est que Burri, plus qu'aucun homme que l'on sache, est sensible aux prestiges de la suie, de la cendre, du plâtre, de la poussière et des choses de rebut. Depuis qu'il vit à Rome, et qu'il n'a souci que de peindre (au sens le moins étroit du mot), les marchands de "fournitures pour artistes" ne l'ont pas vu souvent chez eux. Car ses matériaux favoris sont des vieux sacs (usés, coupés, recousus), des agglomérés de liège en poudre et de sciure (qu'il creuse, dentèle, effrite comme une souris rongeuse), divers gravats, et puis des couleurs industrielles, des colles, des enduits cellulosiques. Il s'enferme avec tout cela, travaille furieusement. Le résultat étonne, qui du format de la carte de visite à celui des panneaux les plus larges a pris un air violent, inimitable, qui est la marque de l'auteur. A première vue, et superficielle, on pourrait juger que ces tableaux bizarrement absurdes, scandaleux parfois en ce qu'ils rappellent des pansements souillés ou des éjaculations et sécrétions qui ne se peuvent dire dans le langage poli, sont le produit d'un goût attardé à "dada", qu'ils tiennent au Picabia de cette époque-là, à Kurt Schwitters, mais l'oeil vite est frappé par la beauté des tons, ne fussent-ils que de goudron et de chanvre brûlé, par les accords qui gouvernent l'assemblage, par le dessin précis d'un espace créé seulement de quelques traits ou taches de couleur, et alors il faut bien admettre que l'on est en présence de ce rare phénomène: un grand peintre moderne encore très peu connu. Quoiqu'il n'y ait pas de "figures" discernables dans ses tableaux, Burri ne saurait être considéré comme un peintre abstrait. Par la matière, qui est généralement le déchet de la vie humaine, c'est un peu au-dessous de celle-là que l'on pourra fixer le lieu de son œuvre, et il ressort de ses compositions une poésie cruelle qui leur donne une intensité à laquelle n'atteindront jamais les tentatives purement picturales. Le sujet, ici, est avant tout la blessure, psychique autant que physique, et je ne pense pas me tromper en écrivant que Burri, dans sa présente manière, est le peintre de la désolation et de la mort, le peintre des mondes inférieurs, sinon même du monde infernal. Certains le lui ont reproché, qui supportaient mal cette fenêtre ouverte sur l'obscur et le froid de la zone infra-humaine; pourtant il est assez connu que ce qui est en bas tient de près à ce qui est en haut, et que les instruments démoniaques font la contrepartie de la musique des anges. Passons. L'important est que la plupart des toiles de Burri, dans l'extrême simplicité, soient tellement suggestives. Deux sacs cousus comme un linceul, ton foncé sur ton clair, liés par le paraphe de la ficelle, deux éclaboussures ailées ou crochues, rouge l'une, l'autre blanche, en voilà assez pour nous mettre de plain-pied avec ces bas-reliefs égyptiens qui montrent la migration des âmes. Burri, d'ailleurs, est un homme gai, comme il semble que l'étaient les anciens habitants de l'Ombrie, son pays, qui peignaient des diables très affreux sur la paroi des tombeaux.

Milton Gendel, "Burri Makes a Picture," *Art News*, no. 8, December 1954.

[. . .] The Italian painter Alberto Burri often "paints" pictures that have little or no paint in them. Expert in the ways of underbrush, particularly its cast skins and tissues, he has created many pictures in a medium of old sacks, bits of rag and string, which he redeems with a sort of Franciscan piety. Although the incorporation of actual materials in a picture is a familiar practice, the nature of Burri's materials still occasions shock or protest. A Milanese collector who prides himself on the completeness of his collection of contemporary Italian painting has steadfastly resisted the idea of including a Burri. To defend his judgment he has classified Burri as a non-painter: "Painting? Filthy sacks! Mold! Garbage!" Even appreciative art chroniclers are apt to be amused by his technique (which sometimes includes sewing) and the materials employed. Reviews of his shows have been titled "Burri Patches a Picture" or "The Doctor-Painter Sticks to Sutures." Solitary by temperament, Burri is indifferent to categorizations of himself or his work. Tranquilly convinced that he has come home to painting, he treats references to his abandoned career as a physician without a tinge of regret, and rejects suggestions that his was a romantic decision. With playful humor he will reply to an acquaintance's apologetic or provocative request for medical advice by saying that he is always glad to prescribe but cannot promise the latest remedies. Ten years ago, while a prisoner of war in Hereford, Texas, he made up his mind to be a painter and quit medicine. His serenity about the rightness of his choice survived the barrage of protests from family and friends that greeted him on his homecoming to the ancient walled town of Città di Castello, in Umbria. It was counted tragic to write off, at the age of twenty-nine, years of study and the status of a professional career, particularly that of a doctor, for something so uncertain as painting. "For his own good" he was urged to think it over, to set up practice and paint on the side—evenings and Sundays. His reply, which must have taxed the patience of his advisers, was, "I will not be a Sunday painter." One ally, a cousin who is a musician, accepted Burri's decision, invited him to Rome and tried to put him in touch with art circles.

[. . .] This summer Burri, who had been working on a series of compositions in variations on black, decided to do a *sacco rosso*, a painting in sacking and red. (In speaking about his work he has adopted a simple terminology that covers the major directions explored in his ten years of painting. He refers to his "sacks" [*sacchi*], "molds" [*muffe*], "blacks" [*neri*], "whites" [*bianchi*], "reds" [*rossi*], "crackles" [*craquelés*], and to combinations of any of these). While he was selecting a large rectangular stretcher from a stack against the wall, the idea of working with a very large red area insistently presented itself, and just eluding consciousness was a correlated idea which emerged as he stretched and fastened a piece of thin black cloth, bought in a dressmaterial shop, horizontally across the stretcher. The second idea was to vary the red area with protuberances. Before stretching and securing the cloth vertically, he twisted a length of thick wire into a double curve, inserted it behind the fabric and nailed it to the stretcher. The cloth now swelled up in two places on the right. It first occurred to Burri to create real swellings in the picture plane in 1949, when he spent several months painting in a shepherd's hut at Le Fienaie, a lonely spot in the mountains near Città di Castello. To increase the effect of tension he was aiming at in a painting composed of ovaloid and parabolic forms in grey, black, brown and white, he inserted two small branches crosswise between the stretcher and the canvas. Drumhead taut and highly varnished, the canvas came forward in a prominent hump, conveying the desired feeling of strain. Burri added this procedure to his technical repertory and frequently makes use of it. For one thing, it is a logical extension of his practice of punching holes in some of his pictures, either literally or by suggestion; for another, it is a major expression of his treatment of the picture as an object in itself, and in this sense his paintings verge on constructions and sculpture, inviting the spectator to walk around them. Burri's paintings are seen most clearly as manipulated objects while he is working on them. He rejects the usual formal relationship between painter and painting, where the canvas remains fixed and the painter moves around. With Burri, both he and the canvas are in movement. [. . .]

1955

James Johnson Sweeney,
Burri, L'Obelisco, Rome, 1955.

Qui laisse une trace,
laisse une plaie
Henri Michaux

But out of a wound beauty is born. At any rate in the case of Burri. For Burri transmutes rubbish into a metaphor for human, bleeding flesh. He vitalizes the dead materials in which he works, makes them live and bleed; then sews up the wounds evocatively and as sensuously as he made them. What would have remained with the cubists a partial intensification of a painted composition—with the dadaists, a protest—with the surrealists, an illustrational fantasy—with Kurt Schwitters, a Merzbild—becomes with Burri a living organism: flesh and blood. The representation of the human form in keeping with the trend of our times may not appear in his pictures; but a suggestion of what gave that form life still remains—a suggestion of flesh and blood; and, more important still, a deep sense of order which relates the human form to a higher level of things, the spiritual. From Burri's art only the superficial resemblance to living creatures is absent. Actually Burri is the St. Januarius of the collage: one can imagine on his feast day every red gash in his compositions liquefying and streaming blood. The martyr's blood in the phials of the Cappella del Tesoro of the Cathedral in Naples melts and bubbles only when put in sight of the head of the Saint himself on certain religious occasions during the year. But the flesh of Burri's pictures pulses in the sight of the sympathetic viewer, everywhere. For if the Paris cubists of the early century and Russians such as Tatlin in a period of fragmentation of pictorial shapes employed collage elements to give a sense of reality, Burri through his collages provides a sense of carnality in an age of avowed reduction and abstraction. Burri's art brings back a sense of living flesh. In the most elementary view he is providing a sensuous—perhaps more truly, sensual experience in a period when art is being threatened with the anaemia of modish intellectualism. His compositions are not reductions or abstractions. His texture-interests are not limited to the surface. They suggest a body and depth with a fuller life beneath. He is an artist with a scalpel—the surgeon conscious of what lies within the flesh of his compositions and moved by it to the point that he can make the observer also sensitive to it. He knows that the surfaces he has sewn together with his sutures enclose a world of invisible forms, mysterious and vital. But the vitality, carnality and intensity of Burri's work is not all it offers. Perhaps they constitute his personal signature; but not more than this. What is most important in his work is the objective metaphors he creates through it. This is where the poet shows himself in his painting.

[. . .] Burri is a poet, a surgeon who knows and feels with intense visualization what lies within the fleshy surface of his compositions and an artist who is able to suggest this to the sympathetic observer. Collage with Burri has taken on another dimension. It is no longer a primarily compositional activity, a *jeu d'esprit* or a gesture; he has given it a living quality, a sensuous character. Within the limits of his medium he taps the sources of enjoyment Rembrandt drank from so deeply in his *Flayed Beef*, Rubens in the flesh of his nudes, Géricault in his corpses. At the same time his work shows a sensibility and delicacy of expression in its most successful examples which gives it for our age and in crudest of materials some of the qualities of a Redon pastel or a Renoir rose. Sensibility to texture contrasts, a subtly disciplined palette, broad, simple compositional organizations and draughtsmanship that controls a sewn thread as effectively as Alexander Calder's leads a wire through space, are the artisan features of Burri's work. But what Burri gives us of most importance is something more. For in Yeats's words "the thing seen is never the vision" as "the thing heard is never the message." To Burri we are indebted for a new visual metaphor: a poet, he brings refreshment to the eye.

1957

Francesco Arcangeli, in *Opere di Alberto Burri*, exhibition catalog (Turin, Galleria La Bussola, 22 November–5 December 1957), La Loggia, Bologna, 1957.

Nonostante, anzi in ragione, delle tele di sacco, delle stoffe varie, delle cuciture di filo, delle lamiere, dei legni combusti (mettete in conto, se volete, come "boutade", la chiusura-lampo usata in una sua grande tela esposta alla Biennale del '56; o il bottone che compare nel *Tutto nero* del '56), nonostante i rigonfiamenti della superficie, i buchi, i crateri, le smagliature; nonostante le materie, gli espedienti – chiamateli trucchi, se vi aggrada – che Burri ha voluto e vorrà usare, a noi pare evidente che si tratta d'un pittore, d'un vero pittore. Consigliamo i visitatori di questa mostra (che ci pare notevolmente rappresentativa degli ultimi cinque anni dell'artista) a non rifiutarsi a quella specie di trauma che un gruppo di opere di Burri inevitabilmente produce su chi abbia gli occhi aperti. A me capitò di provarlo, la prima volta, alla Quadriennale romana del '55-'56. Non avevo mai veduto, fino ad allora, un solo originale di Burri; e, da qualche riproduzione, m'ero anzi formata l'idea che si trattasse di più o meno abili trucchi; forse di balordaggini. Appena entrato nella sala che accoglieva le sue opere, l'idea cadde immediatamente: l'urto più o meno forte, più o meno gradevole, che ogni opera di vera pittura, d'ogni secolo e tendenza, produce nell'occhio dello spettatore qui si verificò immediatamente, con un'intensità che mi parve anche profonda. Non ho dovuto pentirmi, a tutt'oggi, di quella prima imperiosa impressione.

Alberto Burri è nato a Città di Castello nel 1915. È medico, non ha fatto studi accademici. Non partecipò, anche per essere arrivato abbastanza tardi alla pittura (la sua prima personale, a Roma, è del '47) alle più note manifestazioni di gruppo, non si inserì nei movimenti che toccarono la sua generazione, promossi da pittori, se non erriamo, "professionisti". Presto intrattenne rapporti con gli Stati Uniti (già nel '53 espose alla Galleria Frumkin di Chicago). Anche per tutte queste ragioni Burri, in confronto ai coetanei, ha un carattere pressoché unico: qualche cosa di inedito, di diretto, di non compromesso con altre tradizioni che non siano quelle dell'arte più moderna, liberamente cercate e intuite. Non si pensano antefatti, alla sua opera, di vecchio stampo. Noi escluderemmo qualsiasi influenza, sul suo lavoro, delle esperienze astratte italiane, del resto quasi sempre saltuarie o praticate da emigrati; rammenteremmo, se mai, come nomi non irrelativi, anche se non determinanti, Prampolini, per quella sua fedeltà alla tradizione dell'avanguardia europea, e per una certa propensione al comporre il quadro in zone vaste, e Cagli, nel senso d'una suggestione verso la forza tuttora sconosciuta dell'area artistica americana. Ma Burri, almeno dal 1952 in poi, è decisamente personale. Compare in questa mostra il *Grande sacco* del 1952, che è uno dei suoi primi esempi tipici. Che in questa, e in altre opere consimili, giochi il senso della trovata, oltreché da parte dell'autore, anche nel senso dell'urtare, irritare, sorprendere, potrà darsi; ma questa fu la storia, ormai vecchia d'una cinquantina d'anni, del "collage" moderno, fin dalle prime esperienze dei cubisti. Certo si è che in Braque e in Picasso, come in altri, l'uso di materie estranee alla pittura comunemente intesa era assorbito in effetto di pittura; vale a dire, il collage era un gioco brillante, eccezionale, per riconfermare quelle leggi, quei rapporti, che quei talentosi maestri non pensavano in fondo a distruggere; quasi anzi a rendere più amabili variandone e aerandone una possibile o presunta "routine". Nel gesto di Burri che tende sul telaio le grandi tele di sacco è, invece, qualche cosa che viene dopo "dada": dopo, cioè, l'atteggiamento anarchico di alcuni ingegni d'Europa che coll'arte come si era intesa da secoli voleva farla finita, surrogandola con la "boutade", col paradosso giocato sul nulla, con la bizzarria della trovata e dell'espediente. Tuttavia, nemmeno a questi uomini, che si servirono anche del "collage", Burri è veramente legato; e in questo senso il rilancio che attualmente si fa a Roma dello stravagante tedesco Schwitters e dei suoi "papiers collés" sembrerebbe voler intorbidare acque che non sono quelle di Burri. Questi fa sempre, del "collage", uso singolare, nel senso d'una scoperta personale della bellezza, qualità, suggestione delle materie impiegate, mettendole in sapiente dialogo, talvolta per contrasto, con le zone dell'opera tradizionalmente dipinte. Per Burri non si tratta di incollare dipingendo, o di evadere o riconfermare la pittura giocando; si tratta, prima, d'intendere la frusta bellezza della superficie d'un sacco, o il cupo brillare dei legni, o il rigido e opaco splendere d'una lamiera; e poi, cucendo sottilmente, calcolatamente bruciando e tingendo, e soprattutto alternando gli spazi di materia con gli spazi di pittura, dialettizzando i neri neutri d'un fondo con i neri brutalmente viventi e infetti di cenci e residui d'abbigliamento, dare a tutto questo una nuova e diversa vita; sottolinearne una cupa e vivente sostanza, o una incredibile possibilità di grazia. È soltanto issando sulla parete il *Grande sacco* del '52 (un'opera che a terra sembrava bruta materia, scoraggiante per la sua irredimibile apparenza materiale) che ci si accorge di quanto le due sole brevi zone dipinte, un bianco e un nero più intensi, respingano sapientemente la grande superficie del sacco entro un velo di tono, malinconico e trattenuto. La materia compare, allora, vera ma altra da sé; affiora la bellezza della sua sostanza al di là della sua sostanza. Ma, ammesso che, con queste considerazioni, io avessi aiutato qualcuno a intendere, o a intendere meglio che Burri è un pittore, resta a vedersi che cosa significhi ed esprima la sua pittura. Non manca chi lo accusa di estetismo, di eccessi di raffinatezza, di compiacersi cioè della pittura per la pittura. Noi crediamo, invece, che quasi sempre la sua arte esprima. Se Burri è un artista astratto, a me pare tuttavia che egli non lo sia soltanto nel senso che fu, per ora insuperabilmente, definito da Kandinsky nel suo libretto del 1910. Si sa che l'opera astratta non raffigura nulla di comunemente riconoscibile, ma, appunto per il fatto di non distrarre l'attenzione dello spettatore con la cosa raffigurata, porta, con la composizione delle sue forme e dei suoi colori, all'espressione diretta le emozioni spirituali che vivono nell'uomo interiore. Quando, davanti all'opera, lo spettatore domanda: "Che cosa vuol dire?", chiede all'artista quel che l'artista non ha voluto dare; e dovrebbe chiedersi, piuttosto: "Mi emoziona?"; o, al più, "Che significato ha?". Noi non siamo pieni d'entusiasmo per i presunti valori di libertà sconfinata che i fautori dell'astrattismo sembrano promettere all'artista con questa concezione; ne ammettiamo tuttavia la legittimità. Ancora meno vagheggiamo l'atteggiamento per cui la pittura dovrebbe trasformarsi in grafia automatica, ad esprimere direttamente la presenza della personalità; sarebbe grave, per esempio, che qualche perito calligrafo molto versato in materia stabilisse, dalla lettura dei segni e degli intrecci, che l'autore dell'opera è un cretino. È una sorte che non potrebbe mai toccare a Burri, la cui arte, eccezionalmente, non scade nemmeno di fronte a quell'idea tutt'ora piena e complessa, impegnata non solo in un astratto lirismo, ma anche in un giudizio e in una partecipazione agli aspetti del mondo, che noi continuiamo tutt'ora a caldeggiare come la più valevole per l'arte. In Burri l'espressione non figurativa delle emozioni va al di là di un fragile e solitario lirismo; è spesso così nutrita, così implacabile, da diventare la metafora diretta, quasi oggettiva, d'un mondo pieno di significati, d'un suo contenuto non eludibile. Quando, nel '55, Burri invia al Premio Esso una tela di sacco intitolata *Umbria vera*, siamo convinti che non bara. La materia prescelta allude così direttamente al gravare monotono, infinito, di qualche costiera desolata, forata di grotte, dell'Umbria (là dove, salendo, si tramuta di verde in squallidamente terrestre) da valere, così trasferita, quando e più d'una comune interpretazione naturale (e questo trasferimento, questo non imitare direttamente pur essendo così veri, permette anche di vedere altre immagini nell'opera; a me accade di pensare a sai logorati di fraterie, a occhiaie d'incappati o di flagellanti). Del resto, parlando del manto d'un seicentesco san Tomaso, un grande critico vedeva, nel 1926, la luce e l'ombra "distribuire ad un panno comune gli stessi semplici onori che si veggono rivestire brulli le lande tufacee di certe contrade di Spagna". È evidente che alla profonda capacità visuale del Longhi non interessava, in quel momento, che quel Velázquez raffigurasse un san Tomaso, quanto l'imparziale unificazione, sotto il segno della materia, del panneggio d'un manto e degli anfratti d'una "sierra". Così in Burri, che molto spesso usa il collage come asserzione intensa d'un moderno concetto di materia, la tela d'un sacco può direttamente trapassare allo squallore d'un declivio. Ma non vorremmo tirare tutte le acque al nostro mulino di sostenitori d'un "ultimo" o d'un "nuovo naturalismo". Anche se un suo notissimo critico, lo Sweeney, afferma che "Burri con i suoi collages ci dà un senso della materia vitale in un'epoca di riconosciuta riduzione ed astrazione", o che "l'arte di Burri ci ricorda il sentimento della carne viva", è anche da dire che noi non riusciamo a vederci quella "freschezza" di cui parla il critico americano. A differenza dei più tipici pittori di materia (alludo a un Fautrier, a un Dubuffet, o a un Morlotti), in cui vive un concetto di apparente "antistile", e il tentativo di modellare direttamente una forma organica e non intellettualistica, non c'è dubbio che Burri frena assai spesso le sue punte implacabilmente materiali entro quel "vasto e semplice ordinamento della composizione" che gli riconosce lo Sweeney. È allora che nell'opera di Burri, al di là delle suggestioni del moderno astrattismo razionale, riaffiora con violenza un volto anticamente, quasi ciecamente, italiano.

1959

Enrico Crispolti, "La pittura di Alberto Burri," *Il Verri*, no. 1, February, 1959.

[. . .] La durezza e violenza di Burri si dichiarano interamente piuttosto nei catrami, esposti ad "Origine", a Roma, nel '50. Sul "tutto nero" di superfici appena accentuate nella loro ruvidezza, l'evidenza di alcuni elementi, quasi macchie circolari (lontane ascendenze delle piaghe successive), cromaticamente distinti. Ciò segnava nel panorama italiano un'assai radicale divergenza dalle elaborazioni post-cubiste poco prima raggruppate dal "Fronte Nuovo delle Arti" e che si risolveranno in buona parte nella formulazione venturiana dell'"astratto-concreto" [1952]; e su piano internazionale, con il grafismo emblematico allora così teso, di Capogrossi [1949-50] e le imminenti libere ricerche di Fontana [1950], una delle rare mozioni iniziali italiane della nuova condizione *autre* europea. E Burri definiva così la propria clandestinità di fronte al corso ufficiale della nuova arte italiana: clandestinità venuta meno soltanto da pochissimi anni (è ancora pacificamente ignorato nel '56 in *Pittori Italiani dal Futurismo a oggi* di Ballo!), dapprima per l'apprezzamento critico straniero, soprattutto nord-americano (che risale già al '53), e per l'estesissima influenza sulla successiva generazione artistica italiana ed europea, che lo ha scoperto quale effettivo maestro, infine, ma poco più che recentissimamente, all'effettivo ed adeguato interesse della nostra stessa critica. Fra il '51 ed il '52 la visione di Burri si chiarisce definitivamente. Nel '51 sviluppa la tecnica del collage, connettendo zone dipinte, o a sabbia e gesso, a stracci e tele. Il dipinto si articola irregolarmente, a larghe campiture distinte appunto dalla diversità di materia, e tuttavia tende ad un certo ordine compositivo. Nel '52 l'intensità aumenta, il contenuto si precisa. In larghe campiture, spesso bianche, si circoscrivono ed acutizzano episodi ulteriormente accentuati da materie a corpo, rapprese, da zone improvvisamente slargate, quasi nella cute stessa delle precedenti; altrove si sovrappongono vere colature di gesso, o sabbie intrise. Prevalgono qui rossi, neri, bruni. Spesso ne nasce il senso immediato dell'escremento, della benda lorda, ma riportati ad una comune origine fisiologica, ed insieme ad un potenziale espressivo ulteriore, per la sua universalità, la loro mera oggettiva verità. L'*ordure*, che in Fautrier è sottile e raffinata ipotesi di alternativa ad una grazia estrema e già fatiscente, diviene tragica constatazione di materia, verità palpabile, non figurata sia pure in una attiva presenza di percezione. L'irrazionalismo di Burri è infatti ulteriore; la sua disperazione rifiuta anche il gesto di salvezza, infine un po' compiaciuto, d'un patrimonio culturale. Qualsiasi effettivo riferimento al polimaterismo futurista, ai *collages* cubisti, o al polimaterismo sperimentale dada e surrealista – di Schwitters soprattutto – è dunque subito esterno e irrelativo rispetto agli interessi reali di Burri, come al suo stesso processo operativo.

[. . .] Nello stesso '52 Burri realizza i primi grandi "sacchi". La sua preferenza va da allora per dipinti di grandi dimensioni, della più ampia efficacia e presa esistenziale. Come in Pollock, in Rothko, in Kline, in Francis, in Still, l'ampiezza dimensionale, in rapporto alla scala umana, del campo d'espressione diventa elemento di primaria importanza. Il dipinto è nello spazio stesso dell'uomo, qualità del suo ambiente quotidiano: non vi si contrappone in una diversa ipotesi di spazio, di diversa ed ideale natura. Si coglie dunque una concomitanza espressiva di Burri con i problemi della nuova pittura ed in genere della cultura nord-americana. Non unica; anche se i riferimenti ulteriori vanno piuttosto a particolari situazioni del realismo cinematografico (penso sempre a violenti primi piani di Kazan), alla strumentazione scenica del teatro, forse del balletto, all'accentuato radicalismo realistico di un Dos Passos, di un Faulkner. Tuttavia il timbro problematico di Burri è prettamente europeo. Perciò il riferimento a Sartre, eventualmente a Camus, e magari al "Gran Genio" dell'informe che si affaccia in *Bilder* di Benn, risulta infine più necessario. È proprio Burri anzi a rinnovare perentoriamente l'opposizione di una tragica e disperata alternativa all'ottimismo vitalistico prevalente nell'attuale cultura figurativa nord-americana.

[. . .] Ma la verità e storicità di Burri è nella constatazione che quest'inferno non è presentita ipotesi escatologica, ma realtà pressante, quotidianamente travolgente l'uomo contemporaneo, nel crollo attuale d'ogni possibilità d'ulteriore certezza culturale o di etichette ideologiche, di presupposti conoscitivi o di verità imposte e sbandierate. Burri non ha mai fatto professione di ideologismo o di profetismo; ma la sua azione, strettamente di pittore (non a caso nella sua dichiarazione di "poetica" contenuta in *The New Decade. 22 European Painters and Sculptors*, The Museum of Modern Art, New York 1955, ha insistito sulla intrasferibilità in parole della sua pittura, e sulla caratterizzazione di questa soltanto per ciò che sicuramente esclude), tocca la verità esistenziale, travolgendo sovrastrutture, comode e convenzionali certezze. Dal '52 al

'56 la stagione dei "sacchi": accentuazioni organiche della materia (*S 5 P Roma* '53, *M M A Roma* '54, ecc.) sviluppi quasi scenici d'una nuova possibilità immaginativa drammaticamente coattiva (*4 B Roma* '53, *N. I 1 Roma* '53, *Sacco e bianco* '55, ecc.) sottili allusioni e sviluppi d'ironia (*R 1 Roma* '53, *Sacco e verde* '56, ecc.), tragiche dichiarazioni d'una realtà superstite d'un evento umano (*Grande sacco* '52, *S 5 Roma* '55, ecc.). Sempre la presenza ineluttabile della materia, il riferimento diretto al sacco, prescelto non solo per ragioni di intrinseca ricchezza cromatica, ma in tutta la sua entità nozionale, come materia fra le più comuni e misere, fra le più cariche di immediata allusività a vicende, situazioni, destini umani, a eredità stesse culturali (il francescanesimo, più volte citato per Burri, come il suo ascendente in una perentorietà medioevale umbra quasi iacoponica). La tela, lo straccio, spesso brandello d'un indumento. L'*ordure* che segna il passaggio dell'uomo, in tutta la sua verità. Il potenziare di volta in volta questi elementi al massimo in riferimenti e traslati, e sempre ritornando alla loro iniziale imminenza materica. Il connettere l'invenzione allusiva, il rosso tutt'altro che di "pittura" di certe piaghe (ricordo il passo di Sartre citato all'inizio), il nero artificiale, come d'un pannello di cui si dichiari a priori la convenzionalità (pur caricata di elementi allusivi: nero-lutto), ad elementi invece altrettanto esplicitamente "veri", il sacco sudicio, così come raccolto, i suoi strappi, le sue smagliature: dunque l'artificio che diviene realtà, e la realtà che si volge in artificio. Nell'estrema raffinatezza l'eleganza che immediatamente si corrompe, si volta in putrescenza, ancora in *ordure*, ed in questa poi riaffiora. "La tela diviene allora come un muro di base tenebrosamente proliferante e sinistro, su dalla mortale opacità, dalla stasi dei fondi astratti l'occhio coglie ancora qualche cosa muoversi, generarsi, strapparsi, sanguinare" [F. Arcangeli, F. Arcangeli, pres. in cat. pers. a La Loggia, Bologna, ottobre-novembre 1957]. Spesso il senso macabro del trofeo. Se nel '52-'54 si registra una certa giustapposizione e quasi ordinata presentazione di elementi esistenziali, disinnestati dalla loro situazione originaria e disposti in reciproca tensione (caricati dunque d'una allusività ancora relativa ad una situazione originaria dell'oggetto, anziché, come poco dopo, suscitata immediatamente dalla conformazione e significazione nuova di questo nel contesto del dipinto), e parallelamente una certa impronta quasi di vaga discendenza neo-plastica nell'ideazione e strutturazione generale del dipinto, nel '55 e '56 prevale, per l'incalzare d'una dapprima sotterranea, infine determinante mozione espressionista, una più intima connessione di rapporti, trasferendosi appunto l'esistenzialità dall'origine materica degli elementi (sacco, ecc.) alla loro nuova vicenda sul dipinto. L'allusività non giunge al dipinto, ma parte da questo. Allora la conformazione delle materie, degli stracci, ecc. si fa irregolare, di volta in volta nuova, pur nella sua raggiunta univocità: *Tutto nero*, *Sacco e verde*, *Martedì grasso*, *Grande Rosso* del '56, capolavori. Ciò segna un accrescimento del campo espressivo, dell'area analogica, una più pertinente assimilazione d'una situazione e d'un destino esplicitamente esistenziali.

Maurizio Calvesi, "Alberto Burri," *Quadrum*, no. 7, Brussels, 1959.

Il sospetto, benché minimo, di trovarsi di fronte ad un trucco preclude ogni possibilità di penetrazione nella visione di Burri, proprio perché essa è, invece, radicalmente autentica. Né tuttavia per autenticità, specie nel caso di Burri, si può intendere chiarezza, trasparenza di visione, diretta individuabilità di contenuti e di processi; ché anzi il timbro, o uno dei timbri, di tale autenticità va proprio cercato nella sua non dissimulata ambiguità, nella sua disorientante e scoperta polivalenza. Anche se mai s'è posto esplicitamente l'accento su un tale aspetto, sta di fatto che le interpretazioni date della sua pittura – ivi comprese le oralmente espresse – risultano aperte su molteplici tasti, o, se centrate su un motivo, non di rado l'una contraddittoria per l'altra. Emilio Villa, il primo ad intuire la portata di Burri, ne ha dato con le sue immagini letterarie un'introduzione suggestiva, che rimane tra le più aderenti, una sorta di precisione dell'impreciso, un'approssimazione analogica che ha punte, tuttavia, direttamente penetranti al difficile centro focale.

[. . .] Il passaggio di Burri al "non figurativo" si realizza dal '47 al '48. Se un futuro storico dell'arte dovesse rinvenire, senza indicazioni attributive, un gruppo di piccole tempere dal '48 in su, fino ad anni recenti, che oggi Burri conserva presso di sé, avrebbe di che scervellarsi, specie se l'immagine che dell'artista si sarà tramandata dovesse risultare inchiodata all'incrocio delle classificazioni "informale" – "surreale" – "esistenziale". È raro incontrare qualcosa di più squisitamente pittorico, di più dipinto di queste tempere; e con una qualità che non la cede ad altri tra i grossi maestri contemporanei. La personalità di Burri naturalmente c'è in pieno, nella fermezza e nella concisione della sua eleganza, nel suo quintessenziale amore per la pittura, nella chiarezza infallibile della pagina astratta: nel suo stringente e gagliardo ordine formale senza altre implicazioni, qui almeno, che di un'attivante fantasia. Le pitture di Burri tra il '48 e il '50 non sono forse di una qualità così pura, ma profondamente significative, anche per la sua formazione. L'interesse per la materia vi è scoperto: smalti sempre più compositi, sabbia e olio cotto, catrame. Il dipinto è già un organismo, riarso ma cupamente lucente, nero-blu rosso e terroso, con le sue crescenze e contrazioni, borchie di pigmento incrostato e pezzature, ferite ed innesti, operati incidendo nello strato del colore, o sovrapponendo bordature più scure. C'è dentro, a volte, un senso divagato e sorprendente, quasi di favola ma come trattenuto nell'agguato della materia.

[. . .] Cercare i tramiti della formazione di Burri al di fuori di quell'ambiente romano fra cui in realtà egli viveva, operava, discuteva, sarebbe inavveduto storicamente, e quasi ingenuo. Occorre certo, come per ogni personalità eccezionale, tener presente che le intuizioni individuali risultano soverchianti (anche se non fino al punto da obliterarne la fisionomia) rispetto ai dati direttamente offerti o mediati dall'ambiente, dati che a quelle intuizioni fornirono una piattaforma di appoggio e di discussione stimolante. Persino la pulizia categorica e quasi talvolta artigianale che caratterizza il "polimaterismo" di Prampolini e dei secondi futuristi, vale a dire il dato contro cui Burri più violentemente e personalmente reagisce, ha un suo preciso valore, sia perché impostando staticamente e limitativamente il problema poteva offrire lo spunto ad una reazione più dinamica ed estesamente implicante, sia perché lo strutturalismo cui tale esigenza è annessa circoscriveva, anche se snaturandolo, l'apporto "dadaista" e surrealista in una zona di energico equilibrio formale, di discendenza, appunto, cubistafuturista e astratto-razionale. Ed è qui, credo, una delle ineliminabili radici che vietano a Burri di operare come "surrealista", definizione impropria per la sua arte, quanto diffusa, e di cui l'artista è, anche per formazione mentale, insofferente. Non si fa questione, certo, di "dare" e "avere", ma si tenta d'individuare l'importanza di un clima e di un ambiente, un ambiente di cui Burri, ovviamente, fu parte attiva e determinante.

[. . .] Delle fantasie più fosche e rosse di Scipione, ed anche dei tratti più decantati, quasi in un difficile parallelo con Morandi, del pescoso "tonalismo" romano, Burri s'è alimentato a suo modo, nutrendo di inediti fermenti timbrici e di sottili risorse tonali la sua elementare tavolozza. In questa direzione di "neo-tonalismo" Burri s'affianca ad un'altra rilevante personalità di questa stagione romana, Afro. Agganci e parallelismi che vanno proposti, ed intesi, con le dovute cautele, ma che restano tuttavia innegabili, e ben caratterizzanti per l'ambiente in cui Burri storicamente si produce. Uno dei primi "sacchi" di Burri che io conosca, forse il primo da lui fatto, è del 1950: già vi risulta il senso personale della tela largamente campita, di uno squadro largo, robusto, l'accento oscuramente innervante delle grosse giunture di corda, quello insinuante delle cuciture di filo leggero. Il sacco, non esprime ancora "in sé"; l'ordito tonale è perseguito con sporcature di colore, impasti spalmati di sabbia e olio. L'effetto è tuttavia così essenziale, il tessuto pittorico così intelligentemente consunto che si comprende come l'attivo controllo del gusto, già attento alle suggestioni più intrinseche della materia, potesse guidarlo a una più profonda scoperta. Sarà quando – verso il '52 – egli passa ad alternare sul telaio, a zone di pittura, i suoi sacchi grezzi, senza sovrapporre i due elementi distinti e dialetticamente accordati. La materialità delle logore pezze di juta, più sacchi che mai anche dopo tirati sul telaio, non va distrutta, né velata o riconfusa con altre materie: ma invece evidenziata, mettendo l'accento sulla particolare qualità della sua intrinseca e propria bellezza. Tra un nero matto, sonante, e un bianco di calce, robustamente incastrati ai margini del dipinto, la luce abbassata, carica di suggestioni torpidamente risvegliate, che le fibre del sacco decantano, è luce di una logora e compromessa resistenza; sudore del tempo; ma anche assaporamento, di quel tempo, in una durata godibile di tono; quasi il recupero e il trasalimento, e di nuovo l'oblio, di una condizione verificata nel profondo di se stessi. Ancora materia è già pittura; qualcosa (azzardo) se non di analogo di non completamente diverso dalle bottiglie di Morandi; non però le bottiglie dipinte, ma le bottiglie mentre le dipinge, mentre nell'oblio dell'immagine si sciolgono i motivi più addentrati e riposti dell'affezione dell'artista a quegli oggetti impolverati. Se fino qui Burri aveva, ma con prepotente personalità, elaborato i dati di una cultura, se già aveva molto inventato, è ora che egli trova: è ora che la sua ricerca ci interessa in sé (non meno del risultato), che la sua novità s'identifica con un'autentica scoperta. Qualcosa che fa punto e a capo. E ci si può immaginare l'emozione, profonda, di questa scoperta, anche se egli dovette giungervi seguendo soltanto il richiamo di un istinto, quasi naturalmente forse. Ma la scelta, in realtà, impegnava le forze della sua coscienza, coinvolgeva le istanze più impellenti del suo inconscio. L'impaginato largo, fermo di Burri (il "vasto e semplice ordinamento della composizione" cui allude Sweeney) è una sua precisa caratteristica, praticamente constante, sinora; meno apparente in taluni aspetti della sua produzione '56-'57, ma di nuovo spiegata nei "ferri" del '58. Si può notare che negli esperimenti più antichi, prima dei "sacchi" cioè, questa modalità di composizione non è decisamente denunciata; pur discendendo, quindi, da una radice astratto-razionale di cui abbiamo tentato di definire le linee, non si tratta di un dato culturale inerte, che Burri si porti dietro, ma è qualcosa che trova la sua maturazione e il suo equilibrio proprio nel trapasso dalla pittura "dipinta" alla composizione di materia: come una necessità concettuale, una configurazione mentale della scelta sensibile.

[. . .] Le tele di sacco, cose sempre esistite e intensamente esistenti, senza tempo ma logorate dal tempo: immagini, forse, di noi stessi, del nostro essere antichi, del nostro essere presenti, e soprattutto del nostro essere transeunti, "già" invecchiati, e "già" morti. Come il volto della terra che ci genera, ci alimenta e ci ingoia. Su per l'efficace ossatura del quadro, così robustamente autoportante – quasi un ancestrale paradigma di spazio – le cuciture sottili, le pezzature, le gore muffite, i lembi sbrindellati, accendono ad un richiamo intensissimo di vita e di memorie la muta effigie, quasi accasciata, del sacco, riverberata di grigi e di verdi. A tratti è qualcosa che può suggerire il fermento, il brulichio di una carcassa marcescente; ma sull'oscura suggestione fioriscono, preziose e persino dolci, le modulazioni dei toni, in un accordo austero e decantato, poeticamente liberante. Le materie che Burri sceglie per comporre i suoi quadri, sono l'occasione della sua pittura: come per l'artista tradizionale la realtà esterna, il paesaggio o la figura. Ma qui l'occasione è ben più imperiosa, coinvolgente. Siano materie che egli trova, o che egli cerca, l'incontro con esse o la loro scelta non credo infatti che si determinino senza collegamento con l'inconscio. Istanze e "presenze" della psiche, che il processo di elaborazione cui le materie saranno sottoposte, verrà a mettere più sottilmente a fuoco, e nel contempo a purificare, ad esaltare in una sorta di *transfert* squisitamente pittorico. Dunque una "sublimazione" dell'impulso inconscio in una "qualità" artistica? Come abbiamo osservato, il polimaterismo di Burri nella sua prima accezione (tra il '48 e il '51, circa) è un'eredità culturale, sia pure assunta con forte originalità, e con una coscienza e responsabilità del problema già autonome e personalmente approfondite. La maturazione del problema, il passaggio cioè da un polimaterismo di suggestione più genericamente pittorica (dove le zone dipinte restano sostanzialmente equivalenti agli inserti materici, tanto che ad essi il colore si sovrappone sovente, rinforzandone sì, e non eludendone, le intrinseche suggestioni, ma pur sempre in qualche modo snaturandone e riassorbendole in un "idea" di tono) ad una diretta espressione di materia (dove gli interventi del colore sono in precisa funzione di essa, non più dunque filtrando ed alterando tale espressione, ma potenziandola e investendola in una sfera estetica, inquadrandola insomma nella tensione sensibile e concettuale di un organismo pittorico); tale maturazione e tale passaggio possono anche corrispondere, appunto, ad una diversa tendenzialità d'assunzione della materia: invece che come dato puramente sensibile (e perciò equivalente al colore, perfettamente intercambiabile con esso), come dato stimolante di un processo psichico, reattivo ad un'istanza dell'inconscio. Direi anzi che l'avvertimento, segreto, di una nuova ed inconscia attrazione per la materia (in questo caso, il sacco), possa essersi fatta tutt'una con il definitivo accertamento delle sue qualità pittoriche intrinseche, allo stato grezzo; e la simultaneità di questi riflessi potrà motivarsi nella natura dialettica della stessa istanza inconscia, già potenzialmente atta a sublimarsi (cioè a travasarsi in un'istanza estetica) e compiutamente avvertibile dalla coscienza, anzi, soltanto attraverso questo processo di sublimazione. È un classico schema freudiano, che prendiamo a prestito perché ci sembra che possa calzare al caso di Burri, o che comunque ne aiuti la difficile interpretazione. Ma anche se vi insisteremo, e se tenteremo d'affiancarvi a rincalzo altre ipotesi di simile radice (non certo con sufficiente sistematicità e coerenza, né so con quale proprietà strumentale e tecnica) non è alla diagnosi che puntiamo, anzi ne rifuggiamo; per questo una tale proprietà non ci preoccupa né ci sta a cuore. Ci interessa invece lo spunto, la base minima di appoggio, non ad un'analisi parascientifica, ma ad un'intuizione critica: anche se, per nostro limite d'agilità, il discorso potrà sfiorare l'aridità di un'analisi, e peccare d'insufficienza sotto il profilo critico. Converrà allora, perché esso acquisti almeno la validità di uno stimolo all'altrui intuizione, avvertire che la verosimiglianza del processo psicanalitico va comunque subordinata alla verosimiglianza del processo estetico: questo, nella povertà dello schema psicanalitico, non potrà certo trovare la sua giustificazione, né probabilmente la sua spiegazione, ma sì, almeno, l'indicazione della complessa base psichica, su cui il processo estetico indubbiamente si articola, e trova la sua continua integrazione.

[. . .] Egli non "rappresenta" l'istanza inconscia, bensì la sua opera si configura attraverso il processo dinamico per cui tale istanza si trasforma in atto estetico. La sua metodologia, anzi, consiste nell'assumere soltanto, e direttamente, ciò che di quel processo affiora alla coscienza; e così i dati della sua scelta inconscia (materia) si riorganizzano nei valori pittorici integrati dalla coscienza: al di fuori, è vero, di un "sistema" formale astratto ed idealmente precostituito, ma pur sempre nell'ambito di una nozione inveterata di forma e di spazio che, come abbiamo accennato, fa tutt'uno con la sua coscienza, ne costituisce il sedimento più solido e antico. Dunque il rapporto di nozione ed esperienza (cioè, interamente al dipinto di dato mentale e di dato di gesto, di dato formale e dato informale) si risolve in parallelo, ed in stretta connessione, al rapporto di processo estetico e processo psichico, di qualità artistica e quantità inconscia. Si tratta anzi, in realtà, di un processo unico e più complesso, che si determina nella continua integrazione dialettica di momenti schematicamente isolabili: forma come nozione, atto come esperienza, forma come simbolo, atto come simbolo, idea estetica, istanza inconscia. Anche se le diverse tappe di Burri, lungo il suo percorso e sviluppo artistico, sembrano rispecchiare la prevalenza ora dell'uno ora dell'altro momento. Dai primissimi "sacchi", dove l'idea estetica ha il deciso sopravvento, ci si inoltra in una fase di più esplicita "azione": gli strappi e le cuciture sembrano sempre più ferite, quasi carnalmente rimarginate; la materia patisce infinite lacerazioni e sfibramenti. L'atto distruttivo-costruttivo (subito teso, per sublimazione, ad un vibrante esito estetico, talvolta persino delicato) di lacerare, di cauterizzare, di slabbrare, di trapassare ed imbastire con l'ago, s'inquadra nella tensione tonale e timbrica della pagina: a cui ora il colore, lucidamente decantato nella sua pregnante carica di *libido*, partecipa allo stesso livello della materia. Le divaganti ellissi, bordate di scuro, che nel *Bruno* del 1949 ancora sapevano di cifra astratta (da una matrice culturale reperibile tra Arp e Prampolini), nelle *Combustioni plastiche* del '56 e del '57 ricompaiono in un'accezione scopertamente (forse solo più scopertamente?) – quanto inconsciamente – simbologica: non più impresse o sovrapposte alla superficie del dipinto, ma aperte nel suo spessore lùbrico e cupamente splendente, slabbrate ed emergenti più dal profondo; sebbene cadenzate secondo un ordine ancor più rigoroso e scelto, squisito. Non si tratterà, allora, di forme direttamente allusive, ma di schemi formali "ricaricati", infusi di un significato che è altro da quello originario; e se è vero che, nel ricambio onirico, abituali nozioni s'investono di altri significati che premono dall'inconscio, non sarà assurdo credere che, nel processo creativo di Burri, si sia verificata un'analoga trasposizione. Così, mentre comportano un'implicazione del subconscio, quelle lacerazioni restano cadenze spaziali, scansioni di forme e di colori; pure e raffinate "immagini", invece che figurazioni di piglio surreale. Se in partenza poteva essere l'incontro con una materia ad attrarre una scelta, in questa fase ulteriore si direbbe che l'iniziativa passi alle attivizzate energie del subconscio, che esse stesse intervengano a suggerire l'invenzione di particolari materie. La plastica, densa e cedevole, che Burri (nella sua configurazione più "infernale") adotta per le "combustioni" del '56-'57, è appunto una materia pensata per essere violentata, plasmata, modulata, cioè totalmente e quasi sfrenatamente posseduta. Ma, pressoché contemporaneamente, da questo polo estremo si trapassa, come per rivalsa, all'estremo dialetticamente opposto dell'eleganza. Le piccole "combustioni" su carta possono risultare, in questo senso, quasi dimostrative: da un atto così brutale, e simbolicamente distruttivo, come la bruciatura, sortisce un risultato di pura raffinatezza; il significato inconscio è rovesciato con fermezza in un'affermazione di squisito controllo, di sottilissima civiltà.

Paul Wember, in *Alberto Burri*, exhibition catalog
(Krefeld, Museum Haus Lange, May–June 1959), Museum Haus Lange, Krefeld, 1959.

Alberto Burri does not paint paintings, he makes works. These often surprise in their technique and their materials. Let us begin with the *Sacchi*. Fragments of sacking of various coarseness in the thread and different types of weave are brought together here. Torn parts are sewn, sometimes finely machined, sometimes with edges rolled, or again with big clumsy stitches and ends frayed. In places where the thread has failed to catch the fragments hang apart. Many of the sacks have holes, small or big, and almost all bad parts. Seams, patches, darns chase one another across the surfaces. The artist tacks on extra bits of staff and as by accident fragments with printed words. But Burri's pictures are not made only from these rags. Their bases are respectable stretched canvases. Where gaps or holes in the sacking occur and where towards the edges it does not reach out, this canvas ground is painted up in oils. There is some underpainting underneath the sacking too, in black and white, green sometimes and red frequently. In this attitude to the material, an esthetic principle appears. As Michel Seuphor puts it: "Burri knows how to combine apparent clumsiness with perfect taste." Burri began by finding his material in the miller's yard of Città di Castello, a little Umbrian town. Soon he went on to timber merchants and sawmills. It was his *Legni* that he started to compose. Once more the elements are carried on a canvas ground, prepared and in part painted too. On this the artist brings together flat pieces of wood, rough or warped, and strips of veneer. He exploits all the splits, knot-holes and splintered edges there may be. He scorches parts of the wood, obtaining irregular lines and a colour—black—not out of the tube, as contrasts with the light surrounding tone. The next to follow were the pictures in plastic materials. Burri uses the physical nature of the plastic sheets for his own ends, snapping off parts and pushing them together, driving round holes with the edges pushed out. These works are just the same in principle as those in wood or sacking, but plastics bring new visual possibilities and they have their surprises too. The shiny sheets being prepared for table-tops, containers or utensils leave waste parts; and these, under the impact of the artists thought and fantasy, are changed to an expressive medium. The changes which take place in them are arbitrary, not accidental, calculated in the foreknowledge of an effect before the material is transformed by heat. The artist's will makes a symbolic composition out of them. At a certain point in Burri's work, then, the *Ferri* appeared. Fragments of iron sheeting, large or small, right-angled or oblique, curved or irregular in form, these replaced the other materials. Once more an effect was achieved to the observer new and strange. Burri can build his pictures out of all of the materials which men use for their needs, but every time the aim is slightly different. He sees the waste which falls from iron sheeting as it passes through industrial processes or over the workbench with different eyes from those of the technician and with a spirit which is different from any of the existing movements in art. And in this new direction he carries the spectator along with him. Nowadays these different materials and techniques are used by Burri simultaneously. In some works he mixes them. In others painted surfaces play a considerable part. Here Burri works the pigment with the same skill, born of long experience, using splits and breaks and bubbles and a calculated crackelure. But even in the pictures where the waste materials dominate, it is colour which plays the chief part. Indeed, it could hardly be otherwise. Picture-making knows no limitations of technique or of material; what matters is artistic aim and the achievement of a harmony. Burri's works possess a fascination difficult to grasp at first. The old balance is gone and that which they express is new. The artist does not so much destroy as bring back to life that which was destroyed previously. He builds his art out of the apparently worthless, from materials of the rubbish heap. We have often used the word “waste”. It [is the] name given to all the products of the manufacturing and technological process which are not used. But in reality the thing does not exist. This has been gradually recognised until today the practically-minded industries use “waste’” for the production of their new materials. For example wood-splinters go for building-board, cork waste into linoleum, slag from blast-furnaces is used for building-blocks. Parings of metal, melted down, become sheets once again. Manure and glue derive from bones and bakelite and the miraculous Perlon from the phenol produced in the refining of benzol. What Burri does then is the same as industry, but with artistic not utilitarian aim. That is his privelege. Those who see in his work only the waste-products which he has utilised have their minds made up in advance. A sack is not just a container made out of material, it is a purposeless stuff too. A veneer is just a neutral piece of wood which becomes what one makes of it. Iron scrap or tin are, in a sense physical as philosophical, first [of all] specifically composed materials. In Burri’s work, destroyed material has been used, or material destroyed for use in building something new. An old sack may carry its bad patches as the traces of its former use; but sacking, plastics, wood or metal have been changed and destroyed with intention and aim. In the light of results the idea of waste falls away. The industrial product is an implement, a tool, Burri’s product is a technical-esthetic composition. In the first case the aim is practical and in the second spiritual. The *Ferri* are the least inclined to make us think of waste because they suggest things we know. Yet if one compares a *Ferro* with an iron sculpture by Gonzalez—who used scrap too—there are important differences between the two. Gonzalez took finished industrial products, a screw for a nose, a T-iron for a foot, a stove-pipe for a head. Burri contents himself with worthless iron scraps and gives them a new form, making neither a dancer nor a woman with a basket out of them, but a pure composition with formal values of its own. Burri began to paint at twenty-nine. At forty came the climax of his collages of material. Now he is forty-four. One cannot catch him in the category of a style, for he has made his own. With the Tachists on one side and the geometric painters on the other, with those such as Hartung, Winter and Soulages who work with Signs, Burri has nothing to do. The idea of de-naturing objects of use he found, to be sure, in Gonzalez on the one side and in Schwitters, the Dadaists and the Surrealists on the other. But Burri’s wealth of sensibility led somewhere else. He is not aiming at Dada or at the comic chock but at a new sensuous harmony. He points to unsuspected values with a symbol-making power, standing for spiritual freedom and creative work. Like all creators he is only free within a certain area. He is bound by the laws which his discoveries established. Yet his use of new technological materials makes him a pioneer. To some Burri’s works have already the dignity of old masters, while others have their doubts. It is good so, for Burri is no old master, but as a form-creator and a picture-maker most contemporary. If one can see certain sources for his work, it still has opened possibilities which are new, unexplored and even by himself not yet thought out right to the end.

1960

Giulio Carlo Argan, *Alberto* Burri, in XXX *Biennale Internazionale d’Arte*, La Biennale di Venezia, Venice, 1960.

[. . .] A quanti, si chiedono se le opere di Burri debbano ancora considerarsi pittura, si può rispondere che la materia e la fattura di queste opere possono anche non essere la materia e la fattura tradizionali della pittura, ma l’obiettivo finale, e assolutamente esplicito, dell’artista rimane il “quadro”. L’oggetto che Burri compone con quelle strane materie non è figurazione né rappresentazione, ma non è neppure l’oggetto plastico del Cubismo o l’oggetto a funzionamento simbolico del Surrealismo; è un quadro o, se si vuole, la finzione di un quadro, una sorta di *trompe-l’œil* a rovescio, nel quale non è la pittura a fingere la realtà, ma la realtà a fingere la pittura. Per quanto possa parere paradossale, l’immagine tende sempre a rientrare in una superficie, ad adeguarsi a quello che il Francastel chiama lo “schermo plastico a due dimensioni”. È vero che l’immagine ha sempre una sua tangibile plasticità, sicché buca o rigonfia la superficie, mantiene il contatto con la realtà esistenziale, con un di qua e un di là, rispetto ai quali la superficie del quadro, come tale, perde ogni concretezza e vale soltanto come un termine medio, un imponderabile piano di passaggio tra la serie positiva e la serie negativa dei valori: ma lo scopo della ricerca di Burri è appunto di portare la materia, una reale e concreta materia, al punto critico di una condizione-limite, al di là della quale, se mai potesse varcarla, dovrebbe cessare di essere quella che è: reale e concreta materia. E proprio qui si profila il problema: per quanto il processo sia ancora, incontestabilmente, un processo di pittura dal quale è logico aspettarsi una catarsi o una trasformazione della materia in rappresentazione, questa trasformazione non si produce e la materia prelevata dal mondo reale e trasposta nel quadro rimane pericolosamente affacciata e sospesa al confine del nulla, in una condizione di evidente impossibilità spaziale e temporale. Allora è chiaro perché mai la geometria e la materia dei quadri di Burri, pur essendo legate da una relazione tesa e profonda, non si risolvano l’una nell’altra e rimangano sempre distinte e separate, negando a chi guarda sia l’orrore di vedere la geometria sopraffatta e travolta dalla materia, sia il sollievo di veder la materia inquadrarsi e rarefarsi nella struttura geometrica: la presenza della materia contraddice e distrugge lo spazio, così come la presenza della geometria contraddice e distrugge il tempo. Ora, poiché spazio e tempo sono le grandi coordinate dell'esperienza o della vita, la distruzione dello spazio e del tempo determina una sospensione della vita, instaura una condizione "autre", la condizione del "nulla". Ma va notato, a questo punto, che i quadri di Burri non sono né tragici né disperati: benché possiedano un'estrema lucidità e intensità d'immagine, non suscitano forti emozioni o, per essere più precisi, non suscitano emozioni che coinvolgano immediatamente, e mobilitino, i nostri interessi morali. La loro luce è abbagliante ma fredda, come quella di una scintilla elettrica scoccata nel tubo di vetro di un apparecchio di sperimentazione. L'artista ha tentato, e con successo, un'esperienza molto rischiosa: si tratta di vedere che cosa, propriamente, si proponesse di dimostrare.

Egli è certamente riuscito a produrre una condizione di vuoto fisico; ha eliminato o almeno sospeso, contrapponendo geometria e materia, ogni possibilità di pensiero o di vita. Ma qualcosa seguita a esistere, anzi qualcosa comincia ad esistere; il quadro nasce in una dimensione che non è più quella della vita, ma, si badi, nel quadro non v'è altro che quella materia: quella geometria, e non già nella loro relazione (quella che dà luogo alla conoscenza positiva del mondo secondo le categorie del tempo e dello spazio), ma nella loro concreta, fenomenica, irrelativa "presenza". Disgiunte, materia e geometria non possono certamente più organizzarsi in una natura, significare ciò che comunemente si chiama "la vita"; ma esistono tuttavia, e ciò che importa non è la loro verità a priori ma la loro flagrante presenza nel quadro, il loro porsi come dato, e non soluzione, del problema. Poniamo la domanda in tutta la sua gravità: ammessa, e non si può non ammettere, l'evidenza della dimostrazione, qual è la sua portata sul piano morale, quale il suo peso nella situazione storica attuale? Certo la poetica di Burri non è una poetica dell'"engagement" e non è una poetica dell'indifferenza e dell'evasione. Per cercare di chiarirla, bisogna indubbiamente rifarsi a quei due termini, materia e geometria, e vedere che cosa veramente significhino nell'arte di Burri. La materia, anzitutto: quei sacchi ammuffiti, quegli stracci sordidi, quei legni bruciacchiati, quelle lamiere nude, in cui certi critici vogliono vedere la prova d'una colpevole indulgenza, non priva di qualche sarcasmo, per i gusti decadenti degli intellettuali borghesi. La scelta non è casuale, ma non è compiaciuta; le materie che Burri presceglie sono per lo più i resti di cose che hanno avuto una lunga storia nel mondo, una lunga consuetudine con gli uomini, e da questi sono poi state abbandonate, affidate al flusso di un'esistenza senza storia che le riporta passo passo al terriccio informe, alla polvere. Non entra, in questa scelta, il gusto malato del degradato e del corrotto; ma v'entra, certamente, il pensiero che non bastano, quell'abbandono e quella decadenza, a decretare e sanzionare una fine, un'irrimediabile uscita dall'orizzonte dell'esistenza. Il gesto di Burri le ferma sul confine tra vita e morte, e subito l'insopprimibile spinta dell'esistenza prende il sopravvento sull'inerzia della morte. È allora che le toppe e i rammendi dei sacchi scoprono una geometria segreta, i cenci infetti aprono piaghe di carne viva, stillano sangue i legni bruciati, le saldature delle lamiere gonfiano e bruciano come escare di ferite mal chiuse. Così in quella corruzione o degradazione, mentre si consuma l'ultima traccia della cosa, si compie un recupero lento e graduale dell'organico; e non nel senso di cruda naturalità ma nel senso, più umano, di un sentimento ritrovato, di un'ancor timida, ma schietta, proposta di convivenza o di simpatia. Ma quel nuovo valore dell'"organico" è tutt'uno con il "geometrico", come se la nuova esistenza della materia spontaneamente si organizzasse secondo i ritmi profondi, gli appelli più semplici e persuasivi della ragione; e infatti, quella di Burri non è una geometria dedotta da postulati dati e accettati, ma una geometria allo stato nascente, in fieri, e che nel suo farsi si formula prima in figura che in principi di numeri. Dimostrare come, lungo il pendio stesso di una discesa fatale e di un sempre più oscuro confondersi già si ricomponga un disegno e già si formino i germi di una sicura rinascita, o sia pur soltanto di una reincarnazione: ecco, crediamo, il profondo sostrato morale della poetica di Burri. Ma non deve giungersi, partendo da queste premesse, a una interpretazione in chiave di simbolo, che potrebbe essere pericolosa e arbitraria; come se nella singolare vicenda di quelle cose consumate dalla storia, abbandonate al flusso e riflusso del reale, e poi dalla pittura riscattate alla luce della esistenza, dovesse leggersi un'allegoria profetica della vicenda umana. Sarebbe ancora un confondere il simbolo, che è pur sempre trasposizione dal concreto all'astratto, con il segno, ch'è indicazione diretta o addirittura constatazione, toccar con mano. La pittura di Burri non è pittura di simboli, ma di segni; non è pittura che voglia prefigurare o annunciare una situazione, ma pittura che vuole, appunto, toccar con mano. E come segno della condizione di coscienza degli uomini del nostro tempo, non potrebbe essere più esplicito e veritiero.

Herbert Read, in *Alberto* Burri, exhibition catalog (London, Hanover Gallery, 29 March–29 April 1960), Hanover Gallery, London, 1960.

Basic black

to Alberto Burri

florida cry crew cry memory
masterly most crimson silt
shy masculine myrtle endeavour
sever christ cavalier host
gonads ghost sob linger

alleys lost singular wing
veins of love never ever cease
keep keep crestfallen thy cruise
of dastard sap till sessions eventual
droop leman dry mortal entrance
wild hollow winter bruises
vocal allow illyrian avowals
kiss o homily merciful thy keel
england vesicles of delight
lost ever
ever ever white pyx
residues of lust
lost ah wax lack

Human sensibility, if confined to a narrow path, eventually reaches a point of satiety. The mind refuses any longer to register vivid sensations. This is particularly true of the artist's sensibility: his style may be constant, but his nerves are liable to exhaustion. The muscles with which he paints may still work, but automatically. He becomes slick: he is in danger of becoming popular. Style can remain constant and the sensibility keen if the materials of art are changed. To discover and exploit new materials is a rare talent. Picasso, who possesses it in abundance, has changed from painting to sculpture, from sculpture to engraving, but that was not enough. He then invented a completely new type of art, the *collage*: an exercise of sensibility on readymade materials, scraps of paper, oilcloth, rags. Kurt Schwitters was another pioneer in the same extension of the frontiers of sensibility. Burri has advanced still farther into unknown territory. He came to art with unusual qualifications: the skill of a surgeon, the experience of war, and an awareness of the futility of academic conventions in the Age of Hiroshima. In a prisoner-of-war camp the only material to hand was old sacking. Burri's sensibility seized on its irregular texture, its subtle variations of tone, its capacity to stretch in vital tensions, and he began to sew pieces of this burlap into patterns—as a surgeon sews up incisions or wounds. The cicatrices were somehow expressive—of where pain had been, of where miraculous healing had taken place. But above all these seams were sensitive edges to entrancing areas of colour. The faded lettering on the sacks, a touch of scarlet sealing-wax or of goldleaf for rich contrast, some meandering threads—by these means in the first years after the war Burri created a new world of form; and it seemed that the more degraded the raw material of his experiments, the more his sensibility was challenged and the more surely it triumphed. No purer works of art have been created by any artist in the past fifteen years. But Burri did not remain content with this improbable victory. He passed to equally original experiments: to scorified laths of wood, to blistered panels of plastic, and now to welded and blasted sheets of metal. Whatever he does—and this is the wider aesthetic significance of his work—his sensibility dominates the intractable material, to such an extent that a transmutation takes place, an alchemical process in which rubbish is redeemed in the alembic of the artist's sensibility, to become the "perfect body" of a work of art. I could carry this alchemical analogy much farther, for art has always been a kind of alchemy, and the work of art a "treasure hard to attain". The first thing to learn about art, if we would understand it, is that it is essentially such a process of transmutation, and Burri, by the very extremity of his chosen means, demonstrates this truth with an incomparably deft elegance.

Marisa Volpi, "Appunti sull'interpretazione critica di Burri," *Arte Oggi*, year 3, no. 10, March–April 1961.

La rapida assimilazione di idee e di prodotti artistici caratteristica del nostro tempo fa scontare gravemente ai critici e al pubblico ogni sia pur minima intempestività di giudizio. L'artista costituisce oggi un fatto quasi irrelativo, quindi è tanto insostituibile come presenza, quanto esiguo come storia interna del linguaggio. Ci aggiriamo tra Wols, Pollock, Hartung, Burri, De Kooning, Fautrier, Kline ecc. come tra nemici dichiarati, ai quali non potremo singolarmente manifestare un'adesione adeguata senza negare tutti gli altri, e tuttavia sentiamo che tradurre la loro esperienza, senza presunzioni idealistiche, è ancora il modo migliore di costituirne le effabilità (che è in definitiva piano ideologico comune, sulla base di un passato e di un futuro operanti). Porre in relazione i diversissimi linguaggi è venire incontro a ciò che distingue profondamente l'arte di oggi dalle mistiche irrazionali romantiche: il suo sperimentalismo sofferto, la sua responsabilità morale schiacciante. Poiché la pittura di Burri è tra le meno accette al pubblico medio, divenuta (a suo onore) quasi simbolo di scandalo per il benpensante, e viceversa ha una ricca e complessa letteratura critica italiana ed internazionale, sarà bene precisare che, nel panorama dell'arte italiana del secondo dopoguerra, egli rappresenta il ruolo sconcertante dell'anticonformismo che si sviluppa su un innesto di rude e schivo disingaggio sociale, della qualità pittorica eccezionale che si realizza nell'uso azzardato di materie inabbordabili, se non con atto clamorosamente anti-pittorico, e viceversa di un gesto esistenziale di denuncia che rifiuta pubblicità e si presenta solo in condizioni maturate interiormente, di così raffinata bellezza, da generare ambiguità ed equivoci sul suo significato iniziale. Certo il senso polemico dell'opera di Burri è unico e insopprimibile: dinanzi alla strumentalizzazione progressiva dello uomo, alla distruzione incontrovertibile dei suoi "valori" gerarchicamente stabiliti da una tradizione basata sulla trascendenza, Burri si propone di introdurre nei materiali residui, logorati dall'uso e ormai divenuti inservibili, un valore che a sua volta è il meno fungibile, per la piattaforma delle qualità a cui l'individuo è costretto a riferirsi nel giudizio dalla società odierna: il valore estetico. Ciò spiega l'interesse per Burri di critici che non postulano nessuna sublimazione ipotetica dell'esperienza contemporanea e colgono nell'arte d'oggi soprattutto gli elementi conclusivi, se non involutivi, di una civiltà figurativa, come Cesare Brandi; o di critici di dichiarata origine culturale romantica come Francesco Arcangeli. Viceversa la tensione che si sprigiona dalla condizione di "vuoto fisico" realizzata dai quadri di Burri è stata afferrata nella sua precisa inanità simbolica e morale, nel suo carattere "sospensivo" e aggiungerei neurotico, da un critico che vive i problemi dell'arte contemporanea senza riserve, come Giulio Carlo Argan: vogliamo ripetere con lui che la condizione di coscienza presupposta dal quadro di Burri è comune a diversi livelli di cultura. E molti di coloro che arretrano davanti alla formulazione datane dal pittore italiano, la vivono quotidianamente, con la lucidità anemotiva in cui le qualità umane sopravvivono come gusci secchi e vuoti, materiali trasportabili a piacere, privo di moto proprio; mentre il fondo istintivo che le suscitava, privo ormai di ogni potere su di esse, paga l'organizzazione della loro attrezzatura pubblica, con una crescente disintegrazione e lacerazione. Peraltro tale condizione di coscienza è la ragione della ambiguità di ogni gesto estremisticamente polemico dell'individuo-artista contemporaneo, e del pathos della perseveranza con la quale esso reagisce all'alienazione e prospetta le sue ipotesi irreversibili di linguaggio. Il primo interprete di Burri è stato il poeta Emilio Villa che viveva a Roma la stessa congiuntura politica e culturale: l'Italia dopo la disfatta bellica, tra le nazioni dell'area del piano Marshall, quindi in via di subire la pressione ideologica americana. Villa dei quadri di Burri dà una versione immediatamente suggestiva in metafore illuminanti, occasionalmente verificate oltre la suggestione di una interpretazione letteraria (1953, "Arti visive", n. 4-5). Intorno a questa data si sviluppa un interesse di pubblico e di critica soprattutto in America: la pittura di Burri, a grandi dimensioni, con il suo carattere di esibizione impudica, anche se silenziosa, trovava negli Stati Uniti l'ambiente più consono alla comprensione dei suoi procedimenti tecnici inusitati e dei significati espressionistici.

1962

Pierre Restany, "Un art brut soumis à l'esprit de géométrie: Alberto Burri," *Cimaise – Art et architecture actuels,* year 9, no. 59, May–June 1962.

La carrière d'Alberto Burri a été brillante et rapide. En 1944, à 30 ans, ce médecin italien découvre la peinture – ou plutôt la toile (de sac) – dans un camp de prisonniers de guerre au Texas. De retour en Italie en 1945, il se fixe à Rome et se met au travail. Dix ans plus tard c'est la consécration new-yorkaise, dont J.J. Sweeney fut l'enthousiaste artisan: et au-delà de la métropole américaine, c'est bientôt la gloire tout court, avec son cortège habituel de suiveurs et de plagiaires.

Succès amplement mérité, en dépit de ses paradoxes, et qui d'abord ne doit pas grand'chose à l'Europe. Car son Italie natale l'a longtemps tenu à l'écart, jusqu'au moment où elle a dû s'incliner devant les lauriers étrangers glanés par ce fils prodige; et aujourd'hui encore, elle n'est pas très généreuse à son égard. En 1960, à la XXXe Biennale de Venise on lui avait joué le mauvais tour de l'inviter, en même temps que Vedova, il aurait été le grand perdant de la compétition, si un jury international de critiques d'art (dont faisait partie l'auteur de ces lignes) ne lui avait attribué in-extremis une honorable compensation. Quant à Paris, n'en parlons pas: sa première exposition, en 1956 à la galerie Rive Droite (avec César) ne suscita aucun écho. Les rares personnes qui l'avaient remarqué, à l'époque, ceux qui somme toute "l'introduisirent" en France furent Michel Tapié et Herta Wescher. La distance qui sépare les deux personnalités précitées en dit long sur l'ambiguïté du cas Burri. Si Herta Wescher (dont on ne mentionnera jamais assez le rôle dans le renouveau du collage abstrait) voyait alors dans Burri le continuateur expérimental de Schwitters, c'était pour Tapié une variante informelle de l'art brut. L'œuvre de Burri s'est ainsi développée dans un contexte confusionnel: chaque commentateur explique Burri à sa façon, et les explications sont fort diverses. On est attiré par l'effet de matière, la spéculation sur la toile de sac et ses reprises, la matière plastique coulée, le bois en combustion, le fer découpé au chalumeau. Pour d'autres, au contraire, l'art de Burri réside dans une transcendance absolue des moyens employés, la dématérialisation du jute, du tissu, du bois ou du métal. Burri, nous dit-on est un poète symboliste au lyrisme ardent maîtrisé à grande peine. Mais c'est aussi, au-delà de tout baroquisme du matériau, un esprit "géométrique" dans toute sa rigueur. Bref toutes les références critiques y sont passées. Il ne manquait que la psychanalyse. Mais c'est désormais chose faite, et je lis, sous la plume appliquée de Françoise Choay ("Art International", V /5-6) ces mots plaisants: "Le traumatisme par effraction dans la chair du patient est l'expérience de base du chirurgien, Burri l'a vécu physiquement avant de le reprendre dans sa peinture où à nouveau le traumatisme devient fondement puisque c'est autour de lui et à lui que s'ordonnent et se subordonnent les éléments du tableau". Voilà qui vous ouvre de curieux aperçus sur la vocation artistique des médecins-poètes: du sadisme fonctionnel! En fait, des nombreux exégètes de Burri je crois que G.C. Argan a été le plus lucide, car il a su apprécier l'exacte envergure intellectuelle et psychique de la démarche (je pense notamment à sa préface de l'exposition *Burri* au Palais des Beaux-Arts de Bruxelles en 1959). L'humilité est la qualité fondamentale de la personnalité créatrice de Burri. C'est une qualité générale qui se manifeste sur le plan intellectuel et sur le plan psychique à la fois. Burri a une "tête bien faite", comme dirait Montaigne. Cet autodidacte, venu tard à la peinture, a toujours eu le souci de ne pas excéder ses moyens. Il préfère en faire moins que trop. Il est parti de bases simples et il entend s'y tenir. La simplicité des points de départ est une garantie de bases stables. L'aventure n'est pas folle, on ne se lance à corps perdu que dans le travail. Le grand événement est bien entendu la rencontre avec la toile de sac, le choc déterminant de l'aventure expressive. Une anecdote célèbre court à ce sujet. Burri prisonnier n'avait pas d'autre matériau sous la main. Il apprit ainsi à voir la toile d'emballage. Il avait découvert la réalité sous un autre aspect, tout aussi fondamental, mais plus directement sociologique. Faire part de cette découverte au monde était un droit et un devoir. C'est par ce "privilège du regardeur" que Burri est devenu peintre. Toute sa justification est là: nous donner à voir des images nouvelles. Pour bâtir son langage original, Burri a eu recours à des bases très simples. Il a établi une fois pour toutes un schéma structurel géométrique, suffisamment souple pour s'adapter au baroquisme intrinsèque des divers matériaux employés. Et en ce sens on peut parler de rigueur: l'image est structurée pour ainsi dire, elle ne naît jamais des seuls accidents de la matière; la forme est toujours préconçue, son organisation est toujours réductible à un nombre limité d'éléments géométriques (agencement des plans en profondeur, répartition des surfaces planes, équilibre des contours, cassures ou failles). Alberto Burri a un disciple direct en la personne de Robert Rauschenberg, chez qui, très significativement, on retrouve une propension analogue à la rigueur géométrique dans la composition et les structures internes. Mais cette rigueur est exploitée chez Rauschenberg à de toutes autres fins: elle constitue l'élément stabilisateur et compensateur qui permet la surenchère expressive, la débauche baroquisante, l'excès volontaire dans l'emploi des moyens. Chez Burri, au contraire, on n'assiste à aucun phénomène analogue de surexpressivité. Là où l'Américain claironne, l'Italien s'en tient à la mezza voce. Le traitement de la matière n'est jamais agressif: Burri ne recherche pas le choc, il est très loin de tous les phénomènes d'extroversion systématique du néo-dada américain. Même dans sa période la plus misérabiliste, celle des sacs de 1953 (où viennent parfois s'incorporer, sur la toile peinte, des débris de jute réduits à l'état de loques) il ne se départira jamais de cette fondamentale retenue vis-à-vis de la matière: plutôt que de céder à ses immédiates exigences, plutôt que de profiter des accidents et des hasards heureux (l'art brut à la Dubuffet), il cherche à dégager, par une stricte structuration de l'image et une présentation habile, l'expressivité interne de chaque matériau. La parole est à la matière, mais du dedans, dans sa densité et son intériorité spécifique. "L'image" de Burri est une mise en page expressive; comme l'a bien dit Argan: "la peinture de Burri n'est pas une peinture de symboles mais de signes; elle ne désire ni préfigurer ni annoncer une situation, mais veut précisément 'faire toucher du doigt'". Et il faut reconnaître que Burri atteint pleinement son objectif. Il sait admirablement "faire parler" la matière, nous rendre sensibles à telle ou telle qualité de grain du tissu, à l'encrage au pochoir d'un chiffre ou d'une lettre, aux veines et aux noeuds du bois, aux coupantes arêtes des lames de métal. Mais ce langage a une syntaxe dont il n'enfreint jamais les lois. Le langage de la matière, aussi riche soit-il, demeure discret, subtil, il est toujours allusif et secret, parfois à peine perceptible. La vision d'un Burri est une entreprise hasardeuse pour le spectateur que guette à tout instant la faute d'inattention. Regarder un "sac" ou un "bois" est une longue patience, et la saveur n'en est vraiment perçue qu'au terme d'une minutieuse lecture. Burri n'est pas non plus un coloriste. Son registre chromatique est très sommaire, les couleurs naturelles des matériaux employés mises à part. Il porte presqu'unanimement sur le blanc, le noir et le rouge. Les tons sont généralement froids et neutres, bien qu'il sache merveilleusement jouer des oppositions de valeur dans le même ton. C'est en 1955-56 que les préoccupations chromatiques se sont manifestées chez Burri avec le maximum d'intensité. Certains tableaux de cette époque ont des titres significatifs: *Tutto nero*, *Due neri*, *Tutto rosso*, *Tutto bianco*, *Sacco e rosso*, *Combustione legno e nero*, *Bianco verticale*. Mais là encore, couleur et matière s'équilibrent et se complètent mutuellement. La somme harmonique des deux éléments se situe toujours au niveau moins et non au niveau plus. La couleur uniformément distribuée ou concentrée en des points précis du tableau, tend à neutraliser l'effet de matière. La matière exalte en revanche la couleur, dont elle réchauffe la froideur et rehausse l'assourdi des tons. Burri emploie la couleur comme une chape qui vient masquer l'extroversion de la matière. Et quand le matériau accuse de lui-même un penchant à l'uniformité (certains grands sacs, certaines combustions de bois, certains fers), c'est le phénomène rigoureusement inverse qui se produit, la couleur localisée en un accent précis jouant alors le rôle d'un accord lyrique et d'un stimulant vibratoire. Lorsqu'enfin l'artiste réalise des effets de valeurs contrastées dans le même ton, et notamment le noir, il se sert de collages de tissus différents (toiles satinées, velours, drap lisse) comme support des effets alternés ou combinés de matité et de brillance. Autre contrôle de la matière: l'imagination formelle et la sélection des éléments de base. La démarche de Burri n'est jamais *dénaturante*. Il est trop respectueux du potentiel d'expressivité intrinsèque de la matière pour songer à en altérer l'organicité profonde. Mais il tient à en contrôler jusqu'au bout les manifestations et les effets. C'est pour cela qu'il évite résolument le stade objectivé de la matière. Les lames de bois brut à demi-calcinées qui sont collées telles quelles à même le support ne sont altérées dans leur organicité par l'ajout d'un quelconque artifice; mais elles n'ont plus aucun lien avec la caisse ou le madrier originels. Les tôles de fer se métamorphosent sous l'effet des brisures, des trous, des soudures; les sacs n'évoquent plus des emballages complets; et si l'auteur emploie de véritables chemises dans certains de ses collages de tissus, il fait bien de nous le signaler par le titre de l'œuvre: la schématisation du découpage les rend en effet malaisément reconnaissables. Burri se sert du matériau brut dans son état tout venant, c'est-à-dire le moins individualisé: bois, linge, tissu, métal, c'est la matière première à l'état pur, telle quelle. Sa présence est celle d'un échantillon anonyme contenant toutes les caractéristiques de l'espèce: sans plus, mais pas moins. Burri évite délibérément le stade objectivité de la matière, l'objet organisé, le contour organique de la forme. Il n'assemble pas des objets, il construit une image objective, c'est-à-dire une image d'ensemble qui s'objective au niveau de la synthèse. Il évite ainsi l'écueil du fétichisme objectif. Ses tableaux ne sont, à aucun moment, "des objets d'envoûtement intemporels". Ses images, fortement structurées et subtilement agencées ne se réfèrent pas non plus à une symbolique générale de la récupération du déchet, du rachat de la ruine. L'artiste s'interdit de spéculer sur l'humanité fondamentale de ces choses "consumées par l'histoire, abandonnées au flux et au reflux du réel et rachetées ensuite par la peinture à la lumière de la vie". Au niveau d'élémentarité originelle à partir duquel est traitée la matière, cette trace de l'usage humain s'estompe et se perd. Les signes que Burri nous fait "constater" à travers des images synthétiques issues d'une géométrie en perpétuel devenir, sont les manifestations immédiates d'une conscience pleinement éveillée au monde: d'une conscience réaliste, qui assume la grandeur de son humilité. Voilà sans doute pourquoi, malgré des centaines de copistes disséminés aux quatre coins du globe, Burri reste inimitable, solitaire, unique: un grand personnage au cœur d'une grande œuvre.

1963

Cesare Brandi, *Burri* ("Maestri del XX secolo" series), Editalia, Rome, 1963.

[. . .] Burri non inizia col *collage*: i primi quadri del '48 sono tutti dipinti, ma proprio in uno dei primi (presso l'Autore), che è anche il primo *Nero*, con un quadratino celeste (ed elementi rotondi o ovali), il trapasso stesso dal nero lucido all'opaco, non è in funzione di colore ma di materia, come il dritto e il rovescio di un raso. E il quadratino celeste, così chiaramente di origine costruttivista, non ha il valore puramente topico di dislocazione spaziale, né quello di un *inserto*: si sovrappone. Ma non si sovrappone materialmente, a *collage*: *mima* un *collage*. È forse allora una spazialità stratificata e intersecata di tipo cubista che vuol suggerire? Niente di tutto questo. Il lucido e opaco come dritto e rovescio di una stessa stoffa, il quadratino celeste collocato in alto e non "applicato", ma come in transito, hanno l'ufficio primo di attirare lo spettatore su un colore-materia, come la mosca sullo zucchero. La variazione luminosa dal lucido all'opaco non intende di risolversi definitivamente e senza residui nell'ambito strutturale del dipinto: pone allo spettatore il compito di avvistare la variazione dove un occhio disattento non avrebbe rilevato che un'unica tinta di nero. In una parola, attira lo spettatore nel dipinto. Il quadratino celeste completa l'allarme: è un segnale, non sta nel quadro, trascorre, trapassa sul quadro. Ma nello stesso tempo che il contrasto lucido-opaco mette in sospetto lo spettatore, e il quadratino celeste trasmette un segnale ignoto, la struttura del dipinto non si disintegra affatto, resta rigorosa come in un quadro di Malevič. La *balance*, che istituisce, è impeccabile anche dove rientrano elementi surrealisti, gli ovoidi, le conformazioni amebiche, sicché può sorgere il dubbio di avere visto prima quel che non c'era. Se la variazione lucido-opaco non fosse data sul piano, ma in superficie: è offerta all'occhio come al tatto, non ha rapporto con l'intelaiatura spaziale del dipinto: né con la sua trama luminosa. Il quadratino celeste non si pone certo fuori ritmo e tuttavia si colloca di qua dal piano del quadro, è come intercettato al suo passaggio. Lo spettatore deve accollarsi in proprio questi elementi, in quanto si eccettuano come oggetti a se, respingerli o accettarli; ma non in quanto si innestano nella strutturazione spaziale del dipinto. Questa resta ineccepibile, non fa una grinza. Una tale provocazione dello spettatore nel quadro è il fatto più nuovo e conturbante delle opere del primo Burri: designa il suo circospetto moto di individuazione per come intende, ancora oscuramente, di definirsi a se stesso. Dove questa *provocazione* non compaia, il dipinto, che può anche essere più formalmente raggiunto, inesplicabilmente scade.

[. . .] un primo dipinto (presso l'Autore) in cui appare un frammento di sacco con un lacerto di bandiera americana e una scritta (Europa). Fin qui non c'è niente di diverso, a parte la materia, di quello che accadeva nei *collages* cubisti con pezzi di giornale, lettere, numeri, etichette. È probabile che, a quel tempo, se avessimo visto il dipinto, non ci avremmo notato niente di più. Ma il tempo è passato, e noi possiamo rintracciare anche la preistoria di quella tela rozza stampigliata di caratteri.

[. . .] qui l'inserto è fatto in modo da abolire "a vista" la struttura stratificata e interpenetrata del *collage* cubista. Una greve listatura contorna sia i pezzi di sacco sia le altre irregolari zonature. L'effetto è un po' quello del piombo che rilega le vetrate, ed è un effetto che mira a stabilire il piano della pittura come un diaframma trasparente, quindi in una speciale accezione del piano formalmente inteso. Ciò che è sottolineato da un altro particolare: in alcuni casi la listatura non inquadra un colore diverso dalle zone contigue, ma proprio lo stesso colore di fondo con una "ritagliatura" diversa. Ora, ciò non provoca nessun *colore di posizione* ma solo un ritmo astratto, come una battuta vuota: quindi, la listatura è usata sia per abolire la stratificazione del collage, sia per deprezzare, ritogliere, la diversità cromatica delle altre zone. Restano le scritte frammentarie della tela *Unrra* con una presenza non soltanto figurativa, un'aggressività e un palese dispregio: ossia si provoca, in quel punto, l'integrazione forzosa dello spettatore al dipinto, come, più velatamente, si è visto per l'alternanza lucido-opaco, per gli elementi come *in transito* sul quadro. Resta ora da vedere il momento finale, quando la tela perderà le stampigliature, riducendosi al povero straccio: ma prima di arrivare al Sacco, dobbiamo esaminare altri elementi che corrispondono ad altrettanti punti di forza delle strutture di Burri. Questi elementi sono i Crateri, le lacerazioni, le efflorescenze o Muffe. Come si è già visto per il *collage*, che non nasce come *collage* ma solo gradatamente assume la veste del *collage*, così i Crateri non nascono come crateri, ma risultano da un'*interpretazione* che Burri dà agli elementi ovoidali o curvilinei che aveva accettato in primo luogo da Miró. [. . .] È singolare come in Burri i tondi e gli ovoidi, anche soltanto dipinti sulla tela, tendano ad acquistare un orlo, un bordo, a scendere sotto il livello del quadro. È, in un certo senso, il procedimento inverso al *collage*. Finché il bordo o l'ovoide verrà ad essere ritagliato materialmente: è il cratere, questa improvvisa dimensione in profondità che non è, in primo luogo, una profondità come dimensione interna al dipinto, ma dimensione della materia di cui è fatto il dipinto. Ed ecco che, in un quadro del 1950 (presso l'Autore), insieme ai tondi ritagliati, compare una lacerazione, con i bordi a rilievo in gomma-plastica, e i bordi sono aperti come le labbra di una ferita. Come le labbra di una ferita o come quelle secrezioni gommose che si addensano negli spacchi dei tronchi di certi alberi da frutto. Che l'allusione alla ferita o a fatti naturali del genere vi sia, è certo: che addirittura qui compaia anche l'inserto medico, nel modo in cui si ostentano aperti i bordi in membrana di plastica, al modo, cioè, che si rovesciano, tenuti dalle pinze, i lembi di un taglio operatorio, è anche probabile. Ma il moltiplicarsi delle *allusioni*, che qui registriamo, è anche un approfondirsi del senso del quadro, e non nel senso di un abusato sensibilismo surrealista, seppure proprio la finzione illusionistica di materie, secondo la mitografia surrealista, stia qui all'origine del procedimento. Quanto separa il cratere e la ferita di Burri dalla pittura surrealista, è proprio questo darsi *in proprio*, nella lacerazione reale, nella materia plastica effettiva, non in modo allusivo, affabulatorio, quindi, ma in una presenza immediata che tocca la sfera stessa esistenziale dello spettatore, come foro praticato nella tela, come materia indubitabile non meno delle gomme che secernono gli alberi o dei lembi aperti di una ferita. E passato lo stupore del primo incontro, questa messa in contatto non richiesta e sgradita, ecco che il dipinto si ricompone nella sua struttura formale tesissima, in cui quindi il foro, la ferita, la materia plastica passano a elementi figurativi e non già a segni simbolici, onirici, come nel dipinto surrealista.

[. . .] Si è giunti così all'inizio del '51, quando Burri forma con Colla, Capogrossi, Ballocco il gruppo Origine. La riunione dei nomi, quasi più delle parole del manifesto, dice che cosa rappresentasse, almeno per Burri, il raggruppamento: un modo di porsi su una certa linea di frontiera, se non d'avanguardia. Nulla di comune ha mai avuto la pittura cifrata di Capogrossi e la plastica di Colla con l'arte di Burri. Le parole stesse del manifesto designano chiaramente solo una presa di posizione, un obiettivo da raggiungere per vie diverse. "La rinunzia ad una forma scopertamente tridimensionale" va bene per Capogrossi ma non per Colla: la "riduzione del colore alla sola funzione espressiva più semplice" è giusta per Capogrossi che usa un colore tipografico, in nessun momento per Burri. Lo stesso si dica per "l'evocazione dei *nuclei* grafici" e il "raccoglimento umile ma concreto": se un'attitudine può desumersi dai quadri di Burri fino al '50, non è certo un'attitudine umile. Forse la sola parola che gli si attaglia è quel *concreto*, che tuttavia, nel contesto, vuol dire altra cosa che la concretezza materica a cui aspira Burri. Insomma, il gruppo come gruppo era un raccoglimento fittizio, e che l'editoriale del primo numero di "Arti Visive" ('52), la rivista del gruppo divenuto Fondazione Origine, maggiormente accentua nelle espressioni vaghe e nelle asserzioni ubiquitarie.

[. . .] In questa recisa negazione di una componente simbolica in Burri (del resto già negata da Argan e Restany) rientra anche la negazione del tentativo semplificatorio, da più parti tentato anche in veste psicoanalitica, di estrarre la pittura di Burri dalla sua originaria professione medica. Come si sa, un'interpretazione psicoanalitica di un'opera d'arte, e, attraverso l'opera d'arte, del suo autore, è sempre possibile, ma resta sempre una esperienza collaterale che non riesce a inserirsi costituzionalmente nell'atto con cui l'osservatore fonda a sé l'opera come opera d'arte.

[. . .] Lo strappo e la toppa del Sacco sono strappo e toppa, e non ferita e cerotto, medicamento. E dove abbiamo trovato una ferita con i labbri rovesciati, è una ferita data, lo si è rivelato, come su un albero che geme la gomma. Qualsiasi interpretazione simbolica non si lega al contesto chiarissimo del quadro: ancorché si sia agli inizi di Burri e la sua tematica sia in fase di organizzazione. Questa ostensione integralmente oggettiva della materia in Burri è stata allora sentita esattamente nelle reazioni prime del pubblico, che proprio si irritava per vedersi dato in pasto una materia vile e non per gli eventuali simboli sessuali che conterebbe. Per ciò i Sacchi hanno sollevato più indignazione che le aperte allusioni oscene dei dipinti di Dalí: innocui divertimenti per borghesi che credono di avere rimosso il proprio traumatismo. A questo punto apparirà chiaro perché Burri sia risalito al *collage* dalla pittura, in quanto che nel *collage*, rispetto a come lo riceveva da una tradizione figurativa ormai lunga e polisensa (erano già passati 40 anni, nel 1950, dalla nascita del collage), toccava alla zona dipinta ad acquistare la natura ambigua di materia in vista, quasi pulsante, capovolgendo il processo cubista.

[. . .] Ad un certo punto, Burri, invece di limitarsi a scavare crateri, aprire ferite, imporre toppe, forza da tergo il dipinto ad assumere protuberanze, rigonfi, addirittura servendosi, in certi casi, di rami nodosi e storti, inseriti a croce di sant'Andrea da dietro il telaio. Questi rigonfi e protuberanze non hanno niente a che fare, apparentemente, con la stesura, che resta non meno severa e calibrata, del dipinto: sono un disturbo inopinato, una malformazione sgradevole, invocano la mano pietosa che ne rimuova la causa… Ed è qui che la lucidità della coscienza dell'artista ancora una volta colpisce. Infatti, codesto novatore che non solo non licenzia poetiche ma neppure spreca su se stesso una parola di più, aveva capito fin dall'inizio il ruolo presentificante che doveva assumere la materia nella sua pittura, e come a questo ruolo teneva e non alla materia in sé e per sé, ecco che, con l'ingobbatura dei dipinti ne dava la dimostrazione più eloquente. Il disagio che producono, sulle prime, quei bozzi e quelle protuberanze inattese, è dello stesso stampo del disagio che trasmette la materia repulsiva e vile dei catrami e delle muffe: dunque proprio i quadri Gobbi confermano il ruolo della materia in Burri, che è quello di forzare alla reazione diretta lo spettatore. Che poi, finito questo primo incarico, la *gobbatura* del quadro avesse anche una ragione formale, è pacifico. Proprio nella intercambiabilità di pittura e scultura che iniziava il collage cubista sta la possibilità di riinserire nella stesura piana del dipinto l'oggetto *apparentemente* in rilievo.

[. . .] Le lamiere che Burri taglierà e salderà sono lamiere nuove, uscite appena dai laminatoi industriali. Non può non avere importanza questo fatto, che già in sé contrappone i Ferri ai Sacchi. Nei Sacchi era la tela consunta, strappata, macchiata, carica di uso anonimo se non di storia: e proprio questa stracciata bandiera dell'epoca passava a simboleggiarne l'arte. Nei Ferri, nonché i rottami del tempo, non ci sarà neppure più la consunzione in atto, che di se stessa, con l'atomica, fa la nostra sciagurata civiltà, parodia di se stessa. La Combustione, l'orma di fuoco di Hiroshima stampata sulla pelle degli innocenti con il disegno stesso, supremo dileggio, delle stoffe a fiori. Nei Ferri il fuoco serve a saldare sciaveri contrastanti di lamiere, avvampa il metallo con l'alito arroventato, lo chiazza, lo rende cupamente partecipe di aurore infernali e di magma vulcanici. La materia nuova ed intatta sembra sottoposta al martirio come per farne cambiare la natura, nella sfida di un'alchimia impossibile che dalla sua lamina inerte faccia affiorare l'oro e la speranza. Resta la pagina chiusa, saldata come una ferita rimarginata male, e, nelle fitte e nelle ammaccature, quasi col clangore di colpi disperatamente battuti alla sua porta: che è la porta sul vuoto, sul nulla. Ma se questo è il sottofondo o l'immediato corredo associativo che i Ferri suscitano, non si pensi che in ciò consistano, figurativamente, i Ferri medesimi. Nei Ferri c'è piuttosto l'esasperazione della struttura spaziale del quadro, portata, come sforzata sul letto di Procuste, a valere sul piano: con geometrizzazioni rigide, dove nelle suture il metallo sobbolle e ricresce come la carne nelle staffilature a sangue: piaghe rimarginate e ancor più spaventose. La struttura spaziale del quadro è tesa dunque fino a ridursi al piano: ma solo per un momento. Ingobbature inattese, lacerti liberi e taglienti che sembrano sfuggire al controllo e alla fiamma. Improvvisamente uno spacco non richiuso, un lembo che scatta come un coltello a serramanico, mentre forzano lo spettatore quasi a difendersi, a stare in guardia, e dunque a partecipare ad un evento non concluso, problematicamente in atto, offrono in realtà un approfondimento della struttura spaziale, negano il piano, appena proposto, in quanto tale, come struttura bidimensionale del quadro. [. . .] nei Ferri di Burri lo spettatore è invitato a tenersi alla larga per non ferirsi, ma allo scopo di non forzare la figuratività del quadro e di riconoscere, in quel momento, la figuratività al di là dell'esistenzialità.

1977

Gerald Nordland, in *Alberto Burri. A Retrospective View 1948–77*, exhibition catalog (Los Angeles, The Frederick S. Wight Art Gallery University of California, The Regents of the University of California, 25 September–4 December 1977), The Frederick S. Wight Art Gallery, Los Angeles, 1977.

Burri first explored the use of the crackled paint effect in the 1940s. From time to time he would use the technique and occasionally he would exploit it more fully as in the painting, *Two Shirts*, 1957 (Catalog no. 31). In *Grande Legno*, 2, 1958 (Catalog no. 32) from the Aluminum Company of America Collection, he developed a crackled pattern from corner to corner and edge to edge in a nearly two-meter square canvas. Burri affects the size of the *cretti* by the dilution of the mixture he forms, the thickness of his application of it, and the artisan's touch which comes from experience. The expressive vehicle of the painting is the medium which makes the impasto crack under drying conditions. The actual crackling pattern depends upon chance and the artist's sensibility while making the application. When the cracking process develops the appearance he wants to keep, he suspends the process with a Vinavil (glue) application. Where the artist originally made his craquelure patterns with zinc white and suspended them with vinavil, he has in recent years utilized earth (kaolin) in his *cretti* process. The *cretti* are, like all of Burri's materials, familiar to us. The crackle of old paints and varnishes, the aged wall, and the dried river bed have impressed us with images which are unforgettable. Burri then programs a natural process in the one material or the other which he later suspends when he is satisfied with its development and that is preserved either in the natural material color of the medium or is painted in either of his absolute colors, black or white. The emerging pattern does not follow the symmetry of the spider web, but rather an asymmetric development of smaller and larger units, and meandering fissures, which finally achieve a remarkable natural balance in monochrome with a shadowed line. These *cretti* are entirely different from and yet reminiscent of overall composition in the modern tradition—mysterious, wholly invented and yet the echo of nature from micro to macrocosm. The *cretti* are worked flat on raised sawhorse tables and examined from time to time each day during the crackling process. The artist doesn't like to work with the material flat because he is used to taking every square inch of the work into consideration as he develops a composition, adjusting this, repainting or forming that, keeping every element in consideration at all times. Having the large *cretti* reposing flat does not give him his customary vision and sense of control. It is interesting to think of the *cretto* process as a simile for the burnings Burri has celebrated in recent years. Obviously, he has controlled those burnings with care, and has not burned his studios. He has however accepted images which could not have been imagined. He has accepted some of them and has modified others, improved them, added to them in finding his way to a completed work. He has come to enjoy the challenge of working with the unexpected and the apparently valueless. If we can think of the *cretti*'s drying process as an ultimate solicitation of chance, the meaning of the simile for burning will be clear: the artist has set about a "slow burn" that is proceeding on its own fire course. He likes some effects of the process and may not like some others. When will he stop it in order to get a desireable balance between the acceptable and the hoped for? One must not forget for a moment that this chance is not a single incident or effect in the work but it is indeed the entire surface, the whole imagery: the dynamic operation of the process is the object of the relief painting. Burri has learned to compose his *cretti* in the abstract. He has then found a new ability to accept nature as a collaborator just as one tries to use the principles of healing to bring about a recovery in prescribing for a patient. The crackles are not symbolic references to the dry soil of Italy or the vast ravines of the American Southwest which Burri knows so well and enjoys so greatly. He is concerned only with the construction of a new work of communicative power, of esthetic quality and discipline. If there is one distinctive aspect of Burri's career that should be emphasized it would be that: he has always been concerned with controlling and evaluating all of the elements in his composition. He has not been unaware of his colleagues in the fine arts and their experiments and discoveries. He has found himself responsive to new pictorial directions (such as Minimalism) and he has been both amused and offended by the imitations of his own experiment on more than one side. Despite his importance as an innovative intelligence in the area of material painting and in the development of whole new areas of experiment, Burri's greatest contribution is in his compositional genius. Whether it is geometrical, sensuous-baroque or refined to the point of minimalism, it is his compositions which express the grand continuity of the art tradition. Many of his once provocative materials have lost their capacity to shock. We now read only the essential structure and order of the paintings. *Cretto*, 1973 (Catalog no. 58), is one of the ten works the artist chose to represent his work in his unprecedented *Opere di Burri* exhibition in the Sacred Convent of San Francesco at Assisi in 1975. Formed as a triptych, the work was the most ambitious *cretto* of the artist's life until that time.

[. . .] Burri had used the Cellotex building panels for many years and in the last few years (1966–72) had used them almost exclusively in working his burned acetate and acrylic paintings. The cellotex material is an industrial particle board composed of compressed sawdust and glue and whatever stretchers and strengtheners are necessary. It is closer to the synthetic sheets of plastic than it is to veneers of wood, plates of iron or jute sackings. Nonetheless, the Cellotex has a natural appearance and it has a similarity to the coloration of some sacks. With that background and based on the experience Burri had enjoyed with the paint and acetate compositions on Cellotex, he began to work with Cellotex as a new medium in 1975. Though the artist is tireless in his willingness to work and re-work an image to realize the success he senses as potential within it, he is also extremely economical in his use of both time and materials. He finds it possible to give a painting life by merely choosing the right proportion in which to divide the panel with a varnish treatment which distinguishes the ground plane from the sky. As he progressed in working with the Cellotex, he came to work most often with two pictorial elements, either a carved and roughened Cellotex with contrast to the relatively smooth factory finish or matte and shiny oppositions achieved entirely with black paint. To be sure there are combinations in which the artist cuts into theCellotex to build a relief so that a roughened and depressed area takes on one light-absorbing black in contrast to the same paint on the smooth surface or a darker and more reflective black on a third area. As has occured in recent years, landscape suggestions abound but so also do references to images first found in the acetate on Cellotex works of the prior years, even including some paintings which use a drawing manner which has existed in the artist's watercolor experiments since the late 1940s. [. . .]

1980

Nemo Sarteanesi, "Alberto Burri, il Viaggio," in Nemo Sarteanesi and Erich Steingräber, *Alberto Burri, il Viaggio*, Electa, Milan, 1980.

Un viaggio nello spazio, senza tempo, nella profondità silenziosa, dove il moto si identifica con l'immobilità. È questa la prima impressione che ci investe nell'incontro con le dieci superfici che Burri ha dimensionato nella dilatata espansione spaziale, di gotica reminiscenza, di un grande "contenitore" industriale, un ampio vano costruito per altri usi quindi, e realizzato con componenti che mostrano evidenti le elementari strutture geometriche di sostegno. Uno spazio disponibile, non precisato, sfuggente, che trova puntuale comprensione nella dimensione dell'opera che l'artista vi ha inserito. Agli inizi del '78 uscirono dal forno i grandi tagli in ceramica di quello che, ricomposto, sarebbe divenuto il *Grande Cretto* ora al Museo di Capodimonte. Fra i pochi amici presenti ebbi modo di assistere al complicato "assemblaggio". Il grande muro nero (cinque metri per quindici) trovò posto in questo vano e per la prima volta credo che Burri si sia trovato davanti al fascino che emana da questo vuoto, proprio nel rapporto spaziale che si andava chiarendo a mano a mano che il lavoro andava assumendo le sue reali dimensioni. La grande ceramica, pezzo per pezzo, prese forma sostenuta da complessi accorgimenti, una appassionata invenzione strutturale realizzata con la caparbia fantasia dell'artigiano che sorregge sempre l'opera di ogni artista autentico. Nelle ore trascorse ad osservare l'evolversi delle azioni che hanno portato il lavoro a termine, nella vigile attenzione con cui Burri seguiva la messa in opera, sembrava di rivivere lo stesso impegno e la stessa perizia che, in altri tempi, i grandi maestri avevano messo nella preparazione dei grandi supporti, come Cimabue nel seguire la preparazione del grande crocifisso fiorentino. Ma qui l'opera nasceva di pari passo, contemporaneamente alla strutturazione del sostegno. Comunque la grande superficie costituì certamente un precedente all'attuale "itinerario": il primo elemento che impose un dialogo con lo spazio circostante che, nella sua pur grande dimensione, lasciava vuota la massima parte del fondo a cui era appoggiato. Perché l'interesse è nato sulla superficie, nello sviluppo di questa grande superficie che ancora poteva essere a sua volta piano di appoggio per altre serie di opere. Una superficie, due dimensioni entro le quali coerentemente si è andato allineando il "viaggio" che ci è dato di percorrere. Anche questa volta primo a vedere la luce è stato il cretto. L'ho visto nascere e ho constatato come solo un grande mestiere riesca a guidare la lacerazione della superficie cretacea, senza produrre risultati casuali. Le dosi del legante, che stanno alla base del risultato, devono essere accuratamente verificate insieme alla quantità di materia inerte impiegata e solo l'artista è in grado di darne la valutazione così come, evidentemente, la distribuzione degli spessori che dovranno provocare la crettatura di diverso aggetto e frazionamento. Un cretto senza particolari modulazioni emotive. La materia lasciata immutata nel colore della sua sostanza, livellata, sorretta e "fermata" al massimo della carica di energia endogena dalle due suture verticali, che congiungono le tre parti su cui è fissata, segni inscindibili della struttura portante. È stata la "stazione" di partenza che, forse non a caso, si è subito situata nel punto del percorso temporale in cui era stato innalzato il *Grande Cretto* '78. A questo inizio ha fatto seguito la tempera che si pone in assoluto contrasto con il cretto. Una tempera mai eseguita prima d'ora in queste gigantesche proporzioni. L'estrema tensione che si sviluppa al suo interno, nelle accese stesure di colore comprese entro nitidi contorni, è la stessa che si stabilirà tra quadro e quadro. Il contrasto della materia, nella sua insita particolare violenza, è il timbro con cui si sono andate allineando via via le dieci scansioni. È una delle costanti, questa, che ci accompagna con immutata energia per tutto l'itinerario. Dieci immagini, non successioni di eventi ma evento unico, ci investono con lucido distacco ricomponendosi nello spazio da cui emergono, uno spazio che è stato l'inizio della loro genesi e che viene dalle stesse dominato, fermato, cristallizzato. È il sottile motivo che lega i grandi riquadri in un unico contesto. Un viaggio cosmico, ci è dato di immaginare, dove le forme ridotte al limite della loro esistenza portano con sé vibrazioni quasi impossibili, compenetrandosi le une nelle altre in una successione silenziosa "fuori del tempo": il dopo fermato nel presente e nel passato, momento unico di astanza. Le forme si stagliano "fermate" nel momento massimo di tensione, una tensione sempre rinnovata nella dissonanza con cui i dipinti sono accordati fra loro. La complessa esperienza dell'artista si rivela nel grande mestiere che ha reso sensibile tutta la carica espressiva della materia, una materia presentata, nei vari aspetti, con connotazioni apparentemente non emergenti ma sottolineata dal suo profondo vigore. Fuori dal velo atmosferico, tutto si staglia con assoluta definizione; i colori della grande tempera acquistano purezza di timbro altissimo e i neri la profondità del vuoto cosmico. Una materia senza corpo, più luce che sostanza, è il colore steso al limite della purezza che si "inserisce" tuttavia puntualmente in un contesto di timbro monocromo. Con la stessa sicura percezione è collocato il "ferro". Una materia richiamata, svestita dalle remote ossidazioni, con una presenza rigorosa sostenuta dalle implicite sottili variazioni della sostanza, precisata nei bordi taglienti, slabbrati e sottolineati da una strisciata di rossa cromia e riportati sulla superficie dalla sottile connettitura delle lastre avvitate. Una materia quindi priva di allusioni, spoglia, presente più che mai nella forza oscura della sua natura da cui discende la semplice forma ritagliata. Anche la plastica è ritornata ed è entrata in questo viaggio di tensioni controllate. La sua illimitata inconsistente trasparenza, nel quadrato, è precisata e resa immobile dal cerchio tracciato dalla fiamma con un procedere sottile e solido quanto un filo di ferro, definitivo nella sua evidenza privo com'è di bruciature marginali. I cellotex hanno preso forma via via rapidamente, condotti sempre da un grande mestiere che ha messo a nudo le superfici aride di una materia spenta, quasi lucido minerale proveniente da mondi senza vita, supporto a nere forme concluse entro un segno netto, limite invalicabile. Il cellotex è la materia attualmente più vicina alle sollecitazioni creative di Burri. La sua superficie viene modificata pur lasciandone inalterato l'aspetto naturale che si avverte anche sotto la pittura e acquista un'ulteriore carica anche dopo le tormentate "spellature". La spartizione di geometrica purezza del cellotex, da cui emerge la forma del "quadrante" di oro zecchino, ha trovato perfetta opposizione subito dopo la tempera (il cretto, la tempera e questo cellotex sono stati i punti fissi, l'impaginazione di partenza attorno a cui ha fatto seguito la collocazione degli altri quadri). Le sue commensurate sensazioni di equilibrio ci richiamano il fascino delle antiche speculazioni estetiche sulla sezione aurea. In questa ultima successione, in cui i rimanenti cellotex sono condotti con uguale rigore di forme elementari, si colloca una materia nuova, una intuizione che Burri ha molto sofferto: l'acciaio, una soluzione venuta fuori dopo varie versioni rifiutate, dopo molti tentativi in cui la materia è andata via via qualificandosi nella ricerca dell'estrema dissonanza. Agghiacciante, lucida e opaca allo stesso tempo, priva di alcun segno, sostenuta solo dalle doppie file di viti poste lungo le due connessioni che tengono il metallo aderente alla superficie. Con la sua totale astrazione, chiusa nella grigia corazza, ci conduce verso il termine del viaggio. Un viaggio fuori della logica terrestre e lontano dalle sue riduttive strettoie, grandioso intarsio con cui, sul bianco sviluppo del fondo, si collocano le dieci figure di un'unica grande pittura, materia nuda carpita all'alba della creazione la cui polita definizione la conduce ai limiti dell'infinito. Tutti i moti in essa generati si bloccano in un momento unico, nel silenzio di uno spazio inerte, ridotti nelle sue dimensioni della superficie. Una immobilità assoluta che ci rimanda con il pensiero alle remote ibernazioni pierfrancescane. Una odissea al limite dell'astrazione, sintesi totale, la cui dimensione spirituale ci richiama i grandi cicli pittorici che hanno segnato le Presenze della Storia.

Italo Tomassoni, in *Beuys/Burri*, exhibition catalog (Perugia, Rocca Paolina, 3 April 1980–November 1981), n.n., Perugia 1980.

[. . .] Nella mitologia collettivistica dell'avanguardia non è caduto Burri che sa, come Nietzsche, che il volere, là dove diventa liberatore, si scontra col passato. Così egli narra il sogno impossibile di un'iscrizione non separata, corpo di una traccia che incarna la lettera nella sutura della superficie e non si incorpora al simbolico. Egli ha descritto l'immagine che sprofonda in se stessa, il luogo dove si gioca l'abbandono di sé. Ha materializzato l'urlo che Baudelaire attribuisce all'artista prima della morte. Ha vissuto nello choc la separazione del corpo per immaginare l'esistenza. Ha tentato di sottrarre l'arte al reale bordeggiando la risalita dell'immagine alle sorgenti di una sapienza anteriore alla filosofia e alla rappresentazione, il significarsi della forma dentro al proprio vuoto analogico che annuncia nell'Altro irrappresentabile l'impossibile modificazione del reale. Ma anche la pragmatica di Beuys avviene fuori dallo statuto dell'avanguardia. Azzerando la creatività nel flusso (*fluxus*) e spingendo sull'orizzonte del quotidiano l'affondo della equivalenza arte/vita fino all'antropologia, egli introduce una ritualità verticale che solo l'eroe custodisce: perciò ignora l'inconscio collettivo (romantico) come pienezza collettivistica e attraverso l'*ich* gioca sul sosia, cioè sull'archetipo impossibile da rintracciare, su un se stesso/altro che mediante la manipolazione di un sapere post filosofico e post storico produce il linguaggio puro cioè la perturbazione delle lingue, delle poetiche e delle filosofie nell'immaginario. Come per Artaud, la festa di Beuys è un atto politico proprio perché avviene al di fuori del reale, al di là dell'articolazione strumentale del linguaggio, cioè della rappresentazione che sta per supplenza, delega. Anche politica. Perché egli, proclamandosi opera prima, autoinvestendosi genesi dell'arte, impedisce ogni volta, in virtù del primato assoluto accordato al flusso che si origina dal demiurgo, la banalizzazione del quotidiano ma anche la chiusura del senso tipica della metafisica, dell'etica del sociale e di ogni altro postulato della razionalità borghese. Ricominciando sempre il gioco del plasmare a partire da sé egli, Adamo incessante, inganna il linguaggio dal suo interno guardando, come Giano, in due direzioni e contraendo nella caduta spezzata del discorso il movimento del progresso. Oramai possiamo dire che l'avanguardia è stato il contrassegno di un'epoca dominata dal principio di un'organizzazione istituzionale del sapere attuata attraverso l'impegno e l'organicità dell'intellettuale come intellettuale di servizio. Lo specialismo fondava il supporto teorico della corporazione come garanzia della verità di tutti rispetto alla menzogna dell'individuo. Oggi interviene un codice interdisciplinare senza coperture ontologiche né sicurezze universalistiche, mosso da un erotismo dell'estraneità. Questo codice articolato nel desiderio attinge anche alle implicazioni analitiche che, radicandosi nel soggettuale, situano il linguaggio tra ciò che non è dominabile. Dell'avanguardia e delle sue strategie le grandi organizzazioni internazionali dell'arte (Venezia, Kassel) hanno rappresentato l'esemplificazione mondana; esse hanno posto il presidio di un'efficiente amministrazione sul luogo dell'arte garantendo attraverso la critica militante il sopravvento operativo della razionalizzazione. Perciò oggi queste organizzazioni sono in crisi e sopravvivono ancora solo come tecniche di adescamento manovrate dal potere politico. La Biennale o Documenta hanno rappresentato una delle molteplici incarnazioni alienanti del potere; la classificazione dell'arte attraverso la sua reale amministrazione. Ciò che è stato l'università per il pensiero inteso come istituzione e come insegnamento: luoghi al riparo dei quali lavorano l'universalismo e la verità, in nome di un servizio reso al corpo sociale. La odierna coscienza culturale non si riconosce in questa realtà anche se la rispecchia. Mettendo in gioco ciò che è estraniante, la questione del linguaggio è, oggi, prioritariamente la questione del soggetto, il luogo che produce la sua verità e che non si pone al servizio della verità. Così il testo ha a che fare almeno con due verità, per questo è paradossale. Proust narra di aver intuito la memoria involontaria mangiando un biscotto; questo può significare che l'io parlo passa attraverso l'io sono cioè il suo effetto; e che tanto la scrittura che la lettura implicano l'imbattersi in un *hic et nunc* che prescinde dalle modalità della ricerca, postulato, questo, tipico dell'avanguardia. Se il linguaggio è un atto e ogni atto possiede la sua verità non c'è spazio per la mistificazione. Al di qua e al di là. La barra che congiunge/separa la traumatofilia di B. e B. lungo il passo sdoppio del loro incedere instaura il luogo errante,lo specchio che non riflette, il punto di deriva del testo dopo la fine degli ismi, l'allusione dove il linguaggio non precede mai il proprio senso e la scrittura mette in scena la parata della sua interna lacerazione costituendosi come barriera tra il soggetto e il reale. Ma al di qua e al di là; di che cosa? Queste riflessioni non si propongono di dimostrarlo. Tra i bordi dell'arte si spalanca la sparizione dell'arte, il suo vuoto, il suo inattuale prefigurarsi non come oggetto di rappresentazione ma come segno del proprio sparire nel darsi. B.e B. sono vissuti da ciò che li spossessa; tatuaggio o corpo sociale, liquido amniotico o folla solitaria, essi tracciano il geroglifico che annulla tutto ciò che li tiene a distanza dalla forza oscura e nascosta dell'origine. Attraverso lo sconfinamento fino all'invisibile (Beuys) e la regressione all'Es (Burri) aprono ad un inconscio ove l'epos omerico si è liberato dell'ultimo velo mitologico: il telos e la storia come sogno del dominio. Burri, il cui percorso passa attraverso l'esplorazione della morte e del mito classico, è vissuto, attraverso l'asola nera dell'afasia, dalla singolarità inaudita di un *Ur-Sprache* percepibile nel senso biologico ma mai rapportabile ad un significato originario. Beuys, percorrendo nell'andatura della frammentazione la moltiplicazione delle lingue a partire dal proprio corpo costituito in oggetto, sospende nell'aforisma ogni senso, si fa oggetto di enunciazione absoluta che emerge dall'orda, dalla parola e dal tempo per proiettarsi, attraverso la parabola antropologica, verso una folla invisibile su cui stampa l'impronta rovente della propria energia creativa. La scrittura di Burri è il tatuaggio, il gioco sulla pelle contrassegnato da una irriducibile potenza intransitiva, disvelamento di un'energia che si rivolta contro il corpo o invade la natura e la pietrifica. Come nella carcassa di Gibellina che egli inonda di senso per destrutturarla e impedirle di tornare ad essere natura o storia; bloccandola, allo stesso modo del linguaggio, tra presenza e assenza. Rubando l'arte all'arte, Beuys sottrae se stesso al testo concluso; mettendo in scena l'altro e facendo del sosia il suo oggetto, accede alla parola prima, liberata dalla sua funzione di segnale; e a quella ultima, oltre l'economia politica. Egli sa che solo quando il segno muore al segnale nasce al linguaggio e così dice se stesso. È in questo modo che egli allarga il sistema dell'arte: abolendo i segni previlegiati, emancipando il senso, usurpando il ruolo della critica, rapinando la parola e destandola dal suo sonno di segno per rifarla aria, pneuma, fantasma. È qui che apre il dialogo tra il discorso creativo e il corpo sociale passando attraverso il corpo, facendolo a pezzi, divenendo nella propria parola e nel proprio soma un'opera, un oggetto che può ripercorrere nella voce il passaggio di una lettera tagliente che, attraverso il suo sdoppiamento, parla dell'arte, della sua nascita e del suo passaggio esplorando l'enigma del loro manifestarsi nel mondo. [. . .]

1984

Carlo Pirovano, "Un pittore stoico," in *Burri*, exhibition catalog (Milan, Pinacoteca di Brera, 24 May–8 July 1984), Arnoldo Mondadori, Milan, 1984.

Secondo i parametri consueti, la reazione del gusto corrente nei confronti di una creatività sorprendente e atipica come quella di Burri fu sempre quella del contrasto e dello scandalo, spesso rumoroso e volgare; e ora, al volgere di un quarantennio di attività febbrile e di profonde innovazioni, tecniche e formali, essenziali e insostituibili per la storia dell'arte del dopoguerra, nella latitudine di tutta la cultura occidentale, par di cogliere un attonito disappunto per la rarefatta essenzialità iconica con cui l'artista sembra voler suggellare, in olimpica semplicità stilistica e formale, una lunga peripezia di furori, la contrastata discesa agli inferi della degradazione storica dell'uomo quanto il proteico recupero della vitalità implicita e spontanea della materia, e perfino l'espressività medianica del prodotto artificiale. In tal modo sembra riproporsi, in termini rovesciati, l'ineluttabilità di uno iato fra la liberissima invenzione di un artista per il quale non esistono termini di arrivo ma solo pretesti di partenza, e una cultura, sia specialistica che di massa (comunque inguaribilmente catalogica, vivida solo quando può attenersi a etichette o a scompartimenti scolastici) che si arrabatta per codificare rispetto a formule standard un'esperienza che continuamente travalica se stessa e contraddice gli schemi interpretativi che di volta in volta le vengono cuciti addosso. Ora l'occasione eccezionale di questa amplissima rassegna milanese è quella di oltrepassare l'immediata percezione di nuove proposte visive e la reazione dialetticamente contrastata del rinnovamento di stereotipi critici che si operano a ogni nuova acquisizione figurativa, per rivisitare in più dilatata prospettiva storica, senza condizionamenti contingenti, tutta la parabola del fenomeno Burri, sia nella sua intrinseca consequenzialità interna, sia nelle diramate interferenze con la cultura, figurativa, filosofico-letteraria, scientifica, italiana e internazionale. E come di primo acchito risulterà adamantina e necessitante la logica interna del mondo poetico personale (a tal punto che le linee-essenziali delle opere dei primi anni romani sembrano esplicitate e come parafrasate in sofisticata orchestrazione "alla grande" nelle composizioni degli ultimi anni) allo stesso modo ci si dovrà rassegnare ad ammettere che ogni tentativo di omologazione di questa esperienza peculiare nelle semplificazioni astratte di movimenti o scuole risulterà inattendibile, irto di contraddizioni e di confusioni, totalmente sterile. Ma nello stesso tempo la lettura analitica dell'opera, diretta e spregiudicata, non potrà che rivelare nessi fittissimi con la cultura figurativa, antica e attuale, espliciti e reconditi, dichiarati in superficie o rimanipolati e stravolti in una cultissima voracità di stampo primordiale. E di converso l'esercitazione critica non avrebbe nessuna difficoltà a inseguire e rintracciare in amplissimo raggio, geografico e temporale, nella produzione artistica internazionale di questi ultimi trenta anni, echi vistosi e puntuali (a volte scimmiottature sterili, ma spesso anche stimoli fecondi e dinamici) delle fertili invenzioni dell'artista umbro. Un'arte, dunque, di saldissime matrici colte (di una cultura d'immagine, ovviamente, per nulla libresca o scolastica) che ha avuto incomparabile potere dirompente per le esperienze innovatrici del dopoguerra, in Europa e in America. Le parole, le disquisizioni verbose, si sa, difficilmente si attagliano alla poetica di Burri: finiscono spesso per incrostarvisi sopra come superfetazioni ingombranti o pretestuose; meglio attenersi alla franca evidenza delle immagini e seguirle nella loro logica intrinseca, piuttosto che accumulare pretesti interpretativi che a lungo andare denunciano la loro contingenza e il fiato corto della cronaca. I recenti cellotex monocromi, come il monumentale *Nero* del 1982 che conclude questa rassegna, interpretati attraverso le plastiche del '65, come i ferri del '58 o i sacchi della metà degli anni cinquanta, dichiarano esplicitamente quella che è una linea maestra dell'opera di Burri, quasi rigida intelaiatura architettonico-spaziale che sottende e innerva ogni trasposizione figurativa, qualunque sia il veicolo, il pretesto materico attraverso cui si esplicita. È questa l'anima razionale, calvinisticamente rigorosa e inflessibile, che determina la composizione in semplificazioni facilmente riconducibili a schemi geometrici, quadrati o rettangoli, in specie. Come se gli antichi aforismi di un Malevič, di un [Doesburg], di un Mondrian, perfino, ritrovassero linfa e vigore nuovi, ma in stravolgenti applicazioni. Perché l'aspirazione suprema all'"astratto assoluto" che fu già di quei patriarchi dell'arte moderna è come sfidata e quasi irrisa, nella dialettica interna e specifica delle componenti del quadro, quando l'artista non ne simula una trascrizione intellettuale attraverso una raffigurazione ottenuta con un mezzo a ciò convenzionalmente deputato (il colore come trascrizione e surrogato, la forma come simbolo) ma direttamente, brutalmente, coinvolge nell'operazione l'antagonista principe dell'astratto, la materia (per di più storicizzata, comunque sia, da una traccia, da un residuo dell'intervento umano) e la piega a una proposizione epifanica di se stessa, quasi a una amplificazione stupefacente dei suoi valori primordiali. In questa lucida provocazione intellettuale che vuole demonizzare gli assiomi essenziali della cultura figurativa moderna (nei poli opposti del più rigido purismo formale e del diapason dell'espressività), con il suo tasso altissimo di rischio e di sfida, credo vada individuato uno dei termini fondamentali del linguaggio di Burri, che spiega la durata provocatoria, fastidiante e inarrestabile, del suo messaggio. E ne consegue anche un'altra sensazione sottile e quasi inesplicabile in termini strettamente dialettici: quella di un'ambiguità irrisolta e quasi dolorosa, altamente drammatica, lo scacco tragico, privo d'ogni riscatto metafisico, di una razionalità caparbiamente provocata e riprovata, violentata, perfino, nella correlazione diretta e senza diaframmi con i lacerti del fenomenico e del sensitivo. È abbastanza evidente come questa attribuzione di tensione ambigua non vale tanto e non solo per quel complesso di referenze evocative, di suggestioni e allusioni che spiegano il coacervo di interpretazioni tra letterarie e scientifiche che spesso hanno infiorato la lettura dell'opera di Burri (dalle motivazioni psicologiche interpretate in chiave psicanalitica all'aneddotica corrente legata alla prigionia o alla professione medica) ma tocca l'essenza stessa del suo linguaggio, si connatura direttamente e inestricabilmente al modo stesso di far pittura. Il frammento di tela o il pezzo di legno, come il ferro, o la sabbia, o la plastica, nel momento in cui si amalgamano nella composizione, valgono ovviamente per i loro effetti formali, segno, colore, volume; ma nello stesso tempo non occultano o trasfigurano la loro natura prima, nella sintesi estetica non si cancella la loro vita anteriore (che è una realtà altrettanto veridica e duratura). E quando, lungo il suo percorso fantastico che sdegna la ripetitività delle esperienze o si alimenta sempre del gusto dell'inesplorato e dell'imprevisto, Burri depura le componenti del suo mezzo linguistico dai referti diretti della "materia materiata e storicizzata", più sofisticate e sottili diventano anche le trasposizioni mimetiche delle percezioni sensoriali e insieme la loro codificazione in una vitalità formale totalmente autonoma e autosufficiente; e il processo fantastico sembra riproporre a ritroso, in una eterna, assillante indeterminatezza esistenziale, il percorso che già si era riproposto provocatoriamente dalla materia grezza e volgare all'idealità estetica; ora dalla forma intellettualmente pura e incorruttibile si diramano allusioni suasive e conturbanti che coinvolgono esperienze caduche e condizionate, di nuovo, dalla fragilità dell'esperienza empirica e della memoria storica, con tutte le componenti di incertezza e di provvisorietà; e se la salda, quasi ingrata architettura elementare dei cretti (pochi elementi di semplificata geometria che ricordano il ridotto vocabolario figurale della tradizione popolare italica, per esempio nelle sagome usate per dar forma al pane) si inquina poi per quella componente diabolica e conturbante della lievitazione e della fessurazione che inevitabilmente evoca processi organici *in fieri* e misteriosi assestamenti spaziali in una dimensione temporale fissa e allucinata, quasi desolati paesaggi di una terribile stagione apocalittica (o forse, all'opposto, perché no, l'ardua definizione aurorale di una forma di un definito, dall'inerzia vana del caos...); ancor più sfuggente e inestricabile è la legge interna delle sulfuree suggestioni trascorrenti che sprigiona la fiamma che tormenta e vivifica i fogli di plastica. In effetti solo la virulenza provocatoria delle "sperimentazioni d'avanguardia" dei primi lustri del dopoguerra (di cui Burri stesso, suo malgrado, fu protagonista in persona prima) possono aver prodotto una tale assuefazione quasi narcotizzante da far quasi passare in sott'ordine il peso stravolgente dell'intervento dell'artista su questi materiali che per sua natura e per codificazione intrinseca vanno considerati fasulli, artificiali, provvisori. Ebbene, Burri li modella (figurativamente) con gli stessi preziosismi capziosi e sottili con cui i doratori medievali cesellavano le lastre delle porte delle cattedrali o gli artigiani delle botteghe comunali inseguivano suntuosi fantasmi di seriche trasparenze orientali negli apparati liturgici e nei cristalli traslucidi carpiti alle mense regali. Ma l'azione distruttiva del fuoco che pure infonde linfa vitale a questa amorfa, deprimente invenzione della tecnologia moderna, vi incide anche il marchio incontestabile di una dolorosa conflittualità storica, l'impronta di una tensione e, inevitabilmente, di una distruzione: è senza dubbio casuale (ma non certo in termini di elaborazione formale), dovuto forse all'altissima potenzialità evocativa degli elementi primi di queste immagini, bruciature e trasparenze sul bianco puro, e alla capacità mimetica nel senso quasi di larvale germinazione fenomenica, il recupero di "topoi" classici della figurazione pittorica occidentale, da Piero della Francesca a Rembrandt a Matisse. Rinvio per una puntuale disamina delle varie tappe del lavoro di Burri alle pagine documentate e ricche di intuizioni che gli hanno dedicato via via storici come Brandi, Argan, Calvesi, anche se la tentazione di ritornare ogni volta a una rilettura metodica delle componenti squisitamente pittoriche oltre la trama elaborata dei mezzi insoliti riserva sempre stimolanti sorprese. Per vero sarebbe un esercizio di sottile sperimentazione visiva l'inseguire attraverso i conturbanti fantasmi pittorici che la materia di Burri riesce a evocare (non pittura che restituisce la verosimiglianza della natura, ma natura che mina la pittura, come è stato acutamente rilevato) certi archetipi classici della tradizione figurativa occidentale; se l'ossessiva esercitazione dei bianchi sui bianchi, degli smalti e delle sabbie cavate dalla pietra pomice dei primi anni cinquanta possa essere intesa come commosso omaggio a certe abbacinate partiture di Piero della Francesca ad Arezzo, le slargate partiture dei grandi sacchi e di taluni cellotex evocano la pregnante monumentalità e l'amplificazione timbrica del matissiano *Calme Luxe et Volupté*; e certo qualche virtuoso dell'erudizione riuscirà a inseguire attraverso i cataplasmi di una plastica combusta la sagoma oppressiva del *Bue squartato* di Rembrandt, già evocata dalle rivisitazioni di un Soutine e dei nostri pittori neoromantici degli anni trenta. Ma il filo della citazione, salvo il precisare e ribadire la non casualità delle invenzioni di Burri e la loro coerenza in una continuità storica di salde radici "classiche", non aiuta molto a sviluppare la densità poetica che trasfigura il dato naturale e le referenze culturali. E tanto meno potranno essere effettivamente illuminanti le divagazioni letterarie che riducono queste immagini malinconiche a una complicata simbologia di pretesti esistenziali. Personalmente sono convinto che la pregnanza poetica di un'opera si rifletta anche sull'ampiezza e la varietà, ma anche la contraddizione delle interpretazioni che riesce a provocare e nessuna lettura critica sarà mai esaustiva rispetto alla creazione, quando sia veramente poetica: ma con altrettanta sicurezza penso che sia compito dello storico illuminare il contesto, l'ambito culturale, le premesse di pensiero e di sentimenti per evitare assunzioni di significati e di attributi assolutamente estranei e devianti. Nel caso specifico di Burri penso che uno dei malintesi più radicati, coltivato soprattutto da certa critica impressionistica e vitalistica, sia quello di vederne l'opera attraverso la codificazione scolastica dei movimenti (il gergo degli ismi è la maledizione della storiografia attuale) facilitata indubbiamente dalle vicende cronachistiche legate alla divulgazione delle sue opere (clamorosamente contrastate, come si diceva) e dalle necessità riduttive del mercato artistico che abbisogna sistematicamente di sigle, di semplificazioni mnemoniche. In particolare ritengo deviante la rilettura dell'opera di Burri nel profilo dell'Informale e più ancora nella prospettiva dei movimenti vitalistici che tanta fortuna hanno avuto nella recente cultura occidentale, egemonizzata, se non dal pensiero, dalla prassi americana. [. . .]

Daniel Abadie, "Burri. La violence et la grâce," in *Alberto Burri: Cretti e Cellotex*, exhibition catalog (Nice, Galerie Sapone, 14 February–24 April 1984), Rubini e Petruzzi, Città di Castello, 1984.

[. . .] Pour qui, à première vue, regarde l'œuvre de Burri, celle-ci semble n'être que temps successifs correspondant à l'emploi de matériaux jusqu'alors inusités en peinture: le goudron en 1948 et 1949, les sacs et autres textiles pendant les années 50, conjointement à l'utilisation du bois (à partir de 1955) et du fer (enire 1958 et 1960), le plastique, préoccupation majeure de la décennie suivante, les résines craquelées à partir de 1973, le cellotex enfin sur lequel depuis près de huit ans s'inscrit l'essentiel de son travail. A cette classification *élémentaire*, comme à celle qui ne tiendrait compte que des *méthodes* (assemblage, combustion...), l'œuvre même, dans son détail apporte un démenti. Sacs brûlés ou révélant sous une déchirure une nappe de couleur voilée de plastique, film transparent collé telle une peau au cellotex, craquelures observées comme accident de la peinture sur la toile ou la plastique avant d'être cultivées pour elles-mêmes, il semble, à y bien regarder, que le travail de Burri progresse en fait par contaminations, du fortuit à l'essentiel, du hasard à la décision créatrice.

Une telle attitude affirme la primauté du regard, la faculté de voir dans ce qui est aux autres insignifiant la qualité inédite. Exemplaire à cet égard est son expérience de la toile à sac: prisonnier de guerre des Américains et interné dans un camp au Texas, il commence à peindre en autodidacte, faute de matériaux adéquats, sur de vieux Sacs de marchandises récupérés. Cinq ans plus tard, la toile de jute ne sera plus le support médiocre de l'image mais deviendra l'essentiel du tableau, son image même.

Le respect des objets dépréciés, du rebut, l'écoute attentive de leurs qualités tels que les manifeste Burri sont à l'opposé de la volonté iconoclaste des artistes Dada ou de leurs héritiers. Ils participent plutôt, dans le climat général de l'après-guerre, de cette célébration des valeurs décriées, du très banal, à laquelle se consacre également, à cette époque, Jean Dubuffet. "Je ne peux me défendre du sentiment, écrit ce dernier, que les choses les plus proches, les plus constamment sous nos yeux, sont aussi celles qui ont été de tout temps les moins aperçues". Pour Burri, cet ancrage dans la réalité du matériau est manière de dépasser, sans en renier la charge émotive, l'expérience quotidienne pour donner libre-cours à l'invention plastique, à une forme inédite de la peinture abstraite.

La critique a souvent associé le travail de Burri à une sorte d'état ultime du collage tel que l'ont défini avec les *papiers collés* les peintres cubistes. C'était méconnaître la nature contradictoire de leurs approches. Dans le papier collé, il s'est agi de juxtaposer à la peinture un élément hétérogène, de tester par là-même la valeur et la précision du fait pictural. Pierre de touche du travail du peintre, l'élément collé, aussi intégré soit-il à la composition, s'en différencie toujours pour mieux dialectiquement faire exister l'élément dessiné: le paquet de tabac ne vaut que comme garant du dessin de la pipe qu'il accompagne. Pas d'artifice semblable dans l'œuvre de Burri: ici, le matériau importe pour lui-même et la peinture n'est que sa mise en œuvre.

Etrangère à la toile et aux pinceaux, l'œuvre de Burri ne laisse cependant aucun doute quant à sa nature picturale: composition, science des valeurs, passages... y sont présents au même titre que chez les peintres qui utilisent alors classiquement les matériaux traditionnels de la peinture. D'être ainsi transposés au moyen de matières de rebut, les procédés picturaux gagnent encore, par contraste, en raffinement. Tout l'œuvre de Burri joue ainsi paradoxalement de la tension des extrêmes conciliés. Rien de plus apparemment immédiat que les éléments constituant du tableau, mais soumis à une géométrie sous-jacente, à une structure rigoureuse, ils sont à vrai dire plus nécessaires qu'hasardeux.

A l'apparition claire de formes géométriques – dans les cellotex par exemple – correspond un relatif effacement des effets de matière, alors que l'évidence de celle-ci, qu'il s'agisse des *Sacs* ou des *Craquelures*, fait passer au second plan l'organisation volontaire des formes. Ces successives prépondérances font du travail de Burri une expérimentation continue. Entre les termes opposés qui régissent sa peinture se définit en fait l'espace d'une poétique. La violence, non dénuée de sentiment érotique, mise en œuvre dans ses toiles fait des moyens de destruction – déchirure, éclatement où brûlure – le mode même d'élaboration du tableau. Au périssable et au fragile succède ainsi l'incorruptible temps de l'art. Ce sont dépouilles opimes, celles de la victoire de la vie, que fixent, en lambeaux glorieux, les œuvres d'Alberto Burri.

1987

Alberto Zanmatti, "Testimonianze: Alberto Zanmatti, il Cretto di Burri," in *Rotary Club di Città di Castello*, catalog, Tipolitografia Petruzzi & C., Città di Castello, 1987.

Gibellina vecchia, distrutta dal terremoto, rimarrà per coloro che l'hanno abitata un luogo di continuo e rispettoso pellegrinaggio in memoria dei loro morti e della vita passata. Il grande "cretto", come nuova immagine della vecchia Gibellina coerente con le ultime ricerche di Burri, è in una dimensione che interviene concretamente nel paesaggio e si fa architettura. Il "cretto" o crepa, quasi figurazione della terra che ha tremato, diventa percorso dove si ritrovano le vecchie strade, labirinto della memoria che ripropone una vita.

Attraverso i cretti-percorsi la gente potrà arrivare dove esisteva la chiesa e la "piazza" dove si faceva festa. Il progetto prevede di ricoprire buona parte del vecchio centro distrutto, con una superficie rettangolare di circa 300 x 400 metri di lato, un'area quindi di poco meno di 12 ettari, riutilizzando le macerie raccolte in blocchi e ricoperte di cemento bianco. I percorsi pedonali fra i blocchi alti in media circa un metro e sessanta, seguiranno in parte i tracciati delle vecchie strade principali e in parte i cretti spontanei dell'opera di Burri.

Le zone non interessate direttamente da questo intervento verranno ripulite da ogni maceria e utilizzate a verde basso che si confonderà col verde circostante, isolando l'opera. Land-art, scultura, architettura, urbanistica, opera d'arte totale, fatta dalle macerie del passato, ricoperte quasi per conservarle, è riproposta alla gente di Gibellina per ritrovarsi sia nella memoria del passato che nella realtà ritrovata.

1988

Eva Menzio, in *Alberto Burri: Assegai*, exhibition catalog (Turin, Galleria Eva Menzio, 8 November 1988–15 January 1989), Galleria Eva Menzio, Turin, 1988.

Ho conosciuto Burri più di vent'anni fa nella sua casa di Grottarossa. Ricordo poco di quel primo incontro, se non l'impressione che mi aveva fatto la casa, il luogo e la soggezione provata nei confronti dell'artista famoso e schivo. Quando ragazzina andai a trovare Morandi provai sensazioni analoghe. Morandi mi era apparso con la grande figura nel vano di una porta troppo piccola per lui. Mi ero chiesta allora come potesse con le grandi mani, con la statura, che mi era parsa smisurata, fare quei quadri tutti così piccoli. Burri non era tanto alto, e smisurata, in senso contrario, mi sembrò la casa di Grottarossa, la campagna all'intorno. Ma i due incontri avevano qualcosa in comune.

Provai di fronte ad entrambi la stessa soggezione, conscia dell'importanza dei due personaggi. Nei piccoli spazi di via Fondazza, come nell'aperta campagna di Grottarossa, sentii la stessa spiritualità, la stessa distanza dall'attualità, dalla moda, la stessa grandezza. Fu allora che cominciai ad amare Burri come anni prima avevo amato Morandi.

La nostra frequentazione continuò negli anni successivi. Senza mai perdere la deferenza che avevo per lui, comincia quella complicità scherzosa che ancora oggi sussiste tra noi. Mi piaceva andare a trovarlo nella sua casa di montagna, sopra Città di Castello, passare per quelle colline disabitate, vedere quel taglio del cielo in alto, che mi ricordava certe divisioni dei suoi quadri. Mi affascinava l'atmosfera delle Casenuove, punto di partenza di Burri e dei suoi amici per la caccia. La casa, severa, rigorosa, ma funzionalissima, mi è sempre parsa rispecchiare il carattere di Burri che rifugge categoricamente il superfluo. Gli opposti si attraggono. Come potevo quindi non essere attirata da lui io che non conosco neppure il significato della parola rigore? La nostra amicizia continua tra una trasgressione e l'altra, tra una sigaretta che si fuma, quando non si potrebbe fumare, tra un ennesimo bicchiere di ammazzacaffè che si beve, quando non si dovrebbe più bere. "Scrivi tu qualcosa per la mostra" mi ha detto Burri. "Non voglio critici, ché le parole sono inutili a spiegare la pittura". Così mi sono ritrovata davanti alla macchina da scrivere a cercare di parlare del mio amore per lui.

1994

Giuliano Serafini, "La misura e l'entasi," in *Alberto Burri. Il polittico di Atene. Architetture con cactus*, exhibition catalog (Athens, Mouseio Alexandrou Soutzou, Ethnikí Pinakothìki, 11 May–30 June 1994), Athens.

"Bisogna nascondere la profondità sulla superficie..."
Hugo von Hofmannsthal

La vera leggenda di Alberto Burri è di non avere leggende. Nessun altro artista di questa seconda metà di secolo ha saputo forse segnare tra sé e il mondo tanta distanza e tanto silenzio. "È la mia opera che parla per me", ebbe a dichiarare in occasione della mostra "The New Decade: 22 European Painters and Sculptors" presentata da A. Carnduff Ritchie al Museum of Modern Art di New York. Era il 1954, l'epoca dei *Sacchi*, e la sua fama cominciava a consolidarsi tra Europa e Stati Uniti. Da allora non si sono avute altre dichiarazioni pubbliche da parte sua: solo quarant'anni d'attività che hanno cambiato la coscienza estetica del nostro tempo, in un isolamento intransigente e aristocratico che gli ha meritato la reputazione di personaggio difficile. Quando anche quello, e forse soprattutto quello, era un segnale preciso, un contributo sostanziale all'opera, un modo cioè d'elevarla a un'assolutezza dove estetico ed etico sono la stessa cosa, secondo un'intuizione che da Odysseas Elytis rimanda all'universalità del pensiero classico. Attraverso gli anni, quel silenzio ha permesso alla pittura di Burri di manifestarsi in *crescendo*, d'emergere sovrana in virtù del *diminuendo* a cui l'artista si era votato in quanto individuo e persona. È stata un'immersione totale, un autentico transfert che l'ha fatto diventare "luogo" della propria opera, esattamente agli antipodi di quella figura di artista-opera che le tendenze concettuali avevano partorito intorno agli anni settanta: colui cioè che fa del proprio comportamento e della propria presenza fisica il mezzo stesso dell'azione creativa... Viene facile pensare a Beuys, "l'altra metà del cielo", la polarità opposta di Burri, come la critica ha ampiamente riconosciuto. Nel 1981 si sono incontrati a Perugia, a confermare l'irriducibilità della loro posizione rispetto la storia, ma anche a confrontare due diversità complementari che sembrano l'identikit stesso di questa fine di secolo. Curiosa storia la loro. Entrambi provenienti dagli studi di medicina, hanno voltato le spalle a una carriera sicura negli stessi anni (1945-46). Per l'uno e per l'altro l'arte doveva diventare veicolo di sopravvivenza, nel recupero di quella dignità che la guerra appena trascorsa aveva tolto al genere umano. C'è dell'eroico in questa scelta, forse del romantico. Fatto è che solo da artista Burri sapeva di poter riconquistare quella posizione di equidistanza dalle dialettiche umane e recuperare la propria unicità. Come scrive Ralph W. Emerson: "L'Eroe è sempre centrale". Allo stesso modo la storia dell'arte contemporanea ha dovuto tener conto della qualità irradiante che questa opera ha finito per assumere rispetto le varie correnti non figurative sviluppatesi tra i due continenti nell'immediato dopoguerra. [. . .]

[. . .] Per l'artista italiano la materia non nasconde invece significati. La tela di sacco, il legno, il ferro degli anni cinquanta, così come la combustione e la plastica del decennio dopo, fino al cretto e al cellotex degli anni settanta, tutto è facilmente riconoscibile, verificabile all'occhio e al tatto. Ed è su questo contesto di pura *esistenza* che Burri opera la grande, fondamentale trasformazione: là dove era solo rifiuto, oscura traccia del nostro quotidiano, intercetta i segni inconfondibili della bellezza, lo splendore della forma, mettendo in azione quello che ancora Calvesi chiama "un processo di risalita dalla muta, squallida presenza della materia al livello dell'arte". È un intervento di sublimazione con cui l'artista ci apre gli occhi su quanto era sfuggito alla nostra percezione e alla nostra coscienza; aiutandoci a cogliere nella materia qualità estetiche così compiute da far cadere la tradizionale antinomia idealistica che la vedeva contrapposta, in arte, alla forma. In definitiva la rivoluzione di Burri consiste nell'aver fatto coincidere materia e pittura a uno stesso grado espressivo. Cito un famoso scritto di Giulio Carlo Argan, dal catalogo della Biennale di Venezia del 1960: "Per Burri si dovrà parlare di *trompe-l'œil* alla rovescia, nel quale non è più la pittura a fingere la realtà, ma la realtà a fingere la pittura". Ed è solo pittura, nient'altro che pittura, il rammendo che ricuce gli stracci miserabili, il buco che si apre come una notte abissale, la sbavatura di fuoco minerale che ferisce la tela di sacco. E non è tutto: quello che al primo sguardo ci appare uno sconvolto evento materico, in realtà finisce per essere governato da un ordine che sa ricomporre la forma in termini di definizione spaziale, in ritmi e rapporti che rendono tutto intelligibile, come per un desiderio d'appagamento, di calma suprema. Dunque un'altra antinomia, quella che vede contrapposti il dionisiaco e l'apollineo, sembra cadere. La tentazione di una lettura in chiave simbolica della pittura di Burri in fondo viene rimossa da questo prevalere, in ogni sua fase, del fattore formale. Questa è la sua costante maggiore e questa anche la ragione della sua straordinaria unità. Così, quando l'artista ammette che tra il suo primo quadro e l'ultimo non c'è differenza, non possiamo che dargli ragione: perché l'arte rinasce sempre da se stessa, non ha bisogno di futuro. Anche qui Burri sembra dare scacco matto alle avanguardie storiche la cui colpa maggiore è stata d'aver concepito l'arte come una sorta di sorpasso continuo, sull'esempio dei processi evolutivi della scienza. [. . .]

2003

Marco Vallora, "C'è. E basta," in *I "neri" di Burri*, exhibition catalog (Acqui Terme, ex Kaimano, 20 July–14 September 2003), edited by Marco Vallora, Mazzotta, Milan, 2003.

[. . .] Curiosamente, tutte le volte che Burri torna a parlare del "silenzio" che esige intorno alla sua opera vilipesa, e spesso proprio dall'entusiasmo critico, quasi meccanicamente, istintivamente, lo collega però poi, inscindibilmente, anche al fantasma della sacra, degradata Parola. Come nel dialogo con Milton Gendel. "Le *parole* non significano niente, per me: esse parlano intorno alla pittura. Ciò che io voglio esprimere appare *nella* pittura". Burri non ama i contorni, i dintorni, le circonvoluzioni che guardano dall'esterno. Ama gettarsi dentro l'opera, essere l'opera, non "guardarla dal di fuori" (anche se molti esegeti disturbano la distanziazione "epica" di Brecht, per spiegare la sua posizione di oppositore perenne). E poi, nella sua eccezionale "dichiarazione di poetica", nel catalogo della mostra 1956 al MoMA, dal titolo "The New Decade": "Le *parole* non mi sono d'aiuto, quando provo a parlare della mia pittura. Questa è un'irriducibile presenza che rifiuta di essere tradotta in qualsiasi altra forma di espressione. È una presenza nello stesso tempo imminente e attiva. Questa è quanto essa significa: esistere così come dipingere. La mia pittura è una realtà che è parte di me stesso, una realtà che non posso rivelare con parole". La poetica è assolutamente montaliana: "Sarebbe più facile per me dire ciò che non è necessario dipingere, ciò che non riguarda la pittura, ciò che io escludo dal mio lavoro talvolta con soddisfazione". A quella presenza sacra e vilissima, appunto, il nero pesto e tumefatto e trionfante, è dedicata la mostra: ad una "presenza" attiva, imminente, cerimoniale e fecondante, che non smette mai di inquietare e di vivificare le fibre della pittura, di esplodere beneficamente dentro quelle tele sontuose, come l'apocalittico lenzuolo di ceralacca di *Rosso plastica*, 1962 (altro che suggestioni irrefrenabili di morte! Arcangeli parla infatti di "sinistro obitorio, dove qualcosa ancora si muove, si genera, sanguina, si strappa". Ma è ovviamente un degrado, una deliquescenza, che è vita). Appunto, la presenza, dirompente e magnetica, magmatica, del "nero", che dilaga ovunque, catramoso: "tetra necessità medianica". Proprio così, dunque: i "neri" di Burri, con minuscola e virgolette, confidenzialmente (allo stesso modo con cui Villa spegne le sue maiuscole quando parla di "frammenti e riverberi di una serena bisanzio per tutti"). I "neri intensificati" e drammaturgici, contrappesati e sfidanti, dirimpetto gli "infiniti bianchi" e i rossi, laceranti e sanguinosi, che non smettono di fiorire mai sulla carnagione purulenta della sua pittura. Non tanto, quindi, e soltanto, i *Neri*, in senso istituzionale, titolato, quello dei quadri intorno agli anni ottanta, che così esplicitamente si nominano, o che comunque s'aggirano intorno a quei dintorni semantici, quali *Annottarsi*, o i *Nero Cellotex*, o i *Grande Nero*. (Tra l'altro opere per lo più inamovibili dalle stanze di Palazzo Albizzini o dagli ex Essiccatoi, là dove l'arte dell'*accrochage* di Burri li ha posti per sempre e difficilmente salperanno ancora, per nobilitare delle mostre). No, proprio in senso più affabile e confidenziale, i "neri" intesi e concertati in tutta la gamma sinfonica dello spettro scuro, il ventaglio più vario e generoso, dei mille "neri" inventati, che a Burri capitò di manipolare, di far dialogare tra loro, di far "accadere". Neri lucidati, bituminosi, festosi, tragici, operati, sabbiosi, opachi, gessati, frullati, abbrustoliti, disciolti, aggettanti, brutali, delicati, fantastici, realistici, contrastati, sferzanti. Neri mantecati di pomice od impaniati di vinavil. Neri omicidi della plastica e ferocemente ulceranti, quasi inscenando il demonico rito del pennello-delitto da fiamma ossidrica (in parallelo con Yves Klein) biblica ustione che moltiplica paesaggi trasparenti e cedevoli vedute stratificate, visionarie, trasognate. Il nero spaccato e laccato dei cretti immobili, come greti cementati di immemorabili fiumi africani. Il nero sottile e ricamato dei cruciverbi labirintici e gracilissimi di materia. Il nero appeso degli stracci, depositati sulla tela come volatili della notte, pipistrelli raccapriccianti o il nero pustoloso dei *cellophan* masticati dalla pittura, nelle campiture lunghe ed usurate degli appezzamenti sconfinati, trafficati di solitudine. E ancora, neri velati di calzamaglia ed improvvisamente ingobbiti di pelle d'oca. Neri-lapilli e brace-carbone. Neri porosi e piangenti, come quelli del *Nero* 1951, una lieve parentela con Kupka, Vieira da Silva e De Staël.

[. . .] Nero-eros, infine, nelle grandi arature cosmologiche dei *Cellotex*, scosciati e rablesiani, dei tardi anni ottanta, su cui rapidamente va ad annottare la mostra. Apparentemente anemici e tracciati michelangiolescamente sopra i vasti campi atoni del legno truciolato (ricordo lontano del Texas mai redento?). In verità, ed in definitiva, del dio-colore, Burri, l'innamorato delle forme, non ha un'idea così nobile, fondante, trascendente. "I colori sono così dentro la mia testa che potrei farli al buio. Si potrebbe obiettare che gli impressionisti dovevano andarli a vedere con i propri occhi. Ma io il bianco ce l'ho nel cervello. E come il bianco, il nero, il rosso. Potrei fare i miei quadri al buio... è difficile da spiegare, bisogna esserci nati così, non c'è niente da fare". Quasi un daltonismo dell'anima. Talvolta basta infatti a Burri una minima, infima sferetta di nero-morte, o di nero-luce, un microbico pallino da sparo, una punta, un graffio di colore, un'apertura di pagina e di sguardo (vedi ad esempio l'opera *Pagina*, del 1953-54, concertata per un libro d'artista con lo stesso Villa) per orientare l'intera partitura, l'intera vicenda espressiva. E qui davvero non ha alcuna importanza la mutevolezza incontrollabile delle dimensioni dell'opera, come bene aveva intuito Brandi, ne *Il Nero di Burri*, 1967. La "grandiosità" minimale ed intrinseca del fare di Burri prescinde dalle banali misurazioni canoniche. "La monumentalità con cui Burri impiantava anche le sue carte bruciate era dovuta al rapporto interno del quadro, non alle proporzioni. Nelle grandi misure dei quadri Burri non si 'ingrandisce', afferma il suo metro, ma per il fatto detto prima, anche un quadro di modeste proporzioni è monumentale". (Così lui stesso annota: "'Leggerino' è per me un lavoro che non fa della pittura una grande, solida costruzione. La pittura deve essere ogni volta una costruzione di idee, di spirito, di materiali, non può essere tre o quattro macchie da una parte o dall'altra"). Allo stesso modo egli amministra valorosamente il gioco duellante dei bianchi e dei neri, "dialettizzando i neri neutri d'un fondo con i neri brutalmente viventi e infetti di cenci e di residui d'abbigliamento", come suggerisce felicemente Arcangeli. E Crispolti disturba addirittura Sartre e Camus, per spiegare questa polarità originaria, basica che – lo sottolineerà anche Vittorio Rubiu – si risolve ogni volta in "due forze in contrasto, due 'mezzi', e non per farne scaturire un accordo, ma per la forza, appunto, che si sviluppa dal contrasto". [. . .]

2015

Carlo Bertelli, "Burri, ovvero il ruolo della materia," in *Alberto Burri. Catalogo generale.* Vol. III, *Pittura 1979-1994*, Fondazione Palazzo Albizzini Collezione Burri, Città di Castello, 2015.

[. . .] La materia che Burri inserisce nel discorso dell'arte non è mai presentazione di qualche reperto naturale. Burri non raccoglie ciottoli né scortica tronchi d'albero. Né Burri ci sorprende per ironiche analogie visive. Non vede in una spazzola un bruco. Che la superficie fessurata in innumerevoli crepe che i Cretti presentano non sia un fatto naturale, ma metamorfosi di una materia artificiale, ovvero prodotta dall'uomo, prodotto industriale anonimo e informe che cambia per un intervento deliberato, divenne di dominio pubblico quando, in seguito al terremoto del 1968, nel Belice, su committenza del sindaco di Gibellina Ludovico Corrao, Burri coprì le macerie della città distrutta con un autentico sudario di cemento bianco. Come solchi in una sommità collinare fatta di cemento, trincee più profonde dell'altezza di un uomo spaccano i metri quadrati della vasta superficie urbana, ricalcando i luoghi delle strade scomparse. Accompagnano pigramente le curve di livello della collina, o cambiano quota in ripidi percorsi. Rallentano o affrettano il passo. In ogni punto la loro rete complessa sottintende un intreccio di umane relazioni drammaticamente interrotte. Vi è una dolorosa concretezza in questa topografica astrazione. La Gibellina di Burri sugella la memoria d'una città estinta e intende conservarla per le generazioni future. Oggi la pioggia ha scurito il bianco cemento, mentre cespugli, arbusti, erbe stanno invadendo i percorsi delle antiche strade, rompendo a volte le dure placche di cemento. È la materia che si prende una rivalsa. Credo che Burri avesse previsto che qualcosa sarebbe successo. Non certo la distruzione della sua opera, ma una sua dimostrazione di vitalità. Anche questa resa fa parte della sua malinconia. Se non per un suo sentire ogni opera come un pezzo di spazio, Burri non avrebbe altrimenti potuto immaginare la città morta di Gibellina, che come una perenne memoria domina la vallata. Ho avuto la fortuna di allestire insieme a lui la grande mostra antologica a Milano in Palazzo Citterio. Come un bracco in battuta di caccia, Burri fiutava i punti di vista più appropriati, li fotografava prima di scegliere le opere e non gli dispiaceva (con dolore dei prestatori) di scartare lavori che non combinavano con gli spazi prescelti, o che non avrebbero aggiunto molto a un discorso che a lui appariva già compiuto. La materia è spazio occupato e spazio e materia sono i due poli in cui si è cimentata l'arte del XX secolo. A incominciare dai cubisti. Il cantiere del palazzo in cui fu realizzata la mostra milanese presentava scabre pareti ancora non ricoperte d'intonaco, gradini di cemento, nudi pilastri e travi di cemento armato e, per contrasto, finestre chiuse da maniglie ottocentesche neobarocche. Era un ambiente in formazione, ancora in attesa di essere definito e ci sembrava molto congeniale alla presentazione dell'opera di Burri. Brera era a due passi e frequenti furono le visite di Burri alla pinacoteca. Ricordo una sua sosta pensosa davanti alla piccola *Flagellazione* di Luca Signorelli firmata "opus luce". Commentammo quella *luce*. Allora era da pochi anni che aveva preso forma la distinzione netta, nella professione della storia dell'arte, tra storici del passato e critici del contemporaneo. Il problema di una storia dell'arte del XX secolo non si poneva quando il secolo era ancora in corso e il concetto di arte non era stato posto in discussione. Rari erano dunque gli storici che erano anche critici militanti. Tra questi un ruolo eminente ebbe Cesare Brandi, storico dell'arte e teorico, direttore dell'Istituto Centrale del Restauro, che era una sua creatura. Brandi fu uno dei primi ad apprezzare l'opera di Burri e fu particolarmente attratto dalle sperimentazioni del Maestro nel campo della grafica, che Burri rivoluzionò radicalmente, facendo della stampa non la riproduzione delle sue opere, ma un'invenzione originale. Tanto che nel 1973 Brandi fu, con Argan, sostenitore dell'assegnazione a Burri del Premio Feltrinelli per la Grafica dell'Accademia dei Lincei. Anche la carta diventava per Burri materia, specialmente quando la stampa a rilievo "scavava" dentro lo spessore della carta. La lezione di Burri non poteva non servire da stimolo a esplorazioni nuove. Burri aveva indicato la potenzialità della materia, aveva scoperto l'opposizione della materia all'imitazione della realtà. Cosicché il discorso di Burri finì per indirizzare anche la posizione contemporanea rispetto alle opere d'arte del passato. Sino alla rivoluzione di Burri, le opere pittoriche erano soltanto immagine. Con Burri tornarono ad essere materiate, cioè ad essere percepite come muro, tavola, tela. Il vanto dei restauratori era stato l'abilità nello strappo della superficie pittorica dal suo supporto, che, quando si trattava di tavole, veniva spesso distrutto. Poi la consapevolezza dei conservatori cambiò profondamente. Salvo controindicazioni, gli affreschi rimasero sui muri, le tempere sulle tavole. Su queste ultime, le eventuali lacune non furono più stuccate e coperte di nuova pittura, eventualmente considerata "neutra", ma lasciate al vivo, mettendo in evidenza le gallerie dei tarli e le venature del legno. Né le tavole furono sempre costrette nelle armature che ne impedivano i naturali movimenti. Attribuire questa inversione d'indirizzo al solo Burri sarebbe ardito, ma sicuramente Burri aveva inciso profondamente nel gusto e nel rapporto tra l'immagine e la sua costituzione materiale. Jannis Kounellis ha spesso ricordato l'importanza che ebbe Burri per la sua "uscita dal quadro" e il suo incontro con le risorse sceniche della materia. Burri aveva operato nella stagione inaugurata dalle riflessioni di Benjamin sull'opera d'arte nell'epoca della sua riproducibilità tecnica e aveva negato che quella riproducibilità fosse sempre possibile. La materia vi si opponeva. Burri è stato determinante per una presa di coscienza in un tempo in cui le consolidate strategie della rappresentazione dello spazio non convincevano più. Uno dei primi ad acquistare un'opera di Burri fu Lucio Fontana. Senza dubbio fu un gesto dettato dall'ammirazione e dalla solidarietà. Eppure i due grandi Maestri hanno operato su campi opposti. Lucio Fontana ha lavorato per "smaterializzare la materia". Fendendo la tela con tagli di rasoio, e con questo gesto dando valore di segno al vuoto. Immaginando l'irraggiungibile immensità spaziale, fatta d'intangibili nebulose e orbite stellari. Tracciando nei soffitti astratti arabeschi di neon, o inserendovi frammenti di vetri e di smalti per accogliere ed emettere la luce, oppure, nel caso di un soffitto all'Elba, ora nel Museo del Novecento a Milano, per riflettere l'instabile palpito delle onde. Fontana è tanto proteso all'energia quanto Burri alla materia. Nella stessa scultura Fontana negava la solida consistenza tridimensionale. Ora ricoprendo il volume di tessere musive d'oro, ora semplicemente passandovi sopra un colore azzurro. Al contrario, Burri trovava una trascendenza nella materia stessa, quasi che tra i due grandi Maestri del XX secolo si svolgesse un dialogo, una elegante gara di scherma. Ai colori fangosi dei sacchi di juta, cui talvolta Burri aggiungeva una placca rossa o una foglia d'oro, all'incontro tagliente di strati di ferro di Burri (cosa di più vicino alle armature di Piero negli affreschi di Arezzo?) Fontana opponeva la linea casuale sulla tela di frammenti di salgemma. Altra era la leggerezza da cui Burri era partito e che con insistenza sarebbe tornata nella sua opera. Burri aveva abbandonato i primi esperimenti figurativi venendo incontro alle forme aeree di Miró, alle sagome astratte di Arp. Questo riferimento di fondo traspare nelle composizioni del 1948 e passa dalle Muffe alle Combustioni, in un gioco di pieni e di vuoti. Il desiderio di forma, in rapporto spontaneo con la tradizione del Quattrocento, si manifesta nei Cretti centinati, dove il quadro da galleria è negato nel nome della classica pala d'altare. Il bianco boreale dei Cretti terminanti in un arco acquista allora un senso nuovo e fa sì che lo sguardo si perda abbagliato da una luce d'ignota sorgente. Continuava la ricerca nei materiali industriali e la sfida a nobilitarli. [. . .]

Chiara Sarteanesi, "La grafica di Alberto Burri fra tradizione e innovazione," in *Alberto Burri. Catalogo generale.* Vol V, *Opera grafica 1949-1994*, Fondazione Palazzo Albizzini Collezione Burri, Città di Castello, 2015.

[. . .] Alberto Burri si dedica alla grafica dopo la metà degli anni cinquanta insieme a Enrico Castelli, ingegnere di professione, ma anche valido scultore che, nell'immediato dopoguerra, nel suo studio romano di via Flaminia fonda la Stamperia Castelli. Mettendo a frutto la sua elevata inventiva meccanica, unita a notevoli capacità tecniche, Castelli trasforma in torchio da stampa una macchina per produrre pasta alimentare, avuta in cambio di alcune sue opere. In seguito progetta un'architettura, Palazzo Castelli in via Prenestina, concepita fin dall'inizio come struttura per ospitare la stamperia e diversi studi per artisti. Negli anni cinquanta è una delle più importanti stamperie di Roma che riproduce opere di artisti come Afro, Birolli, Burri, Corpora, Fazzini, Guttuso, Gentilini, Rotella, Scialoja e altri.

Le opere che Burri stampa con Castelli sono due: *Muffa* del 1957 e *Combustione* del 1959, realizzate entrambe con l'utilizzo di due tecniche non facili da conciliare, quali la litografia e l'acquaforte. Nella serie *Muffa* è possibile riscontrare delle differenze tra una copia e l'altra, nelle dimensioni delle campiture di colore, dovute al procedimento di stampa a mano sperimentale e all'alterazione dell'inchiostro bianco particolarmente instabile, causata dalla luce. Queste opere hanno una "presenza" che deriva dalla fase progettuale e dalla fase esecutiva e non rappresentano per Burri un punto di arrivo. Egli non considera mai l'opera grafica come un'attività minore, una sorta di divago, ma qualcosa di profondamente meditato, voluto, pesato anche nell'azzardo della forzatura delle tecniche tradizionali. Il rapporto fra Burri e Castelli andò oltre la realizzazione delle grafiche: l'artista umbro coinvolse Castelli nella sistemazione della Plastica realizzata da Burri nel 1968, per la chiesa del convento francescano a Sion, nella complessa progettazione del *Teatro Continuo* per la Triennale di Milano del 1973 (distrutto nel 1989 e ricostruito in occasione del Centenario della nascita di Alberto Burri), nonché nella realizzazione della prima scultura in ferro, Cretto del 1978. Nel 1962 Burri inizia la collaborazione con la 2RC di Roma diretta da Valter ed Eleonora Rossi che avevano avviato la loro stamperia solamente un anno prima. Ciò che persuade Burri a questa cooperazione è la considerazione dei Rossi per la grafica come vero e proprio genere artistico, quali pittura e scultura, e non un'estensione di queste ultime. Lavorano con la 2RC Burri, Fontana, Pomodoro, Capogrossi, Turcato, Santomaso, Consagra, Beverly Pepper, Afro, de Kooning e Calder, questi ultimi introdotti dallo stesso Burri. Il primo lavoro edito nel 1962 con la 2RC sono le tre acqueforti per il libro di poesie di Emilio Villa: *17 Variazioni su temi proposti per una pura ideologia fonetica*. L'opera era stata progettata dall'artista con il poeta stesso già nel 1953, ed ebbe una lunga gestazione. Inizialmente era previsto che ognuna delle copie fosse arricchita da tre opere originali di piccolo formato e di grande valore (copertina e due pagine interne). Burri interrompe l'edizione quando si rende conto che chi ne entrava in possesso estraeva le opere per incorniciarle, travisando la loro primaria funzione che le vedeva di illustrazione propria del libro. Nel 1955 dei 99 esemplari stampati, ne vennero completati solo 24 corredati da fogli illustrativi e relative copertine. Nel 1962 Burri ripensa ad una nuova edizione del libro, corredata da limitate opere grafiche con la 2RC. I poeti, prima della critica, hanno fatto luce sulla portata della pittura di Burri. Libero De Libero e Leonardo Sinisgalli presentano la sua prima mostra romana nel 1947 alla galleria La Margherita, dove erano esposte le prime opere ancora "figurative"; Emilio Villa già nel 1951, secondo solo a Christian Zervos che l'anno precedente aveva segnalato Burri fra i giovani dell'arte italiana in "Cahiers d'Art", scrive: "Io medito su questo pittore che ho perduto venendo in questo nuovo continente, ma che certo ancora opera con rabbia che dovrebbe essere feconda, nel tempo per il dopo, e per il dopo del dopo, fino all'inane e al terribile, come su un audace protagonista. Secondo me, accanto allo statunitense Gorky [. . .] Alberto Burri è già da noverare oggi tra i testimoni della superiore amara iniziativa: del cominciare oggi generando, ma né la vita né la morte. Non rappresentando, ma facendo. Questo io dico: che bisogna fare".

Burri e Villa sono uniti da affinità elettive, *outsider* del linguaggio, l'uno artistico, l'altro poetico, fanno *tabula rasa* del passato, rimanendo fuori dal sistema dell'arte. Rifiutano l'appartenenza in genere, poco amanti delle "parole", ritenute assolutamente inutili a definire l'arte in tutti i suoi aspetti, fuori dalle mode e dai salotti "buoni". Entrambi si sottraggono alle sovrastrutture e privilegiano il rapporto diretto con l'individuo, alla cui sensibilità affidano l'accesso della propria poetica.

La dichiarazione di Burri, pubblicata per la prima volta nel catalogo della mostra "The New Decade" del 1955, lo accomuna alle convinzioni di Villa riguardo all'impotenza delle parole.

Ed è ancora Emilio Villa, nel testo in catalogo della personale di Burri alla Fondazione Origine del '53, a dare lumi sull'assoluta sua modernità: "ecco un'opera che poteva essere fatta solo oggi, ecco un'azione che poteva essere compiuta oggi soltanto, non ieri, non domani". Seguiranno ulteriori collaborazioni fra Villa e Burri.

Nella *Combustione* del '63-64 e nella serie di sei *Combustioni* del 1965, realizzate con incisione, acquaforte, acquatinta, si evidenzia il risultato più sorprendente del binomio Burri-Rossi. La difficoltà era simulare l'effetto di una bruciatura in assenza del fuoco e rendere indefiniti i punti anziché la linea, o meglio rendere sfumati i punti che crea l'acquatinta.

Tale tecnica consente di fare, anche in una stessa matrice, granìture differenti, usando polveri di diversa grossezza e con ripetute morsure per ottenere una superficie ruvida, ma non l'effetto di rilievo che occorreva per simulare le parti bruciate. Burri, insieme a Valter Rossi, prova ad aggiungere rame nella lastra, anziché asportarlo, al contrario di ciò che la tecnica prevede: l'acquatinta, ritenuta una tecnica "in cavo" fino ad ora, diviene "in rilievo".

Prima di approdare a tale soluzione Burri aveva suggerito prove di ogni tipo, usando sistemi empirici, anche molto interessanti, con l'impiego di sabbie, *carborundum* a diverse grane, anche per dimensione, e incollate con leganti di volta in volta diversi. Tali esperimenti si rivelarono per la 2RC molto utili per la realizzazione grafica di opere di altri artisti.

Si rese necessario anche l'utilizzo di un torchio in grado di esercitare una pressione tale da rendere visibile tutto ciò che altrimenti sarebbe rimasto nascosto nelle lastre di rame. Il risultato desiderato dall'artista venne raggiunto solo dopo mesi di tentativi e intenso lavoro. Compiuto il prototipo, il problema era procedere alla stampa: questa fase, normalmente di *routine*, diventava difficile e insidiosa, proprio per le variazioni apportate alla tecnica di base.

Ma a Burri piacevano le sfide, consapevole che da grandi difficoltà non potevano che sortire grandi risultati [. . .].

Gabi Scardi, *Il Teatro Continuo di Alberto Burri*, La Triennale di Milano–Corraini, Milan, 2015.

"Ecco il disegno per il *Teatro Continuo*. La piattaforma in cemento, le quinte in ferro, colore naturale delle lamiere da un lato, dall'altro dipinte di bianco (il colore può essere cambiato quando si voglia) saranno girevoli comandate a distanza, indipendenti. L'amico Enrico Castelli che è un fenomeno per la meccanica, studierà il meccanismo. È uno scheletro di teatro ma penso che sia l'essenziale."

Con questo appunto, chiaro e sintetico, scritto nel 1972, Alberto Burri accompagnava lo schizzo assonometrico di un'opera da costruirsi al centro del Parco Sempione di Milano. Il progetto era destinato alla città di Milano. Su invito di Giulio Macchi, curatore della sezione della XV Triennale di Milano, "Contatto Arte – Città", Burri elabora e propone un'idea di teatro all'aperto. Alla sintetica descrizione di Burri fanno da contrappunto le parole di Macchi che ben esprimono il ruolo sociale e politico del teatro quale spazio rappresentativo del rapporto dell'individuo con la città. "Il teatro nella città antica aveva una sua collocazione urbanistica ben evidente e calcolata così come altri edifici sociali essenziali: il granaio, il tempio, l'arena, il granaio era presente controllabile da tutti i cittadini all'incrocio fra cardini e i decumani, il teatro era oggetto-scultura sempre presente sia se usato dagli artisti che vuoto. Ho pensato di inserire l'idea-teatro fra quelle da proporre agli artisti e ai cittadini. Alberto Burri ha raccolto con entusiasmo la proposta di ideare un palcoscenico all'aperto, essenziale e soggetto a tutte le variazioni volute dall'attore o dal pubblico. Scenario-parco o volendo scene mobili, quinte ruotanti che reagiscono diversamente alla luce nelle loro superfici da una parte specchianti dall'altra opache. La materia essenziale nell'opera di Burri, è il cemento e l'acciaio."

[. . .] Se il testo di Macchi interpreta lo spirito della manifestazione, lo stile conciso, tipico di Burri, corrisponde al registro formale dell'opera. L'intero progetto viene infatti improntato sulla logica di economia dei mezzi. Burri parte da un'analisi della situazione esistente e vi iscrive un'opera semplice e sobria nella forma, ruvida nella realizzazione, progettata con geometrica esattezza, rigorosamente *site specific* nella concezione, nella collocazione e nelle proporzioni: un teatro realizzato per sottrazione, ridotto all'indispensabile, sfrondato di ogni accessorio e di ogni possibile sovrastruttura. Il risultato è una struttura ortogonale, simmetrica, composta da elementi nettamente delineati, prodotti industrialmente: una piattaforma orizzontale di cemento sollevata da terra in modo da risultare sospesa, e sei pannelli verticali in metallo, rotanti su se stessi, imperniati lateralmente sulla piattaforma, tre per lato, a scandire lo spazio a mo' di quinte. L'adozione, da parte dell'artista, di questo linguaggio sintetico e misurato corrisponde a una duplice istanza: da un lato, nel momento in cui si trova a pensare un'opera pubblica per un contesto sensibile e già organizzato quale è il Parco Sempione, Burri assume un atteggiamento di rispetto. Nell'intento di enfatizzare le caratteristiche dell'esistente, asciuga il proprio linguaggio da ogni accento espressivo e adotta una soluzione formale disciplinata, limitando gli elementi compositivi allo stretto necessario. Dall'altro, il trattamento riservato alle superfici, lisce ma non levigate, monocrome ma non lustre, risponde alla scelta di evitare ogni magniloquenza. Con *Il Teatro Continuo* Burri opta per una semplicità che, corrispondendo a chiarezza di idee e di obiettivi, si risolve in una perfetta corrispondenza tra forma, senso e funzione. E, con la scelta del nome dell'opera, esplicita, come meglio non potrebbe, quali siano questo senso e questa funzione. Il Teatro è Continuo perché capace di accogliere nel tempo il desiderio di rappresentarsi, spontaneo o organizzato, di una città e di una società. È continuo esso stesso, e cangiante a seconda di ciò che vi si svolge; capace di persistere pur nella transitorietà delle azioni cui si presta; e in sintonia con il flusso della vita, con la sua transitorietà e con il suo incessante rigenerarsi. È un'opera che dura attraverso le generazioni e che mette in scena il divenire e la trasformazione. [. . .]

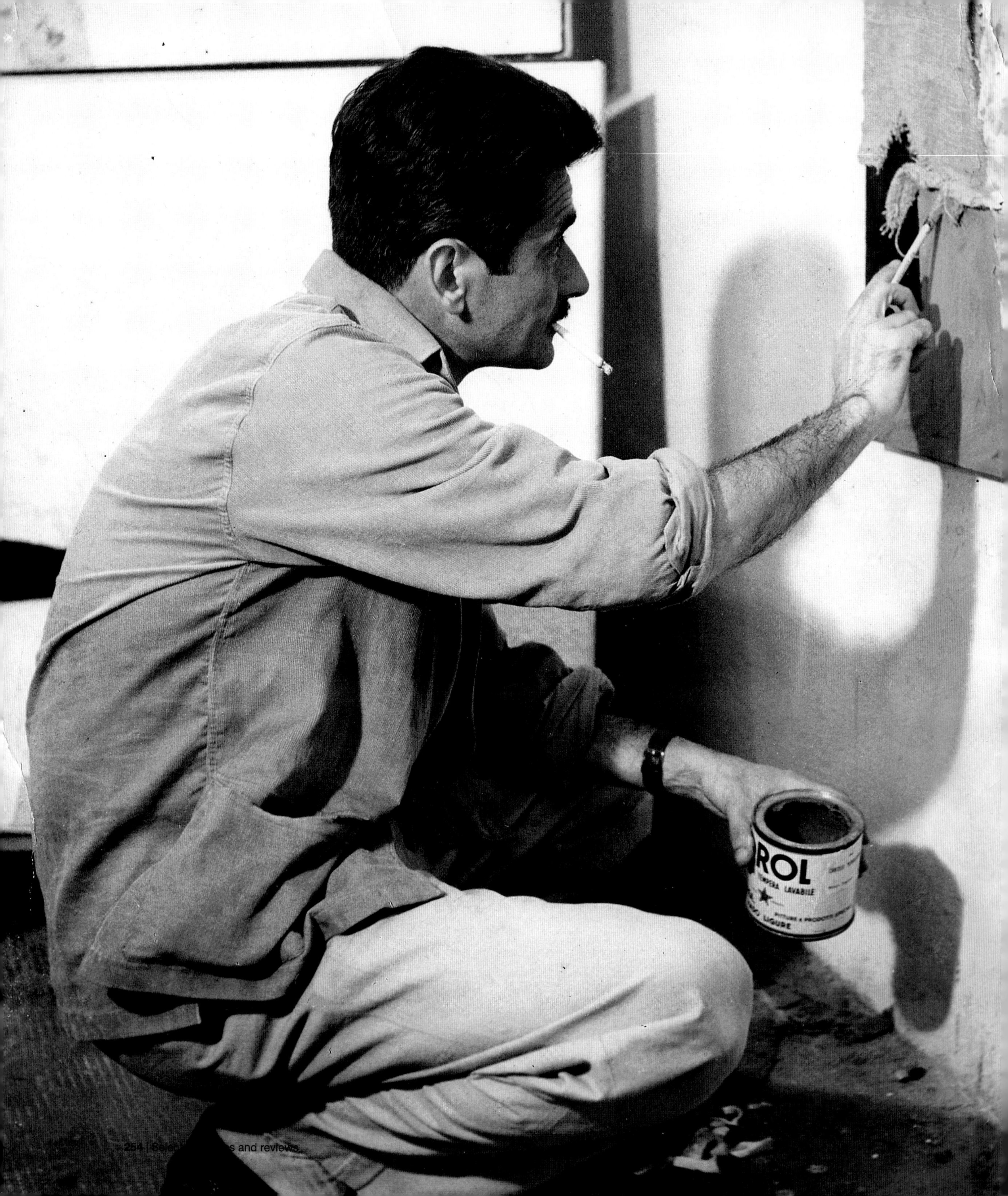
ROL
LAVABILE
LIGURE

Solo Exhibitions

Alberto Burri, Via Aurora, 1945

Scan the QR code to access Alberto Burri's comprehensive bibliography as well as all the group exhibitions he took part in.

Dots indicate exhibitions touring a number of cities

1947
• *Alberto Burri*, La Margherita gallery, Rome, opening on 10 July.

1948
• *Alberto Burri*, La Margherita gallery, Rome, opening on 17 May.
• [*Burri*], Galleria dell'Angelo, Città di Castello, September.

1949
• *Mostra di dipinti di Alberto Burri*, Galleria dell'Angelo, Città di Castello, 29 August–12 September.

1950
• Galleria dell'Angelo, Città di Castello.

1952
• *Neri e Muffe*, L'Obelisco gallery, Rome, opening on 3 January.
• *13 Opere di Burri*, Galleria d'Arte Contemporanea, Florence, opening in April.

1953
• *Alberto Burri. Paintings and Collages*, Frumkin Gallery, Chicago, 13 January–7 February.
• *Burri*, Fondazione Origine, Rome, 18–30 April.
• *Alberto Burri*, Stable Gallery, New York, 23 November–12 December.

1954
• *Burri*, L'Obelisco gallery, Rome, opening on 16 April.
• *Alberto Burri. Recent Paintings*, Frumkin Gallery, Chicago, 19 April–15 May.

1955
• *Burri*, Stable Gallery, New York, 23 May–8 June.
• *The Collages of Alberto Burri*, curated by J.P. Byrnes, Fine Arts Center Colorado Springs, Colorado Springs…, 4–31 October (touring exhibition: Oakland Art Museum, …Oakland…, 12 November–4 December; Otto Seligman Gallery, …Seattle…, 4–29 February 1956; Fine Arts Gallery at the University of British Columbia, …Vancouver…, 13–31 March 1956; Pasadena Art Museum, …Pasadena…, 5–20 May 1956; Haggin Art Galleries, …Stockton, opening on 3 June 1956).

1956
• *Burri*, Galleria del Cavallino, Venice, 17–26 September.
• *Burri peintures, César sculptures*, Galerie Rive Droite, Paris, 6 November–8 December.

1957
• *Alberto Burri*, Galleria del Naviglio, Milan, 12–21 January.
• *Burri: Combustioni*, L'Obelisco gallery, Rome, 14–23 May.
• *Opere di Alberto Burri*, Galleria La Loggia, Bologna..., 22 October–1 November (touring exhibition: Galleria La Bussola, …Turin…, 22 November–5 December; Galleria Alberti, …Brescia, 12–23 January 1958).
• *Paintings by Alberto Burri*, curated by J. J. Sweeney, Museum of Art Carnegie Institute, Pittsburgh..., 11 November–29 December (touring exhibition: The Arts Club of Chicago, …Chicago…, 30 January–7 March 1958; Albright Art Gallery, …Buffalo (New York)…, 8 April–20 May 1958; San Francisco Museum of Art, …San Francisco, 17 June–3 August 1958).

1958
• *Burri*, Galleria La Salita, Rome, opening on 12 March.
• *Burri: Ferri*, Galleria Blu, Milan, 1–31 December.

1959
• *Alberto Burri*, Galerie Marie-Suzanne Feigel, Basel, 14 February–19 March.
• *Burri*, Palais des Beaux-Arts, Brussels, 11–22 April.
• *Antoni Tàpies Alberto Burri*, Galerie Beyeler, Basel, May–June.
• *Alberto Burri*, curated by P. Wember, Museum Haus Lange, Krefeld…, May–June (touring exhibition: Museum am Ostwall, …Dortmund, July–August).
• *Burri*, La Tartaruga gallery, Rome, opening on 13 May.
• *Mostra di Alberto Burri*, Galleria La Loggia, Bologna, 11–22 May.
• *Burri*, Wiener Secession, Vienna, 14 July–9 August.

1960
• *Burri*, Martha Jackson Gallery, New York, 2–27 February.
• *Burri*, Hanover Gallery, London, 29 March–29 April
• *Colección Torcuato Di Tella. Premio Pintores Argentinos. Muestra Individual de Alberto Burri*, Museo Nacional de Bellas Artes, Buenos Aires, 1–30 October.
• *Burri*, Galerie Änne Abels, Cologne, 10 November–8 December.

1961
• *Burri. Mostra antologica. Opere dal 1948 al 1955*, La Medusa gallery, Rome, opening on 14 January.
• *Burri*, Galerie de France, Paris, 14 April–May.

1962
• *Alternative attuali. Omaggio a Burri*, curated by A. Bandera and E. Crispolti, Castello Cinquecentesco, L'Aquila, 26 July–August.
• *Burri*, Marlborough Galleria d'Arte, Rome, December–January.

1963
• *Alberto Burri*, Marlborough New London Gallery, London..., October (touring exhibition: Marlborough-Gerson Gallery, …New York, February 1964).
• *Alberto Burri*, The Museum of Fine Arts, Houston (Texas)..., 16 October–1 December, (touring exhibition: Albright-Knox Art Gallery, …Buffalo (New York)…, 7 January–2 February 1964; Walker Art Center, …Minneapolis…, 14 February–29 March 1964; San Francisco Museum of Art, …San Francisco…, May 1964; Pasadena Art Museum, …Pasadena, 25 August–27 September 1964).

1964
• *Burri, Plastiche*, Galleria Blu, Milan, opening on 9 March.

1965
• *Plastiche di Burri*, Galleria La Bussola, Turin, opening on 16 January.

1966
• [*Dante e Burri*], Galleria Toninelli, Milan..., [January] (touring exhibition: Il Segno gallery, …Rome, February 1966).
• *Alberto Burri*, XXXIII Esposizione Biennale Internazionale d'Arte Venezia, Giardini di Castello (personal room), Venice, 18 June–16 October.
• *Alberto Burri and Lucio Fontana*, Wells College, Aurora (New York)..., 23 September–9 October (touring exhibition organized by the Museum of Modern Art, New York: Kenyon College, …Gambier…, 21 October–3 November; Wilmington College, …Wilmington (Ohio)…, 20 November–11 December; Portland Art Museum, …Portland…, 6–29 January 1967; Ringling Museum of Art, …Sarasota…, 22 May–18 June 1967; University of South Florida, ...Tampa..., 7–30 July 1967; State University College, …Oswego (New York)…, 17 September–8 October 1967; Root Art Center Hamilton College, …Clinton (New York)…, 22 October–12

November 1967; Colorado Springs Fine Arts Center, …Colorado Springs…, 27 November–18 December 1967; University of Iowa, …Iowa City…, 3–24 January 1968; Columbus Gallery of Fine Arts, … Columbus (Ohio), 8–29 February 1968).
• [*Alberto Burri Combustioni*], Palazzina Vitelli, Città di Castello, opening on 31 December.

1967
• *Alberto Burri*, Kunsthalle, Darmstadt, 8 April–14 May.
• *Alberto Burri*, Museum Boijmans Van Beuningen, Rotterdam, 9 June–23 July.
Burri, La Tartaruga gallery, Rome, opening on 4 December.

1968
• *Opere recenti di Burri*, Galleria Blu, Milan, January.

1969
• *Alberto Burri*, Galleria Sanluca, Bologna, 12 March–15 April.
• *Burri opere recenti*, Galleria Notizie, Turin, 5 December 1969–15 January 1970.

1971
• *Alberto Burri*, curated by A. Passoni, Galleria Civica d'Arte Moderna, Turin, 7 October–31 December.

1972
• *Alberto Burri*, Musée National d'Art Moderne, Paris, 26 May–10 July.

1973
Alberto Burri, Galleria Notizie, Turin, opening on 9 May.
• *Opere recenti di Alberto Burri*, Galleria d'arte Sanluca, Bologna, 27 October 1973–3 January 1974.

1974
• *Alberto Burri. Œuvres récentes*, Galerie Jacques Benador, Geneva, 11 February–March.

1975
• *Opere di Burri*, sacro convento di San Francesco, Assisi, 3 May–2 June.

1976
• *Alberto Burri*, curated by B. Mantura and G. De Feo, Galleria Nazionale d'Arte Moderna, Rome, 15 January–14 March.
• *Burri. Disegni, tempere e grafiche 1948-1976*, Palazzo Ducale, Pesaro, 25 September–30 November.

1977
• *Alberto Burri*, curated by B. Mantura and G. De Feo, Calouste Gulbenkian Foundation, Lisbon, February[–March].
• *Burri Cellotex 1974-1977*, Galleria Sanluca, Bologna, 2 February–31 May.
• *Alberto Burri*, Palacio de Velázquez Parque del Retiro, Madrid, April–May.
• *Alberto Burri. A Retrospective View 1948-77*, curated by G. Nordland, The Frederick S. Wight Art Gallery University of California, Los Angeles..., 25 September–4 December (touring exhibition: Marion Koogler McNay Art Institute, …San Antonio…, 8 January–19 February 1978; Milwaukee Art Museum, …Milwaukee…, 31 March–21 May 1978; The Solomon R. Guggenheim Museum, … New York, 20 June–27 August 1978).

1978
• *Alberto Burri*, curated by R. Causa, Museo di Capodimonte, Naples, May–September.

1979
• *Alberto Burri "I sacchi 1952-1958". Mostra Omaggio ad Alberto Burri*, curated by B. Lorenzelli, Galleria Lorenzelli, Milan, 1–28 February.
• *Alberto Burri: Cellotex, Cretti, una scultura, 1978-1979*, curated by F. Caroli and G. Marconi, Studio Marconi, Milan, 17 May–July.
• *Alberto Burri 1978-1979*, James Corcoran Gallery, Los Angeles, 5 June–7 July.
• *Alberto Burri, il viaggio*, Seccatoio del tabacco tropicale, Città di Castello…, 5 December 1979–January 1980 (touring exhibition: Staatsgalerie moderner Kunst, …Munich, 13 March–20 April 1980).

1980
• *Beuys/Burri*, curated by I. Tomassoni, Rocca Paolina, Perugia, 3 April 1980–November 1981.
• *Alberto Burri Orsanmichele*, curated by V. Bramanti, Orsanmichele, Florence, 15 November 1980–11 January 1981.

1981
• *Alberto Burri 1 Scultura 10 Multiplex*, L'isola gallery, Rome, 4 June–30 July.
• *Alberto Burri. Teatri e scenografie*, curated by F. Mancini and A. Burri, Teatro Rossini – Sala della Repubblica, Pesaro, 10 September–30 November.
• *Alberto Burri, Antoni Tàpies*, FIAC – Grand Palais, Paris…, 16–25 October (touring exhibition: Galerie Marie-Louise Jeanneret – Art Moderne, …Geneva, 26 November 1981–15 February 1982).
• *Alberto Burri. Cellotex und Multiplex*, curated by D. Ronte, Galerie im Taxispalais, Innsbruck..., 15 December 1981–20 January 1982 (touring exhibition: Künstlerhaus Salzburger Kunstverein, …Salzburg…, 26 January–20 February 1982; Palais Liechtenstein Museum Moderner Kunst, …Vienna…, 10 March–25 April 1982; Kärntner Landesgalerie, …Klagenfurt, 5 May–6 June 1982).

1982
• *Alberto Burri,* curated by K. Plake, Palm Springs Desert Museum, Palm Springs (California), 26 January–14 March.
• *Alberto Burri, il viaggio*, Columbus Museum of Art, Columbus (Ohio)..., 27 February–11 April (touring exhibition: Brooklyn Museum, …New York…, 8 May–18 July; San Francisco Museum of Modern Art, …San Francisco, 30 September–1 November).
• *Alberto Burri. Cellotex e multiplex*, Galleria Sanluca, Bologna, 27 February–15 April.
• *Alberto Burri 16 opere grafiche e 3 quadri*, Galleria d'arte contemporanea La Nuova Città, Brescia, 6 March–7 April.

1983
• *Morandi e Burri, disegni/grafica*, META Centro Culturale, Florence, 29 January–February.
• *Burri Sestante*, curated by G. C. Argan, Ex Cantieri Navali, Venice, 7 May–18 September.

1984
• *Alberto Burri, Cretti e Cellotex*, Galerie Sapone, Nice, 14 February–24 April.
• *Alberto Burri Rosso e Nero*, curated by P. Falicon with the collaboration of P. Barrau, Galerie des Ponchettes, Nice..., 12 May–31 June (touring exhibition: Musées de Toulon, …Toulon, 5 June–3 July 1985).
• *Burri*, curated by C. Pirovano, C. Bertelli, and V. Maderna, Pinacoteca di Brera, Milan, 24 May–8 July.
• *Burri Grafica – piccoli dipinti*, Galleria delle Arti, Città di Castello, 27 December 1984–27 January 1985.

1985
• *Alberto Burri. Opere recenti*, Galleria Sanluca, Bologna, 26 January–12 May.
• *Burri. Combustioni, Cretti, Cellotex 1964-1984*, Galerie Artcurial, Paris, 7 March–30 April.
• *Alberto Burri opere recenti. Annottarsi*, Galleria Sprovieri, Rome, 3 December 1985–30 January 1986.
• *Alberto Burri. Le opere e i giorni/ Lo spazio/ La scena/ Le opere 1969-1985*, curated by F. Moschini, A.A.M./Coop. Architettura Arte Moderna, Rome, 9 December 1985–1 February 1986.

1986
• *Burri 18 paintings 1953-1986*, Di Laurenti Gallery, New York, 13 March–26 April.

1987
• *Burri. Il Viaggio, Sestante, Annottarsi*, Ex Stabilimento Industriale Peroni, Rome, 12 May–13 September.
• *Burri. Monotex, Multipli, Grande Ferro K*, Palazzo del Rettorato, Museo Laboratorio dell'Università degli Studi La Sapienza, Rome, 12 May–13 September.

1988
• *Il Luogo degli Artisti*, XLIII Esposizione Internazionale d'Arte. La Biennale di Venezia, curated by G. Carandente, Padiglione Italia, personal room, Venice, 26 June–25 September.

• *Burri S. Vitale*, curated by C. Spadoni, Museo Nazionale Complesso San Vitale, Sala del Refettorio, Ravenna, 9 July–30 October.
• *Alberto Burri Non ama il Nero*, Galleria Sprovieri, Rome, 11 October–November.
• *Alberto Burri Annottarsi (Up to Nite)*, curated by P. Sprovieri, The Murray and Isabella Rayburn Foundation, New York, 4 November 1988–7 January 1989.
• *Assegai*, Galleria Eva Menzio, Turin, 8 November 1988–15 January 1989.

1989
• *Burri 3 Cellotex*, Galleria Lia Rumma, Naples, 15 October–31 December.
• *Wien Modern 89. Burri 1953-1968 4 Pitture Wien*, Museum Moderner Kunst, Vienna, 30 October–26 November.
• *Wien Modern 89. Burri 1984 Rosso e Nero Wien*, Istituto Italiano di Cultura, Vienna, 31 October–26 November.
• *Burri*, Galleria Milart, Rome, November–December.
• *Burri 25 grafiche 1 scultura*, Galleria delle Arti, Città di Castello, 8 December 1989–20 January 1990.
• *Burri*, Galerie Sapone, Nice, 20 December 1989–31 January 1990.

1990
• *Burri's Palm Springs Desert Museum Cycle*, Salvatore Ala Gallery, New York, 21 April–26 May.
• *Burri*, Galerie Sapone at FIAC, Paris, 25 October–1 November.

1991
• *Alberto Burri*, Palazzo Pepoli Campogrande, Bologna..., 27 September–10 November (touring exhibition: Casa Rusca, ...Locarno, 15 December 1991–1 March 1992).
• *Burri Cellotex 91*, curated by I. Gianelli, Castello di Rivoli, Rivoli, 2 October–1 December.

1992
• *Alberto Burri: nel segno della materia*, Palazzo dei Capitani del Popolo (Sala dei Savi), Ascoli Piceno, opening on 11 January.
• *Alberto Burri œuvres 1949-1992*, Galerie Sapone at FIAC, Paris, 24 October–1 November.

1993
• 48° Concorso Internazionale della Ceramica d'Arte, *Burri-Nero e Oro* (Donation of one work of the Maestro to the Museo Internazionale della Ceramica), Palazzo delle Esposizioni, Faenza, 18 September–24 October.
• *Alberto Burri, la pittura come materia vivente, opere dal 1949 al 1966*, curated by C. Cerritelli, Galleria d'Arte Niccoli, Parma, 30 October 1993–5 January 1994.

1994
• *Alberto Burri – Το Πολυπτυχο των Αθηνων. Αρχιτεκτονικη και κακτος / Il Polittico di Atene. Architetture con cactus / The Polyptych of Athens. Architectures and Cactus*, curated by G. Serafini, Mouseio Alexandrou Soutzou, Ethnikí Pinakothìki, Athens, 11 May–30 June.
• *Alberto Burri – Arquitecturas con cactus / Architetture con cactus*, curated by G. Serafini, Istituto Italiano di Cultura, Madrid, 30 November 1994–10 January 1995.
• *La donazione Burri* (donation of works of the Maestro to the Galleria degli Uffizi), Galleria degli Uffizi, Florence, 10 December.

1996
• *Burri Fontana 1949-1968*, curated by B. Corà, Museo Pecci, Prato, 13 April–30 June.
• *Burri opere 1944-1995*, curated by C. Christov-Bakargiev and M. G. Tolomeo, Palazzo delle Esposizioni, Rome..., 9 November 1996–15 January 1997 (touring exhibition: *Burri 1915-1995. Retrospektive*, Lenbachhaus, ...Munich..., 5 February–6 April 1997; Palais des Beaux-Arts, ...Brussels, 6 June–17 August 1997).

1998
• *Alberto Burri. Vom Unikat zum Auflagenwerk / Dall'opera unica alla moltiplicata*, curated by C. Sarteanesi, P. L. Siena, and A. Hapkemeyer, Museion-Museo d'Arte Moderna, Bolzano, 12 June–30 August.
Alberto Burri: "Cretti", Museo Civico, Gibellina, 10 October–10 November.
• *Alberto Burri 1948-1993*, curated by A. Bonito Oliva and C. Sarteanesi, Zonca & Zonca Arte Moderna e Contemporanea, Milan, 22 October–31 December.

1999
• *Burri Giacomelli*, Galleria Anna d'Ascanio, Rome, 2 June–31 July.
• *Omaggio ad Alberto Burri. Grafica e scultura*, curated by Edizioni Bora, Bologna, and Galleria delle Arti, Città di Castello, Comune di Colonnella, Colonnella, 30 July–15 September.
• *Burri. Segni di un percorso opere 1949-1987*, curated by V. Rubiu, F. Bacci, and G. Pauletto, Galleria Sagittaria,Pordenone, 4 December 1999–6 February 2000.

2000
• *Alberto Burri opere 1956-1992*, Galerie Sapone at Arte Fiera, Bologna..., 27–31 January (touring exhibition: Arco, ... Madrid, 10–15 February).
• *Alberto Burri Cellotex 1980-1992*, curated by A. Sapone, Galerie Sapone at Miart, Milan, 5–8 May.
• *Burri*, curated by M. Kitatani, T. Kitagawa, C. Sarteanesi, and T. Kanai, Toyota Municipal Museum of Art, Toyota, 6 June–20 August.
• *Burri inedito*, curated by M. Calvesi, Ex Seccatoi del Tabacco, Città di Castello, 24 June–30 September.
• *Burri Multiplo*, curated by C. Sarteanesi, Centro Umanistico Incontri Internazionali Antonio e Aika Sapone, Bellona, November 2000–January 2001.

2001
• *Burri*, curated by M. Calvesi and C. Sarteanesi, Sala Espositiva Chiostri San Domenico, Reggio Emilia, 18 November 2001–7 January 2002.

2003
• *Burri*, Galerie Sapone at Arte Fiera, Bologna, 22–27 January.
• *I "neri" di Burri*, curated by M. Vallora, Palazzo Liceo Saracco, Acqui Terme, 20 July–14 September.
• *Burri. Tutta la grafica*, curated by C. Sarteanesi, Ex Seccatoi del Tabacco, Città di Castello, 11 October 2003–11 January 2004.
• *Alberto Burri. Tra Materia e Forma. Opere scelte 1948-1993*, curated by A. Pia, G. Davide, and L. Mazzoleni, Mazzoleni Galleria d'Arte, Turin, 17 October–31 December.
• *Burri Cellotex* (long-term loan), curated by M. Calvesi, Parco della Musica Auditorium Arte, Rome, 20 October 2003–14 December 2005.

2004
• *Burri Dottori "opere rare"*, curated by L. Amadei, Galleria delle Arti, Città di Castello, 13 March–13 June.

2005
• *Burri il cellotex ha un cuore antico*, curated by G. Serafini, Galerie Sapone at Arte Fiera, Bologna, 27–31 January.
• *Burri. Viaggio al termine della materia*, curated by G. Serafini, Tornabuoni Arte, Florence, 12 May–12 July.
• *Burri e l'opera grafica*, curated by N. Vernizzi, Galleria Civica Villa Valle, Valdagno, 19 November 2005–15 January 2006.

2006
• *I Cellotex nell'autobiografia di Burri*, curated by M. Calvesi, Galerie Sapone at Arte Fiera, Bologna, 26–30 January.
• *Alberto Burri*, curated by M. Calvesi and C. Sarteanesi, Museo Nacional Centro de Arte Reina Sofía, Madrid, 14 March–29 May.
• *Alberto Burri: la sezione aurea dei Cellotex*, curated by I. Tomassoni, Museo Fondazione Luciana Matalon, Milan, 25 November 2006–31 January 2007.

2007
• *Burri opere 1949-1994. La misura dell'equilibrio*, curated by B. Corà and C. Sarteanesi, Fondazione Magnani-Rocca, Mamiano di Traversetolo, 8 September–2 December.
• *Alberto Burri*, Mitchell – Innes & Nash, New York..., 29 November 2007–18 January 2008 (touring exhibition: De Pury & Luxembourg, ...Zurich, 16 February–29 March 2008).

2008
• *Alberto Burri*, curated by M. Calvesi and C. Sarteanesi, Triennale di Milano, Milan, 11 November 2008–8 February 2009.

2009
• *Alberto Burri. Equilibrio – Struttura – Ritmo – Luce*, curated by F. Poli, Palazzo Clemente, Fondazione Malvina Menegaz per le Arti e le Culture, Castelbasso, 20 June–30 August.
• *Burri Colore Omaggio*, Galleria delle Arti, Città di Castello, 29 August–29 November. *Burri e Fontana. Materia e Spazio*, curated by B. Corà, Fondazione Puglisi Cosentino, Palazzo Valle, Catania, 15 November 2009–14 March 2010.

2010
• *Alberto Burri Art Paris + Guest 2010*, curated by B. Corà, Grand Palais Galerie Sapone, Paris, 17–22 March.
• *Alberto Burri. Cretti neri*, curated by M. Calvesi, Luxembourg & Dayan, New York, 10 May–30 July.
• *Burri e Fontana a Brera*, curated by S. Bandera and B. Corà, Pinacoteca di Brera, Milan, 16 June–3 October.
• *Combustione: Alberto Burri and America*, curated by L. Melandri and M. Duncan, Santa Monica Museum of Art, Santa Monica, 11 September–18 December.

2011
• *Alberto Burri dalla concretezza reale all'incanto della forma*, curated by F. Poli, Mazzoleni Galleria d'Arte, Turin, 21 October 2011–31 January 2012.

2012
• *Alberto Burri Form and Matter*, curated by M. Duranti, Estorick Collection of Modern Italian Art, London, 13 January–7 April.
• *Alberto Burri primi ed ultimi*, curated by P. Sapone, Galerie Sapone at Arte Fiera, Bologna, 27–30 January.
• *Alberto Burri da una raccolta privata, quattro opere inedite, multiplex, cretti e serigrafie*, curated by P. Parri, Galleria Pananti – Archivio del Novecento, Florence, 20 June–20 July.
• *Alberto Burri. Opera al Nero Cellotex 1972-1992*, curated by B. Corà, project and realization by M. Di Carlo and A. Sapone, Galleria dello Scudo, Verona, 15 December 2012–31 March 2013.

2013
• *Alberto Burri. Black Cellotex*, curated by A. Sapone, Luxembourg & Dayan, New York, 8 March–20 April.
• *Burri Grafica*, curated by L. Amadei, Galleria delle Arti, Città di Castello, 30 November 2013–30 March 2014.

2014
• *Alberto Burri-Hans Hartung*, Galerie Sapone at Arte Fiera, Bologna, 24–27 January.
• *Burri Unico e Multiplo*, curated by G. Agnisola, Pinacoteca Comunale di Gaeta, Gaeta, 14 June–12 October.
• *Rivisitazione: Burri incontra Piero della Francesca*, curated by B. Corà, Museo Civico, Sansepolcro, 31 October 2014–12 March 2015.

2015
• *Alberto Burri: Oro e Nero*, European Parliament, Brussels, 28 January.
• *Burri e Pistoia*, curated by B. Corà, Palazzo Sozzifanti, Pistoia, 10 May–26 July.
• *Burri e Signorelli. Giornata di studi e mostra storico-documentaria*, curated by C. Cecchetti and A. Iori, Oratorio di San Crescentino, Morra, Città di Castello, 30 May.
• *Burri. I Cretti*, curated by B. Corà, Museo Regionale d'Arte Contemporanea Palazzo Belmonte Riso, Palermo, 25 July–20 September.
• *Sironi – Burri. Un dialogo italiano (1940-1958) / An Italian Dialogue (1940–1958)*, curated by C. Caliandro, Spazio Arte CUBO, Centro Unipol, Bologna, 28 July–18 October.
• *Alberto Burri Grafica*, curated by S. Adamowicz, O. Marciano, T. Margalit, and A. Matthews, Luxembourg & Dayan, New York, 17 September–24 October.
• *Alberto Burri. The Subject of Matter*, curated by C. Piscitelli and F. Cigola, Ierimonti Gallery, New York, 2 October–23 November.
• *Alberto Burri*, curated by Mazzoleni Art, Mazzoleni Art, London, 2 October–30 November.
• *Alberto Burri. The Trauma of Painting*, curated by E. Braun, M. Fontanella, and C. Stringari, Solomon R. Guggenheim Museum, New York…, 9 October 2015–6 January 2016 (touring exhibition: Kunstsammlung Nordrhein-Westfalen, K21 Ständehaus, …Düsseldorf, 5 March–3 July 2016).
• *Alberto Burri. I colori del silenzio, opere grafiche 1965-1985*, curated by G. Agnisola, Spazio COMEL arte contemporanea, Latina, 7–29 November.
• *Alberto Burri e i poeti. Materia e suono della parola*, curated by B. Corà and T. Sicoli, MAON, Museo d'Arte dell'Otto e Novecento, Rende, 11 November 2015–28 February 2016.
• *I Mixoblack di Alberto Burri nella Galleria Tesori d'Arte di San Pietro in Perugia*, curated by Fondazione Palazzo Albizzini Collezione Burri, Università degli Studi di Perugia, and Fondazione per l'Istruzione Agraria, Galleria Tesori d'Arte, Perugia, 21 November 2015–5 January 2016.
• *Burri e Brandi un'amicizia informale*, curated by V. Brandi Rubiu, promoted by Comune and Università di Siena; Polo Museale Regionale della Toscana; Soprintendenza Belle Arti e Paesaggio per le Province di Siena, Grosseto e Arezzo; Santa Maria della Scala, Villa Brandi a Vignano, Siena, 21 November 2015–31 January 2016.

2017
• *Alberto Burri. Gli arazzi per la Regione Emilia-Romagna*, Regione Emilia Romagna, Atrio di viale Aldo Moro, Bologna, 25–30 January.
• *Burri. L'Opera Grafica Permanente*, curated by B. Corà, Ex Seccatoi del Tabacco, Città di Castello, opening on 12 March.
• *Burri posters*, curated by B. Corà, Casa Italiana Zerilli-Marimò, New York University, New York, 26 October–8 December.

2018
• *Alberto Burri*, Tornabuoni Art, Paris, 19 October–22 December.
• *Burri cicli scelti dell'opera grafica*, Vistamare, Pescara, 16 December 2018–15 March 2019.

2019
• *Action / Abstraction Alberto Burri – Lucio Fontana*, curated by Tornabuoni Art London, Tornabuoni Art, London, 8 February–30 March.
• *BURRI la pittura, irriducibile presenza*, curated by B. Corà and C. Sarteanesi, Fondazione Giorgio Cini, Isola di San Giorgio Maggiore, Venice, 10 May–28 July.
• *Burri la ferita della bellezza*, curated by M. Recalcati, exhibition setup design by A. Sarteanesi and M. Chiavarini, Museo Carlo Bilotti – Aranciera di Villa Borghese, Rome…, 22 March–9 June (touring exhibition: MAG – Museo Alto Garda, … Riva del Garda, 21 June–3 November).

Bibliography

Dots indicate exhibitions touring a number of cities

1947
• *Alberto Burri*. Leaflet, texts by Libero De Libero and Leonardo Sinisgalli. Rome, Galleria La Margherita, opening on 10 July 1947.

1948
• *Alberto Burri*. Leaflet. Rome, Galleria La Margherita, opening on 17 May 1948.

1949
• *Mostra di dipinti di Alberto Burri*. Leaflet. Città di Castello, Galleria dell'Angelo, 29 August–12 September 1949.

1952
• *Neri e Muffe*. Leaflet. Rome, L'Obelisco gallery, opening on 3 January 1952.

1953
• *Burri*. Leaflet, text by Emilio Villa. Rome, Fondazione Origine, 18–30 April 1953.

1954
• *Burri*. Leaflet. Rome, L'Obelisco gallery, opening on 16 April 1954.

1955
• *The Collages of Alberto Burri*. Leaflet, text by James P. Byrnes. Colorado Springs..., Fine Arts Center Colorado Springs, 4–31 October 1955.

1956
• *Burri*. Leaflet, text by James Johnson Sweeney. Venice, Galleria del Cavallino, 17–26 September 1956.
• *Burri peintures, César sculptures*. Leaflet, texts by Michel Tapié and Alain Bosquet. Paris, Galerie Rive Droite, 6 November–8 December 1956.

1957
• *Alberto Burri*. Leaflet, text by André Pieyre de Mandiargues. Milan, Galleria del Naviglio, 12–21 January 1957.
• *Burri: Combustioni*. Leaflet. Rome, L'Obelisco gallery, 14–23 May 1957.
• *Opere di Alberto Burri*. Leaflet, text by Francesco Arcangeli. Bologna..., Galleria La Loggia, 22 October–1 November 1957.
• *Opere di Alberto Burri.* Leaflet, text by Francesco Arcangeli. Turin..., Galleria La Bussola, 22 November–5 December 1957.
• *Paintings by Alberto Burri*. Catalog edited by James Johnson Sweeney. Pittsburgh: Carnegie Institute. Pittsburgh..., Museum of Art Carnegie Institute, 11 November–29 December 1957.

1958
• *Burri*. Leaflet. Rome, Galleria La Salita, opening on 12 March 1958.
• *Burri: Ferri*. Catalog. Milan, Galleria Blu, 1–31 December 1958.

1959
• *Alberto Burri*. Leaflet, foreword by Egon Vietta. Basel, Galerie Marie-Suzanne Feigel, 14 February–19 March 1959.
• *Alberto Burri*. Catalog. Krefeld: Museum Haus Lange. Krefeld..., Museum Haus Lange, May–June 1959.
• *Antoni Tàpies Alberto Burri*. Leaflet. Basel, Galerie Beyeler, May–June 1959.
• *Burri.* Catalog, foreword by Giulio Carlo Argan. Brussels: Palais des Beaux-Arts. Brussels, Palais des Beaux-Arts, 11–22 April 1959.
• *Burri*. Catalog, text by Paul Wember. Vienna: Wiener Secession. Vienna, Wiener Secession, 14 July–9 August 1959.
• *Mostra di Alberto Burri*. Leaflet. Bologna, Galleria La Loggia, 11–22 May 1959.

1960
• *Burri*. Leaflet. New York, Martha Jackson Gallery, 2–27 February 1960.
• *Burri.* Catalog, text by Herbert Read. London: Hanover Gallery. London, Hanover Gallery, 29 March–29 April 1960.
• *Burri*. Catalog, text by Paul Wember. Cologne: Galerie Änne Abels. Cologne, Galerie Änne Abels, 10 November–8 December 1960.
• *Colección Torcuato Di Tella. Premio Pintores Argentinos. Muestra Individual de Alberto Burri*. Catalog, text by Jorge Romero Brest. Buenos Aires: Istituto Torcuato Di Tella. Buenos Aires, Museo Nacional de Bellas Artes, 1–30 October 1960.

1961
• *Burri. Mostra antologica. Opere dal 1948 al 1955*. Exhibition notice, text by Enrico Crispolti. Rome, La Medusa gallery, opening on 14 January 1961.
• *Burri*. Catalog, texts by Le Piéton de Paris (from *L'Observateur*, 20 April 1961) and M. Ragon (from *Arts*, 19 April 1961). Paris: Imprimerie du Compagnonnage. Paris, Galerie de France, 14 April–May 1960.

1962
• *Alternative attuali. Omaggio a Burri.* Catalog edited by Antonio Bandera and Enrico Crispolti. Rome: Edizioni dell'Ateneo. L'Aquila, Castello Cinquecentesco, 26 July–August 1962.
• *Burri*. Catalog, text by Cesare Brandi. Rome: Editalia. Rome, Marlborough Galleria d'Arte, 6 December 1962–January 1963.

1963
• *Alberto Burri*. Catalog, text by Cesare Brandi. London: Marlborough New London Gallery. London…., Marlborough New London Gallery, October 1963.
• *Alberto Burri*. Catalog, text by James Johnson Sweeney. Houston: The Museum of Fine Arts. Houston (Texas)..., The Museum of Fine Arts, 16 October–1 December 1963.

1964
• *Burri, Plastiche*. Catalog, text by Cesare Brandi. Milan: Galleria Blu. Milan, Galleria Blu, opening on 9 March 1964.

1965
• *Plastiche di Burri*. Catalog, text by Cesare Brandi. Turin, Galleria La Bussola, opening on 16 January 1965.

1966
• *XXXIII Esposizione Biennale Internazionale d'Arte Venezia*. Catalog, foreword by Gian Alberto Dell'Acqua, text on Burri by Vittorio Rubiu. Venice: La Biennale di Venezia. Venice, personal room, Giardini di Castello, 18 June–16 October 1966.
• *Alberto Burri and Lucio Fontana*. Leaflet, text by Renée Sabatello Neu. Aurora, New York..., Wells College, 23 September–9 October 1966.

1967
• *Alberto Burri*. Catalog, texts by Hans G. Sperlich and Bernd Krimmel. Rotterdam Darmstadt, Kunsthalle, 8 April–14 May 1967.
• *Alberto Burri*. Catalog, texts by Renilde Hammacher-van den Brande and Bernd Krimmel. Rotterdam: Museum Boymans-van Beuningen. Rotterdam, Museum Boymans-van Beuningen, 9 June–23 July 1967.

1968
• *Opere recenti di Burri*. Catalog. Milan: Galleria Blu. Milan, Galleria Blu, January 1968.

1969
• *Alberto Burri*. Catalog, text by Francesco Arcangeli. Bologna: Galleria Sanluca. Bologna, Galleria Sanluca, 12 March–15 April 1969.

• *Burri opere recenti*. Leaflet. Turin, Galleria Notizie, 5 December 1969–15 January 1970.

1971
• *Alberto Burri.* Catalog with selected reviews edited by Aldo Passoni. Turin: Galleria Civica d'Arte Moderna. Turin, Galleria Civica d'Arte Moderna, 7 October–31 December 1971.

1972
• *Alberto Burri*. Catalog, foreword by Jean Leymarie, text by Aldo Passoni. Paris, Musée National d'Art Moderne, 26 May–10 July 1972.

1973
• *Opere recenti di Alberto Burri*. Catalog. Bologna: Galleria d'arte Sanluca. Bologna, Galleria d'arte Sanluca, 27 October 1973–3 January 1974.

1974
• *Alberto Burri. Œuvres récentes*. Catalog with selected reviews. Geneva: Galerie Jacques Benador. Geneva, Galerie Jacques Benador, 11 February–March 1974.

1975
• *Opere di Burri*. Catalog, text by Cesare Brandi. Rome: Editalia. Assisi, Sacro Convento di San Francesco, 3 May–2 June 1975.

1976
• *Alberto Burri.* Catalog, foreword by Italo Faldi, text by Bruno Mantura, works catalogation by Giovanna De Feo. Rome: De Luca Editore. Rome, Galleria Nazionale d'Arte Moderna, 15 January–14 March 1976.
• *Burri Disegni, tempere e grafiche 1948-1976*. Catalog edited by Valter Rossi, text by Maurizio Calvesi. Pesaro: Il Segnapassi. Pesaro, Palazzo Ducale, 25 September–30 November 1976.

1977
• *Alberto Burri*. Catalog, foreword by Italo Faldi, text by Bruno Mantura; works catalogation, biography, exhibition list, and bibliography by Giovanna De Feo. Rome: De Luca Editore. Lisbon, Calouste Gulbenkian Foundation, February–March 1977.
• *Alberto Burri*. Catalog, foreword by Italo Faldi, texts by Vicente Aguilera-Cerni, Giulio Carlo Argan, and Bruno Mantura. Madrid: Ministerio de educacion y ciencia. Madrid, Palacio de Velázquez Parque del Retiro, April–May 1977.
• *Alberto Burri. A Retrospective View 1948-77.* Catalog edited by Gerald Nordland. Los Angeles: The Regents of the University of California. Los Angeles..., The Frederick S. Wight Art Gallery University of California, 25 September–4 December 1977.
• *Burri Cellotex 1974-1977*. Catalog. Bologna: Galleria Sanluca. Bologna, Galleria Sanluca, 2 February–31 May 1977.

1978
• *Alberto Burri*. Catalog, texts by Giulio Carlo Argan and Raffaello Causa. Naples: Amelio Editore. Naples, Museo di Capodimonte, May–September 1978.
• *Alberto Burri. A Retrospective View 1948-1978*. Leaflet, text by Hilarie Faberman. New York: The Solomon R. Guggenheim Foundation. ...New York, The Solomon R. Guggenheim Museum, 20 June–27 August 1978.

1979
• *Alberto Burri 1978-1979*. Catalog, text by Robert Hauston. Los Angeles: James Corcoran Gallery. Los Angeles, James Corcoran Gallery, 5 June–7 July 1979.
• *Alberto Burri: Cellotex, Cretti, una scultura, 1978-1979*. Exhibition notice, text by Flavio Caroli (drawn from *Burri, La forma e l'informe*. Milan: Mazzotta-Studio Marconi, 1979). Milan: Studio Marconi. Milan, Studio Marconi, 17 May–July 1979.
• *Alberto Burri "I sacchi 1952-1958". Mostra Omaggio ad Alberto Burri*. Exhibition notice, text by Mario Perazzi. Milan, Galleria Lorenzelli, 1–28 February 1979.
• *Alberto Burri, il viaggio*. Leaflet, text by Nemo Sarteanesi. Milan: Alfieri Edizioni d'Arte Electa. Città di Castello..., Seccatoio del tabacco tropicale, 5 December 1979–January 1980.

1980
• *Alberto Burri, il viaggio*. Catalog, text by Erich Steingräber. Milan: Electa International. ...Munich, Staatsgalerie Moderner Kunst, 13 March–20 April 1980.
• *Alberto Burri, Orsanmichele.* Catalog edited by Valter Rossi, text by Vanni Bramanti. Milan-Rome: 2RC. Florence, Orsanmichele, 15 November 1980–11 January 1981.
• *Beuys/Burri*. Catalog edited by Italo Tomassoni. Perugia: n.n. Perugia, Rocca Paolina, 3 April 1980–November 1981.

1981
• *Alberto Burri 1 Scultura 10 Multiplex*. Catalog. Rome: Galleria L'Isola. Rome, L'Isola gallery, 4 June–30 July 1981.
• *Alberto Burri, Antoni Tàpies*. Catalog, selected reviews with texts by André Pieyre de Mandiargues and Rainer Michael Mason. Paris..., Grand Palais F.I.A.C., 16–25 October 1981.
• *Alberto Burri, Cellotex und Multiplex*. German/Italian catalog, text by Dieter Ronte. Città di Castello: Rubini e Petruzzi. Innsbruck..., Galerie im Taxispalais, 15 December 1981–20 January 1982.
• *Alberto Burri. Teatri e scenografie*. Catalog, text by Emilio Villa. Pesaro: n.n. Pesaro, Teatro Rossini, Sala della Repubblica, 10 September–30 November 1981.

1982
• *Alberto Burri*. Catalog, text by Jan Butterfield. Palm Springs: Palm Springs Desert Museum. Palm Springs, Palm Springs Desert Museum, 26 January–14 March 1982.
• *Alberto Burri. Cellotex e Multiplex*. Catalog. Bologna: Galleria Sanluca. Bologna, Galleria Sanluca, 27 February–15 April 1982.
• *Alberto Burri, il viaggio*. Catalog, foreword by Marco Miele, text by Nemo Sarteanesi. Milan: Electa International. Columbus (Ohio)..., Columbus Museum of Art, 27 February–11 April 1982.

1983
• *Burri Sestante*. Catalog edited by Giulio Carlo Argan with selected reviews edited by Vanni Bramanti. Milan: Electa. Venice, Ex Cantieri Navali, 7 May–18 September 1983.

1984
• *Alberto Burri, Cretti e Cellotex*. Catalog, text by Daniel Abadie. Nice, Galerie Sapone, 14 February–24 April 1984.
• *Alberto Burri Rosso e Nero, Nizza 1984*. Catalog edited by Pierre Falicon, texts by Daniel Abadie, Pierre Falicon, and Claude Fournet. Nice: Musées de Nice. Nice..., Galerie des Ponchettes, 12 May–31 June 1984.
• *Burri*. Catalog, texts by Carlo Bertelli and Carlo Pirovano. Milan: Mondadori. Milan, Pinacoteca di Brera, 24 May–8 July 1984.

1985
• *Alberto Burri opere recenti. Annottarsi*. Catalog, Rome, Galleria Sprovieri, 3 December 1985–30 January 1986.
• *Burri, Combustioni, Cretti, Cellotex 1964-1984*. Catalog, text by Jean Leymarie. Paris: Artcurial. Paris, Galerie Artcurial, 7 March–30 April 1985.

1986
• *Burri 18 Paintings 1953-1986*. Catalog, text by Gerald Nordland. New York, Di Laurenti Gallery, 13 March–26 April 1986.

1987
• *Burri. Il Viaggio, Sestante, Annottarsi*. Catalog, forewords by Ludovico Gatto, Simonetta Lux, Antonio Ruberti, Elisa Tittoni, and Rosella Siligato, text by Maurizio Calvesi. Città di Castello: Petruzzi Editore. Rome, Ex Stabilimento Industriale Peroni, 12 May–13 September 1987.
• *Burri, Monotex, Multipli, Grande Ferro K*. Catalog, foreword by Antonio Ruberti, texts by Maurizio Calvesi, Simonetta Lux, and Marisa Volpi. Città di Castello: Petruzzi Editore. Rome, Palazzo del Rettorato, Museo Laboratorio

dell'Università degli Studi La Sapienza, 12 May–13 September 1987.

1988

• *XLIII Esposizione Internazionale d'Arte. La Biennale di Venezia. Il Luogo degli Artisti*. Catalog edited by Marie-George Gervasoni, foreword by Paolo Portoghesi, text edited by Giovanni Carandente, texts by Guido Ballo, Achille Bonito Oliva, Roland Barthes et al. Milan: Fabbri Editori. Padiglione Italia, personal room, Venice, 26 June–25 September 1988.

• *Alberto Burri Annottarsi (Up to Nite)*. Catalog, foreword by Isabella del Frate Rayburn, text by Mary Jane Jacob. New York: The Murray and Isabella Rayburn Foundation. New York, The Murray and Isabella Rayburn Foundation, 4 November 1988–7 January 1989.

• *Alberto Burri Non ama il Nero*. Catalog. Rome: Galleria Sprovieri. Rome, Galleria Sprovieri, 11 October–November 1989.

• *Assegai*. Catalog, text by Eva Menzio. Turin: Galleria Eva Menzio. Turin, Galleria Eva Menzio, 8 November 1988–15 January 1989.

• *Burri S. Vitale*. Catalog edited by Claudio Spadoni. Ravenna: Edizioni Essegi. Ravenna, Museo Nazionale complesso San Vitale, Sala del Refettorio, 9 July–30 October 1988.

1989

• *Burri*. Catalog. Rome: Galleria Milart. Rome, Galleria Milart, November–December 1989.

• *Burri 25 grafiche 1 scultura*. Leaflet. Città di Castello, Galleria delle Arti, 8 December 1989–20 January 1990.

• *Burri 3 Cellotex*. Leaflet. Naples, Galleria Lia Rumma, 15 October–31 December 1989.

• *Burri.* Catalog. Nice: Galerie Sapone. Nice, Galerie Sapone, 20 December 1989–31 January 1990.

• *Wien Moderner 89. Burri 1953-1968 4 Pitture Wien*. Catalog, texts by Claudio Abbado and Dieter Ronte. Vienna: n.n. Vienna, Museum Moderner Kunst, 30 October–26 November 1989.

• *Wien Moderner 89. 1984 Rosso e Nero Wien*. Catalog, texts by Claudio Abbado and Dieter Ronte. Vienna: n.n. Vienna, Istituto Italiano di Cultura, 31 October–26 November 1989.

1990

• *Burri*. Catalog. Città di Castello: Petruzzi Editore. Paris, Galerie Sapone at FIAC, 25 October–1 November 1990.

1991

• *Alberto Burri*. Catalog edited by Carlo Pirovano, texts by Andrea Emiliani and Carlo Pirovano (foreword by Pierre Casè in the catalog of the Locarno exhibition). Bologna: Nuova Alfa Editoriale. Bologna..., Palazzo Pepoli Campogrande, 27 September–10 November 1991.

• *Burri Cellotex 91*. Catalog edited by Ida Gianelli. Milan: Fabbri Editori. Rivoli, Castello di Rivoli, 2 October–1 December 1991.

1992

• *Alberto Burri œuvres 1949-1992*. Catalog. Nice: Galerie Sapone. Paris, Galerie Sapone at FIAC, 24 October–1 November 1992.

1993

• *Alberto Burri, la pittura come materia vivente, opere dal 1949 al 1966*. Catalog with selected reviews edited by Claudio Cerritelli. Parma: Galleria d'Arte Niccoli. Parma, Galleria d'Arte Niccoli, 30 October 1993–5 January 1994.

1994

• *Alberto Burri - Arquitecturas con cactus / Architetture con cactus*. Spanish/Italian catalog edited by Tonia Giannoudaki, texts edited by Giuliano Serafini. Madrid: Ministero degli Affari Esteri-Istituto Italiano di Cultura. Madrid, Istituto Italiano di Cultura, 30 November 1994–10 January 1995.

• *Alberto Burri – Το Πολυπτυχο των Αθηνων. Αρχιτεκτονικη και κακτος / Il Polittico di Atene. Architetture con cactus / The Polyptych of Athens. Architectures and Cactus*. Greek/Italian/English catalog edited by Tonia Giannoudaki, texts by Giuliano Serafini. Athens: Mouseio Alexandrou Soutzou-Ethnikí Pinakothìki. Athens, Mouseio Alexandrou Soutzou, Ethnikí Pinakothìki, 11 May–30 June 1994.

• *La donazione Burri (Donazione opere del Maestro alla Galleria degli Uffizi)*. Leaflet, texts by Antonio Natali and Giuliano Serafini. Florence, Galleria degli Uffizi, 10 December 1994.

1996

• *Burri Fontana 1949-1968*. Italian/English catalog edited by Bruno Corà, coordination by Jole De Sanna and Chiara Sarteanesi, texts by Enrico Crispolti, Rudi Fuchs, Italo Tomassoni, Chiara Sarteanesi, et al. Milan: Skira. Prato, Museo Pecci, 13 April–30 June 1996.

• *Burri opere 1944-1995*. Catalog with critical chronology edited by Carolyn Christov-Bakargiev and Maria Grazia Tolomeo, with the collaboration of Chiara Sarteanesi, Teresa Mulone, and Raffaella Ridolfi, texts by Bruno Mantura, Mario Perniola, Ferderica Pirani, Carlo Pirovano, Nemo Sarteanesi, and Italo Tomassoni. Milan: Electa. Rome..., Palazzo delle Esposizioni, 9 November 1996–15 January 1997.

1997

• *Burri 1915-1995. Retrospektive*. Catalog edited by Carolyn Christov-Bakargiev and Maria Grazia Tolomeo, with the collaboration of Chiara Sarteanesi, Teresa Mulone, and Raffaella Ridolfi, texts by Bruno Mantura, Mario Perniola, Federica Pirani, Carlo Pirovano, Nemo Sarteanesi, and Italo Tomassoni, critical chronology with annexes in French and Dutch. Milan: Electa. Lenbachhaus, ...Munich..., 5 February–6 April 1997.

1998

• *Alberto Burri 1948-1993*. Catalog edited by Achille Bonito Oliva and Chiara Sarteanesi. Milan: Skira. Milan, Zonca & Zonca Arte Moderna e Contemporanea, 22 October–31 December 1998.

• *Alberto Burri: "Cretti"*. Leaflet. Gibellina, Museo Civico, 10 October–10 November 1998.

• *Alberto Burri. Vom Unikat zum Auflagenwerk / Dall'opera unica alla moltiplicata*. German/Italian catalog edited by Andreas Hapkemeyer, Chiara Sarteanesi, and Pier Luigi Siena. Bolzano: FOLIO. Bolzano, Museion-Museo d'Arte Moderna, 12 June–30 August 1998.

1999

• *Burri. Segni di un percorso opere 1949-1987*. Catalog edited by Francesca Bacci, Giancarlo Pauletto, and Vittorio Rubiu. Pordenone: Centro Iniziative Culturali. Pordenone, Galleria Sagittaria, 4 December 1999–6 February 2000.

• *Omaggio a Alberto Burri. Grafica e scultura*. Catalog with selected reviews. Bologna: Edizioni Bora. Colonnella, 30 July–15 September 1999.

2000

• *Alberto Burri Cellotex 1980-1992*. Catalog with selected reviews. Nice: Galerie Sapone. Milan, Galerie Sapone at Miart, 5–8 May 2000.

• *Alberto Burri opere 1956-1992*. Catalog, text by Paola Sapone. Nice: Galerie Sapone. Bologna..., Galerie Sapone at Arte Fiera, 27–31 January 2000.

• *Burri*. Italian/Japanese catalog edited by Tadashi Kanai, Tomoaki Kitagawa, and Masao Kitatani, texts by Maurizio Calvesi, Chiara Sarteanesi, and Masao Kitatani. Toyota: Toyota Municipal Museum of Art. Toyota, Toyota Municipal Museum of Art, 6 June–20 August 2000.

• *Burri inedito*. Italian/English catalog edited by Chiara Sarteanesi with the collaboration of Maria Sensi, text by Maurizio Calvesi. Milan: Charta. Città di Castello, Ex Seccatoi del Tabacco, 24 June–30 September 2000.

• *Burri Multiplo*. Catalog with selected reviews edited by Chiara Sarteanesi. Città di Castello: Petruzzi Editore. Bellona, Centro Umanistico Incontri Internazionali Antonio e Aika Sapone, November 2000–January 2001.

2001

• *Burri*. Catalog edited by Chiara Sarteanesi, forewords by Maurizio

Festanti and Nemo Sarteanesi, texts by Maurizio Calvesi, Giuliano Serafini, Chiara Sarteanesi, and Italo Tomassoni. Città di Castello: Petruzzi Editore. Reggio Emilia, Sala Espositiva Chiostri San Domenico, 18 November 2001–7 January 2002.

2003
• *Alberto Burri. Tra Materia e Forma. Opere scelte 1948-1993*. Catalog, foreword by Francesco Poli. Turin: Mazzoleni Galleria d'Arte. Turin, Mazzoleni Galleria d'Arte, 17 October–31 December 2003.
• *Burri Cellotex*. Catalog edited by Maurizio Calvesi. Città di Castello: Petruzzi Editore. Rome, Parco della Musica Auditorium Arte, 20 October–14 December 2003.
• *Burri Grafica. Opera completa*. Monographic catalog edited by Chiara Sarteanesi, texts by Maurizio Calvesi, contributions by Lorenzo Canova, Valter Rossi, Marianna Vecellio et al. Città di Castello: Petruzzi Editore. Città di Castello, Ex Seccatoi del Tabacco, 11 October 2003–11 January 2004.
• *I "neri" di Burri*. Catalog with selected reviews edited by Carlo Repetto and Marco Vallora, texts by Maurizio Calvesi and Marco Vallora. Milan: Mazzotta. Acqui Terme, Palazzo Liceo Saracco, 20 July–14 September 2003.

2004
• *Burri Dottori "opere rare"*. Catalog edited by Luigi Amadei. Città di Castello: Petruzzi Editore. Città di Castello, Galleria delle Arti, 13 March–13 June 2004.

2005
• *Burri il cellotex ha un cuore antico*. Catalog, text by Giuliano Serafini. Città di Castello: Petruzzi Editore. Bologna, Galerie Sapone at Arte Fiera, 27–31 January 2005.
• *Burri. L'opera grafica*. Catalog edited by Nathalie Vernizzi. Valdagno: Comune di Valdagno. Valdagno, Galleria Civica Villa-Valle, 19 November 2005–15 January 2006.
• *Burri. Viaggio al termine della materia*. Catalog edited by Giuliano Serafini, photos by Aurelio Amendola. Florence: Tornabuoni. Florence, Tornabuoni Arte, 12 May–12 July 2005.

2006
• *Alberto Burri*. Catalog, texts by Maurizio Calvesi and Federica Pirani. Madrid: Museo Nacional Centro de Arte Reina Sofía. Madrid, Museo Nacional Centro de Arte Reina Sofía, 14 March–29 May 2006.
• *Alberto Burri: la sezione aurea dei Cellotex*. Catalog edited by Italo Tomassoni, forewords by Floriano De Santi and Luciana Matalon. Milan: Fondazione Luciana Matalon. Milan, Museo Fondazione Luciana Matalon, 25 November 2006–31 January 2007.
• *I Cellotex nell'autobiografia di Burri*. Catalog, text by Maurizio Calvesi. Città di Castello: Petruzzi Editore. Bologna, Galerie Sapone at Arte Fiera, 26–30 January 2006.

2007
• *Alberto Burri*. Catalog, texts by Germano Celant. New York: Mitchell-Innes & Nash. New York..., Mitchell – Innes & Nash, 29 November 2007–18 January 2008.
• *Burri opere 1949-1994. La misura dell'equilibrio*. Italian/English catalog edited by Chiara Sarteanesi and Simona Tosini Pizzetti with the collaboration of Stefano Roffi and Rita Olivieri, texts by Bruno Corà and Chiara Sarteanesi. Cinisello Balsamo: Silvana Editoriale. Mamiano di Traversetolo, Fondazione Magnani-Rocca, 8 September–2 December 2007.

2008
• *Alberto Burri.* Catalog edited by Chiara Sarteanesi, forewords by Davide Rampello and Nemo Sarteanesi, texts by Vittorio Brandi Rubiu, Maurizio Calvesi, Bruno Corà, Rita Olivieri, Chiara Sarteanesi, and Italo Tomassoni. Milan: Skira. Milan, Triennale di Milano, 11 November 2008–8 February 2009.

2009
• *Alberto Burri. Equilibrio – Struttura – Ritmo – Luce*. Italian/English catalog edited by Francesco Poli. Milan: Mazzotta. Castelbasso, Fondazione Malvina Menegaz per le Arti e le Culture, Palazzo Clemente, 20 June–30 August 2009.
• *Burri Colore Omaggio*. Leaflet, text by Chiara Sarteanesi. Città di Castello, Galleria delle Arti, 29 August–29 November 2009.
• *Burri e Fontana. Materia e Spazio.* Catalog edited by Bruno Corà. Cinisello Balsamo: Silvana Editoriale. Catania, Fondazione Puglisi Cosentino Palazzo Valle, 15 November 2009–14 March 2010.

2010
• *Alberto Burri Art Paris + Guest 2010.* Catalog edited by Chiara Sarteanesi, texts by Bruno Corà and Chiara Sarteanesi. Nice: Galerie Sapone. Paris, Grand Palais Galerie Sapone, 17–22 March 2010.
• *Alberto Burri Cretti neri.* Catalog edited by Maurizio Calvesi, foreword by Daniela Luxembourg & Amalia Dayan. New York: Luxembourg & Dayan. New York, Luxembourg & Dayan, 10 May-30 July 2010.
• *Burri e Fontana a Brera.* Catalog edited by Marina Gargiulo, texts by Sandrina Bandera, Maurizio Calvesi, Bruno Corà, and Marina Gargiulo. Milan: Skira. Milan, Pinacoteca di Brera, 16 June–3 October 2010.
• *Combustione: Alberto Burri and America.* Catalog edited by Lisa Melandri and Michael Duncan, foreword by Elsa Longhauser. Santa Monica: Santa Monica Museum of Art. Santa Monica, Santa Monica Museum of Art, 11 September–18 December 2010.

2011
• *Alberto Burri dalla concretezza reale all'incanto della forma.* Catalog edited by Francesco Poli, photos by Aurelio Amendola. Turin: Mazzoleni Arte Moderna. Turin, Mazzoleni Galleria d'Arte, 21 October 2011–31 January 2012.
• *Alberto Burri Form and Matter.* English/Italian catalog edited by Massimo Duranti, texts by Andrea Baffoni and Massimo Duranti. Perugia: EFFE Fabrizio Fabbri Editore. London, Estorick Collection of Modern Italian Art, 13 January–7 April 2012.

2012
• *Alberto Burri da una raccolta privata, quattro opere inedite, multiplex, cretti e serigrafie.* Catalog, text by C.L. Florence: Edizioni Pananti. Florence, Galleria Pananti - Archivio del Novecento, 20 June–20 July 2012.
• *Alberto Burri Opera al Nero Cellotex 1972-1992.* Italian and English catalog edited by Bruno Corà, texts by Maurizio Calvesi, Bruno Corà, Aldo Iori, Laura Lorenzoni, Rita Olivieri, and Vittorio Rubiu, interview by Manuela De Bernardis. Verona-Milan: Galleria dello Scudo-Skira. Verona, Galleria dello Scudo, 15 December 2012–31 March 2013.
• *Alberto Burri primi ed ultimi*. Catalog, text by Bruno Corà. Perugia: 3Arte ali&no editrice. Galerie Sapone at Arte Fiera, 27–30 January 2012.

2013
• *Alberto Burri. Black Cellotex*. Catalog, text by Antonio Sapone. New York: Luxembourg & Dayan. New York, Luxembourg & Dayan, 8 March–20 April 2013.
• *Burri Grafica*. Leaflet, text by Luigi Amadei. Città di Castello, Galleria della Arti, 30 November 2013–30 March 2014.

2014
• *Alberto Burri-Hans Hartung*. Catalog, text by Bruno Corà. Arezzo: Magonza editore. Bologna, Galerie Sapone at Arte Fiera, 24–27 January 2014.
• *Burri Unico e Multiplo/Unique et Multiple.* Italian/French catalog edited by Giorgio Agnisola, foreword by Bruno Corà, texts by Giorgio Agnisola and Marcello Carlino. Arezzo: Magonza editore. Gaeta, Pinacoteca Comunale di Gaeta, 14 June–12 October 2014.
• *Rivisitazione: Burri incontra Piero della Francesca*. Italian/English catalog edited by Bruno Corà, texts by Carlo Bertelli and

Bruno Corà, critical apparatuses by Simonetta Riccardini and Annamaria Rosi. Città di Castello: Fondazione Palazzo Albizzini Collezione Burri. Sansepolcro, Museo Civico, 31 October 2014–12 March 2015.

2015

• *Alberto Burri*. Catalog, foreword by Giovanni Mazzoleni, texts by Cesare Brandi (reprint of *Burri*. Rome: Editalia, 1963) and Vittorio Brandi Rubiu. London-Turin: Mazzoleni. London, Mazzoleni Art, 2 October–30 November 2015.
• *Alberto Burri e i poeti. Materia e suono della parola*. Catalog edited by Bruno Corà and Tonino Sicoli, texts by Bruno Corà, Chiara Sarteanesi, and Tonino Sicoli. Città di Castello: Fondazione Palazzo Albizzini Collezione Burri. Rende, MAON – Museo d'Arte dell'Otto e Novecento, 11 November 2015–28 February 2016.
• *Alberto Burri Grafica*. Catalog, foreword by Daniella Luxembourg & Amalia Dayan. New York: Luxembourg & Dayan. New York, Luxembourg & Dayan, 17 September–24 October 2015.
• *Alberto Burri. The Subject of Matter*. Catalog edited by Christian Piscitelli, coordinated by Francesca Cigola. New York: Ierimonti Gallery. New York, Ierimonti Gallery, 2 October–23 November 2015.
• *Alberto Burri. The Trauma of Painting*. Catalog edited by Emily Braun with Megan Fontanella and Carol Stringari, forewords by Richard Armstrong, Emily Braun, and Bruno Corà, texts by Emily Braun, Megan Fontanella, and Carol Stringari, annexes by Ylinka Barotto. New York: The Solomon R. Guggenheim Foundation. New York, Solomon R. Guggenheim Museum, 9 October 2015–6 January 2016.
• *Burri e Brandi, un'amicizia informale.* Catalog edited by Vittorio Brandi Rubiu et al., texts by Massimo Bignardi, Vittorio Brandi Rubiu, Elisa Bruttini et al. Siena: Santa Maria della Scala.-Siena, Santa Maria della Scala, Villa Brandi in Vignano, 21 November 2015– 31 January 2016.
• *Burri e Pistoia*. English/Italian catalog edited by Bruno Corà, texts by Aurelio Amendola, Bruno Corà, Giuliano Gori, and Chiara Sarteanesi, photos by Aurelio Amendola. Pistoia: Gli Ori. Pistoia, Palazzo Sozzifanti, 10 May–26 July 2015.
• *Burri e Signorelli. Giornata di studi e mostra storico-documentaria*. Catalog edited by Catia Cecchetti and Aldo Iori, texts by Catia Cecchetti, Bruno Corà, Aldo Iori, Federico Mancini, Chiara Sarteanesi et al. Città di Castello: Fondazione Palazzo Albizzini Collezione Burri. Città di Castello, Morra, Oratorio di San Crescentino, 30 May 2015.
• *Burri. I Cretti*. Catalog edited by Bruno Corà, texts by Bruno Corà, Valeria Patrizia Li Vigni, and Italo Tomassoni. Città di Castello: Fondazione Palazzo Albizzini Collezione Burri. Palermo, Museo Regionale d'Arte Contemporanea Palazzo Belmonte Riso, 25 July–20 September 2015.
• *I Mixoblack di Alberto Burri nella Galleria Tesori d'Arte di San Pietro in Perugia*. Catalog, foreword by Franco Moriconi, texts by Fondazione Palazzo Albizzini Collezione Burri and Cristina Galassi. Passignano sul Trasimeno: Aguaplano. Perugia, Galleria Tesori d'Arte, 21 November 2015–5 January 2016.
• *Sironi – Burri. Un dialogo italiano (1940-1958) / An Italian Dialogue (1940–1958)*. Italian/English catalog edited by Christian Caliandro. Bologna: CUBO Centro Unipol Bologna. Bologna, Spazio Arte CUBO, 28 July–18 October 2015.

2017

• *Alberto Burri. Gli Arazzi per la Regione Emilia-Romagna*. Leaflet. Bologna, Regione Emilia Romagna, Atrio di viale Aldo Moro, 25–30 January 2017.
• *Burri. L'Opera Grafica Permanente*, edited by Bruno Corà, texts by Chiara Sarteanesi, bibliographical update by Greta Boninsegni. Città di Castello: Fondazione Palazzo Albizzini Collezione Burri.
• *Burri posters*. Catalog edited by Bruno Corà. Rome: De Luca. New York, New York University, Casa Italiana Zerilli-Marimò, 26 October–8 December 2017.

2018

• *Action / Abstraction Alberto Burri – Lucio Fontana.* Catalog edited by Tornabuoni Art. London: Tornabuoni Art. London, Tornabuoni Art, 8 February–30 March 2019.
• *Alberto Burri*. English/French leaflet. Paris, Tornabuoni Art, 19 October–22 December 2018.

2019

• *Burri la ferita della bellezza*. Catalog edited by Massimo Recalcati and coordinated by Alessandro Sarteanesi; texts by Aldo Iori, Gianfranco Maraniello, Massimo Recalcati, and Alessandro Sarteanesi; visitors' response edited by Roberta Bramante, Romano Manescalchi, Patrizia Rocchi et al. Catalog design by Alessandro Sarteanesi and Moira Chiavarini. Arezzo: Magonza. Rome…, Museo Carlo Bilotti – Aranciera di Villa Borghese, 22 March–9 June 2019.
• *BURRI la pittura, irriducibile presenza*. Catalog edited by Bruno Corà and Chiara Sarteanesi, editing supervision of Philip Rylands, texts by Luca Massimo Barbero and Bruno Corà. Florence: Forma Edizioni. Venice, Fondazione Giorgio Cini, Isola di San Giorgio Maggiore, 10 May–28 July 2019.